POLITICAL THEORY
AND THE RIGHTS OF
INDIGENOUS PEOPLES

This book focuses on the problem of *justice* for indigenous peoples and the ways in which this poses key questions for political theory: the nature of sovereignty, the grounds of national identity and the limits of democratic theory. The chapters are by leading political theorists and indigenous scholars from Australia, Aotearoa/New Zealand, Canada and the United States, who show how the different historical circumstances of colonisation in these countries nevertheless raise common problems and questions for contemporary political theory. The book examines ways in which political theory has contributed to the past subjugation and continuing disadvantage faced by indigenous peoples, while also seeking to identify resources in contemporary political thought that can assist the 'decolonisation' of relations between indigenous and non-indigenous peoples.

Duncan Ivison is Lecturer in Philosophy at the University of Sydney. He is author of *The Self at Liberty* (1997) and various articles in the history of political thought and contemporary political theory.

Paul Patton is Associate Professor in Philosophy at the University of Sydney. He is the author of *Deleuze and the Political* (2000), and the editor of *Nietzsche, Feminism and Political Theory* (1993) and *Deleuze: A Critical Reader* (1996).

Will Sanders is Fellow at the Centre for Aboriginal Economic Policy Research at the Australian National University, and also co-ordinator of the Institutions of Aboriginal Australia strand of the ANU's Reshaping Australian Institutions Project. He is co-editor, with Nicolas Peterson, of *Citizenship and Indigenous Australians* (Cambridge University Press, 1998), editor of *Mabo and Native Title* (1994) and author of *Unemployment Payments, the Activity Test and Indigenous Australians* (1999).

POLITICAL THEORY AND THE RIGHTS OF INDIGENOUS PEOPLES

EDITED BY

DUNCAN IVISON
University of Sydney

PAUL PATTON
University of Sydney

WILL SANDERS
Australian National University

CAMBRIDGE
UNIVERSITY PRESS

PUBLISHED BY THE PRESS SYNDICATE OF THE UNIVERSITY OF CAMBRIDGE
The Pitt Building, Trumpington Street, Cambridge, United Kingdom

CAMBRIDGE UNIVERSITY PRESS
The Edinburgh Building, Cambridge CB2 2RU, UK
40 West 20th Street, New York, NY 10011–4211, USA
10 Stamford Road, Oakleigh, VIC 3166, Australia
Ruiz de Alarcón 13, 28014 Madrid, Spain
Dock House, The Waterfront, Cape Town 8001, South Africa

http://www.cambridge.org

First published 2000

Printed in Australia by Brown Prior Anderson

Typeface New Baskerville (*Adobe*) 10/12 pt.   *System* QuarkXPress®   [PK]

A catalogue record for this book is available from the British Library

National Library of Australia Cataloguing in Publication data
Political theory and the rights of indigenous peoples.
Includes index.
ISBN 0 521 77048 3.
ISBN 0 521 77937 5 (pbk.).
1. Indigenous peoples – Politics and government.
2. Aborigines, Australian – Politics and government.
3. Maori (New Zealand people) – Politics and government.
4. Indians of North America – Politics and government.
5. Indians of North America – Canada – Politics and government.
I. Ivison, Duncan 1965– .
II. Patton, Paul.
III. Sanders, Will.
342.0872

ISBN 0 521 77048 3 hardback
ISBN 0 521 77937 5 paperback

Contents

Contributors

MANUHUIA BARCHAM is a PhD student in the Department of Political Science in the Research School of Social Science, Australian National University. He is a member of the Ngati Kahungunu, Te Arawa and Ngati Tuwharetoa Iwi of New Zealand. His PhD thesis critically examines the comparative political economy of development in Australia and Papua New Guinea, and he has an ongoing interest in the intersection of political theory and political practice, particularly in the analysis of notions of indigeneity and social change.

JOHN BERN is Professor of Sociology and Director of the South East Arnhem Land Collaborative Research Project at the University of Wollongong. He has undertaken extensive ethnographic research with Aboriginal people in Australia's Northern Territory. The major foci of his research are the national politics of indigenous people, issues of indigenous governance and land ownership, and socio-political developments in remote Aboriginal communities in the Northern Territory.

WILLIAM CONNOLLY is Professor and Chair of Political Science at Johns Hopkins University. His *The Terms of Political Discourse* (1974) received the biennial Lippincott Award in 1999 for the 'best book in political theory still influential fifteen years or more after publication'. His most recent publications are *The Ethos of Pluralization* (1995) and *Why I am Not a Secularist* (1999).

SUSAN DODDS is a Senior Lecturer in Philosophy at the University of Wollongong and joint co-ordinator (with John Bern) of the Public Policy: Civil Society and State Institutions research group within the Institute of Social Change and Critical Inquiry. Her work is primarily within the areas of moral and political philosophy. She has published papers on a range of topics, including indigenous justice and citizenship, property rights, reproductive technology, personal autonomy and research ethics.

AUGIE FLERAS is Associate Professor in sociology at the University of Waterloo in Canada. He has long-standing interests in race, ethnic and aboriginal relations, with particular emphasis on policy and politics. He is currently working with Roger Maaka on a host of issues pertaining to Maori–Crown relations.

DUNCAN IVISON teaches in the Department of Philosophy at the University of Sydney. He is the author of *The Self at Liberty* (1997) and various articles in the history of political thought and contemporary political theory.

WILL KYMLICKA is a Queen's National Scholar in the Philosophy department of Queen's University in Kingston, and a visiting professor in the Nationalism Studies program at the Central European University in Budapest. He is the author of four books published by Oxford University Press: *Liberalism, Community, and Culture* (1989), *Contemporary Political Philosophy* (1990), *Multicultural Citizenship* (1995), and *Finding Our Way: Rethinking Ethnocultural Relations in Canada* (1998). He is the editor of *Justice in Political Philosophy* (Elgar, 1992), *The Rights of Minority Cultures* (1995), *Ethnicity and Group Rights* (NYU, 1997) and *Citizenship in Diverse Societies* (2000).

ROGER MAAKA is Head of the Department of Maori at the University of Canterbury and a member of the Waitangi Tribunal. He has research interests in Maori political and social development and change. He has published several studies on Maori society, including a study on the effects of urbanisation. Roger is currently on the Tribunals hearing the Mohaka ki Ahuriri region land claims and the Indigenous Flora, Fauna and Intellectual Property Rights claim.

PAUL PATTON is Associate Professor in Philosophy at the University of Sydney. He is the author of *Deleuze and the Political* (2000), and has published several articles on the implications of native title in Australia.

PHILIP PETTIT is Professor of Social and Political Theory at the Research School of Social Sciences, Australian National University. He is the author of a number of books on philosophy and political theory, including *The Common Mind: An Essay on Psychology, Society and Politics* (1993) and *Republicanism: A Theory of Freedom and Government* (1997).

JOHN POCOCK is Professor Emeritus of History at the Johns Hopkins University, where he taught from 1974–94. He has held posts as Professor of Political Science at the University of Canterbury and Professor of History at Washington University, St Louis. His publications include *The Ancient Constitution and the Feudal Law* (1957), *The Maori and New Zealand Politics* (1969), *Politics, Language and Time* (1971), *The Machiavellian Moment* (1975), *Virtue, Commerce and History* (1985), and *Barbarism and Religion I: The Enlightenment of Edward Gibbon, II: Narratives of Civil Government* (1999).

WILL SANDERS has been, since 1993, a Research Fellow at the Australian National University's Centre for Aboriginal Economic Policy Research, where he has also been co-ordinator of the Institutions of Aboriginal Australia strand of the ANU's Reshaping Australian Institutions Project. He has worked on several areas of Australian public policy relating to indigenous Australians, including housing, employment, income support, health, local government and inter-governmental relations.

AUDRA SIMPSON is a PhD candidate in the Department of Anthropology, McGill University. Her doctoral research examines the relationship between discourse, narrativity and nationhood. She is a Kahnawake Mohawk.

SONIA SMALLACOMBE is an indigenous Australian and a member of the Maramanindji peoples from the Daly River region of the Northern Territory. She is undertaking a PhD at ANU in Canberra, and also manages the Indigenous Cultural and Intellectual Property Task Force within the Aboriginal and Torres Strait Islander Commission (ATSIC).

JAMES TULLY is Professor of Political Science at the University of Victoria, Victoria, British Columbia. His publications include *Strange Multiplicity: Constitutionalism in an Age of Diversity* (1995, revised 1999); and as editor, *Struggles for Recognition in Multinational Societies* (forthcoming).

JEREMY WEBBER is Dean and Professor of Law at the University of Sydney. Until 1998, he was on the Faculty of Law of McGill University. He is the author of *Reimagining Canada: Language, Culture, Community and the Canadian Constitution* (1994) and of other works on cultural difference, indigenous rights, federalism, nationalism, constitutional law and legal theory.

IRIS MARION YOUNG is Professor of Political Science at the University of Chicago, where she teaches political theory and feminist theory. She is author of several books, including *Intersecting Voices: Dilemmas of Gender, Political Philosophy and Policy* (1990). *Inclusion and Democracy* will appear in the Oxford University Press Series in Political Theory in August 2000.

Acknowledgements

The project from which this book emerged was first conceived when the editors were all resident, in various capacities, at the Australian National University in Canberra. Since this is a book concerned to explore the consequences of indigenous peoples' claims and aspirations for contemporary political theory, we would like, first of all, to acknowledge the Ngunnawal people as traditional owners of the land upon which our endeavours began and took shape, and thank them for their interest in and support of the project.

We are especially grateful to the Humanities Research Centre at the ANU, and especially to the Director, Iain McCalman, and the Associate Director, Graeme Clarke, for their unstinting support of our efforts. Without the backing of the HRC this book, and the various seminars and colloquia organised around it, would simply not have occurred. The Centre provided an unrivalled atmosphere in which to pursue our project. The HRC graciously allowed us to offer visiting fellowships to many of our contributors, enabling them to come to Canberra for various lengths of time, and to develop and discuss their papers with each other and the many other visiting and resident scholars from a wide range of disciplines. The administrative staff at the HRC were wonderfully supportive as well, and handled the often complex arrangements involved with great efficiency and good humour. In particular, we would like to thank Leena Messina, Stephanie Stockdill, Julie Gorrell, Ben Penny, Lia Szokalski and Misty Cook.

We would also like to acknowledge the support of our efforts by the Research School of Social Sciences at the ANU, under the auspices of the Reshaping of Australian Institutions Project directed by John Braithwaite and Frank Castles. Further support was provided by the Social and Political Theory Group at the RSSS which enabled us to bring a number of our contributors to Canberra. We are especially grateful to Philip Pettit, Director of the Group, and to Robert Goodin and Barry Hindess for their help in this regard. Additional support for the project was provided by the Nuffield Foundation, the Department of Politics at the University of York and the Australian Foundation for Culture and the Humanities. To all these institutions and organisations, we are very grateful.

Phillipa McGuinness and Sharon Mullins of Cambridge University Press have been receptive and supportive editors ever since we first approached them with the idea of this book, and provided the right combination of incentives and sanctions to help keep us focused on the task at hand. Melissa McMahon provided excellent help in readying the manuscript for publication. We are also grateful to Peter Cook for help in preparing the index.

Finally, we would like to thank the following for their help in realising this project: Mick Dodson, Danny Celermajer, Frank Brennan, Russell Barsh, Roy Perrett, Henry Reynolds, John Wunder, Sidney Haring, Garth Nettheim and Margaret Wilson.

CHAPTER 1

Introduction

Duncan Ivison, Paul Patton and Will Sanders

Contemporary political theory has much to learn from the encounter with its colonial past. The demands of indigenous peoples for justice present far-reaching challenges. Suppose we begin by asking what are 'indigenous rights'? Are these rights as liberal political theorists understand them? If contemporary liberal political thought presents itself as a universal idiom for understanding and reflecting upon social and political relations, where does this leave indigenous political thought and indigenous understandings of their rights to land, culture and self-rule? How can contemporary political theory contribute to a future in which indigenous communities no longer suffer the consequences of colonisation, dispossession and forced assimilation? Can liberal democracy become genuinely intercultural?

These questions do not arise in a vacuum, but in response to a problem of ongoing political concern in many former colonial countries, namely, the relationship between western colonial societies and the continuation and resistance of pre-existing indigenous societies on the same territory. They are not issues of mere academic interest, since they touch upon historically entrenched injustice and social disadvantage. Ultimately, they concern the very survival of indigenous peoples. Such issues should concern any reflective citizen of a contemporary nation state.

What has been the relationship between modern western political theory and the struggles of indigenous peoples over the past 400 years? Each set of peoples and each state has its own particular story with its inherent complexities. The chapters in this book address the legal, constitutional and cultural circumstances of a group of countries colonised under British law: Australia, Canada, Aotearoa/New Zealand and the United States of America. Generally speaking, at various points of history, different strands of western political thought have not only been

1

complicit with, but helped to justify, colonial expansion and imperial control over indigenous peoples and their territories. As much as modern political theory, especially in its liberal and social democratic variants, has emphasised universal human rights, equality before the law and individual and collective freedom, it has also explicitly denied such entitlements to indigenous peoples. Much of modern western political thought has tended to rely on an anthropological minimalism that has in fact been anything but minimal. As we understand it, 'western political thought' refers broadly to that body of political, legal and social theory developed by European, American, Australian and New Zealand authors and practitioners from the beginning of the modern period in Europe to the present. It is a complex and contested body of thought concerned with the normative problem of the justification of government as well as the question of how, in fact, peoples or populations are governed. Thus it includes reflection upon and engagement with practices of self-formation, discipline, education and training as well as upon the sanctions and limits of political power (Tully 1993; 1995).

Western political thought has often embodied a series of culturally specific assumptions and judgements about the relative worth of other cultures, ways of life, value systems, social and political institutions, and ways of organising property. As a result, egalitarian political theory has often ended up justifying explicitly inegalitarian institutions and practices. This history of western, and especially liberal, political thought's entanglement with colonialism has been recently told in much detail and with great force. The emergence of 'postcolonial' theory in English and Cultural Studies, the careful work of historians and legal historians of settler societies and Empire, as well as historians of early modern political thought, have been of particular importance in this regard.[1]

Finding appropriate political expression for a just relationship with colonised indigenous peoples is one of the most important issues confronting political theory today. As important as it is to understand how western and especially liberal political theory is implicated in the justification of colonialism, it is even more important to determine whether this complex tradition of thought might provide space for the contemporary aspirations of indigenous peoples. Typically, these have included claims for the return of traditional lands, the preservation of culture, and the right as well as the means to exercise effective self-government. Western political thought is not necessarily the language of the world's indigenous peoples, although they have often been constrained to use it and there are points at which it overlaps with indigenous conceptions of what is right or just.[2] This book is intended as a contribution to an ongoing intercultural conversation between indigenous and non-indigenous theorists, and between theorists occupying different vantage points within the same general 'language' of western political thought. Our aim is to help create a better understanding of the range of relations between political theory and indigenous rights claims, as well as to contribute to new thinking about the best means to address such claims. What new combination of familiar values or concepts can be constructed to meet indigenous claims? What would it mean to 'do justice' to these claims in ways that are acceptable and accessible to both indigenous and non-indigenous peoples? What do we mean by 'justice' in this context?

Indigenous peoples' claims to prior and continued sovereignty over their territories question the source and legitimacy of state authority. Some states rely on the now discredited doctrine of *terra nullius*; in others, the terms of treaties are not always observed. No doubt most states owe their existence to some combination of force and fraud. However, the issue is not simply a matter of how a state came to be, but of how it can become 'morally rehabilitated', even if it began in an illegitimate fashion. How might the narratives of nationhood be retold, the founding moments of a state reconstituted or its fundamental documents reinterpreted? These issues have broad consequences for philosophical views about the relation between the individual and the state, and the nature of community and identity.

One important issue that emerges at the outset is the problem of distinguishing indigenous claims from the claims of other kinds of cultural or 'societal' groups. In order to 'do justice' to indigenous claims we need an understanding of the distinctive nature of the claims put forward by indigenous peoples. As much as it is true that, historically speaking, liberal democracies have tried to assimilate indigenous peoples and deny them any group-specific forms of recognition, Will Kymlicka points out in his chapter that the same is true with many other minority groups. Basques, Bretons, Scots and Québécois have all, at various points, been victims of state-sponsored discrimination or assimilation. Moreover, these 'stateless nations' have also tended to see themselves not only as a distinct people, as do indigenous peoples, but as occupying territories they have come to think of as their 'homelands'. If we are to distinguish between these groups and indigenous peoples, how can it be done, and according to what criteria? This question leads us into issues of cultural difference, universalism and particularism.

Rights are generally conceived of as securing or protecting fundamental human interests, for example, those to do with property or bodily integrity. Hence they appeal to conceptions of what counts as a fundamental interest and are shaped by the particular contexts and the challenges faced in securing or promoting those interests. They are also embodied and expressed in distinctive conceptions and idioms of law, which in turn require institutional expression. The recognition and

expression of indigenous rights will require accommodation and translation of all these different facets, with the additional burden of doing so
in the context of an imposed non-indigenous legal framework. As Jeremy
Webber points out, whatever else might be said about the character of
indigenous rights, they are 'mediated rights': the recognition of indigenous interests in land as legal or political rights inevitably transforms
those interests.

James Tully suggests that western political theory has consistently
failed to enter into a just dialogue with indigenous peoples and their political traditions and understandings. At the same time, the demand for a
just dialogue between indigenous and non-indigenous peoples presents
a series of difficult challenges. What are the necessary conditions for
such dialogue? On the one hand, it is clearly a presupposition of dialogue that indigenous and western political theories are not utterly
incommensurable. On the other hand, this does not mean that there
cannot be profound differences between their conceptions of social relations, individual rights and obligations and that, as a result, we still face
the problem of finding appropriate translations or reconciliations. Does
this imply that western liberal political theory should renounce its claim
to universality and present itself as based upon one possible set of values
to be considered alongside others, including indigenous ones? And
would this not raise the spectre of cultural relativism? Are we, then, not
in danger of assuming that cultures and traditions are more homogeneous and self-contained than they actually are? Do we not risk losing
sight of the possibility that there may be values concerned with equality,
freedom, autonomy, wellbeing and justice that are shared between cultures and traditions?

Contemporary anthropologists and cultural theorists have shown how
even the most apparently 'traditional' cultures are actually quite complex and fluid (Clifford 1988; Moody-Adams 1997). This seems particularly true in the case of the cultures of colonised indigenous peoples
within contemporary liberal democracies. Conversely, problematic
assumptions about the inherent inferiority of indigenous peoples and
their practices and the inherent superiority of European norms and institutions have been a standard feature of arguments in political theory
since at least the sixteenth century.[3] When we invoke a mysterious 'oth-
erness' or radical difference in referring to indigenous cultures, we are
in danger of simply replaying such prejudices. Deep cultural diversity
and difference is a key feature of many contemporary societies. But that
is not to say that the various cultures and peoples are encased within static and clearly delineated cultural structures and boundaries. Claims of
cultural difference have to be balanced against the dynamic nature of
cultural practices and traditions and the ways in which cultures borrow

and import practices and beliefs from outside of themselves. The chapters by Manuhuia Barcham, Audra Simpson, William Connolly and Jeremy Webber examine the conceptions of identity and difference current in contemporary political thought.

In recent years, there have been genuine attempts from within the liberal tradition to accommodate indigenous claims. These need to be evaluated as much as the earlier forms of complicity with the process of colonisation. Accordingly, this book addresses two general questions. First, in what ways has western political theory contributed to the colonisation, subjugation and continuing disadvantage faced by indigenous peoples in the past and today?

Second, what resources exist in political theory for thinking differently about these relations and about the possibility of 'decolonising' relations between indigenous and non-indigenous peoples? Contributors have been asked to pursue both questions with regard to three general themes – *sovereignty, identity* and *democratic theory* – in each case, with an eye to the fundamental issue of *justice* for colonised indigenous peoples. Some of the chapters touch on all three themes, others focus on one or a combination of them. Each of these themes represents a significant domain within western political theory, and each has been central to the encounter between indigenous and non-indigenous peoples.

Our aim here is to provide a philosophical context within which the reader can situate the essays. We shall consider how indigenous claims have come to be understood and interpreted by contemporary political philosophers, and what they have taken to be the consequences of these claims. Liberal political philosophy looms large, since it has been among liberal political theorists that debate on the nature of indigenous claims from a non-indigenous perspective has become, philosophically speaking, most developed. We aim to provide a sense of both the limits and possibilities within liberal political theory for recognising and responding to indigenous claims.

Responses to Indigenous Claims

Three kinds of response to indigenous rights claims have emerged in recent years. The first argues that liberal political theory need not be reshaped in light of indigenous demands, but instead should hold fast to its individualist and non-interventionist credentials, and ensure that the rights and protections it cherishes effectively be extended to indigenous peoples. The second argues that liberal political thought *can* be remoulded and reshaped to meet indigenous aspirations, but only to the extent of the limits given by liberal conceptions of equality and autonomy. The third argues that the poverty of both previous responses suggests that some reshaping of the conceptual framework of political theory is required in order to do justice to indigenous aspirations.

The first response invokes a form of liberal neutrality and argues that the liberal state should not seek to recognise distinctive cultural or group rights but instead focus on providing effective individual civil rights such as freedom of expression, association, religion, movement and the like. In particular, liberal theorists should be wary of the social ontology of cultures and groups. Groups are not homogenous but dynamic, heterogenous historical associations of individuals (Kukathas 1992; 1997b). To treat them otherwise is to risk empowering elites within groups and creating problems for 'internal minorities'. Hence, it is argued, individuals should be empowered to move around within and, if they so choose, out of the 'associations' in which they grew up in or choose to live. Individuals should be free to form associations with others on the grounds of a shared societal culture or way of life. The state has no business interfering with their choice, but it must ensure that the rights of individuals to express dissent from or exit such associations are protected. This means avoiding entrenching group rights. Rights should not be exercisable over individuals by something like a group or a 'culture'. The link between individual wellbeing and group or cultural membership is contingent and bi-directional. Cultural membership may contribute to individual wellbeing, but group rights can increase the transaction costs of communication in a state by complicating the political process and slowing down effective decision-making. They can also place burdens – material and otherwise – upon majority populations (that is, subsidising alternative legal systems; language programs; separate schools etc.) that can generate resentment and 'backlash', thereby undermining the conditions for granting such rights in the first place (Offe 1997; Hardin 1995; Post forthcoming). Individual and not group rights are what need to be secured. The rights of self-government or self-determination for indigenous peoples are satisfied *ipso facto* upon the provision of their individual rights.

This conclusion suggests why such arguments have been understood by indigenous peoples to be fundamentally hostile to their claims. It appears to reduce what they see to be certain distinctive rights they possess as peoples to the undifferentiated rights of citizens participating in the processes of collective will formation as part of an already constituted 'people'. In other words, they see it as another form of assimilation. So, as much as the fluidity of cultural boundaries and the dangers of the 'dynamic effects' of group rights are recognised, this first approach has been seen as deeply problematic on normative grounds, for it presupposes precisely what is at issue: the nature of 'the people' upon whom rests the legitimacy of democratic authority (see the chapters by Kymlicka, Pettit and Tully).

An alternative response, still from within the liberal tradition, has been to tie the recognition of more extensive rights of self-government and the protection (or return) of indigenous lands to an argument about individual wellbeing. This argument has been developed with considerable skill by Kymlicka (1989; 1995; 1998a). Kymlicka's argument is that indigenous people are owed self-government and title to their lands because without such rights (in addition to traditional liberal rights of freedom of movement, association and expression) they are in danger of losing access to a secure societal culture and hence, to the context in which individual freedom is rendered meaningful. Thus group rights, up to and including self-government, are justified on the grounds of preserving the conditions for the flourishing of individual autonomy and freedom. The same grounds also justify the limiting condition 'liberals can only endorse minority rights insofar as they are consistent with respect for the freedom and autonomy of individuals' (Kymlicka 1995: 75). Justice involves compensating for arbitrary and unfair social disadvantages, as well as promoting and securing the capacities of individuals to pursue and revise their own conception of the good. The value of cultural membership, including in this case a particular relation to land, is fixed relative to a conception of justice in which the value of autonomy is central. To give up on the centrality of autonomy for the purposes of a liberal recognition of difference is to risk tolerating practices that are not simply illiberal, but potentially harmful.

Kymlicka's innovative argument has broken new ground in liberal political theory. It manages to transcend the sterile debate between liberals and communitarians; it addresses the claims of cultural, ethnic and national minorities historically left out of the story of the emergence of the liberal state; and it preserves a fluid and dynamic account of culture that avoids romanticising or 'freezing' cultural practices in time. This is an impressive achievement, given how often liberals are castigated on all these fronts by various critics. Moreover, as Kymlicka himself emphasises, even if the details of his argument or the grounds upon which it is made are rejected, it represents at least an attempt to formulate a distinctly liberal response to indigenous claims. Hence it can be read as an attempt to initiate intercultural dialogue rather than simply as a justification for imposing liberal principles on indigenous communities (Kymlicka 1995: 163–72).[4] Kymlicka sees his argument as actually building upon recent developments within contemporary liberal democracies and, to a lesser extent, international law (1989: 206–19; 1995: 49–74). In his chapter, he shows how a narrow view of 'American multiculturalism' has exerted a detrimental effect on current debates concerning the rights of indigenous peoples and other 'nations within'. In particular, he argues that the tendency to contrast the apparently open, fluid and voluntary nature of American multiculturalism with the closed, static and involuntary conception of 'minority nationalisms' associated with the claims of the Québécois, Basques and various indigenous peoples is empirically and historically mistaken. Moreover, insofar as this contrast is employed internationally to promote 'the American model, it actually inhibits the efforts by many contemporary states to understand and accommodate minority nationalisms'.

Kymlicka's argument has nevertheless been subject to extensive criticism.[5] On the one hand, liberals who are worried about his incorporation of 'culture' into the list of primary goods the liberal state should seek to promote and protect have criticised him for not being interventionist enough with regard to the cultural practices of various groups (Okin 1998; Laitin 1998; Doppelt 1998). If the limiting condition of 'autonomy' is to be interpreted broadly – perhaps even according to standards internal to the particular cultural group – then Kymlicka risks endorsing a form of cultural relativism. Some have queried the grounds for and the need to provide group rights at all, in addition to the basic rights of expression, conscience and association usually promoted by liberals (Kukathas 1992; Offe 1997). On the other hand, some critics have focused on the apparent imperial tenor of Kymlicka's argument, especially his grounding of the case for group rights on the value of individual autonomy. It can be argued that Kymlicka justifies group rights on grounds that only basically liberal groups can meet, and thus his argument is actually less accommodating than often presumed. More seriously, others argue that if the self-government rights for indigenous peoples are meant as a form of internal autonomy within a pre-existing state that continues to claim preeminent sovereignty, then Kymlicka's argument could be said to be perpetuating internal colonisation rather than dismantling it.[6] The presumption of sovereignty anticipates the problem of reconciling two or more peoples on a territory rather than offering a possible solution to it (Kymlicka 1996). The phrase 'nations within' shows the persistence of this problem. As a result, the conditions for a just dialogue between indigenous and non-indigenous peoples are not met by Kymlicka's case for group rights.

In response to such objections, Kymlicka (1998a: 144–46) has argued explicitly that it is our 'most urgent obligation of justice' to 'recognize the principle of the inherent right of self-government' of Aboriginal peoples and to 'negotiate in good faith about its appropriate implementation'. He makes clear his view that existing federal arrangements in Canada are unjust because 'the boundaries drawn up and the division of powers within Canadian federalism took no account of Aboriginal needs and aspirations' (144). Moreover he thinks that it is wrong for liberals to simply presume that it is justified to subject indigenous governments or institutions to the Canadian or American Supreme Court (Kymlicka 1995: 166–67; 1996; 1998b). More decentralised and 'culturally appropriate' forms of judicial review, or even international forums, are arguably more justifiable. However, the greater the scope for self-government Kymlicka is willing to grant to indigenous peoples, the more he seems to be moving away from his commitment to grounding group rights on a liberal interpretation of the value of individual autonomy.

This tension between cultural difference and liberal values leads to the third response to indigenous claims, which sees a need for greater conceptual and practical reshaping of liberal democratic norms and institutions. Part of the reason for this scepticism about existing norms and institutions is that liberal arguments are said to be unable to comprehend what is distinctive about indigenous claims to land and self-government. What is it about the claims of indigenous peoples that is missed by liberal responses, and in what way are indigenous claims distinctive when compared to those of other minority peoples?

Approaches to this issue tend to appeal either to the 'inherent' sovereignty of indigenous peoples, to the history of their relations with settlers, or to their cultural differences with Europeans. Some argue that indigenous peoples exercised historical sovereignty over their lands and communities and therefore possessed an 'inherent' sovereignty that was unjustly taken away and should be returned to them. Similarly, lands that were unfairly expropriated should be returned or appropriate compensation negotiated where this is not possible.

There are two difficulties with this argument. First, other stateless peoples also once exercised historic sovereignty over their lands and communities (for example the Scots and the Catalans) and it is not clear how indigenous claims are any more distinctive than theirs. It might be argued that indigenous peoples have suffered more than other peoples have, and thus there is a remedial case for distinguishing their claims from others (Anaya 1996). But linking self-government rights to degrees of suffering is problematic. The case for remedial rights depends on there being a temporary measure intended to address specific disadvantage caused by historic injustice. But indigenous claims appeal to 'inherent', not temporary, sovereignty. The second problem with the historical sovereignty approach is that it is not clear what is meant by 'sovereignty' in this context, and therefore what should actually be recognised or 'returned' to indigenous peoples.

The relevance of the history of relations between indigenous and non-indigenous peoples is something contemporary theories of justice have been slow to recognise. Jeremy Waldron has argued that the recognition of Aboriginal claims to land or self-government rights should not be about compensating for historical injustice, but about addressing contemporary discrimination and disadvantage (Waldron 1992; Simmons 1995). If it were the historical nature of the entitlements that mattered most, then it wouldn't be clear what the restoration of lands or resources had to do with distributive justice, since the parties might just as well be reasonably well-off, or at least not suffering from any serious disadvantages. Of course indigenous peoples do currently suffer from appalling social disadvantages. Moreover, on the most charitable reading of his argument, Waldron's aim is precisely to acknowledge this point.

But the distinctiveness of indigenous claims, if understood as deriving from their attachment to the land and the history of their relations with the colonial state, is lost or rendered opaque in discussions of distributive justice. Some would argue that this is unavoidable. Justice is about the impartial distribution of goods, and the distinctive identity or history of Aboriginal peoples is only relevant insofar as it affects consideration of their fair share of 'primary goods' here and now relative to other citizens. But this means that there is a risk that the manner in which such lists of primary goods are arrived at, as well as the construction of notions of fairness, will misunderstand not only the particular value of culture or land being appealed to, but also the nature of the moral wrongs upon which the claims are based – the historical legacy of colonialism. Indigenous claims are not just for rights to any fair share of Australian or Canadian resources, but to a particularised share (Simmons 1995: 174); one that must be understood against the background of the denial of their equal sovereign status, the dispossession of their lands and the destruction of their cultural practices.

The final means of distinguishing indigenous claims from those of other peoples involves an appeal to cultural difference. On this approach, indigenous peoples' claims are distinctive because of the nature of their culture and especially their relation to the land, which affects the particular history of their interactions with various settler states. The way we distinguish between indigenous peoples and other 'stateless' nations is that, in the processes of state-building, these other peoples were able to converge along with the majority nation on what Kymlicka has put, in his chapter, as 'certain cultural self-conceptions, and to share certain economic and social needs and influences'. Indigenous peoples remained apart from such convergences, and were only ever integrated by force. Hence their way of life, although not incommensurable from that of other cultures in liberal democracies, is sufficiently different not to be readily assimilated.

One problem with this approach is that focusing on cultural difference risks locking in unrealistic and paternalistic views of indigenous cultures. Notions of custom or culture should not be presumed to exist independently of contemporary indigenous social and political life, which should not be either romanticised or demonised. Recent legal cases have highlighted the danger of interpreting indigenous cultures in ways that locate their practices in supposedly 'traditional' contexts and then attempt to limit any subsequent rights in virtue of them accordingly.[7] The danger here is that of reinstating hierarchical assumptions about the value or 'authenticity' of cultures while deciding which interests should be protected or promoted by various kinds of rights or institutions. These interests should be defined and contested as much as possible by contemporary indigenous peoples themselves, rather than according to assumptions elaborated within various western anthropological, political or legal doctrines. Although, needless to say, these are doctrines of which indigenous peoples might avail themselves.

But this touches on another problem for the difference approach. If indigenous peoples' claims are distinct because of their cultural difference then how deep does this difference run? Should indigenous social and political institutions be exempt from basic human rights legislation or charters of rights? Many commentators argue that although indigenous communities have good reason to be sceptical about the existing legal and political institutions and mechanisms that enforce such rights, this isn't to say they should be exempt from the basic underlying norms of human rights (Carens 1995; Kymlicka 1996). This is seen as especially important with regard to vulnerable members of such communities (often women) and 'internal minorities'. Others insist that indigenous political theory itself contains constraints on indigenous decision-making processes and institutional design that are more than capable of meeting such challenges. If anything, it has been constant colonial interference in these practices that has undermined traditional mechanisms for dispute resolution and the protection of vulnerable members of the community (Alfred 1999a; Canada, Royal Commission on Aboriginal Peoples 1996a, 1996b).

Reshaping Sovereignty, Identity and Justice

New ways of thinking are required with regard to certain crucial conceptual and normative assumptions informing indigenous claims. This is particularly true in three areas: the nature of *sovereignty*; questions of political and cultural *identity and difference* (both individual and collective); and contemporary approaches to distributive *justice* and *democratic theory*. Consider first the spectre of sovereignty that dominates contemporary political theories of the state. It haunts the complex of issues at stake in the conflicts between indigenous peoples and the institutions of colonial societies in a variety of ways.

Roger Maaka and Augie Fleras highlight the issue of the legitimacy of the colonial states in their chapter. On what basis did white settler systems acquire sovereignty over the land and its inhabitants, and by what authority do they exercise that sovereignty? Three answers have been put forward throughout the history of modern colonisation. The first relies exclusively upon the doctrine of discovery, which was the basis on which European nations recognised each other's claims to specific territories in the New World. However, discovery is only a sufficient basis for the acquisition of sovereignty if there were no original inhabitants, or if the inhabitants lived under such rudimentary conditions of social organisation that they could not be considered sovereign peoples. The latter view amounts to the so-called extended doctrine of *terra nullius*, which was invoked by colonial governments and courts throughout the nineteenth and early twentieth centuries to deny that indigenous peoples had any legal or political rights other than those derived from the colonial sovereign. This was the basis on which the British Crown laid claim to its Australian territories. However, since *Mabo* (1992), the High Court of Australia has ruled out any reliance on *terra nullius* with respect to domestic law and the consequences of colonisation, as has the Supreme Court of Canada since *Calder* (1973). Nevertheless, notwithstanding the rejection of the extended doctrine of *terra nullius* by the International Court of Justice in its *Advisory Opinion on Western Sahara* (1975), and in the absence of any declared alternative, it remains the basis of state authority over the indigenous population. The historian Henry Reynolds points to an unresolved issue of legitimacy which, he suggests, is:

the fundamental problem at the heart of Australian jurisprudence. The doctrine of the settled colony only works if there literally was no sovereignty – no recognisable political or legal organisation at all – before 1788. And that proposition can only survive if underpinned by nineteenth-century ideas about 'primitive' people. (Reynolds 1996: 13–14)

Michael Asch argues that a similar contradiction emerges in recent Canadian jurisprudence:

The view that indigenous peoples were uncivilised at the time of settlement was repudiated in *Calder*, and to uphold it in order to explain State sovereignty is not only contradictory; it is also repugnant to contemporary values. The idea is ethnocentric and racist, a direct holdover from the colonial era . . . Yet the State has derived no thesis to supplant it; the government has chosen not to address it; and the court has chosen either to ignore it in the *Calder* era, or to define it away in *Van der Peet*. (Asch 1999: 441)

The second justification of the acquisition of sovereignty under international law stems from the doctrine of conquest. However, few countries are prepared to rely upon the claim of conquest alone.

More common is recourse to the third justification, namely the conclusion of treaties with local indigenous populations. Treaties draw their legitimacy from the fundamental principle of western political and legal thought that actions affecting the interests of others are acceptable only with the consent of those affected. Moreover, as both J.G.A. Pocock and James Tully point out, recourse to treaties presupposes that the indigenous peoples involved are sovereign. However reliance upon treaties as the ground of acquisition of sovereignty over indigenous peoples raises a further set of problems with regard to the interpretation of those treaties. Pocock and Tully question whether or not indigenous signatories to treaties can reasonably be said to have agreed to the transfer of sovereignty rather than the extension of their own sovereignty, or at least consent to share their land and resources with the newcomers.

This raises further questions about the nature of sovereignty itself and the degree to which it is a concept shared between European and non-European traditions of political thought. Sovereignty is by no means an uncontested concept even within western legal and political theory: does it apply, as Iris Young suggests, only to states, or, as Pocock and Tully suggest, can it be applied to peoples independently of whether they exercise their sovereignty through forms of state government? Many indigenous writers have questioned whether sovereignty is an appropriate concept with which to represent the forms of indigenous governance and relation to the land (Boldt and Long 1985; Pearson 1993: 15; Alfred 1999a: 53–69, 109–10). Underlying this problem are the complex issues of cross-cultural translation, which are raised in stark form by the controversy surrounding the interpretation of the founding document of Aotearoa/New Zealand. In the English version of the Treaty of Waitangi signed in 1840 by representatives of the British Crown and some 500 Maori chiefs, the Maori agreed to transfer 'sovereignty' to the Crown in exchange for royal protection of the 'full and undisturbed possession' of Maori lands and estates. Not only is there no concept of sovereignty in the Maori language, but it is not evident how this concept should be aligned with the terms used in the Maori version. What the chiefs consented to transfer to the Crown was kawanatanga, which some argue should be translated as 'governorship'.[8] What they retained was te tino rangatiratanga, which may be translated as full and complete chieftainship or authority (Sharp 1997; McHugh 1991; Kawharu 1989; Orange 1987). Maaka and Fleras argue that the political problem of Maori sovereignty today is precisely the problem of finding political structures adequate for the expression of te tino rangatiratanga.

Over and above these issues of intercultural translation, the assertion of indigenous peoples' rights intersects in a number of ways with other contemporary challenges to the understanding and forms of exercise of sovereignty. Standard definitions of sovereignty point to a range of elements which may or may not be included within the concept: sovereignty as supreme legal authority within a given jurisdiction; sovereignty as comprehensive authority within that jurisdiction; sovereignty as supreme and comprehensive authority over a given territory (Onuf 1991; Philpott 1995; Caney 1999). The prevailing view has tended to connect all three of these elements with the concept of the state as the embodiment and agent of sovereign power in a global political system based entirely upon such states. However, as several of the chapters in this book point out, the idea and the reality of such a system have come under increasing moral as well as political pressure in recent years. Young points to the range of moral considerations that have been advanced against the idea of a global state system as well as the pressures in practice to regulate across national boundaries. Like several other contributors, she points to the sense in which, to the extent that the rights of indigenous peoples are recognised and enshrined in law and legislation, they constitute a form of internal limit to the sovereign power of colonial states. Moreover, since indigenous peoples' demands for autonomy and self-determination rarely extend as far as independent sovereign statehood, they contribute to the need for a reconceptualisation of sovereignty that would separate it from the system of nation states in favour of more diverse arrangements of 'secessionless' sovereignty that is shared among different levels of government. Maaka and Fleras embrace the suggestion that the conception of state sovereignty 'reflects a certain understanding of power and authority, rooted in a particular historically determined configuration of social relations and public space' that may have already run its course. Recent settlements in Aotearoa/New Zealand under the Treaty of Waitangi as well as the recommendations of the Canadian Royal Commission point to the need to separate the issue of the underlying sovereignty of indigenous peoples from that of the appropriate political structures and mechanisms for the expression of that 'sovereignty' (or te tino rangatiratanga) in the present.

Demands for the reshaping of sovereignty lead directly to questions of political and cultural identity. William Connolly argues that the dominant mode of understanding identity in western political thought has involved prioritising relations of identity over difference, which serves to obscure the degree to which identity and difference are fundamentally relational in nature (Connolly 1991; 1995). Their interdependence implies that the attempt to fix some authentic or natural centre to individual or national identity depends upon defining an identity against another who is not the same. And yet the need to fix some immutable centre or authentic identity only serves to inflame feelings of resentment and fear of this very 'other'. As Connolly points out in his piece, this leads to a paradox with regard to national identity:

> the nation is experienced by many as an imperative that must be achieved if cultural belonging is to be secure . . . or if sovereignty is to be stable. But the nation is also an imagination of unity or wholeness that has never been actualised.

Webber also draws attention to the tendency to exaggerate the extent to which national identities require a single, coherent national story. He recommends instead the metaphor of a conversation between different groups, suggesting that 'it often seems that nations are marked as much by the structure of their disagreements as by their agreements'.

This general point about the relations between identity and difference has consequences for thinking about indigenous identities. Manuhuia Barcham, for example, points to the very real problems presented by assumptions about cultural identity with regard to the emergence of the urban Maori in New Zealand, an issue not limited to that country alone (see, for example, Canada, Royal Commission on Aboriginal Peoples 1996a, 1996b). He argues that academic and policy-oriented definitions of Maori tend to be derived from notions of indigeneity contingent upon the possession of 'authentic' cultural norms and traditions. The result is that a socially and politically constructed notion of indigenous authenticity is then used to judge between relative degrees of indigeneity as a means of determining which groups are more deserving of 'indigenous rights' than others. But since all political and cultural identities are historically and socially dynamic, this leaves those groups not fitting the dominant model of indigeneity outside the framework of indigenous rights. Hence 'urban Maori' are set against 'traditional Maori', and denied access to the resources and benefits – such as they are – reserved for 'genuine' indigenous people. And yet, urban Maori represent a significant proportion of the general population of Maori. Barcham argues that any claim based on indigenous identity and culture must accept that they are inherently dynamic and subject to change not only over time, but in relation to institutional and practical frameworks. The institutional forms through which indigenous cultures manifest themselves should also remain open to change; urban-based institutions for Maori should be seen as no more or no less 'authentic' than kin-based institutions. Thus, as Pocock suggests, the model of a postcolonial state may be envisaged, individually and institutionally speaking, as a kind of 'confederacy of shape-changers'.

The chapters by John Bern and Susan Dodds, Sonia Smallacombe, Audra Simpson and Jeremy Webber also point to the interdependencies between identity and difference, and to unavoidable articulation of indigenous interests with the governmental apparatus of the state. Indigenous peoples, like any other group in a liberal democratic state, are subject to a whole range of 'governmental' actions on their actions (not limited to those by the state itself). Using the example of the Australian Northern Territory's *Aboriginal Land Rights Act*, Bern and Dodds show how legislative and policy regimes shape not only indigenous interests in land, but also those who are said to have authority to represent those interests – a point similarly emphasised by Barcham, Smallacombe and Webber.

Smallacombe criticises the way in which the dominant cultural institutions construct and then display 'Aboriginal culture' according to particular western understandings of 'cultural heritage'. Simpson's narratives of different strands of Kahnawake nationhood, glimpses of what she refers to as the 'interior frontiers of Mohawk nationhood', illustrate the practical and conceptual contexts within which claims to identity and difference are made and heard. Drawing on a critical use of Michael Jackson's conception of 'radical empiricism', she points out that these social and historical contexts are difficult to capture through essentialist anthropological discourse. The focus on the dynamics of experience in Jackson's approach, she argues, resonates with Mohawk claims for sovereignty over both their land and representations of their culture (a point made equally forcefully with regard to Australian Aboriginal identity by Smallacombe). Nationhood becomes the 'prism through which Indians view their historical experience, themselves and their aspirations', with the result that, like thought in Heidegger's formulation, '"nationhood" . . . may be understood as a movement toward a clearing'. Emerging here is a conception of sovereignty that has as much to do with the reclaiming and retelling of various histories – of peoples, cultures and institutions – as it does with control over territory and resources.

Webber argues that the common law recognition of native title in *Mabo* (1992) has far-reaching implications for Australian constitutionalism because of the way it implicitly acknowledges the continued existence of distinct Aboriginal and Islander societies with their own autonomous legal traditions. In sharp contrast to the assimilationist views that have dominated policy towards Australia's indigenous peoples, native title law implies that they should be counted as legally and politically autonomous participants in the national story. In common with Barcham, Dodds and Bern, Smallacombe and Simpson, Webber focuses on the need for institutional arrangements intended to protect indigenous cultures and secure self-determination. Whether local, national or international, these arrangements need to be capable of recognising and accommodating the dynamic and fluid nature of indigenous identities.

One lesson we might draw from these discussions is the need to detach ourselves from the paralysing discourse of 'individual versus group rights' that dominates so much of the consideration of indigenous claims in western political theory. This need not mean abandoning the language of rights completely, but one consequence of perceiving the complex relations between identity and difference might be the moderation of our desire to translate every claim into one that can be classified as an individual or group right. Seeing cultural accommodation as mainly about setting the scope and limits of individual and group rights holders provides incentives for the parties involved to telescope cultural and political identities and demands in order to secure the gains associated with rights conceived in a zero-sum fashion. The dynamic effects of such assumptions, especially with regard to 'internal minorities' or the 'constitutional stability' of a state, inevitably leads to a perception of collective and individual interests being diametrically opposed. But this approach tends to underplay points of interdependence and possible forms of accommodation (Post forthcoming). Arguably, processes of cultural accommodation should be seen more as matters to do with institutional innovation and evolution rather than as an extension of the jurisprudence of rights. Disavowing colonialism involves more than assertions and counter-assertions of rights. Rights, understood as powers or instruments to secure or promote individual and group interests, operate and come to be grasped within practical and interpretive frameworks that are partly held in place by historically patterned beliefs and practices. A postcolonial political theory needs to focus as much on these processes as it does on the language(s) of right.

Finally, what does it mean to do justice to indigenous claims within the framework of a democratic and postcolonial state? The 1996 Royal Commission on Aboriginal Peoples in Canada, perhaps the most extensive study of relations between indigenous and non-indigenous peoples ever undertaken, has proposed that these relations be based on principles of mutual recognition, mutual respect, sharing and mutual responsibility (Canada, Royal Commission on Aboriginal Peoples, 1996a: 676–97). A just relationship between indigenous and non-indigenous peoples is one that involves dialogue, which must occur under conditions that are acceptable to both parties. We have referred to the difficulties that arise in a situation where there is disagreement about the relevance of the historical character of injustices. However, there are further difficulties with the conditions under which democratic consensus or legitimacy is arrived at

by the parties involved. Public discourse is always characterised by relations
of power as much as it is by reason. Political settlements are thus much
closer to a kind of *modus vivendi*, as opposed to a deeper 'overlapping
consensus' on constitutional norms (Rawls 1993: 146–72; Ivison 2000).
Consensus is important, but is never a sufficient condition for understanding relations of power since it is often a result of such relations.
The history of indigenous peoples' treatment in the hands of liberal
democratic states provides ample reason for such caution towards the
regulative role of consensus. For this reason, it is appropriate that some
contributors directly address questions of democratic theory by indigenous peoples' claims.

Philip Pettit argues that on a thin 'electoral' conception of democracy,
claims by indigenous people and other minority groups will not fare very
well, since to argue that a minority group needs special rights of self-
government to protect it from the decisions of the majority is to challenge
the principle of the sovereignty of the people. Even if we think general
counter-majoritarian measures such as a Bill of Rights are essential for
the possibility of democracy itself, 'special minority rights' are not similarly justifiable. They appear to come upon democracy from the outside.
Hence the need for a richer account of democracy; a two-dimensional
conception in which there is a demand for not only 'electoral' legitimacy
but a 'contestatory' dimension as well. If the rationale for democracy is
in part to force governments to take their guidance from people's genuine common interests, then it should be organised so as to give standing to all possible common interests. There should be mechanisms to
ensure that where citizens feel they have not been treated as equals they
can contest government decisions and have some confidence of such
decisions being reversed. 'Special' – or perhaps more accurately, specific
– minority rights present just such a mechanism. The justification for
them is tied to the value of equal standing, which in turn is tied to the
value of democratic rule. The more multicultural a state, the greater the
need for such contestatory mechanisms.

However, the question remains whether such 'special' minority rights
are sufficient in order to establish the conditions for just relations with
indigenous peoples, and whether or not thinking of them as 'special' is
not itself part of the problem. Connolly argues for 'a thick public culture
of multidimensional pluralism well oiled by an ethos of engagement
between diverse constituents'. Pettit suggests that the case for specific
rights may extend beyond merely contestatory mechanisms to include
significant powers of self-government in matters affecting the survival of
indigenous communities and cultures.

The strategy of creating space within liberal democracies for indigenous claims therefore leads back to the issue of sovereignty and the

nature and limits of state power. For some, including Tully, Pocock, Simpson and Kymlicka in this volume, there can be no equal standing for indigenous peoples until they are acknowledged as equal sovereigns within a postcolonial constitutional arrangement. For others, such as Young and Fleuras and Maaka, it is the very nature of the sovereign state that must be rethought. Young argues that the challenge posed by the history and current status of indigenous peoples converges with feminism and other movements towards a form of global democracy involving self-determination without sovereign borders.

An important part of the argument in the *Report of the Royal Commission on Aboriginal Peoples* (1996a) is that the principles of mutual recognition and respect can only be realised if they draw on Aboriginal and western values that both sides can accept as legitimate, including the ways in which Aboriginal and non-Aboriginal peoples have acted together in the past. How does the case for the inherent sovereignty of indigenous peoples fit into this framework? On the one hand, self-government is clearly a value central to western conceptions of justice. There is a freedom and equal dignity secured by participation in the government of a political association one not only consents to but in which one feels 'at home' among its institutions and practices (Hardimon 1992; Mason 1999). But these are goods shared by both indigenous and non-indigenous conceptions of justice, albeit developed in their own ways. Generally speaking, the 'currency' of egalitarian justice is one of rights and resources impartially distributed between individuals and groups. This distribution is usually justified relative to some account of the basic capacities or goods needed for citizens to live decent lives, including the capacity to participate freely in the governing of one's society and pursue one's life according to one's own choices and responsibilities. However, the way in which indigenous claims to land and self-government are redeemed according to liberal theories of justice raises a series of difficulties.

On Kymlicka's argument, self-government is justified by virtue of the disadvantages indigenous peoples suffer in view of the vulnerability of their cultural structure – their lands and their cultural practices – to the political decisions of the majority society. These disadvantages stem not from the choices indigenous peoples make but from the way they find themselves relative to the rest of the population. Hence they are a legitimate basis for demands for justice.[9] But it is not clear to what extent this distinguishes their claims from other ethnic groups and thus, how it corresponds to the form of recognition indigenous peoples actually seek. Many migrant groups were unjustly incorporated into 'settler' states. Moreover, the children of migrants who have tried to recreate the cultural structures they have left behind are arguably in a position analogous to that of members of indigenous cultures: neither chose to be members of minority cultures. If what differentiates these indigenous groups from migrants is the fact that the former are much worse off than the latter because they suffer from much greater social and political disadvantages, then once again, the historical nature of their claim seems to be less important than the fact of contemporary disadvantage.

This argument may be effective, but it misrecognises the nature of indigenous claims for the recognition of their inherent rights to self-government, since it grounds the basis of these rights in the facts of contemporary disadvantage relative to an independently derived currency of rights and resources. For some, this is entirely correct. There can be no special pleading on the basis of historical status or cultural difference when it comes to distributing rights and resources. But seeing indigenous claims as so much 'special pleading' against a common currency of justice is, arguably, precisely the problem indigenous peoples are arguing needs to be addressed.

Is there an alternative way of thinking about the recognition of special rights in the case of indigenous peoples? One possibility might be to insist that the recognition of indigenous difference – one grounded in the historical consequences of colonialism and their particular relation to the land – is a necessary precondition of the legitimacy of the very institutions and practices within which rights and resources – the currency of egalitarian justice – are to be distributed. This is a strong precondition. How can we know when it is fulfilled? According to what grounds and in what contexts? The idea of 'recognition' needs content. Does it mean recognising indigenous sovereignty? If so, what does that actually entail? Who or what is to be recognised? And how? We have surveyed some of the possibilities and risks involved, as have many of our contributors. A balance will have to be struck between demands for the preservation of culture and the means to adapt and change the practices involved to suit the times and the diverse peoples for whom culture represents a living, dynamic thing rather than a museum piece.

A crucial aspect of any possible just response to these issues is the manner in which the principles or norms invoked to govern indigenous and non-indigenous relations are related to the concrete practices and contexts in which they occur. The justice or injustice of any set of political arrangements depends as much on how principles and norms are applied and used on the ground as they do on how they are derived or justified philosophically. Unjust political arrangements are often so precisely because of the way in which they have arisen or been imposed on those subject to them. But even apparently just arrangements can be imposed unjustly. Perhaps this is one of the contributions engagement with indigenous claims makes to the practice of political theory. It teaches us that care about the application and use of principles and norms in the world is as important and relevant to considerations of justice as the hypothetical or deliberative process of settling on the principles themselves. The point is not simply a pragmatic or prudential one. Care about the application and use of norms feeds back into the process of how we select or identify the relevant principles and norms in the first place. Ironically, one of the interesting consequences of the encounter between liberalism and its colonial past and present might be a more context-sensitive and multilayered approach to questions of justice, identity, democracy and sovereignty. The result would be a political theory open to new modes of cultural and political belonging. On this approach, universalism and particularism would not be conceived as irreconcilable moral vantage points between which we are forced to choose, but as points of reference between which new forms of coexistence among different peoples and cultures must be negotiated. This is not an easy task, but an important one in liberal democracies striving to become 'postcolonial' in the eyes of all of their citizens.

PART I

Sovereignty

CHAPTER 2

Waitangi as Mystery of State: Consequences of the Ascription of Federative Capacity to the Māori

J.G.A. Pocock

Among the English-speaking political societies for whom indigenous rights are at present problematic in political theory and practice – there are of course other non-English-speaking societies of which this is true – New Zealand occupies a special and, to all appearances, unique position. Australia, Canada and the US are continental confederations. Within this group, indigenous or pre-settlement peoples apart from those in Australia are able to appeal to treaties made with the British Crown before the confederations became self-governing and independent, and to further treaties with state and federal governments during and after that process. Canadian First Nations and Native Americans seek to affirm forms of sovereignty alleged in treaties with federal states whose sovereignty was attained through processes in which indigenous peoples did not play a crucial part. Australian Aborigines were party to no such treaties, and it is doubtful whether they could or should seek one now. There is also the case of the Native Hawaiians, whose claim may be based on the alleged illegitimacy of the overthrow of the Kamehameha kingdom in 1898.

Distinct from these cases, New Zealand (in Māori, Aotearoa) is a unitary state established by the Crown's sovereignty, whose establishment was in turn preceded by the Treaty of Waitangi in 1840, drawn up between representatives of the Crown and rangatira (translatable as 'chiefs') of the iwi and hapū (translatable as 'tribes'), constituting the people or peoples who came to call themselves Māori (meaning 'normal') and who are also termed 'tangata whenua' or 'people of the land and birthplace' – a term conveying some of the meanings of 'aboriginal' (Orange 1987). This Treaty was drawn up and signed before – though its signatories were able to envisage – the massive settlement of New Zealand by the British, Irish and other European colonists known as *pākehā*, now a majority of the people who democratically exercise the sovereignty of the crown, in whose name they perform legislative and judicial acts (Belich 1996).

It is necessary to explain this vocabulary to publics who may be ignorant of it, because a situation has arisen that constitutes New Zealand's uniqueness. The Treaty of Waitangi is now considered fundamental, in the sense that it precedes and establishes the national sovereignty; it therefore furnishes a basis on which Māori may make claims against that sovereignty, reminding it that it is conditional upon fulfilment of a treaty that made promises to the Māori which have not always been honoured (this is to put it mildly). The Treaty is not used to delegitimise sovereignty, but as a reminder of its conditionality and put in its mind claims to which it is urgently concerned to attend. Democratisation has meant that the sovereignty of the Crown is no longer that of a distant imperial authority, but is exercised by a people divided into a *pākehā* majority and an indigenous minority whose understandings of property, sovereignty and history differ sharply from those of the Crown and the majority (Sharp 1997; McHugh 1991; Kawharu 1989). Both sets of understandings are traceable to the Treaty itself. New Zealand/Aotearoa (the order can be reversed) is therefore unique compared to other countries, and may be so in a much larger conceptual category, in having consciously exposed its sovereignty to legal, political and philosophical challenges. All arise from the problem of indigenous rights, but at a time in history when the concept and practical exercise of sovereignty are being globally challenged by forces of an altogether different origin. The case of New Zealand/Aotearoa is therefore interesting and international publics unaware that its history has been going on will do well to study it and learn its vocabulary.

This chapter will be – to use an older terminology – a discourse upon history rather than a history. Without attempting a close narrative of what has been happening in the world of practice, it will draw out and pursue some general implications for politics of the decision to contract a treaty with Māori in 1840, and of the decision to make that treaty a fundamental document nearly 150 years later. The initial decision received the following theoretical support from Lord Glenelg, then Colonial Secretary, in a memorandum dated 15 December 1837:

> They are not Savages living by the Chase, but Tribes who have apportioned the country between them, having fixed Abodes, with an acknowledged Property in the Soil, and with some rude approaches to a regular System of internal Government.[1]

Glenelg was an Evangelical, and this memorandum has its place in a complicated history of liberal Christian attempts to influence governments and settler associations in their dealings with indigenous peoples in various parts of the southern oceans. Among these points of contact were Tasmania and Victoria, and it is possible to view Glenelg's words in the context of settler–Aboriginal history in Australia (Reynolds 1996). However, the 'they' of the opening statement are, in the first instance, Ngāpuhi and other *hapū* living around the Bay of Islands, then the chief point of contact between the Crown and Māori where the Treaty of Waitangi was to be signed later. Glenelg thought of them as 'the New Zealanders', and the effect of these words was soon extended to all peoples living in both major islands who became collectively known as 'Māori'. In saying that they were 'not Savages living by the Chase', Glenelg was making a distinction important in European jurisprudence, political philosophy and anthropology. He was saying that the Māori had left the hunter–gatherer condition, to which the word 'savage' (*sauvage, selvaggio*, forester, bushman) was in theory restricted, and entered a condition supposed to succeed it in natural law and stadial theory: that of agriculture, in which human communities became sedentary upon the land, and by tilling and rendering it productive established property in it and made property the basis of civil society (Pocock 1992; 1998).

In Lockean theory, hunter–gatherer peoples might have property in what they found or captured – 'the deer is that Indian's that hath killed it' – but not in the land over which they travelled in its pursuit (Locke 1988: 289). It is tempting, therefore, to oppose what Glenelg is saying of the Māori to what was being said of Australian peoples whose normal condition was held to be one of walkabout, pursuing songlines in search of sustenance, and to find in this distinction the source of the decision that the land over which they passed was *terra nullius*, unappropriated by agriculture. (Europeans ignored, or were ignorant of, the Aboriginal sense that land might be appropriated by song.) To make such an opposition would be to situate Glenelg's memorandum at a point of bifurcation, from which New Zealand and Australian history begins to become as profoundly different, as in many ways they are. Among these differences would be the circumstance that the Treaty of Waitangi has no equivalent in the history of Australian settlement. The effect of Glenelg's words is to justify entering into treaty with Māori, one that has been made foundational in New Zealand history and is here discovered at its foundation. *Terra nullius* has the effect of denying Aborigines the capacity to make treaties; the federative capacity, derived from *foedus*, the Latin word for 'treaty'.

At this point, however, we must refine the distinctions being made. In European thought, the capacity to establish 'a fixed property in the soil' is the beginning of two processes: the development of civil society and the development of civil government. The former may have reached the point (well known to Locke) where there are known to be claims, rights, disputes and means of resolving them, though the latter has not reached the point where there exists a sovereign authority competent to resolve all disputes. Glenelg says no more of the Māori than they have made 'some rude approaches', but he is saying that they have not developed a sovereign authority or state. The question imposed by the vocabulary he is using may run as follows: treaties are made between sovereigns, so what treaty can be made with peoples as yet lacking 'a regular system of internal government'? In subsequent New Zealand history, the famous Prendergast judgment pronounced that the Treaty of Waitangi lacked binding force in law, precisely because the Māori signatories lacked the authority of sovereign statehood that alone could have made the terms of a treaty with them binding on the Crown and its subsequent judges, officers and subjects.[2]

Faced with this argument, there are strategies modern Māori may adopt to make the Treaty binding on the Crown. One is to intensify, as part of the historical record, the approaches to a regular system of internal government that were being made by Māori before 1840; much may be made of the 'Declaration of the United Tribes' that came into being in 1835 and had a flag of its own.[3] Another – to use terms compatible with the vocabulary of classical *pākehā* political philosophy – is to move from the concept of treaty towards that of contract of government. In classical theory, people possessed of rights and civil society, but as yet of no civil government, may compact to set up such a government, transferring to a sovereign authority the right of enforcing these rights and legislation concerning them, while retaining for themselves the rights they empower government to enforce. A compact of this sort may be held to have occurred at Waitangi, where the Māori signatories recognise the Crown as endowed with *kāwanatanga* – a neologism in *te reo Māori* (the Māori language as cultural instrument), which is a phonetic equivalent of the word 'government' – while the Crown guarantees them the continued possession of *rangatiratanga*, a word more authentically Māori, whose meanings include chiefly authority, property in land and, by extension then and since, the entire fabric of Māori culture and self-possession.[4]

At a culminating point in the ceremonies at Waitangi, Governor Hobson is said to have remarked, 'now we are one people'. His comments can be read as meaning simply that there has occurred a union of head and body; the Māori have become a people in the state of civil government by recognising the Crown as their sovereign. It would follow – as it has – that Māori are entitled to claim that the Crown is bound to maintain *rangatiratanga*, that failure to do so is a breach of the contract of government, and that the consequences of such a breach may extend as far as a Lockean 'dissolution of government', a threat sufficient to maintain the binding force of the Crown's obligation. Māori in the late twentieth cen-

tury have engaged in large-scale symbolic actions approaching civil disobedience, with the precise effect of using such reminders to revive the
binding force of the Treaty, but it does not follow, as it might, that the
Treaty is simply the outward or originatory form of a contract of civil government. There is more to the New Zealand state and its attendant civil
society than the confrontation of *kāwanatanga* and *rangatiratanga*; the
former is not the only threat the latter faces.

Hobson's words at Waitangi need not be read – though they often have
been – as meaning that Māori and *pākehā* 'are now one people'. The reason is that massive *pākehā* presence – intensive colonisation by British settlers intending to appropriate land in their own way, to develop a civil
society of the kind they are used to, and to continue to live under the
Crown as their civil government – is not envisaged at Waitangi or spoken
of in the Treaty. It was, however, beginning to occur. The Crown knew this,
and had its own intentions regarding it, and accusations of bad faith
against the Crown in its dealings at Waitangi begin here. It was the Crown's
intention to establish its sovereignty before settlement began in order to
retain sovereignty over the process. It did so by means of a treaty, or contract of government, with the Māori, but did not make clear to them either
the impact that settlement would have on their *rangatiratanga*, or the
extent to which the Crown would further that process in the act of exercising sovereignty over it. If the Crown did not become the mere instrument of the settlement companies, it came close, especially after 'the
growth of responsible government' meant that its sovereignty was exercised in and by acts of parliament representing the settler majority.

Here we revert to Glenelg. His language ascribes to pre-Treaty and
pre-contact Māori a capacity to create property in land.[5] Property is a
right, here recognised as ancient and aboriginal, rooted in the customs
of an indigenous people. This is crucial to any claim that may subsequently be made that *rangatiratanga* antedates, conditions and obliges
the establishment of sovereignty at Waitangi. However, research into the
language and behaviour of the agents of settlement companies and other
land purchasers then active in various parts of Aotearoa reveals that they
were as anxious as the Crown to ascribe property and original title to the
Māori from whom they sought to purchase land, for the obvious reason
that they needed it to legitimate their purchases in the eyes of a Crown
under whose sovereignty they might soon find themselves.[6] For its part,
the Crown was interested in ascribing to Māori a capacity to hold property and enter into treaties, in order to acquire sovereignty over the
processes of purchase and settlement, over which it did not wish the settlement companies to acquire an authority preceding its own.

The capacity to hold property, to claim rights in it and to enter into
treaties respecting it were understood by Māori in terms of their own

concept of *rangatiratanga*. We now see, however, that they implied – and were operated by *pākehā* in 1840 so that they should imply – a capacity to alienate property with which Māori were not familiar and which might be hostile to their governing values. What went on in the mind of a *rangatira* engaged in what a *pākehā* thought of as a land sale may be hard to recapture, but probably entailed a belief that he was extending his *mana* (the term is stronger even than *rangatiratanga*) over the land in question, not that he was parting with it for money.

Historically, this is the point from which many confusions and injustices – the latter often quite deliberate – take their origin. Jurisprudentially, here begins a history that has to be re-assessed with a view to remedying the injustices, once their existence and origin have been pointed out. Philosophically, at this point we observe that Māori are being involved for the first time in a historical process to which they have not consented, and perhaps in the first historical process they are obliged to recognise as such. Rights in European jurisprudence might exist timelessly or in a process conceived merely to elucidate their character. Property, as a specie of right, required no organisation of time beyond inheritance and custom. The time structure of the Māori world was mythic, composed of ancestral and cosmic images. But the movement of property from possession to alienability entailed a history more drastic than any of the stadial sequences designed to precede it; a process of commodification in which all goods became mobile and *homo* became *mercator*, committed to exchange. As goods became commodities, exchange transformed their use and character. The future became open, at the price of uncertainty. Māori, accustomed to living in a cosmos of reciprocity, justice and revenge (the word for the latter two is *utu*), found themselves living in a process of shifting patterns, in which the new must be undertaken without seeing its outcome, nothing was quite what it seemed, and the Treaty that was supposed to guarantee their *rangatiratanga* became an instrument by which they lost it. The wars fought in Aotearoa/New Zealand during the 1860s were in part between *Kingitanga*, Māori who resisted land sales, and *kūpapa*, Māori who had decided to engage in and control them. But the wars could not check the flood of *pākehā* immigration, and the *kūpapa* sometimes found their lands confiscated, like those of the *Kingitanga* (Belich 1986; 1989; 1996: 229–46).

This is life in the open-endedness of history, a vision of things frighteningly necessary to the open society in which humans seek freedom and self-determination. Neo-conservative historians sometimes point out that even the most barbarous and brutal Europeans encountered by Māori knew things about living in a history of differences, and therefore about being free, unknowable in a closed Māori cosmos that taught no response to them, and that once the sailors had arrived, freedom could only be had by living in a history like – if not identical with – theirs.[7] This may well be, but a history that has been forced on one can only be made one's own by its retelling, and those who enter history with the fragments of a cosmos about them must tell it in terms that not only the fragments, but the knowledge of their former wholeness, provide. There may be ways of relating Glenelg and the Treaty to this process.

Glenelg gives us textual evidence that Māori were thought capable of federative action because they were able to establish and apportion property in the soil, and were therefore approaching the state of civil government (it is noteworthy, in Lockean terms, that the federative capacity here preceded the legislative).[8] There is a further way of stating this capacity, which Glenelg did not use and which does not seem to figure in the discourse attending Māori–Crown settler relationships; it was nevertheless available to *pākehā* engaged in this discourse, and may be introduced into the history as a means of enlarging its philosophical significance. Encounters between the Crown and the indigenous peoples of North America had been going on for two centuries before Glenelg wrote his memorandum, and there had taken shape an elaborate image of the capacity of Mohawk, Iroquois and Huron leaders for war, oratory and reason of state (Colden 1747: *v, viii, xiii*, 106, 135, 150–51, 178–79; Ferguson 1995). It had been pointed out as a paradox that these were hunting peoples – Glenelg's 'Savages living by the Chase' – who should in theory lack all these capacities; their powers of political speech exceeded their powers to command a state's resources. Nevertheless, they could resolve to make wars, treaties and alliances, and could enter into debate with French and British governors and settlers as to whether the wars fought by the latter were just or unjust. It had in consequence been suggested in the literature of empire that hunting peoples might demarcate hunting grounds and fight wars, just or unjust, and terminate these wars by treaties concerning their demarcation (Pownall 1993: 259n, 265–80).

This was an important step away from the supposition that peoples 'living by the chase' lacked political capacity, and toward the proposition that the federative capacity might arise in the order of natural development before the governmental. It could be applied to the historical condition of Māori at the time of contact, who had 'advanced' (as a progress-based discourse would put it) beyond 'living by the chase', and among whom there visibly occurred what a European could recognise as 'wars' and 'treaties' over 'apportionment' of land. The capacity to engage in war, terminate it by treaties, precede it by alliances, and behave wisely or unwisely, justly or unjustly, in the practice of these activities was important in what was termed 'the progress of society' and of the human moral faculty. It constituted the universes of *jus gentium* and 'reason of state', the intellectual universes governing the relations of sovereigns with one another. The sovereign's 'federative' capacity to make wars and enter into treaties was significant in the history of morals and morality.

Against this background, it can be argued that the Treaty of Waitangi and the intellectual preparation for it have had the effect of conceding the Māori presence in the universe of *jus gentium*, whereas the effect of *terra nullius* has been the refusal of such a presence to Aboriginal peoples, deemed unable to appropriate lands or make war and peace, and thus obliging them, even today, to seek their remedies in the universe of *jus naturale*, which has no history. This argument in several ways entails ideal simplifications. The admission of Māori to *jus gentium* was imperfect and often denied, and did not prevent Māori suffering manifold injustices within that universe. To write Aboriginal history as if it had been governed by the *terra nullius* judgment and by nothing else would certainly be inadequate, and modern attempts to reconstitute the mental universes of both Māori and Aborigines at the time of contact have shown them containing elements deeper and more various than those of the universe of *jus gentium* alone – elements to which appeals are now being made.[9] However, the argument does permit the contention that, in virtue of Waitangi, Aotearoa/New Zealand history has, as Aboriginal/Australian history perhaps has not, occurred in a universe of *jus gentium*, where wars and treaties are recognised components of history. In precontact Aotearoa, wars and treaties recognisably occurred. There was a Treaty at the foundation of sovereignty and partly in consequence of its imperfections, wars occurred in the 1860s and were fought by those who knew them to be wars, in both Māori and *pākehā* senses; these wars were not terminated by treaties, but the Treaty is now being invoked as a means of saying they were not properly terminated and of applying various modes of closure which are thought to be needed. It is a strong but minority position that the condition of New Zealand/Aotearoa is one of internal war that has not yet been terminated by Treaty; a much more general position, to which the state itself appears to subscribe, is that the Treaty of Waitangi is to be used as a means of re-assessing history and remedying grievances that have caused wars in the past and arise out of ways in which those wars were terminated (if terminated they were). The rewriting of New Zealand/Aotearoa history in this way appears to have become established, and since it is unlikely that history can be written with finality, it must continue to be practised, and to happen, as well as be rewritten. This is a remarkable characteristic of that polity as it now finds itself.

It is evident at this point that history has become important in the theory and practice of politics. The Māori bring to the Treaty envisaged by Glenelg something other than the history of property and progress in which Glenelg (we may say) thought it would involve them. The Treaty becomes a focal point around which they organise their history as they understand it: the history of the *mana* and *rangatiratanga* which they once created and possessed, the history of their dispossession of *rangatiratanga* contrary to the promises of the Treaty, the history of how *rangatiratanga* and *mana* nevertheless survived and how the Treaty may be used as a means of re-asserting and reclaiming them. (The circumstance that all these concepts are becoming debatable among Māori themselves is important to the politics of history, but will not be discussed here.) This history is a source of both pride and pain, and both are significant when it is brought to the negotiating table that the Treaty provides an occasion for the constant re-assertion of that history. Because it is seen as unfulfilled, it becomes not a single encounter between negotiating peoples whose histories begin again (perhaps as one history) as the outcome of a treaty, but as a means of rendering the encounter and the negotiation ongoing and open-ended, so that they become the history that the negotiants now have in common. At issue is not rights and justice alone, but the identity and history they define. When a New Zealand government some years ago was seen to be offering a cash settlement in return for the closure of all claims under the Treaty of Waitangi, it was told in effect that the history of encounter between Māori and *pākehā* was such that it could not be brought to a closure, that the offer was insulting, and that the history would have to continue in the form of negotiation into an indefinite future in which negotiation and history would be inseparable and nearly identical (Gardiner 1996; Oliver 1997: 135–45).

Here something begins to be said about *pākehā* history, first by Māori and by *pākehā* themselves. The Māori remind the *pākehā* that the history of their settlement as a people entails at every point the dispossession of the Māori from that *rangatiratanga* guaranteed them by the Treaty, and their relegation to a history of dispossession, survival and recovery. They invite the *pākehā* to return to Waitangi and recognise that their legitimacy as a people rests on promises that have not been fulfilled and for whose unfulfilment remedy is necessary and obligatory. Unless their response is one of complete denial, *pākehā* respond that they recognise the history that calls for remedial justice, but – unless their reply is made for them by a critical intelligentsia anxious to unmake every identity including its own – they further respond that their history does not fully arise from the Treaty of Waitangi and does not consist wholly in the undeniable nonfulfilment of its provisions. More pertinently, their identity as a people is characterised but not defined by the dispossession of Māori which the Treaty at every point entails. They point out that the Treaty was made by the Crown before there was a *pākehā* people, that through democratisation they have assumed the obligations of the Crown under the Treaty, but that their self-formation as a people has come about not solely through interaction between them and the Crown or between *pākehā* and

Māori, but also between *pākehā* and *pākehā* – defining their own history
by its own contestations – and between them and the land (in Māori, *te
whenua*) they now inhabit. They acknowledge the central unfairness of
colonial history, that colonisers had a better chance of making their own
history than the colonised, but say that their history is not to be taken
from them merely because it is unfair that they should have it on terms
exclusively their own. When informed by the critical intellect that it is
highly debatable how far their history has been of their own making, they
reply that they have always known that, which is why it is paradoxically
theirs. This debate will be with Māori centrally, but with Māori among
others, and the others will include themselves.[10]

The Treaty as history cannot annul, although it can act upon, the existential imbalance that, for one people, is about the loss, retention and
recovery of its *mana*, but for the other it is not. One group may have its
own *mana* and history, but the Treaty is only a part of that history. One
possible contributing remedy is that Māori may discover a history of
themselves that is not exclusively about *mana* and the Treaty, but has
been made by Māori interacting with Māori, *pākehā* and *whenua*, in a history to be possessed differently. There are signs that such a historiography is taking shape, though only Māori can write it. It will not diminish
the importance of the Treaty in providing an alternative to it, since every
people should possess alternative histories of itself. Meanwhile, the
Treaty debate and process have importance for both peoples. It has been
made a debate over the exercise and character, if not exactly the location, of sovereignty, and if sovereignty is not *mana*, a spiritual and historical essence and identity, it is the place – in Māori the *marae* – where 'we'
(the pronoun may be used)[11] make decisions of a certain finality regarding what 'we' will do and have done, and therefore (insofar as our actions
in history define us) determine who we have been and will be.

The Treaty of Waitangi renders New Zealand sovereignty perpetually
debatable, but recasts sovereignty as a perpetual debate between Crown,
Māori and *pākehā* qualified to engage in it. Sovereignty rests on the
Treaty, but the Treaty remains unfulfilled, and the lack of fulfilment sets
up a process and a debate that extend into an indefinite future. Like a
written or an unwritten constitution, the Treaty is open to perpetual
interpretation by a body identical to neither courts of law nor parliament
(though in procedure it resembles the former), not exercising sovereignty so much as advising it of its perpetually disputable character, the
debate going on (as in the two texts, English and Māori, of the original
Treaty) between two never finally congruent readings of the world and
its Aotearoa/New Zealand history. In conducting this debate, the disputants conduct their history by maintaining its ambivalence.

This is an idealist and historicist account of a situation that actual history – the operation of social, cultural and economic forces – may quite

possibly bring to an end. One may even identify some forces operating to do so. I once suggested, at a conference of the New Zealand Historical Association, that inhabitants of the country might cease dividing themselves into *tangata whenua* (people of the land, or Māori) and *tau iwi* (strangers, or everybody else), on the grounds that both were *tangata waka*, peoples of the ship.[12] A distinguished spokesman of the Ngai Tahu *iwi* of the South Island replied that both might very well find themselves boat people. He meant that economic and cultural globalisation might dissolve them into pools of migrant labourers and consumers, unaware of any history save the fluidity of the global market. Under such conditions, it is reasonable to inquire what it is that sovereignty can do – a reasonable question that too often turns rhetorical in the hands of a cultural criticism insistent on the negotiability of sovereignty and identity, in the evident belief that to negotiate these things is to negotiate them away – into whose hands, we are not usually told. The Treaty process, however, seems to have had some success in supplying New Zealand/Aotearoa with a history where sovereignty has a continuing part to play: the conduct of an unfinishable debate over how it is itself to be exercised.

Suppose, however, that the debate should continue forever in this form: a debate over the encounter between two understandings of history, around which two peoples should crystallise as participants. It might continue forever to produce contested yet sovereign decisions, and still leave unanswered the question: is this a debate among citizens or a treaty between sovereigns?

The politics of difference may dissolve the *polis* or *res publica* into a confederacy, a series of *ad hoc* agreements negotiated between separate identities, each changing but intent on autonomously conducting its own transformation. Thus the Haida Gwaai canoe, in the great sculpture by the late Bill Reid chosen by James Tully to illustrate his *Strange Multiplicity*, is crewed entirely by shape-changers and steered (if at all) by a shaman through whom all changes are mediated (Tully 1993; 1995: *xvii*, 17–29). One recalls the *Hunting of the Snark*, and wonders if they will ever arrive at a collective decision, which the mouth of the steersman (*gubernator*) will enact. Perhaps a confederacy of shape-changers is the best we can hope for in a postcolonial and postmodern world. Perhaps the world market requires us to be no more than shape-changers that may be directed. But if we discover histories that we must debate with one another, even debating the character of the histories in which we are involved and the means of debating them, there may develop transitive, if ambivalent, languages that we speak to one another, a step towards the recovery of sovereignty and – in however strange a multiplicity – of *mana*. It might be done, which is why the reconstitution of New Zealand as Treaty is interesting.

CHAPTER 3

The Struggles of Indigenous Peoples for and of Freedom

James Tully

How does political theory hinder or help the liberation of indigenous peoples? That is, in what ways can political theory help or hinder the struggles of indigenous peoples *for* and *of* freedom?

These are not new questions. They have been raised and answered in various ways since the first encounter of Europeans with indigenous peoples, and they have been raised in, and partly given rise to, the complex language (or multiplicity of languages) of modern, western, non-indigenous political thought.

This chapter is an attempt to address aspects of these complex and difficult questions from a non-indigenous perspective with reference to Canada. Western political theory here is used broadly to refer to the political, legal and social theories, reasoned legal decisions and legislative and policy documents written by European, North and South American, Australian and New Zealand non-indigenous authors from the beginning of the modern period in Europe to the present. These theories make up part of the complex, shared and continuously contested languages of modern, western political thought.

The motley language of western political thought has two well-known characteristics. It is a language woven into the everyday political, legal and social practices of these societies and, in a slightly more technical and abstract key, a language of interpretation and critical reflection on the practices of these societies in the institutions of law, policy and academia. In short, it is the language of both political self-understanding and self-reflection of these societies and their non-indigenous members. It is not the language of political self-understanding and self-reflection of indigenous peoples, even though they are constrained to use it. Indigenous people have, for lack of better terms, indigenous political theories and a complex and contested shared indigenous language of political

thought. These two languages are not closed, incommensurable or independent of each other, but massively unequal in their effective discursive
power in the present. One is the dominant language that presents itself
as a universal vocabulary of understanding and reflection; the other a
subaltern language which, when noticed at all, is normally taken to be
some kind of minority language within the dominant language of western political thought.[1]

The questions I ask at the start do not arise in a vacuum but in
response to a fundamental problem in practice. *The practical problem is
the relation between the establishment and development of western societies and
the pre-existence and continuing resistance of indigenous societies on the same
territory.* This problematic relation takes different forms in Canada, the
US, New Zealand and Australia, varying widely within each of these
societies in relation to different indigenous societies, and also over
time. Despite wide variation, the relation is commonly called the 'internal colonisation' of indigenous peoples by the dominant societies. As
systems of internal colonisation and the arts of resistance by indigenous peoples change over time, they periodically give rise in the dominant societies to the sorts of questions addressed in this volume. (These
questions arise much more frequently in indigenous societies, where
colonisation is the lived reality.) To address them effectively, it is necessary to understand the main features of systems of internal colonisation and practices of resistance, as well as the more specific features
that have become problematic in the present and given rise to critical
reflection. I restrict my investigation to North America and mostly to
what is now called Canada.

Internal Colonisation and Arts of Resistance

Internal colonisation refers, first, to the historical processes by which
structures of domination have been set in place on Great Turtle
Island/North America over the indigenous peoples and their territories without their consent and in response to their resistance against
and within these structures. The relevant institutions of the US and
Canada constitute structures of domination in Weber's sense because
they are now relatively stable, immovable and irreversible vis à vis any
direct confrontation by the colonised population, as the massive display of force at Kahnesatake/Oka, Quebec in 1990 was designed to
show (MacLaine & Baxendale 1991; York & Pindera 1991). They 'incorporate' or 'domesticate' the subordinate indigenous societies. These
two concepts are widely used by indigenous peoples to refer to the form
domination takes: that is, as a matter of fact, and of the coloniser's law
indigenous peoples exist *within* the dominant societies as minorities,

domestic, dependent nations, aboriginal peoples or First Nations *of*
Canada and so on.[2]

Second, within the stable structures of incorporation, internal colonisation refers to the vast array of more mobile and changeable techniques
of government by which indigenous peoples and their territories are governed within the American and Canadian political systems. Techniques
of government refer to the totality of modifiable discursive and non-
discursive ways and means used in strategies for guiding the conduct,
directly and indirectly, and responding to the resistance of indigenous
peoples. Ever since the consolidation of the control of the US and
Canada over two-thirds of the continent and the effective assertion of
exclusive jurisdiction by the mid-nineteenth century, the struggles of
indigenous peoples on the ground have primarily involved attempts to
modify the techniques of government to gain degrees of self-government
and control over some of their territories, rather than direct confrontation with the background structures of domination. There is not a sharp
distinction between structures of domination and techniques of government in practice, as what appears to be a part of the immovable background to one generation can be called into question and become the
object of struggle and modification by another, and vice versa. The former is like the relatively stable riverbanks that change imperceptibly
while the latter is like the changing waters of the river.

The processes of internal colonisation have developed in response to
the struggles of indigenous peoples for freedom both against and within
colonisation on the one hand, and in response to overriding objectives
of the settler societies and the capitalist market on the other. There have
been four major dimensions to these processes.[3] When Europeans
invaded and began to settle in North and South America, they encountered free, vibrant, sovereign indigenous nations with complex forms of
social and political organisation and territorial jurisdictions that were
older (3000–30 000 years), more populous (60–80 million) and more
variegated than Europe. First, through the spread of European diseases,
wars and the destruction of indigenous societies, the interlopers reduced
the population by roughly 90 per cent by the turn of the twentieth-
century (from 10 million to 0.5 million in Canada and the US). Second,
they usurped the existing traditional forms of government and subjected
indigenous peoples to French, British and then Canadian and American
governments, either directly, through various techniques of assimilation,
or indirectly, through setting up systems of internal self-rule (band councils in Canada) governed by special authorities and departments of the
dominant societies.

Third, to build western political societies on the territories and ruins
of indigenous societies, the newcomers gradually displaced the rapidly

decreasing native population to small reserves, appropriated their territories by effectively exercising exclusive jurisdiction over them, and opened them to resettlement by the rapidly increasing immigrant population, and to capitalist development either indirectly (as in the early fur trade) or directly (agriculture, fishing, forestry, mining and other forms of resource extraction). Fourth, in the early stages and again in the present, where indigenous resistance has been effective, usurpation and appropriation have often been preceded or accompanied by treaty-making. This has modified the *processes* to some extent and created relations of cooperation. The long-term effects of these four dimensions for the vast majority of native people in Canada have been to reduce formerly economically self-sufficient and interdependent native societies to tiny overcrowded reserves, inter-generational welfare dependency, substandard housing, diet, education and health facilities, high levels of unemployment, low life expectancy, high rates of death at birth, and predictably, following these conditions on or off reserves that undermine their wellbeing and self-esteem, high levels of substance abuse, incarceration and suicide for native peoples.

This form of colonisation is 'internal' as opposed to 'external' because the colonising society is built on the territories of the formerly free, and now colonised, peoples. The colonising or imperial society exercises exclusive jurisdiction over them and their territories and the indigenous peoples, although they comply and adapt (are *de facto* colonised), refuse to surrender their freedom of self-determination over their territories and continue to resist within the system as a whole as best they can. The essence of internal colonisation, therefore, is not the appropriation of labour (as in slavery), for this has been peripheral, or depopulation (genocide), for indigenous populations have increased threefold in this century, or even the appropriation of self-government (usurpation), for at different times indigenous peoples have been permitted to govern themselves within the colonial system (as in the early treaty system and perhaps again today). Rather, the ground of the relation is the appropriation of the land, resources and jurisdiction of the indigenous peoples, not only for the sake of resettlement and exploitation (which is also true in external colonisation), but for the territorial foundation of the dominant society itself.

In external colonisation, colonies and the imperial society coexist on different territories. The colonies can free themselves and form geographically independent societies with exclusive jurisdiction over their respective territories, as Canada, the US, Australia and New Zealand have done in relation to the former British Empire. With internal colonisation, this is not possible. The problematic, unresolved contradiction and constant provocation at the foundation of internal colonisation, therefore, is that the dominant society coexists on and exercises exclusive jurisdiction over the territories and jurisdictions that the indigenous peoples refuse to surrender.

It follows that the entire system of internal colonisation is seen by both sides as a temporary means to an end. It is the irresolution, so to speak, of the relation: a matrix of power put in place and continuously provoked by and adjusted in response to the arts of resistance of indigenous peoples. The temporary nature of internal colonisation is obvious enough from the indigenous side. They unsurprisingly would prefer to resolve it by regaining their freedom as self-governing peoples. It is not as obvious from the side of the colonising society, and is commonly overlooked in the theoretical and policy literatures, which tend to accept the colonial system as an end in itself and seek to justify and ameliorate it in some new form or another. However, since the beginning, the long-term aim of the administrators of the system has been to resolve the contradiction by the complete disappearance of the indigenous problem: that is, the disappearance of the indigenous peoples *as* free peoples with the right to their territories and governments. There are two major strategies of extinguishment and corresponding techniques of government by which this long-term goal has been and continues to be sought.[4]

The first type of strategy is that indigenous peoples could become extinct, either in fact, as was widely believed to be the trend in the late nineteenth century (through dying out) and is widely heard again today (through intermarriage and urbanisation), or in deed, as the overwhelming power of the dominant society could gradually wear down and weaken the indigenous population to such an extent that their will and ability to resist incorporation would be extinguished, as various marginalisation hypotheses have projected throughout the twentieth century (and as the appalling conditions on most reserves portend today). The second and more common strategy is the attempt to extinguish the rights of indigenous peoples to their territories and self-government.

Over the last three centuries there have been three enduring types of this second strategy of extinguishing the rights of indigenous peoples. The first is either to presume that indigenous peoples do not have the rights of self-governing peoples which pre-exist and continue through colonisation, or to try to demonstrate, once and for all, that they do not have such rights. The presumption of Crown sovereignty, *terra nullius*, the discovery doctrine, and the primitive or less-developed thesis are examples of discursive techniques employed.

The second strategy is to extinguish indigenous rights either unilaterally (through conquest, the assertion of sovereignty and the doctrine of discontinuity, supersession or by the unilateral effect of lawmaking) or voluntarily (through treaties and cession). The third and equally familiar strategy and set of distinctive techniques is to transform indigenous peoples into members of the dominant society through re-education, incentives and socialisation so that they lose their attachment to their identity by outlawing indigenous political and social practices and establishing band councils in their place, residential schools, adoption, exchanging native status for voting rights, programs of de-indigenisation and westernisation, and fostering a co-opted native colonial elite to administer the system.[5]

Once one or more of these strategies of extinguishment is presumed to be successful, a number of different strategies of incorporation of indigenous peoples as members of the dominant society have been put into practice by mobilising a corresponding range of governmental techniques. There are two major competing strategies of incorporation in Canada today. The first is assimilation, where indigenous persons are treated like any other member of the settler society. Difference-blind liberalism, the policy of the Reform Party of Canada, the Statement of the Government of Canada on Indian Policy of 1969, and various forms of delegated, municipal-style self-government are examples of this approach. The second is accommodation, where indigenous people are recognised and accommodated as members of Canada and the bearers of, or at least claimants to, a range of aboriginal group rights, in exchange for surrendering or denying the existence of their rights as free peoples. Recent Supreme Court rulings, the present treaty process, and various policies and influential theories of Canada as a multicultural and multinational society (such as the Three Orders of Government of the failed Charlottetown Accord) are examples of this neocolonial approach. In the latter case, commonly called reconciliation, the prevailing system of incorporation is transformed to a legitimate system of group recognition and rights in the Canadian constitution with the agreement of the indigenous peoples themselves.[6]

These five strategies and techniques make up the dominant side of the complex agonic relation of colonial governance vis à vis indigenous resistance. From the side of the ruling peoples, this Goliath-versus-David relation is a political system that underlies and provides the foundation for the constitutional democracies of Canada, the US, Australia and New Zealand. The aim of the system is to ensure that the territory on which the settler societies is built is effectively and legitimately under their exclusive jurisdiction and open to settlement and capitalist development. The means to this end are twofold: the ongoing usurpation, dispossession, incorporation and infringement of the rights of indigenous peoples coupled with various long-term strategies of extinguishment and accommodation that would eventually capture their rights, dissolve the contradiction and legitimise the settlement (see section 2).

From the side of indigenous peoples, it is a political system that over-
lies and is illegitimately based on making use of their pre-existing governments and territories. It is a system established and continuously
modified in response to two distinct types of arts of resistance and freedom: against the structure of domination as a whole in the name of the
freedom of self-determination, and within it, by compliance and internal
contestation of the strategies and techniques in the name of the freedom
of insubordination and dissent (see section 3).

First, indigenous peoples' struggle *for* freedom as peoples in resisting
the colonial systems as a whole, in each country and throughout the
world of 250 million indigenous people. Given the overwhelming power
of the dominant societies, indigenous peoples cannot confront them
directly in liberation struggles to overthrow occupying imperial powers,
as decolonisation has standardly unfolded in the modern period. Nevertheless, from appeals to the Privy Council in the seventeenth century to
statements to the Working Group on Indigenous Populations of the Sub-
commission on Prevention of Discrimination and Protection of Minorities of the United Nations today, their 'word warriors' have never ceased
to declaim the illegitimate system of internal colonisation and proclaim
their sovereignty and freedom (see section 4).[7]

Second, they exercise their freedom *of* manoeuvre within the system.
In any relation of power by which techniques of government are
mobilised to govern the conduct of indigenous peoples, individually and
collectively, there is always a range of possible comportments – ways of
thinking and acting – that are open in response, from the minuscule
range of freedom of hidden insubordination in total institutions such as
residential schools to the larger and more public displays of the repatria-
tion of powers of internal self-government, health care, education and
territorial control. Over the centuries, indigenous peoples have developed a vast repertoire of infra-political resistance to survive and revitalise
their cultures, nations and federations, to keep indigenous ways of being
in the world alive and well for the next generations, to adapt these ways
and stories to the present strategic situation, to comply with and participate in the dominant institutions while refusing to surrender, to regain
degrees of self-rule and control over their territories when possible, and
so to seek to transform internal colonisation obliquely from within
(Alfred 1999a; Scott 1990).

Legitimations of Internal Colonisation

The practical relation between internal colonisation and practices of
resistance has been the focus of theoretical discussion in the legal, political and academic centres of the dominant societies over the last 30

years because of the capitalist expansion and intensification of the colonial appropriation of formerly neglected or under-exploited indigenous
lands and resources, on the one hand, and the globally coordinated
insubordination of indigenous peoples on the other. The conflicts on
the ground have led to five major types of overlapping forms of conflict
and dispute irresolution: recourse to the domestic courts and international law; legislative and constitutional change; treaty-making and
other forms of political negotiations; unilateral action by domestic and
transnational resource companies, interest groups and governments
despite indigenous rights and protests; and native communities unilaterally governing themselves and exercising jurisdiction over their territories despite the law. Critical and historical reflection on these disputes
has brought to light the long history of the unresolved system of internal colonisation and practices of resistance of which these contemporary struggles form a part.[8]

With this practical context in view, it is possible to consider how western political theory contributes to the colonisation of indigenous peoples. Written within the larger language of political self-understanding
and self-reflection of western societies in general, these theories serve
either to legitimise or delegitimise the colonisation of indigenous
peoples and their territories. When they legitimise internal colonisation
by justifying, defending, or serving as the language of governance and
administration of the system and its conflicts, political theories play the
(sometimes unintended) role of a discursive technique of government in
one or more of the five strategies of extinguishment and accommodation. When they delegitimise the system in one way or another, political
theories are a discursive technique in a practice of resistance. With a few
notable exceptions, western political theory has played the role of legitimation in the past and continues to do so today.

Briefly, in the first two centuries of overseas expansion Europe
emerged from relative obscurity to become the most powerful centre of
nations and empires in the world, based largely on the wealth and power
generated from the settlement and exploitation of indigenous lands and
resources. When the colonies freed themselves from the British empire
and developed modern societies on the continued appropriation of
indigenous lands and resources, many of the colonies' leading legal and
political theorists carried on and elaborated on the traditions of interpretation and justification of the legal and political system of internal
colonisation their canonical European predecessors had begun.

In late nineteenth-century Canada, as the indigenous population was
reduced and marginalised and internal colonisation firmly secured, the
need for further legitimation was correspondingly diminished. The reign-
ing ideology of the superiority of European-derived societies and the

inferiority of indigenous societies served as the taken-for-granted justification for the removal of indigenous populations, who were seen as
obstacles to the progressive exploitation of their lands. The relative disappearance of the issue from the public agenda does not mean that
resistance did not continue in less public ways. It signals that members of
the immigrant society now took the exclusive and legitimate exercise of
sovereignty over Great Turtle Island for granted as the unquestionable
basis of their society. The question disappeared and was replaced by an
abstract starting point for theories of constitutional democracy that had
nothing to do with the way these societies were founded. The prior
existence and sovereignty, as well as the continuing colonisation and
resistance, of indigenous peoples was rarely mentioned until it began to
reappear at the margins during the last decade of the twentieth century
(Turner 1997; Williams 1990; Pagden 1995; Culhane 1998: 37–72; Tully
1993: 58–99; 1994).

   Yet, even in late nineteenth and early twentieth-century conditions of
maximum western self-confidence and dogmatic superiority, a lingering
uncertainty about the legitimacy of the settler society remained unresolved in practice. Under the cover of public complacency, officials none
the less found it necessary to sign a series of extinguishment treaties with
a handful of indigenous peoples who were portrayed in the dominant
discourse as too primitive to have any rights or to require their consent
to take their lands and subject them to colonial rule. Incredibly, the officials asserted that scrawled Xs by a few native people on written documents constituted agreements to cede and extinguish forever whatever
rights they might have to tracts of land larger than the European continent. The signatories were said to agree to this in exchange for tiny and
crowded reserves (which were soon reduced further) and a few usufruc-
tuary rights that exist at the pleasure of the Crown. Indigenous people
understood these treaties in the same way as the earlier peace and friend-
ship treaties: as international treaties among equal nations to agree to
work out ways of sharing the use of land and resources while maintaining
their freedom as nations (Canada, Royal Commission 1995a: 1–59; 1996a:
148–200; 1996b: 9–64; Tobias 1991).

   Although indigenous communities began to rebuild, reorganise and
fight for their rights during the first half of the twentieth century, their
activities did not make a significant impact on the public agenda until the
1970s. The Nisga'a Nation's assertion of their rights to collectively use and
occupy their traditional lands led to the judgment of the Supreme Court
of Canada of *R* v. *Calder* (1973), which is now seen as marking the transition to the present period. Six of seven judges agreed that Nisga'a
Aboriginal rights derived from their occupation of their traditional territories before contact. In the oft-repeated phrase of Mr Justice Judson,

'when the settlers came, the Indians were there, organized in societies and occupying the land as their forefathers had done for centuries. This is what Indian title means.'[9] Three judges went on to say that their Aboriginal rights had been extinguished unilaterally by general legislation; three said Aboriginal rights could not be extinguished unilaterally except by specific legislation; and the seventh decided against the Nisga'a on the traditional British Columbia argument that this case could not be brought against the province of British Columbia without the appropriate legislation. Although the Nisga'a lost their appeal, the Court found that Aboriginal rights existed at the time of contact and was split evenly on whether or not such rights had been extinguished. So, the contradiction at the foundation of Canadian society and its underlying system of internal colonisation once again entered the public agenda.

Two major official strategies of incorporation have been advanced to resolve the contradiction: to incorporate indigenous people by means of assimilation or accommodation. The assimilation approach has support among some federal and provincial parties, the lower courts, economic interest groups and about half the general public, especially when they are polled on more specific and detailed questions about indigenous self-government. The accommodation approach has support in the higher courts, the federal Conservative Party when it was in office, the current Liberal Government of Canada and the province of British Columbia in the current treaty process, and the other half of the general public, especially when polling questions are posed in general terms (Warry 1998: 20–30, 249–55; Smith 1995). Although incorporation by accommodation is legitimated by policies and theories of multiculturalism, it is more illuminating to investigate the basics of the strategy in two fora: the Supreme Court of Canada and the treaty process. While each approach gives different degrees of recognition and accommodation to indigenous peoples, both do so within the indubitable sovereignty of the Canadian state over indigenous peoples and so do not question, let alone challenge, the continuing colonisation of indigenous peoples and their territories, but serve to legitimise it.

In a series of decisions from *R* v. *Sparrow* (1990) to *Delgamuukw* v. *BC* (1997) the Supreme Court has defined the rights of Aboriginal peoples as those rights that are recognised and affirmed in section 35 of the *Constitution Act 1982* (Asch 1997; 1999). The Court advances four main steps to define these constitutional rights.

First, the Court incorporates indigenous peoples into Canada and subjects them to the Canadian constitution in the very act of recognising their rights as rights within the Canadian constitution. In so doing, it reaffirms the system of internal colonisation. The Court does not acknowledge that indigenous peoples possess any rights that pre-exist the assertion of sovereignty by the Crown in 1846 (in British Columbia) over the territory now called Canada; rights which may render the establishment of Crown sovereignty subject to their consent and which may have survived unsurrendered into the present. The rights that Aboriginal peoples have in Canada are said to have their source or foundation in the pre-existence of organised Aboriginal societies, systems of laws and the occupation and use of their territories since time immemorial. Nevertheless, these activities, institutions and practices, which are the universal criteria of sovereignty and self-determination, did not give rise to any rights until they were recognised by the Crown as common law rights until 1982, and as constitutional rights thereafter. As the Court explains with respect to Aboriginal title (the aboriginal right to land):

> from a theoretical standpoint, aboriginal title arises out of the prior occupation of the land by aboriginal peoples and out of the relationship between the common law and the pre-existing system of aboriginal law. Aboriginal title is a burden on the Crown's underlying title. However, the Crown did not gain this [underlying] title until it asserted sovereignty over the land in question. Because it does not make sense to speak of a burden on the underlying title before that title existed, aboriginal title crystallized at the time sovereignty was asserted.[10]

As a result of the nonsense of speaking about rights of indigenous peoples to their territories before the recognition of their rights within common law, there is no reason to doubt that the unilateral assertion of sovereignty by the Crown over their territories, without their consent, constituted the legitimate achievement of sovereignty:

> [I]t is worth recalling that while British policy toward the native population was based on respect for their right to occupy their traditional lands, a proposition to which the *Royal Proclamation of 1763* bears witness, there was from the outset never any doubt that sovereignty and legislative power, and indeed the underlying title, to such lands vested in the Crown . . . [11]

Thus, indigenous peoples are subject to internal colonisation by a combination of a doctrine of *terra nullius* and a doctrine that discovery, settlement and recognition by other European powers constitute legitimate sovereignty and subjection.[12]

The second defining characteristic of the Aboriginal rights that indigenous peoples are recognised as having, only in virtue of being members of the Canadian society and subject to its sovereignty, is that such rights derive exclusively from the distinctiveness of Aboriginal peoples as *aboriginals*. They do not derive from any universal principles, such as the freedom and equality of peoples, the sovereignty of long-standing, self-governing nations, or the jurisdiction of a people over the territory they have occupied and used to the exclusion and recognition of other peoples since time immemorial. The Court explicitly rejects any appeal to such universal general rights of the liberal Enlightenment as a ground of aboriginal rights.[13]

The Court has shown that a wide range of cultural, ceremonial and economic rights, including rights to the land, can be derived from the distinctiveness of Aboriginal peoples and that these rights need not be limited to the distinctive practices, customs and traditions they engaged in at the time of contact. A limited right of self-government within the Canadian constitutional structure may also be derived from aboriginal distinctiveness in future cases. This exclusive ground of Aboriginal rights in the politics of difference (without the universal demand for freedom that underlies and justifies it) has thus ushered in a higher degree of internal autonomy for indigenous people within the colonial system than they have been permitted since the mid-nineteenth century, when administrative intervention in their internal affairs began in earnest. Nevertheless, it denies indigenous peoples the right to appeal to universal principles of freedom and equality in struggling against injustice, precisely the appeal that would call into question the basis of internal colonisation.[14]

The third step in defining Aboriginal rights concerns the content and proof of Aboriginal title (aboriginal rights to land). The right of an Aboriginal people to land is derived from their distinctive occupation of the land at the time of contact and the Crown's recognition of that occupation as a common law and constitutional right. Aboriginal title is a distinctive or *sui generis* proprietary right, yet similar to fee simple. It is a right to the land and its exclusive use, alienable only to the Crown, and held communally. The land may be used for a variety of purposes, which do not need to be distinctive to the Aboriginal community, such as resource extraction, subject to the limitation that the land cannot be used in a manner that is irreconcilable with the distinctive nature of the attachment to the land by the Aboriginal people claiming the right (*Delgamuukw* 1997: 112–39; McNeil 1998: 2–6).

Following from the first two steps, the onus of proof is not on Canada to prove that it has the underlying title to all indigenous territories. This is not a claim but an assertion validated by its acknowledgment by other European powers. Rather, the burden of proof is made to rest with indigenous peoples, who are presumed not to actually possess aboriginal title, but to be making a claim to it before the Court. For an indigenous people to possess and be able to exercise title to their land, they have to prove to the satisfaction of the colonial Court that they occupied the claimed land at the time the Crown asserted sovereignty over them, and that the occupation was exclusive (*Delgamuukw* 1997: 140–59; McNeil 1998: 7–8).

No such proof has been made. Even if such a proof is successful in the future, the structure of the process further entrenches the taken-for-granted colonial relationship in which the claim is presented and the proof granted or withheld.

The fourth and final step is that once a claim to Aboriginal title is proven, and presuming the land and resources have not been developed in the interim, the title has still to be reconciled with the sovereignty of the Crown. That is, the Crown must take into account the justifiable objectives of the larger Canadian society that conflict with an Aboriginal land right, infringe the right accordingly, and compensate the aboriginal people for the infringement. The Court explains in *Delgamuukw* that proven Aboriginal title can be infringed by the federal and provincial governments if the infringement furthers a compelling and substantive legislative objective and if it is consistent with the fiduciary relation between Crown and Aboriginal peoples. The sorts of objectives that justify infringement are:

> the development of agriculture, forestry, mining and hydro-electric power, the general economic development of the interior of British Columbia, protection of the environment or endangered species, and the building of infrastructure and the settlement of foreign populations to support those aims, are the kinds of objectives that are consistent with this purpose and, in principle, can justify the infringement of aboriginal title. (*Delgamuukw* 1997: 165, 166–69; McNeil 1998: 8–14)

It is difficult to see in these objectives much difference from the early justifications of dispossession in terms of the superiority of European-derived societies and their developmental imperatives.[15] The federal and provincial governments are not obliged to gain the consent of the Aboriginal people whose right they infringe (another unique feature of this constitutional right) or to bring them in as partners in the developmental activities. As in the nineteenth century, governments are under a duty only to compensate the Aboriginal people for taking their land. Compensation involves consultation (consent if it involves fishing and hunting regulations) and the compensation paid should vary with the nature of the title affected, the severity of its infringement and the extent to which aboriginal interests are accommodated.

In summary, the underlying reason why the land rights of Aboriginal peoples can be treated in this imperial manner is that Aboriginal societies unquestionably are distinctive colonies incorporated within and subject to the sovereignty of the larger Canadian society:

> Because . . . distinctive aboriginal societies exist within, and are part of, a broader social, political and economic community, over which the Crown is sovereign, there are circumstances in which, in order to pursue objectives of compelling and substantive importance to that community as a whole (taking

into account the fact that aboriginal societies are part of that community), some limitation of those rights will be justifiable. Aboriginal rights are a necessary part of the reconciliation of aboriginal societies with the broader political community of which they are a part; limits placed on those rights are, where the objectives furthered by those limits are of sufficient importance to the broader community as a whole, equally a necessary part of that reconciliation.[16]

That is to say, the internal colonisation of indigenous peoples itself provides the ultimate justification for the infringement of the rights they have within Canadian society.

In *Delgamuukw*, the Supreme Court recommends that the Gitxsan and Wet'suwet'en peoples turn to the treaty process to settle their lands, guided by the framework the Court sets out, rather than returning to an expensive retrial. An example of this alternative strategy is the negotiations of the Nisga'a Nation of Northern British Columbia with the federal government and, after 1990, the provincial government of British Columbia. Twenty years of negotiations led to the *Nisga'a Final Agreement* in 1998, which shows fairly clearly what can be expected from the present treaty process.

The Nisga'a treaty follows for the most part the framework set out by the Supreme Court. The Preamble states that the objective is the same as the Court's – to reconcile the prior presence of Aboriginal peoples and the assertion of sovereignty by the Crown – but to achieve reconciliation by negotiation rather than litigation. Like the approach of the Supreme Court, the Nisga'a are recognised from the outset as Aboriginal people within Canada and subject to the Crown. They are an Aboriginal people or a first nation *of* Canada. Furthermore, the aim of the negotiations is to define the undefined distinctive aboriginal rights that the Nisga'a have under section 35 of the *Constitution Act 1982* exhaustively and completely in terms of the rights and remedies set out and agreed to in the treaty.[17]

In place of the Court's step of infringement of and compensation for the lands they occupied at the time the Crown asserted sovereignty, the Nisga'a voluntarily gave up to the Crown in the negotiations 93 per cent of their traditional territory. Over the remaining 7 per cent (approximately 2000 square kilometres), they are allotted Aboriginal title in the form of an estate in fee simple proprietary right under the constitution, some rights with respect to trap lines, wildlife and migratory birds outside Nisga'a lands, and approximately $200 million in compensation. Unlike the Court, which has not ruled on an Aboriginal right of self-government, but following the federal and provincial government's policies of recognising such a right in principle, the Nisga'a Nation negotiated an Aboriginal right of limited, western-style self-government, with more powers than a municipality yet less than a province, and within the bounds of the constitution.[18]

Like the Court, the federal government has never questioned the legitimacy of the unilateral exercise of sovereignty over the indigenous peoples and their territories.[19] Nevertheless, as we have seen, governments of Canada have always been concerned to extinguish whatever rights indigenous peoples might have independent of the Canadian legal system. Therefore, unlike the Court, which does not acknowledge such rights, the treaty stipulates that the rights set out are the full and final settlement of the Aboriginal rights of the Nisga'a, not only under section 35, but any rights they may have or come to have as indigenous peoples from any other source. For greater clarity, any such rights are either modified and continued in their entirety in the treaty rights or the Nisga'a Nation releases them to Canada (*Nisga'a* 1998: 20–1).

Although the term is 'release' rather than the traditional 'extinguishment', the legal effect is the same. As far as I am aware, this is the first time in the history of Great Turtle Island that an indigenous people, or at least 61 per cent of its eligible voters, has voluntarily surrendered their rights as indigenous peoples, not to mention surrendering over 90 per cent of their territory, and accepted their status as a distinctive minority with group rights within Canada. This appears to be the first success of strategies of extinguishment (release) and incorporation by agreement.[20]

Struggles *for* Freedom

Western political theories need not legitimise colonisation. Political theorists can employ the language of western political thought critically to test these dubious justifications, to delegitimise them and to test the claims of indigenous peoples for and of freedom. This orientation takes up the second question made at the beginning: what resources exist in political theory for thinking about the possibilities of a non-colonial relation between indigenous and non-indigenous peoples?

Recall that indigenous peoples resist colonisation in two distinct ways. First, they struggle against the structure of domination as a whole and for the sake of their freedom as peoples. Second, they struggle within the structure of domination vis à vis techniques of government, by exercising their freedom of thought and action with the aim of modifying the system in the short term and transforming it from within in the long term.

A people can struggle directly against colonisation in two ways: by words and deeds. In this case the recourse to deed – a direct confrontation in a revolution to overthrow the colonial system – is next to impossible. The states against which the revolution would take place are the most powerful in the world and exist on the same territory as the colony.

Turning to direct confrontation by the pen rather than the sword, two underlying presumptions, firmly held in place by the day-to-day activities that reproduce these societies, serve to legitimise the system of internal colonisation. The first is that the exercise of exclusive jurisdiction over the territories of indigenous peoples is not only effective but also legitimate: it was either legitimately established in the past or the present irresolution is in the process of being legitimately resolved today by one or more of the five main strategies. The second presumption is that there is no viable alternative. Given the modern system of independent nation states, each with exclusive jurisdiction over its territory, either the dominant state exercises exclusive jurisdiction or the indigenous people do after a successful colonial revolt, but the latter is impossible. These two presumptions reinforce each other. They are among the 'hinge' propositions around which the political and economic way of life of these modern societies turns.[21]

Although it is impractical to struggle for freedom in deed by direct confrontation, it is possible to struggle in words by confronting and seeking to invalidate the two legitimating hinge propositions. This is the way of indigenous word warriors and of western political theorists who take a critical stance towards the legitimating and deeply embedded myths of their society. This critical activity consists in three major exercises:

- to test if the freedom and equality of indigenous peoples as peoples with jurisdiction and governance over their territories is defensible by the principles of western political thought;
- to test the alleged validity of various legitimations of their incorporation; and
- to show that the second hinge proposition is a false dichotomy that conceals a way of resolving the underlying contradiction of the colonial system: namely, indigenous peoples and settler peoples can recognise each other as free and equal on the same territory because jurisdiction can be shared as well as exclusive.

Dale Turner explains that indigenous word warriors have their ways of engaging in these three exercises by presenting indigenous political theories that draw on the indigenous language of political thought. By listening to and responding to these presentations in critical discussions, members of the dominant society can begin to free themselves from the hold of the hinge propositions and take a critical stance. These intercultural dialogues are the best and most effective way, for they enable Westerners to see their conventional horizon as a limit and the dialogues are themselves intimations of and indispensable groundwork for a future non-colonial relationship between genuinely free and equal peoples (Turner 1997; forthcoming). A second-best, monological approach is to draw on the resources of critical self-reflection available within the dominant western language of political thought to challenge the comfortable and unexamined prejudices of self-understanding and present a non-colonial alternative.

In the second-best approach, employed by indigenous and non-indigenous scholars over the last forty years, the three critical exercises go together. To show that indigenous peoples are self-determining peoples with jurisdiction over their territories entails that the standard legitimations of their colonisation are false, since these legitimations presuppose that indigenous populations are not peoples, and the third exercise then follows. The two most thoroughly researched and reasoned arguments of this comprehensive kind are the prior and coexisting sovereignty argument and the self-determination argument.

The prior and coexisting sovereignty argument begins with a historical investigation of the situation at the time that Europeans arrived on Great Turtle Island and the Crown asserted sovereignty. America was inhabited by indigenous peoples, divided into separate stateless nations, independent of each other and the rest of the world, who governed themselves by their own laws and ways, occupying and exercising jurisdiction over their territories. As a consequence, they met the criteria of free peoples and sovereign nations in the law of nations, and so were equal in status to European nations. The question is, how can the Europeans legitimately settle and establish their sovereignty; that is, acquire their own territory and exercise jurisdiction over it and establish their own political and economic institutions? This is the starting point for an inquiry into justice and legitimacy of governments and jurisdiction in the US and Canada, not the fictitious and counter-factual original position that has dominated most political theory for the twentieth century.[22]

The only defensible answer in accordance with unbiased western principles of international law at the time and today is that the legitimate achievement of non-indigenous sovereignty in North America consists of two steps. First discovery, some settlement, the assertion of sovereignty by an European nation, and the international negotiation of boundaries with other affected European colonising nations is sufficient to establish sovereignty vis à vis other European nations. However, this step has no effect on the indigenous nations of the territories over which sovereignty is asserted because these nations, unlike the other European nations, have not given their consent. To legitimise their exercise of sovereignty on Great Turtle Island, the European nations had next to gain the consent of indigenous peoples. This second step is fundamental to legitimation, for it follows from the basic principle of western law, both domestically and in international relations among independent nations, that the exercise of sovereignty must be based on the consent of those affected by it.[23]

To gain the consent of indigenous peoples, representatives of the Crown are required to enter into negotiations with indigenous peoples as nations equal in status to the Crown. The negotiations are nation to nation, and the treaties that follow from agreement on both sides are, by definition, international treaties. If the Crown pretends that the treaty negotiations take place within its overriding jurisdiction, then it fails to recognise the status of indigenous peoples, and incorporates and subordinates them without justification, rendering the negotiation illegitimate. The indigenous nation in question thus has the right to appeal not only to domestic courts for redress of infringement, but, if this fails, to international law, like any other nation.[24]

Under these circumstances, the indigenous peoples were and are willing to give their consent to the assertion of the coexisting sovereignty of the Crown on three conditions. First, that the indigenous peoples continue to exercise their own stateless, popular sovereignty on the territories they reserve for themselves and the newcomers are not to interfere. Second, the settlers can establish their own governments and jurisdictions on unoccupied territories that are given to them by indigenous peoples in return for being left alone on their own territories. Third, indigenous peoples agree to share jurisdiction with the newcomers over the remaining, overlapping territories so that one party to a treaty does not extinguish its rights and subordinate itself to the other. Instead, they treat each other as equal, self-governing, and coexisting entities, and set up negotiation procedures to work out consensual and mutually binding relations of autonomy and interdependence, and to deal multilaterally rather than unilaterally with the legitimate objectives of the larger society, subject to review and renegotiation when necessary, as circumstances change and differences arise.[25]

Such a stance constitutes a genuine resolution of the problem of internal colonisation. It shows that indigenous peoples were independent peoples or nations at the time of the assertion of sovereignty by the Crown, that this status has not been legitimately surrendered, and, consequently, the prevailing legitimations of exclusive Crown sovereignty are indefensible. The presumption that jurisdiction must be exclusive is replaced with two (indigenous) principles: free and equal peoples on the same continent can mutually recognise the autonomy or sovereignty of each other in certain spheres and share jurisdictions in others without incorporation or subordination. This is a form of treaty federalism with the capacity to negotiate fairly all the legitimate objectives of the now much larger settler society (including obligations beyond Canadian borders) much better than the present system of infringements, protests, lawsuits, negotiations and uncertainty. In summary, prior and continuing 'sovereignty' does not refer to state sovereignty, but, rather, a stateless, self-governing and autonomous people, equal in status, but not in form, to the Canadian state, with a willingness to negotiate shared jurisdiction of land and resources.[26]

Notwithstanding the availability and legitimacy of this resolution, it has been overwhelmed by the drive of colonising states to establish their exclusive jurisdiction and to legitimate it by doctrines of discovery and incorporation and by interpreting treaties as domestic instruments of extinguishment and release. Hence, indigenous peoples have turned to international law to gain recognition and protection of their status as peoples with the right of self-determination. The extensive research and reasoning that support their prior and coexisting sovereignty also, and *eo ipso*, support the recognition of indigenous populations as internally colonised peoples to whom the principle of self-determination applies.[27] The principle or right of the self-determination of colonised peoples is one of the fundamental and universal principles of the United Nations and international law. In Article 1(2) of the Charter and the Covenants of the UN self-determination is equal in status to individual human rights. Moreover, it is in general the principle that has justified decolonisation struggles since the Enlightenment, including those of Canada, the US, Australia and New Zealand.[28]

Indigenous peoples have gained a modicum of support at the UN. In an advisory opinion of the International Court of Justice, *Western Sahara*, the International Court of Justice rejected the doctrine of discovery and asserted that the only way a foreign sovereign could acquire a right to enter into territory that is not *terra nullius* is with the consent of the inhabitants by means of a public agreement. The Court further advised that the structure and form of government and whether a people are said to be at a lower level of civilisation are not valid criteria for determining if the inhabitants have rights, such as the right of self-determination. The relevant consideration is if they have social and political organisations. This line of reasoning calls into question the doctrines that continue to serve to deny the prior and continuing rights of indigenous peoples in Canada.[29] In addition, indigenous peoples managed to have established within the Sub-Commission on the Prevention of Discrimination and Protection of Minorities of the Commission of Human Rights a working group on indigenous populations in 1982. The working group provides a forum for presentations by indigenous peoples and has issued a draft Declaration on the Rights of Indigenous Peoples which states that indigenous peoples have a qualified right to self-determination.[30]

Despite such occasional glimmers of hope, indigenous peoples are not recognised as colonised peoples to whom the principle of self-determination applies. The reason for this is that international law, the UN and its Committees are created by existing nation states that will do everything in their power to deny the application of the principle of self-determination whenever it threatens their exclusive jurisdiction.[31] The four main ways its application to indigenous peoples is denied in international law are analogous to and complement the earlier arguments in domestic law to incorporate and assimilate or accommodate indigenous peoples within the exclusive jurisdiction of existing nation states. As in the domestic case, indigenous and non-indigenous scholars have critically examined these rationalisations, shown them to be dubious, and defended the application of the principle to indigenous peoples.

The first argument is that indigenous peoples do not meet the criteria of 'peoples' but are 'populations' or 'minorities' within states. This strategy is not difficult to employ because there is no official agreement on the criteria and the general guidelines are vague. Even so, studies by Special Rapporteurs at the UN tend to substantiate what independent research has shown: the indigenous peoples of the Americas are peoples in the clear meaning of the term as it is used in the Charter and the General Assembly Declaration on the Granting of Independence to Colonial Countries and Peoples, and thus the principle of self-determination enunciated in the Declaration applies to them.[32] It is difficult to see how peoples who have governed themselves over their territories for millennia and have not surrendered under a few centuries of colonisation can be denied the status of peoples by those who have colonised them, without introducing a biased criterion that the ICJ has said to be inadmissible.

The second argument is the 'saltwater' thesis that the right of self-determination applies only to colonised peoples on geographically separate territories from the imperial country. This notorious and arbitrary thesis in the General Assembly Declaration on the Granting of Independence to Colonial Countries and Peoples neatly legitimises the dismantling of external colonies in the twentieth century while excluding internal colonies, thereby denying indigenous peoples the same right as other colonised peoples and protecting the exclusive jurisdiction of the major drafters of the Declaration.[33]

A more serious argument is that the right of self-determination of colonised peoples is subordinate to the protection of the territorial integrity of existing nation states from disruption.[34] There are two cogent responses to this argument. First, it presupposes what is in question: namely, the legitimacy of the present territorial integrity of existing nation states. The second and more important response is that the recognition of the right of indigenous peoples to self-determination does not entail the disruption of the territorial integrity of existing nation states. This would be the case only if the exercise of the right of self-determination by indigenous peoples took the European and third-world form of deco-

lonisation and the establishment of sovereign nation states with exclusive
jurisdiction over their territories. For indigenous peoples, the exercise of
self-determination consists of decolonisation and the recognition of
indigenous peoples as free, equal and self-governing peoples under
international law, with *shared* jurisdiction over lands and resources on the
basis of mutual consent.[35] This achieves rather than disrupts territorial
integrity (if 'integrity' has any normative content) by amending an illegitimate exclusive jurisdiction into a legitimate shared jurisdiction. This
kind of post-Westphalian, multiple and overlapping governance and
jurisdiction is said to be the general tendency of global politics in many
spheres. There is no non-discriminatory reason why it should be denied
in this specific case, only the tenacity by which existing states hold on to
their exclusive jurisdiction, inherited from an earlier period in which
state sovereignty ruled supreme.[36]

The final and most prevalent argument is that the principle applies
only to colonised peoples, whereas indigenous peoples are said
already to enjoy the right of self-determination within existing nation
states. This comes in two varieties. The first is that the right of self-
determination is satisfied when indigenous peoples are counted as
part of the fictitious, homogeneous sovereign people of a nation state
and are able to exercise the same individual rights of participation as
other citizens.[37] Here, the reduction of the rights of peoples to undifferentiated individual rights of participation is used to gloss over the
existence of more than one people in an existing nation state and so
to legitimise their assimilation. Given the dispossession, usurpation
and cultural genocide this ruse conceals, it is beneath contempt. Even
so, critical liberal theorists have responded that it undermines the
individual liberties and goods that liberal democracy is supposed to
secure, by destroying the appropriate institutions of self-rule in which
they are cultivated and protected.[38]

The more sophisticated version of this argument is that forms of
accommodation that recognise degrees of self-government and land
rights within existing nation states satisfy the criteria of *internal* self-
determination. The right of internal self-determination is the right of a
people within a larger state to govern themselves in a wide range of matters, including culture, religion, education, information, health, housing,
welfare, economic activity, land and resource management, environmental practices and membership.[39] If a people exercise such a right,
they are not colonised but internally self-determining. Only if this right
of *internal* self-determination is thwarted by the encompassing society
may a people in principle exercise the right of *external* self-determination: that is, free themselves from the dominant society and set up their
own nation state. Since societies with systems of internal colonisation

claim to be moving in the direction of recognising the right of internal self-determination, the demand for self-determination is being met and these societies are legitimate under international law.[40]

The response of indigenous people is that this argument perpetuates rather than dismantles the system of internal colonisation by giving international legitimacy to domestic policies of incorporation and accommodation (Venne 1998: 119–22, 138–63). Indigenous peoples are not recognised as peoples under international law, but as peoples under domestic law. Also, their jurisdiction over their territories is not recognised. Rather, they are given a form of proprietary right to a small portion of their territories under the domestic legal system. As a result, they are precluded from appealing to international law as peoples to redress infringement of their rights under the guise of domestic law – the very reason they turned to international law. Finally, the contradiction generated by the presumption of exclusive jurisdiction is reproduced rather than questioned by the distinction between internal and external self-determination, thereby eliding the resolution indigenous people offer.

It follows that internal self-determination is not a valid form of self-determination at all. The principle or right of self-determination is, on any plausible account of its contested criteria, the right of a people to govern themselves by their own laws and exercise jurisdiction over their territories, either exclusively or shared. A people are said to govern themselves, and thus to be a free people, when the laws by which they are governed rest on their consent or the consent of their representatives. The condition of consent holds for legislation and even more fundamentally for the constitution. If the constitution does not rest on the consent of the people or their representatives, or if there is not a procedure by which it can be so amended, then they are neither self-governing nor self-determining, but are governed and determined by a structure of laws that is imposed on them and they are unfree. This is the principle of popular sovereignty by which modern peoples and governments are said to be free and legitimate.[41]

Yet, this principle of popular sovereignty and condition of self-determination is not met by the concept of internal self-determination. An alien constitution, the constitution of surrounding nation state, is imposed over indigenous peoples and their territories without their consent and to which they are subject. Their internal self-determination exists within the constitution, which functions as a structure of domination. They will be free and self-determining only when they governed themselves by their own constitutions and these are equal in international status to western constitutions. Internal self-determination, therefore, is not a form of self-determination or freedom. It is a form of indirect colonial rule, not unlike earlier forms of British indirect colonial rule, which

Canadians, Americans, Australians and New Zealanders found to be an intolerable form of unfreedom and the justification for their own successful and purportedly universal struggles for freedom. Yet, for reasons that do not withstand public scrutiny, they do not hesitate to impose such a yoke on weak and captive peoples within their own borders.[42]

Struggles *of* Freedom

Despite the cogency of research and arguments supporting the freedom of indigenous peoples in domestic and international arenas, the system of internal colonisation remains firmly in place and the two presumptions reinforcing it remain largely unquestioned. One reason for this inertia is the overwhelming power and interest of the existing nation states with internal indigenous colonies. Another is that propositions which play the hinge role in a society – of being presupposed by and legitimising its routine way of political and economic life – are relatively immune from direct criticism. They are background norms of the daily operation and criticism of the institutions and practices, not objects of criticism – the riverbed, not the river (Wittgenstein 1974: 341, 343, 655; Zerilli 1998). The irresolution thus remains in theory and practice, as East Timor tragically illustrates.

If such hinge propositions and the social system they legitimise change over time, they do so obliquely, by means of more local and indirect criticism and modification within the system they frame. The multiplicity of immanent activities of challenging specific strategies and techniques by the democratic means of dissent and insubordination available may not only modify this or that rule of the system, which is important in itself, but may also in the long run bring about the self-overcoming of the system itself (Foucault 1998: 316; Scott 1990). Consequently, the arts of resistance involved in struggles *of* freedom to modify the system of internal colonisation from within are arguably more important and more effective than the complementary arts of legitimising and delegitimising struggles for freedom with which political theorists have been preoccupied.

The diverse range of possibilities of thinking and acting differently vis à vis the relations of knowledge and techniques of government that reproduce the system – of working with and against, of complying and adapting while resisting the allure of the co-opted native, male colonial elite, of indigenising the degree of self-government and land use recovered, of connecting reserve and off-reserve native people, and innumerable other arts of resistance – constitute a vast field of human freedom, not unlike any other colonial system. These arts of words and deeds have been practised since the beginning of colonisation. In addition to the spectacular public displays of resistance mentioned earlier, they are mostly quotidian acts of protecting, recovering, gathering together, keeping, revitalising, teaching and adapting entire forms of indigenous life that were nearly destroyed. The persistence of traditional medicine, healing and child-rearing practices, the revitalisation of justice circles, indigenous languages and political ways, and the astonishing recovery and renaissance of indigenous art are some examples of these arts of resistance and indigenisation that Taiaiake Alfred calls 'self-conscious traditionalism' (Alfred 1999a: 80–8; Simpson, this volume).

These practices of freedom on the rough ground of daily colonisation usually fall beneath the attention and interest of Western political theorists unless they are members of an oppressed group, and it is the big, abstract questions of normative legitimation that tend to capture the attention of most of the field. Yet it is these unnoticed contextual struggles of human freedom in the face of techniques of government and strategies of legitimation that have brought the internal colonisation of indigenous peoples to the threshold of public attention and critical reflection in our time. And it is these which have the potential to lead in the long run to the same kind of freedom for indigenous peoples that western political theorists and citizens already enjoy, but which is currently based on the unfreedom of indigenous peoples.

CHAPTER 4

Beyond Regret:
Mabo's Implications For Australian
Constitutionalism

Jeremy Webber

> To the extent that the common law is to be understood as the
> ultimate constitutional foundation in Australia, there was a
> perceptible shift in that foundation [in the decision of
> *Mabo* v. *Queensland (No. 2)*] away from what had been
> understood at federation.[1]
> Wik Peoples *v.* Queensland *(per* Gummow J)*[2]

In *Mabo* v. *Queensland (No. 2)*, the High Court broke with Australia's long
history of denying indigenous title and recognised indigenous title's
continued existence within Australian law. Like many judgments, *Mabo*
was primarily – and quite properly – backward-looking. It explored the
reasons for the denial of indigenous title, evaluated those reasons in the
light of developments in Australian law and society, and suggested how
the law should be reconceived.[3] My purpose here is to look forward, to
examine the significance of *Mabo*'s recognition of indigenous title for
indigenous/non-indigenous relations over the coming decades. It
explores the shift in Australia's constitutional foundations to which
Gummow J adverted in *Wik*, in the passage quoted above. It describes the
sense of mediated nationhood, of mediated sovereignty, that is implied
in the recognition of indigenous title – for indigenous peoples and for
Australia as a whole.

This chapter is therefore about the impact of *Mabo* on Australian constitutionalism. By that, I do not mean its effect on specific rules of constitutional law, but rather on the general framework of presumptions and
concerns that inform our understanding of public action and that are
used to explain and justify the exercise of governmental power within
any society.[4] Such presumptions operate at a high level of generality and
are closely connected to conceptions of nationhood, but their effects are
not confined to a realm of ideological abstraction. They have a marked

conditioning effect on legal interpretation, governmental practice and institutional reform. I suggest how we should understand the change accomplished by the recognition of indigenous title in *Mabo*, what new constellation that recognition has introduced into Australian constitutionalism, and some of the consequences the recognition of indigenous title should have for legal interpretation and the evolution of governmental structures.

The suggestion that *Mabo* has implications for Australian constitutionalism needs defending, for one often hears a much narrower interpretation of its significance. Indigenous title is frequently discussed as though it were simply another kind of interest affecting land, slipped into the structure of Australian property law.[5] On that view, its implications may be important, but they remain relatively confined. The implications are thoroughly captured by determining the content of indigenous title according to the rules of indigenous customary law, examining to what extent the title has been extinguished by prior acts of the non-indigenous sovereign, and then enforcing the remaining interest. That view of indigenous title is, however, altogether too limited, not just because a more ambitious interpretation should be preferred as a matter of policy, but because it misunderstands what the recognition of indigenous title necessarily involves. Indeed, it mischaracterises the very nature of indigenous title as a legal doctrine.

That doctrine does not merely acknowledge what is, to Australian law, a novel form of title. It operates at a broader level of generality, implying a quite different relationship between indigenous and non-indigenous Australians of significance beyond the bounds of land law. *Mabo* does not purport to describe the incidents of that relationship in detail. Those incidents cannot be described in advance. Rather, *Mabo* initiates a process of mutual adjustment that will continue long into the future (if Australians remain true to the start made in that case). Perhaps it is not quite accurate to say that *Mabo* initiates the process of adjustment, since a measure of mutual interaction has always characterised Australian history. *Mabo* attempts to change the basis on which that interaction occurs, placing it (one hopes) on a more positive, more acceptable foundation.

In emphasising the transformative potential of that change, I do not mean to adopt the more sanguine interpretations of indigenous rights, in which *Mabo* and cases like it represent a chance to restore a pristine Aboriginal sphere. *Mabo* is not about the recognition of two utterly separate spheres – one indigenous, the other non-indigenous – that can go forward in parallel. Indigenous and non-indigenous societies have been thrown together and inevitably affect each other. *Mabo* is about the restructuring of that relationship, in which one hopes that there will be

areas of significant autonomy and continuity of Aboriginal and Torres
Strait Islander traditions, but in which relative autonomy will be combined with a measure of interaction and mutual influence. (One hopes
that the influence will indeed be mutual, and not entirely a matter of
non-indigenous pressure on indigenous traditions.) Thus, the recognition of indigenous title and the mediation of sovereignty that it entails
have a hard institutional edge; it is not enough to praise the recognition
of indigenous traditions of land-holding and affirm their autonomy; one
has to be concerned with the structures through which indigenous and
non-indigenous societies will continue to interact into the future.

I begin by looking at the principal decisions of the High Court of Australia, and particularly at the doctrine of native title elaborated in those
cases, to show that there is more going on than the simple recognition of
a neglected or forcibly suppressed type of land title. I will then move to a
more general plane – indeed, a very general plane – to explore what I take
to be the broad implications for Australians' sense of their country, as well
as their understanding of government and law. Finally, I will attempt to
bring those reflections down to institutional specifics: how should Australia go on, in a manner consistent with the paths opened in *Mabo*?

The Nature of Indigenous Title in Australian Law

In one sense, *Mabo* certainly does recognise a form of land title. Native
title does involve the acknowledgement of a unique set of rights to the
land. Where the conventional view fails is in its treatment of that entitlement as though it were a determinate set of rules that can be ascertained
by hearing evidence on indigenous custom and then enforced by the
common-law courts, much like any other common-law title. There is
more to the recognition of Indigenous title than that.

Native Title/Normative Autonomy/Political Autonomy

To begin, the law of indigenous title recognises not just a set of rights and
obligations with respect to land, but the continued relevance of
autonomous indigenous legal traditions. In one sense, this is patent in
the judgments. The very content of indigenous title is said to be the
product of the laws and customs of indigenous societies, so that the title
is recognised but not created by the common law. In Brennan J's words:

> Native title has its origin in and is given its content by the traditional laws
> acknowledged by and the traditional customs observed by the indigenous
> inhabitants of a territory. The nature and incidents of native title must be
> ascertained as a matter of fact by reference to those laws and customs.[6]

The action of these legal orders is not confined to the past, however. Brennan J acknowledges in *Mabo* that indigenous orders were not frozen at the moment of contact, but that they have continued to evolve and to apportion rights and responsibilities among the community's members. It is this contemporary, not the pre-contact, indigenous custom that provides the content of native title.[7]

This suggests something very different from indigenous title as a confined set of rights, which is simply absorbed into the common law. It acknowledges, at least implicitly, that indigenous societies form autonomous legal orders, and moreover, that those orders change over time. The capacity for change suggests a degree of political autonomy (at least *de facto*), for indigenous societies are able to determine the evolution of their law by their own internal means.

One must be careful not to overstate this implicit recognition of political autonomy. The recognition, though real, need not imply any acceptance that indigenous societies are immune from non-indigenous governmental action. The autonomy may exist on sufferance, liable to erosion or obliteration. In that sense, indigenous societies may lack 'sovereignty' – although whether some partial 'sovereignty' (or other protected right of self-government) might persist in Australia has yet to be squarely addressed.[8] But in any case, until obliterated, a measure of normative autonomy – including the capacity for change, not merely the possession of a static set of rights – certainly exists. The recognition of indigenous title necessarily involves an acceptance, at least provisional, of that autonomy.

If this seems implausible – if one wants to cling to the view that indigenous title merely involves the recognition of a particular form of title – one can arrive at the same conclusion by asking what the content of that title would be. At what time would its content stop evolving and crystallise? The moment when sovereignty was first asserted seems highly artificial, and it is no wonder that that position was rejected in *Mabo*. What other point is appropriate? The moment of judgment is the next most obvious, but if that point is chosen, one must then explain why indigenous title can continue to evolve under the control of the indigenous people themselves up to that point, but then must be utterly displaced to the courts. It would be bitterly ironic if, in the very act of recognising indigenous title, the courts simultaneously extinguished its vitality, especially if this occurred without any clear perception that that was happening or any attempt at justification.[9]

Mediated Law

It is also a mistake to believe that *Mabo* is simply about the *continuation* (in that word's most straightforward sense) of indigenous laws with respect to land. The content of indigenous title is not simply a carry-forward of what was before; the very content of indigenous title has been marked by its encounter with non-indigenous society. This is true not just in the cataclysmic sense that some indigenous rights have been extinguished. Rather, the very content of the rights has been transformed through a process of translation and re-expression.[10]

To begin, the need to express indigenous interests as 'rights' may only arise once indigenous societies are confronted with colonisation. Before then, the interests may well still exist – perhaps in distinctively indigenous conceptions of law, perhaps merely as the way things are – but in a form that is not well described using the common law's language of right. The need to characterise the interests as rights becomes relevant only when they are subjected to the threats posed by colonisation and one is forced to find some means of protection that is comprehensible to and efficacious within a non-indigenous system of law.

This is most obvious in the case of rights to a measure of governmental autonomy, such as the recognition of indigenous societies as 'domestic dependent nations' in American law (a right not yet acknowledged within Australian law).[11] Before colonisation, indigenous societies certainly were autonomous and governed themselves. They were, in that sense, 'sovereign'. But it is questionable whether they would have conceived themselves as having a 'right' to self-government, and inconceivable that they would have thought of themselves as having anything like the qualified rights of domestic dependent nations, except perhaps for those peoples who acknowledged the suzerainty of another indigenous people, as, for example, the Delawares and certain other peoples did with respect to the Iroquois (Jennings 1987: 75). Why would they? That latter right only makes sense within the context of an overarching colonial sovereignty. It is generally the case that the articulation of rights is prompted by some threat or perceived challenge. If there is no threat, why bother articulating it as a right? It is simply the way things are.

That does not mean that they are any less deserving of protection as rights once there is a challenge. The human value of self-government may well be sufficiently important that it deserves legal recognition in some form of right once the conflict of colonising power and indigenous people has arisen. It is not at all unfamiliar to see fundamental interests recognised as rights, once subjected to threat. That progression lies at the origin of virtually all common-law and equitable rights. The whole law of fiduciary obligation, for example, is an attempt to provide legal recognition and enforcement of the distinctive interests and responsibilities inherent in a wide range of relationships, and the law of fiduciary obligation has extended precisely as it has come to grips with new types of relationship (Sealy 1962).

Indeed, something like this process is arguably inherent in the powerful allegories at the foundation of many theories of natural rights. Those theories often claim that rights exist in the state of nature, before the formation of society. Thus, for example, in Locke, the compelling need of individuals to appropriate things in order to eat is held to support a natural right of appropriation, and ultimately a fully elaborated set of property rights (Locke 1986: 327ff). But there is another way of thinking about those allegories, in which the rights themselves do not exist, as rights, in the state of nature. On the contrary, the existence of rights requires precisely the web of social recognition that exists only upon the formation of society. Rather, the need to appropriate exists in the state of nature as a compelling interest – a fundamental prerequisite of survival, which individuals in the state of nature simply act upon. The 'right' is generated when individuals' attempts to appropriate and cultivate come into conflict.[12] The challenge generates the need for a system of obligation. The fact that the right emerges only in response to challenge does not diminish its force in the slightest. I do not mean to adopt here a natural rights theory of property, nor do I mean to suggest that indigenous societies are best conceived as having been themselves in a state of nature before colonisation. That was manifestly not the case, and the rejection of such a bigoted conception has been a major element in settler societies coming better to terms with the presence of indigenous peoples.[13] Rather, the allegory is significant in drawing our attention to the fact that interests are fundamental and rights epiphenomenal – that rights are fashioned in order to protect fundamental interests from challenge, and their particular form is shaped by the specific context and nature of that challenge.

This is also true of rights which, like native title, serve to protect interests that were conceived to be matters of entitlement within the pre-colonial legal traditions of indigenous peoples. Even though native title does protect entitlements that existed pre-contact, it does so within a profoundly changed context, and especially within a superimposed legal system. That context inevitably shapes the rights in a myriad ways. Perhaps the most fundamental is tied up with the very idea of law in the western legal tradition, in which 'law' is generally considered to capture only a subset of social norms, one enforced by specialised tribunals. In indigenous societies, there tends not to be the same sharp differentiation between law and other forms of social normativity; there may not be the same emphasis on the posited quality of law, there may be less emphasis on rules, and of course there may be no specialised agencies for the enforcement of law (Law Reform Commission 1986: 75–8; Maddock 1984; Myers 1986: 103–58; Berndt *et al.* 1993: 58–73). It may be difficult, then, to identify a distinctive category of 'law' apart from methods of social ordering generally. This is not a sign that indigenous societies lack norms worthy of the name 'law' or occupy a lesser stage of development, as was often suggested in the past; it is simply that indigenous methods of social ordering may be structured very differently.[14] But it does pose difficulties to the attempt to recognise and respect indigenous rights within the common law. What is one respecting? All social practices? All those that have, in indigenous societies, an obligatory character? Only those that are analogous to property rights, or perhaps analogous to other conventional elements of a western legal system? That uncertainty underlies a number of the thorny issues in indigenous rights adjudication today. It is especially acute in Canada, where the rights enjoy constitutional protection.[15]

Inevitably, interests that are recognised are expressed in a form that involves some accommodation to the need for the rights to be intelligible within the broader legal framework. This does not necessarily mean that the terms of the accommodation are rigidly set by the non-indigenous legal tradition. The history of indigenous title has involved the recognition of interests and methods of proof that have few parallels with those previously existing in the common law. But there is nevertheless a measure of translation and adjustment in the very act of recognition, and this process may well be unequal. Indigenous rights are mediated rights (Rose 1996: 35).

This is patent in legislative regimes for the recognition and administration of native title. Creating an Aboriginal Land Council, land trust or indigenous corporation involves the establishment of new institutional forms quite different from indigenous forms, through which the interests are henceforth regulated and exercised. This inevitably affects the enjoyment and control of the interest, often conferring a measure of authority on individuals who are not themselves traditional owners of the relevant land. This is especially true when the bodies charged with holding or administering the title are umbrella groupings, comprising many peoples (as is the case with Land Councils). For that reason, one often encounters ambivalence about statutory regimes. As H. C. Coombs (1994: 210) asked at the time of the adoption of the *Native Title Act 1993* (Cth): 'is not the survival of native title in its legislative form simply another mechanism for the progressive extinguishment of Aboriginal title?'[16] Here, I argue that a continual process of adjustment and adaptation is inherent in the recognition of indigenous title – indeed is of its essence – and do not share the view that indigenous interests can be respected in a pristine, pre-contact form (neither does Coombs). But the remaining ambivalence is real, and results from the fact that one is necessarily faced with better or worse accommodations, not the protection of the pre-contact interests themselves.

The fact that the recognition of native title inevitably requires accommodation is also reflected in the judicial decisions. The courts have implicitly acknowledged that new institutions for the management of the title may be required, and have taken that into account in their adjudication of native title. The *Mabo* judgments recognise that the establishment of a trust for the administration of indigenous land does not extinguish that title, even though trusts clearly take many of the prerogatives of ownership out of owners' hands.[17] In the year following *Mabo*, the Federal Court dealt with an action brought by certain traditional owners to prevent the vesting of land in a Land Trust under the *Aboriginal Land Rights (Northern Territory) Act 1976* (Cth), on the grounds that the structures created by that Act would bring about the extinguishment of their native title. Lockhart J, speaking for the Full Court, noted that there was no precise correspondence between the traditional owners on the one hand and the Aboriginal individuals whose views had to be ascertained by a Land Council in its administration of land within a Land Trust on the other. He also acknowledged that the rights and obligations that flow from a grant to a Land Trust are not identical to those of native title. Yet he concluded:

> The establishment of Land Trusts and Land Councils is essentially a modern adaptation of traditional Aboriginal decision-making processes through their communities. The Land Rights Act was created to reflect the rights and obligations that arise from traditional title...[18]

Indeed, the development of new indigenous institutions goes hand in hand with the recognition of indigenous title. This is clear in specialised regimes. The *Aboriginal Land Rights (Northern Territory) Act 1976* (Cth) is founded upon a structure of Land Councils and Land Trusts. The *Native Title Act 1993* (Cth) allowed for the recognition and funding of 'representative Aboriginal/Torres Strait Islander bodies', which could facilitate the preparation of claims and represent claimants in proceedings. The development of effective coalitions of title claimants and the encouragement of agreements to coordinate various interests in the land have become crucial elements of the native title process.[19] Very frequently, these structures have not simply been imposed by legislation, but have emerged out of the process of advocacy for and litigation of indigenous claims. Thus, the Land Councils of the Northern Territory are the descendants of Aboriginal councils established informally during the Woodward commission of inquiry into indigenous land rights,which led to the adoption of the *Aboriginal Land Rights (Northern Territory) Act 1976*. The *Native Title Act 1993* has served as a catalyst for the creation of regional coalitions or working groups to manage today's title claims (Sullivan 1997: 129). Similarly in the Canadian context, the extensive political structures of the

James Bay Crees and the Inuit of Northern Quebec emerged out of their struggle to secure recognition of indigenous land rights in northern Quebec. Indeed, the principal regulatory agency under the *James Bay and Northern Quebec Agreement* of 1975 – the Hunting, Fishing and Trapping Coordinating Committee – is the successor of a subcommittee created to deal with wildlife issues during the negotiation of that Agreement; the negotiating structure was transformed into the regulatory agency (*James Bay* 1976: section 24; LaRusic 1979; Landmann 1988: 15).

The need to struggle with issues of institutional representation is also present in common law actions. The claimants themselves must decide who should bring the action, in the name of what entity (as individual owners? as individuals in a representative capacity? through representative organisations? or, as in *Wik*, in the name of the people – clan? language group? – as a whole?).[20] They have to decide how decisions with respect to the litigation are to be taken. The court can be drawn into these issues if the form of the action or the entitlement to sue is challenged. Moreover, if the action is successful, the court may ultimately have to determine who holds the title, and how that entity can act to avail itself of the interest. Especially when one is dealing with a communal title, held by a collectivity, these questions may involve difficult issues of political organisation and control.

Thus, the recognition of native title is about far more than simply the recognition of a particular kind of land tenure, surviving from the period before contact. It is intrinsically bound up with issues of political organisation and self-government. This is true, first, in that the title is grounded in and its content determined by contemporary indigenous societies, which have their own legal orders and their own continuing capacity for legal change. Indigenous societies are, by the very doctrine of indigenous title itself, contemporary polities with continuing control over their own normative orders (at least until displaced). The recognition of indigenous title is simultaneously a recognition of that political capacity. Second, the indigenous interests are not simply absorbed into the general law in their pre-contact form. They are mediated, translated into forms susceptible to protection within a non-indigenous legal system. Sometimes entitlements are created for the first time in the act of recognition, for the good reason that despite their fundamental character, there was no need for them to be expressed as entitlements before the threats posed by colonisation. Finally, the need to vindicate and administer those interests in the contemporary environment requires that one develop institutions appropriate to those changed circumstances. The recognition of native title involves, as a necessary concomitant, attention to political organisation and the development of institutions. Native title is more about adjustment and adaptation than the conventional view of native title – as simply another property interest incorporated within non-indigenous land law – presumes.

This need for adjustment is also true on the non-indigenous side. *Mabo* involved a reconsideration of the feudal foundations of Australian land law, with the radical title of the Crown being taken henceforth as a notional attribute of sovereignty and an abstract postulate of the doctrine of tenures, rather than an irrebuttable presumption that absolute beneficial ownership had been held, at some historical moment, by the Crown.[21] The common law thereby made room for a kind of title that had its roots outside the system, in the pre-contact legal orders of the indigenous peoples. That much is uncontroversial, but there is good reason to believe that the recognition of native title will require continued reconsideration and adaptation.

That indeed is one of the principal points of difference between the majority and the minority judgments in *Wik*. That case refined our understanding of the nature of pastoral leases – a form of tenure, based on statute, extensively used in Australia. The Court was forced to do so because of the need to decide whether native title could persist on land subject to a pastoral lease.[22] One of the elements upon which the majority and minority disagreed was whether the granting of a pastoral lease immediately vested a beneficial interest in the Crown, namely the reversionary interest that would expand into a full interest upon the ending of the lease. If so, this would have excluded native title, for in effect the Crown would have created two beneficial interests covering all aspects of the land: the interest held by the lessee for the term of the lease; and the balance of the interest in the land, held by the Crown. The notion of the immediate vesting of the reversion was very like the Crown's radical title in *Mabo*: an element of the doctrine of estates, inherent in the common law conception of a lease, and originally developed without any thought for its possible interaction with indigenous title. The majority and minority divided on whether it is appropriate to import that notion into a statutory 'lease', granted out of Crown lands subject to indigenous title, and having incidents that are in some ways materially different from common law leases. The majority held that that was neither required nor appropriate, and therefore declined to do so.[23]

Shortly after the decision in *Mabo*, Brendan Edgeworth (1994) suggested that the case's consequences for Australian land law should be considerably more far-reaching, leading to the abandonment of land law's feudal foundations altogether so that interests in land are seen to be entirely allodial (which he also linked to the movement for a republic). The recasting of land law is unlikely to happen in such a thorough-going fashion. Nevertheless, Edgeworth's suggestion does draw attention to the extent to which native title poses challenges for our understanding of property, even in non-indigenous law. And decisions such as *Wik* may suggest that Australian land law is, in an incremental and lawyerly fashion, emancipating itself from its feudal roots.[24]

Thus, the recognition of indigenous title appears not so much as the cut and dried incorporation of a discrete set of private rights, but the initiation of a longer process of interaction, mutual adaptation and incitement to reflection and reform. Native title is about the co-existence of partially autonomous societies, each with its own system of law, that must in some fashion, good or ill, relate to one another. Because of the challenges of adjustment – because of the sometimes profound differences of context and forms of social ordering – that process may only be achieved through mutual accommodation over the very long term.

Judicial Strategy

This intersocietal, adaptive and, in a broad sense, constitutional dimension of native title is evident in the very way in which the law of indigenous title has been developed by the courts, especially in North America where it originated. If indigenous title were simply another set of rights incorporated into the broader, non-indigenous system of land law, one would expect that the courts would simply articulate that title's incidents and then proceed to enforce them. In other words, the courts would seek to determine precisely the relationship, under the various indigenous systems of law, between specific individuals or groups and specific tracts of land, and they would then enforce these specific entitlements. That indeed appears to be the process envisaged in the first Australian judgments on native title and perhaps in the *Native Title Act 1993* itself. But in fact, the North American courts have traditionally been manifestly unconcerned with determining entitlements within indigenous law. Instead, they have focused purely and simply on the recognition of the title's existence and on the need to respect it. One could summarise the law of Indigenous title with little distortion by stating that it involved:

• the recognition that indigenous societies have title to their lands;
• the proposition that that title should be (or, if the judgment is retrospective, should have been) dealt with before non-indigenous settlement of those lands; and
• regulation of the mode of acquisition (for example, the prohibition on the alienation of indigenous lands except to the Crown). (Slattery 1987)

This point bears emphasis. One searches the North American decisions in vain for any serious discussion of the inner workings of indigenous systems of landholding. The reason is simple: that is not the purpose of the law of indigenous title. That body of law does not seek to have the non-indigenous courts take over and enforce indigenous systems of land law (as though non-indigenous courts were competent to do so). The law of indigenous title is a law of the interface between societies presumed to continue with considerable legal autonomy. It requires respect for indigenous systems of land law. It does not absorb them. It effectively says: 'The indigenous peoples have rights to this land. Deal with them before encroaching, or you will be in violation of those rights. The proper agency to deal with the rights is government, not private parties.' The internal administration of indigenous title is, in very large measure, left to the indigenous communities themselves.

This explains why indigenous title is often said to be 'collective' or 'communal'. Frequently, title to land is not collective if by that is meant that land is, according to the law of the particular community, held in common. There are many indigenous societies in which land is held by individuals or by families, with no overarching proprietary right in the community. That is true of the Meriam Islanders, for example, whose rights were the subject of the action in *Mabo* (*Mabo* 1992: 87; Sharp 1996: 132–35). It is also true of the James Bay Crees of northern Quebec, and indeed of many other North American societies (Tanner 1979: 182ff). But the law of indigenous title is not concerned with that internal attribution of rights. It views those societies from the outside – and viewed from the outside, the societies do hold their land 'collectively', for the internal distribution of rights and responsibilities is left to the communities themselves. In other words the 'collective' nature of indigenous title is an implicit recognition of the political and legal autonomy of indigenous societies, not a description of the actual form of landholding practised within them. The tenure is 'collective' because the common law treats the land as the province of the community concerned; any internal allocation is left to the community.[25]

The effective consequence of indigenous title is therefore the need to manage the interface between non-indigenous and indigenous legal orders, between non-indigenous and indigenous occupation. In the North American context, this once meant the detailed regulation of the mechanism of land acquisition across the cultural boundaries. Indeed, the emergence of the common law of indigenous title was intrinsically bound up with the gradual extension of controls on colonial settlement and the progressive centralisation of the power to acquire indigenous lands (Webber 1995b: 644–47, 651–55). In one sense, one could say that the recognition of one was the premise for the other, but this is probably too tidy. It is more accurate to say that the recognition of indigenous title emerged *through* the imposition of constraints on settlement and the development of a practice of treaty-making.

Even when indigenous title has come before the Canadian courts, the courts have tended to see themselves as simply policing the boundary, with the detailed management of the relationship to be resolved through negotiation. This is patent in a number of the recent decisions, in which the courts have exhorted the parties to negotiate.[26] But the same approach is arguably implicit in the jurisprudence of indigenous rights in Canada as a whole. The courts' consistent strategy has been to rule upon the framework of indigenous title – to ensure that indigenous title is taken seriously as a material interest in the land – but not to enter too deeply into the precise nature of the rights or how those rights should be accommodated. That is left to negotiation. When one thinks of the great Canadian decisions on indigenous title or related rights – *Calder, Sparrow, Delgamuukw* – those decisions operate almost entirely at the level of general principle, not the definition and enforcement of specific interests (*Calder* v. *AG BC* [1973] SCR 313; *Sparrow* 1990; *Delgamuukw* 1997). Even in the most recent and far-reaching of those decisions, *Delgamuukw* v. *British Columbia*, the Supreme Court of Canada did not rule in detail on the claims, although invited to do so on the basis of the most extensive evidentiary record ever presented. Instead, it referred the matter back to trial on the thin ground that the pleadings had been framed as claims by each of the 51 Gitxsan and Wet'suwet'en Houses, not (as ultimately accepted) as amalgamated claims by the Gitxsan and Wet'suwet'en nations.[27] The principal majority judgment concluded with a powerful statement that the matter should be negotiated, not re-tried:

> Ultimately, it is through negotiated settlements, with good faith and give and take on all sides, reinforced by the judgments of this Court, that we will achieve what I stated . . . to be a basic purpose of s. 35(1) [of the *Constitution Act 1982* (Canada), which protects Aboriginal and treaty rights] – 'the reconciliation of the pre-existence of aboriginal societies with the sovereignty of the Crown'. Let's face it, we are all here to stay.[28]

If negotiations are not successful, the courts may be compelled to intervene more vigorously. This is, in effect, what the Supreme Court has done over time, not least in *Delgamuukw* itself. It has by stages defined more of the content of indigenous rights. But it has done so with reluctance, exercising restraint in its pronouncements and encouraging the parties at each point to take matters into their own hands. The set of draft constitutional amendments in the failed Charlottetown Accord of 1992 would have imposed a duty to negotiate indigenous self-government (including control of land) in good faith upon Canadian governments, with the courts exercising a superintending role over those negotiations.[29] One could argue that the courts have already, tacitly, been doing just that.

In Canada, then, the law of indigenous title has been very much concerned with fostering negotiated solutions to issues that are broadly constitutional – concerned with defining and indeed structuring the
interface between indigenous and non-indigenous legal orders – even
though the issues have been framed through the concept of indigenous
title.

What of Australia? The Australian authorities have tended to speak as
though the recognition and enforcement of a proprietary right by the
non-indigenous courts alone were in issue. The Canadian experience is
often distinguished on the basis that Canadian custom is founded on a
practice of treaty-making not present in Australia – without recognising
that the treaty process in North America was not a separate sphere of
'political' interaction but an integral element of the recognition of
indigenous title.[30] The problem lies in the artificially constricted and ultimately inadequate understanding of what is in issue in Australia. The
constitutional dimensions of indigenous title are just as present, notably
the implicit recognition of the autonomous legal orders from which
indigenous title derives and the need to structure the relationship of the
indigenous/non-indigenous boundary. As in Canada, the Australian
courts are faced with the incongruity of an approach to indigenous title
that suggests that they should become the privileged interpreters and
enforcers of indigenous systems of land tenure. They have confronted in
practice (though perhaps not yet in theory) the dilemma that if they do
enforce an indigenous title like any other, they will, by that very act, displace the indigenous institutions on which the title depends. And they
have also begun to encounter the complexities of deciding what precise
entity should be recognised as the holder of the title, how the non-
indigenous legal order might conceive of that entity and of the native
title holder's relationships to non-indigenous institutions, and how decisions with respect to the use of that indigenous title might validly be
made in the future.

Faced with these questions of fundamental constitutional relationship,
the Australian courts and the specialised agencies created under the
Native Title Act 1993 have adopted strategies, implicitly, very like those in
Canada. The courts have confined themselves to ruling upon the general
existence of indigenous title and issues of extinguishment or impairment;
they have not engaged in the detailed specification of the content of
the title, nor decided conflicts between members of a single indigenous
people.[31] In the most extensive judicial discussion of native title in Australia to date, *Ward* v. *Western Australia*, the Federal Court was asked to
determine that certain lands of the Miriuwung and Gajerrong communities were held by subgroups ('estate groups'). The court declined to do
so, finding instead that the communal title was held collectively by all

members of the community. In that decision, Lee J made reference to the
difficulty of proving that the current members of the subgroups were
descended from the pre-colonial owners, but the burden of his decision
rests not upon a question of proof but upon the intrinsic nature of indigenous title at common law – that indigenous title operates at a broader
level of generality and is vested in the entire community rather than in
subgroups. Also in *Ward*, the court declined to rule in detail on how
indigenous title and concurrent non-indigenous interests in the land
should be coordinated, suggesting that the parties should resolve those
questions by negotiation.[32]

Moreover, the proceedings under the *Native Title Act* have moved
increasingly towards mediation and negotiation, with respect to the existence and scope of indigenous title, but also with respect to the coalesc-
ing of indigenous groups in order to bring the claims, the resolution of
conflicts among indigenous parties, the reconciliation of indigenous
land use with non-indigenous interests and public authorities, and, on
occasion, the structuring of institutions to administer indigenous title.
The proliferation of 'regional agreements' and 'Indigenous land use
agreements' is an important manifestation of this process,[33] suggesting
that the precise signification of indigenous title is being defined in practice through a process of adaptation and accommodation, within a broad
framework determined by the courts and the *Native Title Act*.

This reliance upon accommodation may be worrying, especially if one
distrusts the commitment of non-indigenous parties to negotiate in good
faith. I do not mean to suggest that it is ideal, or that it occurs in a spirit
of generosity or even respect. There will always be room for criticism of
negotiating stances, dispute settlement mechanisms, and outcomes,
always cause for ambivalence like that of Coombs', cited previously.[34] Nor
are the accommodations insulated from relations of power in society at
large, although relations of power are not the whole story. Arguments of
justice, consistency of principle and moral appeal remain important
(though by no means determinative), as indeed they have been throughout Australia's recent grappling with indigenous rights.[35] The courts
retain a crucial role in maintaining fundamental elements of principle.
But the issues of intercultural accommodation are sufficiently complex –
the challenges of developing appropriate structures for the administration of indigenous land and the resolution of its relationship to
non-indigenous interests sufficiently difficult – that there is no real substitute for negotiations in the long term.

Judicial Role

Given that indigenous title is bound up with the recognition of indigenous societies as autonomous legal orders possessing their own political

presence, and that this recognition necessarily raises difficult issues of accommodation, is this an appropriate arena for the courts? The question is a live one, for the High Court's decisions have been subjected to fierce criticism from some quarters because of their allegedly 'political' character.[36] The objection, however, is misconceived. Even within much more conventional and familiar areas of the law, there are concepts that play a role similar to that of indigenous title: a fundamental but relatively inchoate claim is recognised, the precise details of which are left to be worked out over time, often through a complex, context-dependent process of adjustment. This phenomenon takes a variety of forms.

First, many of the most familiar legal concepts began with the recognition of an abstract principle, sometimes found to be implicit in a previous body of law. That recognition set in train a long process of reflection and elaboration as the principle's implications were explored in subsequent decisions. The development of the law of negligence provides many good examples, from the first recognition of a general tort of negligence in *Donoghue* v. *Stevenson*, through negligent misstatement, the liability of public authorities, and compensation for pure economic loss. In these situations, one trusts that one will be able to develop more detailed principles over time, as one confronts a diversity of circumstances to which the principle applies, but one does not expect to be able to give a full, certain and detailed account of the law in the early stages. Indeed, common-law judges have generally declined to provide full discussions of an area even after that area has been extensively canvassed in previous decisions, in the belief that a continual, cautious incrementalism is more likely to capture the full complexity of the interests in play.

But second, there are areas of law in which one does not have confidence that there ever can be a detailed elaboration of the applicable principles, because the principles apply to such complex relationships that one's judgments must always be situation- and context-dependent. The principles remain at a high level of abstraction, though nonetheless operative. The principal criterion for child custody decisions – the 'best interests of the child' – is a good example. It has a material impact upon virtually all custody decisions, yet it seems highly unlikely that it will ever be given the kind of detailed elaboration one expects in many areas of the law, simply because the complexity of circumstances makes generalisations very difficult.

Third, there are areas – much rarer than the two already discussed – in which law again operates at a broad level of generality, but where one has little confidence that either incremental elaboration by judges or context-specific adjudication can produce acceptable outcomes. Instead, the content is best filled out through processes of political deliberation or by negotiation – although perhaps the latter word carries too much baggage that suggests an amoral, normless compromise. 'Bilateral deliberation' might be better, although this errs in the other direction. In these situations, there may be broad recognition of the need for a settlement, and a sense of certain general criteria that such a settlement should observe, but substantial differences of interest or principle as to how one should be achieved. The issues may combine an insoluble mixture of corrective and distributive justice. They may involve elements of judgment that are best left to more participatory or more representative institutions than the courts. At times, the differences of perspective may have a strong bilateral character, so that joint conferences may be the best response to issues of detail. Industrial disputes may be a good example, in which even during the heyday of Australia's arbitration regime the essential challenge was to reconcile the different perspectives of employers and employees. Careful attention was therefore paid to balance of representation, and commissioners used negotiations and processes of decision-making that mimicked negotiations to fashion workable solutions, while still asserting an overarching framework of principle.[37] The belief that similar circumstances are present in family break-up may be a crucial element underlying the move towards mediation in that context. The recognition of indigenous title may raise similar challenges: strong justification for the general principle, but great difficulty elaborating the content except through negotiations.[38]

Another way to conceive of these issues is that in indigenous title, the principle has great force, but that principle is consistent with a wide range of possible means of respecting indigenous control and managing the interface between indigenous and non-indigenous institutions. The overarching principles might be termed 'framing norms', in that they operate at a level of abstraction consistent with a wide range of possible instantiations. The choice among the instantiations is best left to negotiation and legislation, as long as the principles are respected.[39]

This means that adjudication must often employ a lighter hand than is usually the case, so that it affirms the principle while leaving room for the parties to work out the detail of co-existence. This does contemplate a closely linked combination of adjudicative and negotiational approaches, the latter with a political cast that may, in the view of some people, cast doubt on the decisional integrity of the former.

But what alternative is there? The simplest would be to avoid the challenge by denying that indigenous peoples retained any right to their lands, affirming that Australia was once again *terra nullius*, and treating Aborigines and Torres Strait Islanders once again as trespassers on their own land. That result hardly seems more just, hardly consistent with our respect for proprietary rights, our commitment to equal respect regardless of race, or the reasons why both common and international law contain principles that protect private rights upon the acquisition of territory. There is, in short, no substitute for a serious grappling with indigenous rights to land, unless one wants to succumb to much greater injustice and normative inconsistency. And if one does take indigenous title seriously, one confronts the fact that the basic questions have an ineluctably constitutional dimension, concerned with how very different societies, each with its own legal order, should coexist within Australia. Indigenous title does have compelling force as a principle of Australian law, but it also inevitably sets in motion a process of intercultural adjustment and accommodation.

The Significance of Indigenous Title for
Australian Constitutional Theory

The recognition of indigenous title therefore has very broad implications for an understanding of the Australian legal and constitutional order. This is patent in the popular debate, where it has provoked a long discussion of the conditions of reconciliation between indigenous and nonindigenous Australians; extensive arguments over the extent of a society's responsibility for its past; and, in the specifically legal domain, the awakening of a multitude of issues with respect to the role of the courts.

Nor have these controversies exhausted *Mabo*'s implications. In *Wik*, Gummow J said that *Mabo* brought about a shift in Australia's constitutional foundations (*Wik* 1996: 230). It is worth understanding the nature of that shift. (In sketching that shift, I do not mean to suggest that it is fully or uniformly accomplished across Australian society. The argument is about the potentialities inherent in the change, about the change's general orientation, not about its current acceptance in popular discourse.)

The recognition of indigenous title clearly has involved the recognition of an autonomous source of legal and political authority within Australia. It is true that indigenous title is recognised by the common law, and in that sense there are 'sources' of indigenous title within the common law. Furthermore, the act of recognition is not an utterly deferential one (such acts never are); in the act of recognising, the law also goes some way towards defining.[40] The common law acknowledges, for example, means by which Indigenous title can be obliterated, and judges ultimately decide who should be considered 'owners'. Indigenous legal orders are therefore portrayed as partially, not entirely, autonomous. But nevertheless, indigenous title involves the recognition of norms whose source lies outside the common law. That source is not confined to the period before contact, but is a parallel social structure with its own bodies of law, which continues post-contact.

This constitutes an extraordinary change in position. Australian nationhood is no longer forged within an exclusively non-indigenous

crucible. Aborigines no longer enter the national story merely as outsiders against whom settlement was established or – to capture the role
that was commonly assigned to Aborigines – as doomed relics of a previous stage of humanity, destined to be utterly displaced. They are no
longer people from another time, co-existing only physically, not morally,
with non-Aboriginal Australians. Bain Attwood (1996a: *xiii–xiv*, 100; 1996b:
101ff) has emphasised that *Mabo* is about the recognition of the contemporaneity of indigenous Australians. That seems absolutely right. If we
take the law of indigenous title seriously, Aborigines and Torres Strait
Islanders are now current participants (partners?) in the Australian story.
They are seen as having a contemporary role, perhaps even a unique contribution, to fulfil. This development is not unprecedented. Indigenous
Australians already have a substantial presence in Australian cultural sym-
bolism. But it does represent a substantial change in their perceived role
within the legal and political spheres.[41]

Some commentators have suggested (or feared) that this might mean
the fracturing of Australian nationhood. In academic discourse, the
great differences of perspective between indigenous and non-indigenous
people are sometimes emphasised, with the suggestion that irre-
deemable difference and mutual incomprehension undermine any possibility of coherent national narrative (Povinelli 1998: 575). In more
popular discourse, some have expressed anxiety that the recognition of
indigenous claims will lead to a devaluing of the country's history.
Indeed, Prime Minister Howard and others have decried a supposed
'black armband' theory of Australian history.[42]

Both these assertions are excessively pessimistic. The first overesti-
mates the isolation between indigenous and non-indigenous people.
The relationship between settler society and indigenous peoples has
indeed been conflictual, marked by severe tensions over land and at
times by extreme brutality. These conflicts have been reflected in, and
perhaps sometimes been the product of, profoundly different beliefs on
the ideological plane. But one can acknowledge these divisions, while
still recognising that there have been important points of connection. In
every era there have been individuals and associations who have sought
to understand, with some success, those on the other side of the divide.
These connections have led to more constructive relationships between
peoples. And it is undeniable that the societies have, over time, shaped
each other. I do not romanticise this interaction. The influence of non-
indigenous on indigenous cultures has often been accomplished by violent and objectionable means.[43] Nor has it been anything like reciprocal.
Today, indigenous societies may well most need respect for autonomy in
order to maintain their cultures and protect their material and spiritual
possessions, not demands that they participate in what has long been an

unequal cultural exchange.[44] But one can acknowledge all that without asserting that there is an unbridgeable gulf between the societies and without denying that more productive relations are possible. To assert such a gulf is not only false; it runs the risk of treating indigenous peoples once again as people from another time, which non-indigenous Australians can observe, but from whom they need learn nothing.

As for the 'black armband', it is true that a re-evaluation of indigenous peoples' place within Australian society requires coming to terms with aspects of Australian history that are not meritorious, and may involve regret for things that were previously praised. But what alternative is there? That one perpetuate the injustices of the past, because one is reluctant to admit the failings? That one build one's national pride upon a deliberate denial of the past? Martin Krygier and Desmond Manderson have argued with great force that if one takes pride in what is good about one's past, one also has to be open to regret (Krygier 1997: 64–98; Manderson 1998: 238–39; Webber 1995a: 10–11, 15, 24–5). Acknowledging the bad does not diminish the good. On the contrary, it may help to identify just what was good, the conditions under which the good was achieved, and the lessons for today. There is much to treasure about Australian society, and one of those things is the frankness and (at its best) the honesty of public debate. That quality should be preserved in our evaluation of the past.

Finally, both pessimistic views exaggerate the extent to which national identity must be founded on a single, coherent, and perhaps static national story. No nation works like that. All change through time. All are marked by internal differences and by vigorous debate, frequently over the most fundamental matters. Indeed, it often seems that nations are marked as much by the structure of their disagreements as by their agreements. I have suggested elsewhere the metaphor of conversation as a way of understanding national identity and indeed cultures generally (Webber 1993: 136–38; 1994: 183–93). Such identities are like conversations through time, in which those who participate share a real commonality in the way in which they frame the questions, in the historical references upon which they draw, in their knowledge of and dependence upon earlier stages of the conversation itself, and in their commitment to continued engagement in that conversation (although the commitment may not be a matter of choice; we often find ourselves in our communities without choosing them). They emphatically do not require that all members believe the same thing, and their very nature involves change. They can accommodate profound disagreements, without necessarily fracturing their commonality.

Understood in this way, indigenous and non-indigenous Australians already share much. The native title debate itself has been shaped by the distinctive ways in which such issues have been framed in this country.[45] In one sense, the struggle of indigenous people has been about *how* they are to take part in that conversation, the degree to which they are going to be able to preserve their own autonomous identities while doing so, and the recognition within the conversation of indigenous peoples' integrity, the value of their beliefs and property, and their entitlement to pass them on to their children. Hence the importance of the apology that indigenous Australians have demanded from the Commonwealth government, especially for the forced removal of indigenous children. Such an apology would serve as a symbolic coming-to-terms with the past. National narratives are always being worked and reworked against the country's past. People draw upon that past in their arguments and their claims, and as they do, they suggest what is most important about the country, what is most valuable, and what should be left behind. The fashioning and refashioning of national identity is, inevitably, a process of moral reflection on the past. We judge the past, at least implicitly. The demand for an apology is an attempt to call those judgments into the open.[46]

The reworking of the national conversation will, if it continues, occur in many forums and across a wide range of issues. This is not the place to explore those dimensions in detail. But I will draw attention to one aspect of special significance for Australian constitutionalism.

For non-indigenous Australians, a constitution is a made order, a product of human will and industry. At the most general level, this is reflected in national myths about the building of the country, which celebrate the material achievements of the society, portraying those achievements as the product of individual and collective effort. It is also present in the strong strain of democratic republicanism in Australia – the sense that good government is about taking one's destiny in one's own hands and making society what one wants. It is evident in the marked positivistic leanings in Australian legal and political culture: its heavy emphasis on procedure, due process and compliance with explicit rules established by the self-conscious action of democratic legislatures; its suspicion of informal norms and processes; and its reluctance to conceive of law as inherently moral, for fear that that will necessarily mean that someone else's morality is imposed. Regardless of whether 'a strict and complete legalism' (conceived as the application of express rules entirely pre-determined by due authority) is an accurate description of judicial decision-making in practice or in theory,[47] it retains a very tight hold over the Australian conception of the rule of law and the justification of authority.

Indigenous title has the potential to upset that presumption. First, the very recognition of a body of law that has its origin outside the system deflects attention from the legislature as the font of law. Second, it initiates a process of adjustment across societies that challenges the conceptual unity and willed rationalism of many Australians' conception of law. Third and most importantly, law for indigenous Australians has traditionally been considered not to be the product of deliberate choice, but an inheritance, determined in The Dreaming or by what has come before, not merely by the desires of those now living.[48] The visions of law could hardly be more different.

Often this is not seen. Its potential for generating misunderstanding and awkwardness of institutional arrangements is missed. But it surfaces, for example, in the unease occasionally affecting the alliance between those committed to reform in general political life (for example, environmental protection, individual rights, the republican movement) and indigenous peoples. The visions of social organisation held by reformers and indigenous peoples can be quite different, the reformers emphasising agency and a purely democratic understanding of legitimacy, the indigenous peoples often more concerned with issues of respect (for ancestors, for elders), restoration and autonomy. I do not mean to exaggerate the difference. Indeed, I believe firmly that there are ways of reconciling them. But it is no accident that in the period of settlement, those on the conservative end of the political spectrum were often more respectful of indigenous rights than those committed to reform, whose belief in development and individual opportunity frequently led them to advocate rapid and relatively uncontrolled expansion of white settlement, and whose commitment to a highly cohesive democratic polity sometimes led them to exclude people of other races.[49] Today comparable tensions occasionally emerge, most obviously over issues of environmental protection once lands are under indigenous control, and over women's place within society.[50]

One of the ways in which this tension will be manifest in the years to come is in contrasting expectations of how issues of indigenous/non-indigenous relations might be resolved. There is often a sense in non-indigenous political life that if there are serious questions of indigenous rights, they should be squarely addressed and exhaustively defined, so that political and economic life can proceed in full certainty of what those rights entail. This attitude was abundantly evident in the political debate surrounding *Mabo* and *Wik*, and was effectively harnessed by the Howard government in its campaign to amend the *Native Title Act 1993* (Brennan 1998; Clarke 1997: 1ff). Among those who favour indigenous rights, one sometimes encounters a similar sense that reconciliation can be achieved by an act of collective will – perhaps a national treaty – refounding the relationship and re-affirming rights.[51] Such dramatic initiatives may indeed be essential as a way of marking new beginnings, of accomplishing a material change in the protection of rights long denied, and of achieving some practical conciliation between indigenous rights and non-indigenous interests. But we should not pretend that they can solve these issues once and for all, at one moment in time. The redefinition of the relationship is a matter for the long haul, and indeed is likely to be a matter of continual adjustment. This is true because of the complexity of the issues, because one is dealing with relations between whole societies that continue to change, and because of the additional reason suggested here: today's indigenous leaders may not see themselves as having such complete authority over their communities' structure and law.[52] There are unlikely to be any quick fixes.

The post-*Mabo* relationship is in part, then, about the encounter between different legal/political philosophies. The management of the interface between societies requires that we conciliate social visions (Pocock 1998; Poirier 1996). This will undoubtedly involve respect for autonomy, although that autonomy should be combined with constructive engagement. The problem is one of restructuring a dialogue – or perhaps it would be more accurate to say 'developing a dialogue', given the largely one-directional nature of influence to this point – not restoring some pre-dialogic purity.

There is substantial potential for that interaction. In drawing the contrast between indigenous and non-indigenous approaches to law, I portrayed the difference as more stark than it is in fact. There are strong elements of tradition in the non-indigenous Australian law, although imperfectly acknowledged. By this I do not mean merely that there are elements we consciously recognise as 'traditional' (although there are these), but that the concept of tradition is a good way to understand the processes of legal reasoning generally. Legal reasoning works with concepts and judgments inherited from the past; it reflects on the significance of those concepts and those judgments for the issues of today, and in the process, the tradition itself evolves (Krygier 1986; 1988; 1991; Parkinson 1994: 10–18).[53] Taking that traditional character seriously may allow a better understanding of the non-indigenous system and the place of intention and inheritance within it. It may also provide grounds for more respectful interaction with cultures in which tradition plays a more obvious role.

Change has also been a larger part of indigenous traditions than has frequently been supposed. Indeed, indigenous cultures have internalised values from non-indigenous cultures, so that now those values are fully part of the indigenous societies (Law Reform Commission 1986: 88–90; Coombs 1994: 93–5; Attwood 1996b: 109–10; Maddock 1984: 234–35; Macdonald 1997). The issue is not one of complete separation or of fracturing. It is about the conditions of interaction, and about the achievement of a national dialogue that is more typified by respect than by imposition.

Institutional Implications

The shift in focus for which I have argued – away from indigenous title as a simple property interest and towards a recognition of the intersocietal and constitutional dimensions inherent in that title – has important practical implications for the determination of native title claims and for the restructuring of Australian institutions. While I will not canvass those implications in detail, a couple of examples will help demonstrate the practical impact of reconceiving indigenous title.

First, there are very significant consequences for the way in which courts and tribunals go about determining native title claims, both how they frame their conclusions and how they conduct the adjudicative process itself. I have shown that courts have, in practice, been reluctant to absorb principles of indigenous landholding into the body of law they administer. They have not treated indigenous title as merely a set of proprietary interests to be interpreted and enforced in the same way that they adjudicate other interests in land. Instead, they have kept their judgments one step removed from this level of detail, ruling on the existence of native title and on its extinguishment, but saying very little about the rights enjoyed under any specific indigenous people's law. I have shown why this approach is right – why it conforms to what is really in issue in indigenous land claims, namely respect for indigenous people not merely as individual or familial proprietors, but as members of societies with their own law, their own cultures and institutions, their own patterns of social order, and their own conceptions of land use and landholding.

I have offered a rationale for the method that the courts and tribunals have themselves adopted when faced with the practical demands of native title determination. That rationale will, I hope, support the courts' approach, encouraging them in adjudication with a light touch, which rules upon the persistence of the indigenous community and its control over resources, but allows the precise determination of those interests to occur (if possible) through more extended processes of adjustment and accommodation. The courts may be driven to intervene more strongly if the fundamental claim is not respected. But the starting point should be that native title operates at a level of generality compatible with a range of possible instantiations, and that it is best if the detail is worked out through the internal procedures of indigenous communities, combined with negotiations with non-Indigenous actors. In other words, that it has the characteristics of the 'framing norms' described previously. Otherwise, the courts will find themselves ruling upon precise questions of indigenous law, the internal requirements of indigenous political action, the specific manner in which indigenous land use must be reconciled with non-indigenous interests, and the design of institutions to bridge the indigenous/non-indigenous divide – for all of which they are poorly suited.

Moreover, the realisation that indigenous title is about the recognition of indigenous societies, rather than about determining the rights of indigenous individuals, has implications for the procedure by which courts should determine indigenous title. In the Yorta Yorta claim, for example, the parties invested enormous energy in attempting to trace the claimants' ancestry to known individuals living in the area claimed at the time of the assertion of sovereignty (the required date being 1788, even though non-indigenous explorers reached the area only in 1824) (*Yorta Yorta* 1998: 52). This degree of individual genealogical research seems hardly necessary if the primary question is one of survival of the society that occupied the land in question. Shouldn't the focus be on the continuation of that society, rather than on biological descent? If, for example, individuals were adopted into that community in the post-contact period, wouldn't they be entitled to participate in the rights of the community? And if the remaining members of several communities coalesced in one community in the period following contact, wouldn't the successor community enjoy the rights of its predecessors? After all, such political consolidations are a common feature of the evolution of all societies, and were especially common in the North American context, without imperilling the persistence of indigenous title there.[54]

Genealogies may become important in situations where the survival of the community as a collectivity is in doubt – as indeed the court found in the Yorta Yorta claim (*Yorta Yorta* 1998). If, for example, one has to determine whether a significantly transformed successor community is descended from the original inhabitants, individual descent may be part of the proof. But surely in the main run of cases, the focus on bloodlines is too narrow, mistaking individual inheritance (according to what law of succession?) for continuity of the society. In fact, most indigenous title cases do deal with descent in a broader fashion than this. They remain concerned with the current claimants' connection to the original holders of the land, but they look at succession through time of the Indigenous community, not the biological descent of individuals.[55]

The recognition of the constitutional dimension of indigenous title also serves to shift the focus away from adjudication towards issues of institutional design. These are, in the end, inseparable from native title, given the need to determine precisely what entity holds the land and how that entity makes valid decisions about it. They become especially important once one realises that the simple enforcement by the courts of interests held under indigenous law would produce detrimental results: it would displace indigenous methods of social ordering, freeze the development of indigenous law, and place the administration of that law in the hands of non-indigenous tribunals. The essential problem becomes, then, one of recognising and respecting autonomy, and this means that institutions have to be developed to provide for the effective management of the indigenous/non-indigenous divide – institutions that can hold indigenous resources, while relating to the broader society in a manner that non-indigenous law can accommodate; structures that can protect indigenous interests in lands that are subject to joint indigenous/non-indigenous use. If native title itself is law of the interface, taking it seriously requires that one develop strong institutions that can structure and protect the indigenous/non-indigenous divide.

The argument in this chapter has implications for the design of those institutions. The various Aboriginal Land Councils have suffered considerable criticism in recent years, sometimes from their friends, because their processes depart from strict control by the traditional owners.[56] It is true that Land Councils do enable people who may not be traditional owners to have a role in determining the use of the land. Some of the most influential Councils cover vast tracts, with membership from many indigenous peoples. The law governing the Councils instructs them to have regard for the interests of the traditional owners (an obligation that the Councils generally take very seriously), but this is certainly less than full and exclusive traditional control.[57]

But is this criticism too precious (if confined to this ground alone)? Isn't it too focused on the proprietary dimensions of native title, insufficiently attentive to the fact that indigenous title is about relations between societies rather than the simple vindication of property rights, and perhaps even too resistant to political change that has occurred in indigenous communities themselves, driven by indigenous leaders? The Land Councils – especially the Northern and Central Land Councils in the Northern Territory – have, without doubt, been more effective in working for the recovery of indigenous lands and in asserting control over those lands than would have been the case had the initiative rested solely with traditional owners, with no overarching political coalition. The Councils have been particularly powerful because of their size, expertise and the resources derived from resource revenues in the Northern Territory. In native title claims in southern Australia, communities have similarly found that combination increases the chances of success. There has, therefore, been a comparable process of political coalescence in the south, driven by the practicalities of making title claims and administering the lands obtained.

This seems to me to be both a necessary and an acceptable process. Just as it makes no sense for non-indigenous courts to turn themselves into adjudicators of indigenous law – indeed, precisely because it makes no sense for that to occur – it is appropriate for indigenous communities to create structures that stand midway between traditional owners on the one hand and non-indigenous institutions on the other. Land Councils do that. They provide a mechanism for holding the land that works well within Australian law, while enabling traditional owners to continue to enjoy their lands, according to indigenous custom, under that umbrella. Rowley made this point in his path-breaking study of indigenous communities in the 1960s and 1970s. He referred to the incorporation of indigenous communities as possibly providing 'the carapace structure within which the members have comparative security from interference, to develop patterns of leadership'. It provides 'an area of security for autonomous adjustment'.[58] Anthropologists have drawn attention to the flexibility, capacity for change, and toleration for multiple and shifting interests that characterises the law of at least some Aboriginal peoples (Myers 1986: 127–58; Poirier 1996; Berndt 1982: 1; Hiatt 1989: 99; Sutton 1995b: 49–60; Langton, in Yunupingu 1997: 84). Land Councils provide a sphere, protected from non-indigenous interference, in which that kind of entitlement can continue to operate without the formalisation and rigidity that judicial enforcement would inevitably entail. They can blend indigenous modes of decision-making with structures that interact well with non-indigenous forms. They permit indigenous land use to meet new challenges, including the need to respond to the dislocation and dispossession of many indigenous people, and to the new ties to country developed by indigenous people who have, following dislocation, long resided on others' land – again under indigenous control.[59]

There is no guarantee of perfection in the handling of these issues. There are occasions when Land Councils have failed their constituents (as, of course, is true of virtually all political authorities). Land Councils are real institutions, with all the factionalism and political manoeuvring that involves. Tensions have led some constituent groups to secede from the Northern Territory Councils. It may be that better institutions can be devised, or existing ones improved. But something like this form of organisation would seem to be essential if the autonomous development of indigenous peoples and indigenous law is to continue.

The recognition of indigenous title in *Mabo* has begun a process that reaches well beyond the simple recognition of a property right. It raises broader considerations of relations between non-indigenous and indigenous societies. It requires that Australian law come to grips with the presence of other legal orders, with their own dynamism and their own mechanisms of change, within Australia. It therefore has a constitutional dimension, raising issues of the mediation of sovereignty, requiring that one attend to the institutions that can appropriately structure the inter-societal interface.

Claims of indigenous self-government are often treated as though they were quite separate from claims of native title. I have demonstrated that they are integrally connected, even though the connection may not be explicit in the judges' reasons. Indeed, Brennan J's judgment in *Mabo* expressly separates the proprietary from the governmental (Grattan and McNamara 1999: 55–8). But indigenous title necessarily involves that one recognises the presence of autonomous legal orders that have their origin outside the settler society's legal system. Once one acknowledges (as the High Court does) that indigenous orders are dynamic entities, with the capacity to develop and change, then the governmental dimension of indigenous communities becomes clear. It is no exaggeration to say that the recognition of indigenous title necessarily involves the recognition of a measure of indigenous self-government. Those governmental mechanisms may not, under the common law, be immune from legislative impairment, but that does not make them any less recognised by law. Native title itself is not immune, yet it is undeniably a legal right. The common law of indigenous title squarely raises the persistence of autonomous legal orders on the Australian continent, and forces us to ask difficult questions about how non-indigenous institutions should respond to that reality.

Indigenous and non-indigenous legal orders therefore interact across a front that is broader than is often realised. The issues are extraordinarily complex, involving respect for indigenous entitlements to land but also the recognition and institutionalisation of spheres of indigenous control, mechanisms for the resolution of jurisdictional conflicts and means of reconciling different forms of land use over the same territory. These issues are best resolved through negotiation rather than adjudication. They require the working out of solutions over the long term. Indigenous title is therefore more about the continual definition and redefinition of a relationship rather than the simple vindication of a property right.

This has important implications for the drive for 'certainty' that has been so much a part of the recent debate over native title in Australia. The issues raised by native title cannot be resolved, once and for all, by an exhaustive statement of that title's incidents. If a court did purport to decree such a result, we would soon find that the issues emerged in other guises, as indigenous people took issue with the interpretations given of their law and asserted their ability to have a continued role, as societies, in the control of their lands. If we do wish to obtain some degree of 'certainty' – some mechanism for conciliating, in a stable and predictable fashion, indigenous and non-indigenous land use – we would do much better to think about institutional responses that provide for a measure of co-determination or mutual adjustment (such as joint management structures in national parks, or the agreements many resource companies now conclude, often without legal compulsion, to secure Indigenous consent to new developments) (Woenne-Green *et al.* 1994; Howitt 1991; Senior 1998). Institutionalised adjustment and collaboration, rather than exhaustive definition, is the path of the future.

What is not open to us is to avoid the issue and return to a vision of a single people, coming together in the simplicity of a common parliament to create the only legitimate law of the land. Australians came to recognise, in *Mabo*, that Australia was made up of the overlay, displacement, inter-penetration, parallel trajectory, dialogue, mutual incomprehension of a set of indigenous societies, each with its own pathways traced across this land, and a newly implanted non-indigenous society whose members have fashioned their own heritage, their own distinctive governmental institutions, and their own deep connection to this country. The task now before us (of which the recognition of indigenous title is one component) is to think how those societies can best relate to one another as communities living in the same time. There are resources on which to draw. We can build productively upon the moral and practical interaction that has been, at times, a part of Australian history, and on the respect that all have for this country. We can also draw upon the tradition of democratic and institutional innovation in this land, which may now have to respond to a deeper diversity and a greater complexity than it has in the past, but which has often shown itself to be highly adaptable. We must also, without prevarication, come to terms with the consequences of denying indigenous connection to the land, of attempting forcibly to sever Aborigines' connection to their heritage, and of even denying, at times, indigenous Australians' humanity. That more wrenching experience holds its own lessons, and has left a legacy that we cannot simply avoid.

But one crucial element is the one emphasised here: that we take indigenous societies seriously as living, dynamic communities, with their own institutions and laws. For the most part, Aboriginal and Torres Strait Islander societies survive, even though they have, like any societies, been subject to change, adjustment and reconstitution over the years since 1788 (and indeed before). Those indigenous societies cannot be wished back into the past.

CHAPTER 5

Engaging with Indigeneity: Tino Rangatiratanga in Aotearoa

Roger Maaka and Augie Fleras

Working through Differences

The emergence of indigeneity as discourse and collective transformation marks a major ideological shift in realigning the postcolonising dynamics of white settler dominions (Maaka and Fleras 1997). The proposed restructuring of indigenous peoples–state relations is animated by the transformational politics of indigeneity, with its politicisation of 'original occupancy' as basis for entitlement and engagement. Recurrent themes pervade the transformational dynamics within these settler cultures: foremost is a rejection of colonialist arrangements in exchange for indigenous models of self-determination that sharply curtail the legitimacy and jurisdiction of the state while bolstering indigenous jurisdiction over land, identity and political voice (Alfred 1995).

The politics of indigeneity resonate with references to sovereignty and self-determination. Particular emphasis is focused on indigenous peoples as fundamentally autonomous political communities, each of which is sovereign in its own right, yet sharing in the sovereignty of society through multiple, yet interlocking, jurisdictions (Asch 1997). To be sure, indigenous claims to sovereignty rarely entail separation or secession but instead a reconstitutionalising of the first principles upon which indigenous peoples–state relations are governed. Nevertheless, the transformational process continues to be compromised by an almost exclusive reliance on 'catch-up justice' ('claims-making') as a basis for renewal and reform – in effect, privileging conflict over cooperative coexistence, outcome over process, and the 'throwing of money' at a problem rather than working through differences. To cut through this impasse requires models of constructive engagement that foster innovative patterns of relative yet non-coercive autonomy without necessarily falling into the trap of secession or confrontation.

Such an assessment would appear to apply to Aotearoa/New Zealand, where the various hapu and iwi ('tribes') who comprise Maoridom continue to contest their relationship with the Crown. Maori–Crown relations are undergoing profound changes in response to the privileging of binary cultural politics as a catalyst for transforming Aotearoa's political contours in ways that have yet to be fully explained or explored (Fleras and Spoonley 1999). Discourses that once bolstered 'society-building' themes of 'community development', 'multiculturalism', 'te taha Maori' and 'institutional accommodation' have been sharply challenged. Endorsed instead are the discursive frameworks of a new constitutional order, including 'Maori sovereignty', 'tino rangatiratanga', 'tangata whenua', 'iwi models of self-determination', 'bi-nationalism' and 'Treaty partnerships'. Instead of a 'needs'-driven agenda that historically framed Maori–Crown interaction – namely, a Crown perception of Maori as a problem to be solved rather than as a relationship to be nurtured – there is a growing commitment to a rights-based discourse involving the principle of tino rangatiratanga as articulated in the Treaty of Waitangi (Maaka and Fleras 1998–99). Emergence of tino rangatiratanga as a constitutional framework for redefining the 'dialogue between sovereigns' has proven to be double-edged: Maori claims to indigenous self-determination may be fortified by virtue of their status as tangata whenua (original occupants), yet such an assertion invariably clashes with state assumptions of unilateral and undivided authority over all of the land. The contesting of these 'duelling discourses' strikes at the core of cultural politics in Aotearoa.

This chapter examines the politics of indigeneity in Aotearoa by refracting debate over Maori sovereignty and self-determination through the prism of tino rangatiratanga. We argue that appeals to tino rangatiratanga go beyond the restoration of Treaty entitlements or resolution of historical grievances *per se*. Engagement with tino rangatiratanga acknowledges Maori indigenous rights as a legitimate source of sovereign authority, a preferred basis for consent, a framework for a new constitutional order and a supportive context for constructive re-engagement. We also argue that principles of tino rangatiratanga are inseparable from Maori initiatives that emphasise 'standing apart' as a precondition for 'working together' as part of a 'bi-national' partnership. This shift in emphasis from entitlement to re-engagement invariably raises questions regarding the extent to which tino rangatiratanga is about relationships rather than rights, about reconciliation rather than restitution, about process rather than results, and about listening rather than legalities (Coates and McHugh 1998). To the extent that tino rangatiratanga reflects and reinforces Maori aspirations for recalibrating the political contours of Aotearoa, its role in reconstitutionalising the interactional basis of Maori–Crown relations cannot be underestimated. In that tino rangatiratanga espouses

Maori models of self-determination through innovative patterns of belonging to society, yet is subject to contested debate over who owns what and why, its potential in advancing the cause of a postcolonising Aotearoa has yet to be realised.

Indigeneity: Discourse and Transformation

Structurally speaking, white settler dominions such as Canada, Australia and New Zealand have much in common. At the core of the colonisation process was the dispossession and disempowerment of indigenous peoples by way of force, policy or persuasion (Stasiulis and Yuval-Davis 1995). But indigenous peoples in these and other postcolonising domains have become increasingly politicised, in the hope of 'unsettling' their relationship with society at large (Dudley and Agard 1993). The now-encapsulated descendants of the original occupants insist on the following demands as a precondition for atonement and reconciliation:

- a special relationship ('nation to nation') with the state;
- repossession of land and resources unless explicitly ceded by treaty, Parliament or conquest;
- acknowledgement that legitimacy rests with the consent of the people rather than state authority;
- moves to restore autonomy and cultural integrity at the level of governance;
- espousal of new patterns of belonging in which sovereignty is shared with society at large (Stea and Wisner 1984; Morse 1992; Alfred 1999a).

Of particular note in this package of proposals are indigenous demands for recognition of indigeneity as integral in sculpting an innovative political order around the primacy of indigenous rights as the basis for engagement and entitlement.

Indigeneity as discourse and transformation can be defined as the politicised awareness of original occupancy as the grounds for reward and relationships. As discourse, indigeneity refers to indigenous peoples as 'first nations', whose customary rights to self-determination over jurisdictions pertaining to land, identity and political voice have never been extinguished but remain undisturbed for purposes of identity, belonging and relations (Fleras 1996). The emergence of indigeneity as discourse entails a discursive shift in the constitutionalisms that historically undergirded colonial domination (Tully 1995). Institutional structures that once colonised the 'nations within' are no longer acceptable; endorsed instead are indigenous models of self-determination that sharply curtail the state while advancing the idea of indigenous peoples as autonomous political communities. The noted Métis scholar, Paul Chartrand, writes to this effect when he says: 'We are political communities in the sense that we are a distinct culture and we want to create political institutions to maintain those very distinct communities' (Chartrand 1999: 100). Also pivotal in contesting the balance of sovereign power are proposals for constructive engagement as an empowering normative framework for sorting out who controls what, and why. Appeals to constructive re-engagement are critical in advancing the cause of a shared sovereignty, involving multiple yet interlocking jurisdictions in working through differences. Inasmuch as indigeneity challenges the paramountcy of the state as the final arbiter of jurisdictional control and absolute authority, the assertion of 'sovereignty without secession' is indeed 'subversive'. In its willingness to work within the system rather than outside of it, a secessionless sovereignty is consistent with the demands of postcolonising society (Fleras 1999).

Indigeneity and the Sovereignty Game

Indigenous challenges to the legitimacy of white settler dominions have eroded political conventions that formerly circumscribed indigenous peoples–state relations (Fleras and Spoonley 1999). With its claims that simultaneously deny yet affirm a sovereign state, indigeneity assumes a political framework that is inherently contradictory of settler state claims to sovereignty (Havemann 1999). Colonialist assumptions about sovereignty have crumbled accordingly. Daniel Salee and William Coleman strike a resonant chord when they repudiate the sovereign mindsets that govern white settler dominions:

> The nineteenth-century idea of sovereignty may have run its course; it is not a natural, or an eternal given. It reflects a certain understanding of power and authority, rooted in a particular, historically determined configuration of social relations and public space. As sociohistorical conditions change, does sovereignty remain an adequate or desirable political objective? (Salee and Coleman 1997: 196)

Discrediting the tacit constitutional assumptions that underpin white settler governance raises a host of questions (Dodson 1994; Spoonley 1995). Legitimacy is the key issue: on what basis and by what authority do white settler systems exercise sovereignty over the land and its inhabitants? (Fleras 1999) In what ways can descendants of white settlers claim rights to citizenship – by discovery, conquest, Treaty, legislation or by default over time (Mulgan 1989)? Does political legitimacy reside first and foremost with the consent of those peoples whose customary rights to land, identity and political voice remain undisturbed (Renwick 1991)? What people have the right to draw a line around themselves and declare sovereign status (Reynolds 1996)? Is sovereignty indivisible or can it be shared without undermining the integrity and cohesion of society (Winichakul 1996)? To what extent can any system accommodate contested sovereignties when social realities are diametrically opposed (Cheyne *et al.* 1997)? How can anyone 'belong together with (fundamental) differences' when absolute sovereignty is withdrawn or divided (Taylor 1992)?

The politics of indigeneity go beyond the simple expedient of creating cultural space or social equity. With its focus on the removal of discriminatory cultural and structural barriers within the existing institutional framework, its scope transcends a commitment to official multiculturalism. Nor does indigeneity simply entail restitution for historical grievances or even restoration of indigenous rights *per se.* Indigeneity as principle and practice is ultimately concerned with reshaping the structure of indigenous peoples–state relations in the hope of crafting a legitimate political order where innovative patterns for belonging can be explored (Taylor 1992; Kaplan 1993; Kymlicka 1995; Tully 1995; Chartrand 1996; Webber 1997). Claims to indigenous sovereignty are a central element in the discourse. Obsolete versions of absolute sovereignty are being discarded for indigenous equivalents that emphasise an autonomy both relative and relational, yet non-coercive (Scott 1996). Several models of sovereignty can be discerned: at one end of the continuum are appeals to absolute sovereignty ('statehood') with complete independence and control over internal and external jurisdictions (O'Regan 1994). In between are models of 'de facto' sovereignty ('nationhood') and 'functional' sovereignty ('municipalityhood') that do not entail any explicit separation ('sovereignty without secession'), but limited only by interaction with similar bodies and higher political authorities. Indigeneity as practice can coexist with the principle of a multiple yet interlocking sovereignty at this level, provided that jurisdictions are defined and divided accordingly. At the opposite pole are sovereignties in name only ('nominal sovereignties'); that is, a 'soft' sovereign option with residual powers of self-determination within existing institutional frameworks. Table 1 provides a somewhat ideal-typical overview of indigenous sovereignty levels by comparing and contrasting their degree of autonomy.

The proliferation of sovereignty discourses makes it important to distinguish nuances in usage. On the one hand, the right of sovereignty applies to all indigenous peoples as the original occupants; on the other, there may be a reluctance to exercise that right because of political circumstances or social conditions (Chartrand 1993). Indigenous sovereignty rarely invokes a call for independence or non-interference: preference is in cultivating relationships as a way of working through differences in a non-combative manner.

Table 1 Levels of indigenous sovereignty

State	Nation
• absolute (de jure) sovereignty • internal and external autonomy • complete independence with no external interference	• de facto sovereignty • control over internal jurisdiction within framework of shared yet interlocking sovereignty • nations within
Municipality	**Institutional**
• functional sovereignty • community-based autonomy • internal jurisdictions, limited only by interaction with similar bodies and higher political authorities	• nominal sovereignty • decision-making power through institutional accommodation

The distinction between the right of sovereignty versus the right to sovereignty is also important. Indigenous peoples have the right of sovereignty by virtue of original occupancy; however, the right to sovereignty in the sense of final authority is more fiercely contested and widely rejected (Daes 1996). Indigenous peoples may not be sovereign in the political–legal sense, but they most certainly are for purposes of entitlement and engagement. Such distinctions confirm that references to sovereignty below the level of statehood constitute a form of 'nested' sovereignty: that is, a people retain the right of self-determination over those jurisdictions of direct relevance to them but in conjunction with the legitimate concerns of other jurisdictions (Clark and Williams 1996). References to the Eurocentric term 'sovereignty' may not correspond with indigenous mindsets, and thus co-opting indigenous peoples into dialogues that do not reflect their culture and realities (Alfred 1999a). Nevertheless, indigenous groups may have little choice except to engage in this discourse if they want to *talk the talk that resonates with results* (McHugh 1999).

Impasse

With so much at stake in the sovereignty game, the restructuring of state–indigenous peoples relations has proven more daunting than anticipated. The era of indigenous rights talk has emerged as a significant feature of contemporary political discourse, but there is no agreement whether the principle of indigeneity has resulted in the constitutionalising of indigenous rights or the indigenising of dimensions of white settler polity (Havemann 1999: 403). At the source of this impasse is the state's persistent intent to maintain colonial control over indigenous peoples and their land, notwithstanding removal of the most egregious aspects of colonialism (Alfred 1999a).

Equally obstructive is the failure to appreciate the implications of indigeneity as a politicised ideology for radical renewal. References to indigeneity are inextricably linked with competition over power – or, more accurately, the transfer of power from those who have it to those who never consented to its extinguishment (Oliver 1995). Indigenous challenges are not about isolated cases of injustice as the Crown went about its legitimate business of colonisation and land alienation; the very legitimacy of the colonising process is contested by challenging Crown authority over peoples, land and governance.

Indigeneity is political in that choices about who controls what, and why, are out in public and subject to debate. It is political because indigenous claims constitute grievances against the state, and because government policy and administration are the institutional correlates of that domination. Indigenous demands are inherently political in radicalising the relationship between indigenous people and the state over the allocation of scarce resources. Finally, recognition of indigeneity as part of the national agenda has had the effect of curbing state jurisdiction over indigenous affairs; it has also advanced the counter-hegemonic assertion that political legitimacy rests with indigenous peoples' consent rather than in the paramountcy of the state (Levin 1993).

The politicisation of indigeneity opens up the governing process to contestation. Politicisation confronts white settler dominions with the most quintessential of paradoxes – by forcing them to justify their very right to existence, the legitimacy of their claims to citizenship and their rationale for rule over land and inhabitants. The state is drawn into the most contentious of all relations, namely, the relationship between co-sovereign equals in the political arena, each of which claims intrinsic authority over separate yet interlocked spheres of jurisdiction (Fleras 1996). Yet state initiatives for engaging indigeneity tend to reflect political discourses that miscalculate the magnitude and intensity of transformational politics (MacDuff 1995; Wickcliffe 1995). Political preference remains mired in the multicultural placement of all minorities in a settled hierarchy of ascending/descending order, with all sectors committed to a common goal as well as a shared set of rules (Sharp 1990). The state appears comfortable with a 'needs'-driven indigenous policy through removal of discriminatory barriers and advocacy of developmental modes; it is less predisposed towards a 'rights'-driven policy (Parata 1994). State perception of indigenous peoples as a disadvantaged multicultural minority has compromised their aspirations as distinct societies of an inherently political nature with the right to participate in crafting a legitimate political order (Chartrand 1996). Inasmuch as indigenous claims against the state are articulated by those who demand recognition not as disadvantaged subjects, but as equals with inherent rights to redefine the basis for belonging, a conflict of interest is inevitable and irreconcilable. According to Salee:

> The points of contention between First Nations and non-Aboriginals do not simply consist of irritants that might be overcome by mere good will, or of territorial claims that might be satisfied if one or the other party showed flexibility or compromised. As the conceptual differences over land partly revealed, the two parties operate within institutional parameters and socio-cultural systems which have nothing in common . . . The contention between Aboriginals and non-Aboriginals rests in fact on a paradigmatic contradiction of which the poles are, a priori, logically irreconcilable. (Salee 1995: 291)

The resultant 'dialogue of the deaf' is known to have transformed indigenous peoples–state relations into a jumble of competing agendas and opposing constituents. Such a politicised climate confirms indigenous policy as a 'contested domain' involving the struggle of opposing interests for definition and control. It also reinforces a view of indigeneity as more than a postmodernist deconstruction of the discursive categories that subordinate and 'hegemonise'. What *we* have instead is a counter-hegemonic vision that articulates a fundamentally 'subversive' way of belonging to society. Such a subversion complicates the process by which interdependent peoples must negotiate the thicket of jurisdictions when sorting out what is 'mine', 'yours' and 'ours'.

Untying the Gordian knot: Toward Constructive Engagement

The resolution of claims is undeniably important as part of a broader exercise in relations repair for righting historical wrongs. But on its own and divorced from the bigger picture of re-engaging state–indigenous peoples relations, corrective justice is fraught with underlying contradictions. A 'winner-take-all' approach (Langton 1999) has the effect of reconstituting the very colonialisms that indigenous peoples are seeking to discredit and discard (Fleras and Maaka 1998). Reliance on results rather than relations appears to have generated as many problems as it solved (McHugh 1998). A preoccupation with contesting claims to the exclusion of engagement has also had the effect of glossing over the key element in any productive interaction: namely, the managing of a relation in the spirit of cooperative coexistence rather than according to the letter of the law (Henare 1995: 49; McHugh 1998). The emergence of a new 'constructive engagement' model of interaction may provide a respite from the interminable bickering over 'who owns what', while brokering a tentative blueprint for a discrete institutional framework that secures the legitimacy of indigenous models of self-determination (Maaka and Fleras 1997; Walker 1999). By embracing a more flexible approach that emphasises engagement over entitlement, constitutionalism over contract, relationships over rights, interdependence over opposition, cooperation over competition, reconciliation over restitution, and power-sharing over domination, constructive engagement provides a catalyst for reconstitutionalising indigenous peoples–state relations (Fleras and Maaka 1998). Among the key planks in forging a commitment to constructive engagement are the following constitutional principles.

- Indigenous peoples do not aspire to sovereignty *per se*. Strictly speaking, they already have sovereignty by virtue of original occupancy, never having relinquished this independence by explicit agreement. Only the structures necessary for its practical expression are subject to debate once the reality of indigenous sovereignty is assumed for the purposes of rewards and relations.
- Indigenous peoples are neither a problem to solve nor a competitor to be jousted, but a partner with whom to work through differences in a spirit of cooperative coexistence. In acknowledging that 'we are all in this together for the long haul', is there any other option except to shift from the trap of competing sovereignties to the primacy of relations between equal partners (McHugh 1998)?
- The bi-culturalism implicit in a constructive relationship is not the kind that grafts a few multicultural bits onto an existing institutional framework. A genuine bi-culturalism ('bi-nationalism') acknowledges a partner relationship between two equals involving power-sharing and distribution of resources (Linden 1994). A bi-national arrangement may more accurately describe the notion of relative yet relational autonomy between peoples, each of which is autonomous in their jurisdiction, yet sharing in the sovereignty of society.
- The reconstituting of indigenous peoples as relatively autonomous political communities is critical in crafting a revised political order based on indigenous rights. Indigenous peoples must be accepted as having their own independent sources rather than being shaped for the convenience of the political majority or subject to unilateral override (Asch 1997).
- Innovative patterns of belonging are integral to constructive engagement. While these patterns will vary in time and place, indigenous proposals for belonging to society entail an expanded citizenship, anchored around a primary affiliation with ethnicity or tribe rather than as individual citizens. Citizenship in the sense of control and consent will need to be expanded and differentiated to foster a belonging through difference.

An adherence to constructive engagement goes beyond the legalistic (abstract rights) or restitutional (reparations), however important these concerns are in building identity and mobilising resources. Reliance on the legalities of rights and reparations tends to emphasise continuities with the past at the expense of social changes and evolving circumstances (Mulgan 1989). Worse still, as Taiaiake Alfred concludes, attempting to right historical wrongs by equalising material conditions ignores the fact that indigenous peoples were essentially autonomous political communities before the wrongs began (Alfred 1999a: *xv*). By contrast, a constructive engagement policy is focused on advancing an ongoing relationship by taking into account shifting social realities. Constructive engagement also goes beyond the dualities inherent in claims-making – dualisms establish a confrontation between two entities, so a choice must be made in terms of this opposition, thus disallowing the possibility that each of the opposing terms requires and draws upon a/the supposed opposite (Fay 1996). A dialectical mode of thinking is proposed under constructive engagement in which differences are not perceived as absolute or antagonistic, but as deeply interconnected in the sense of being held in tension within a larger framework.

'Engagement' is the key. Time will tell if state–indigenous peoples relations can evolve from claims-making to constructive engagement. Acceptance of difference is insufficient; proposed instead is an active engagement with indigeneity as legitimate in shaping outcomes, interaction, relations and identity.

Rethinking Aotearoa: The Politics of Tino Rangatiratanga

Few indigenous peoples have enjoyed as much publicity or notoriety as the tribes ('iwi' and 'hapu') comprising Maori of Aotearoa. Images long extolled Maori as cooperative and congenial contributors to New Zealand's much ballyhooed reputation as a paragon of racial harmony (Blythe 1994). *Recent* representations have accentuated a harder dimension because of Maori protest action from open confrontations to acts of civil disobedience (Walker 1995b; Poata-Smith 1996). The politics of protest bristle with a growing Maori assertiveness over their relational status as 'junior partners' in a bi-cultural project. Maori politics resonate with increasingly politicised calls to rebuild the relationship along bi-national lines. Discourses range from assertion of Maori sovereignty over the *entire country* (Awatere 1984) to the creation of separate Maori institutions (Spoonley *et al.* 1996), with arguments for constitutional-based power-sharing arrangements in between (Oliver 1997). Common to each of these assertions is restoration of tino rangatiratanga as a framework for putting these transformative principles into practice.

Tino Rangatiratanga: A Contested Site

Tino Rangatiratanga! The expression resonates with a lilt that betrays its potency (Hutton 1996). Few words are as likely to elicit such animus or to evoke admiration; fewer still have the open-endedness for spanning the spectrum of meanings from empowerment and change to destruction or deceit, with points of irrelevance in between. Issues of rangatiratanga animate a host of political discourses in Aotearoa/New Zealand, yet the concept remains shrouded in mystery, as Renwick observes:

> But rangatiratanga is still a mystery to a great many Pakeha and it catches them in one of their cultural blindspots. If the task of the 1980s was to rethink the duties of the Crown under the Treaty, the task of the 1990s is to develop ways by which Maori express their Article 2 rights of rangatiratanga as part of the fabric of the wider New Zealand society. (Renwick 1993: 37)

Uncertainty is perhaps understandable: at various times, tino rangatiratanga has encompassed the following: Maori sovereignty, Maori nationhood, self-management, iwi nationhood, independent power, full chiefly authority, chiefly mana, strong leadership, independence, supreme rule, self-reliance, Maori autonomy, tribal autonomy, absolute chieftainship, trusteeship, self-determination. That confusion prevails is less problematic than the refusal to front up to tino rangatiratanga which, in the words of the late Matiu Rata, may well represent 'the most crucial and important means by which Maori can participate fully both in their affairs and in those of the country' (Ihimaera 1995: 89).

For many non-Maori, the expression is often dismissed as offensive or an affront, since references to rangatiratanga not only challenge the foundational myth of 'he iwi kotahi tatou' ('we are one people'). Critics also deplore rangatiratanga as little more than a smokescreen for propping up the 'grievance' industry while capitulating to the impertinent demands of hot-blooded activists.

In contrast are Maori perceptions of tino rangatiratanga. The principle and practice of tino rangatiratanga conjures up a host of reassuring images for restoring Maori as a people to their rightful place in a post-colonising society. The notion of 'tino rangatiratanga' is subject to a host of different interpretations (Melbourne 1995; Archie 1995; Barlow 1996; Durie 1995; Mead 1997). Depending on the person or context, reference to tino rangatiratanga has been used to justify:

- Maori power and empowerment;
- self-determination and control over jurisdictions and destinies;
- bi-culturalism and partnership;
- Maori control over Maori things within a Maori value system;
- restoration of mana Maori;
- Maori cultural autonomy and territorial development.

To complicate matters further are debates over the scope of tino rangatiratanga. For some, tino rangatiratanga resides within the hapu; for
others, the iwi; for still others only Maori as a collectivity; and for yet
others still, within the individual.

Appeals to tino rangatiratanga have leapt to the forefront of Maori
struggles in challenging colonial arrangements and orthodox sovereign
discourses (Ward and Hayward 1999). The essence of rangatiratanga is sov-
ereignty-driven: for some, this sovereignty prevails over the entirety of
Aotearoa; for others, it entails some degree of autonomy from the state; for
still others, it consists of shared jurisdictions within a single framework.
'Radical' views equate tino rangatiratanga with absolute Maori ownership
and political control (Jackson 1997). Maori versions of the Treaty ceded
kawanatanga (governorship) to the Crown, but vested Maori sovereignty
in tino rangatiratanga by guaranteeing exclusive customary rights over
property. Moderate versions suggest a shared sovereign arrangement
involving a division of jurisdiction. According to Sir Hugh Kawharu, the
Treaty established a unique relationship in which Maori sovereignty over
the land was bequeathed to the Crown in exchange for the 'full', 'exclusive' and 'undisturbed' possession of Maori properties (Kawharu 1996).
Also guaranteed under the indigenous rights concept of rangatiratanga
was the traditional mana (authority) of chiefs over tribes to conduct lives
accordingly (Mulgan 1989). This interpretation is consistent with recent
publications of the Waitangi Tribunal in extolling the oppositional tension
between kawanatanga (Crown governance) and tino rangatiratanga
(indigenous rights to self-determination) as a basis for crafting a bi-nation-
alistic partnership (Maaka and Fleras 1998–99).

> (a) In the Maori text the chiefs ceded 'kawanatanga' to the Queen. This is less
> than the sovereignty ceded in the English text, and means the authority to
> make laws for the good order and security of the country, but subject to the
> protection of Maori interests. The cession of sovereignty is implicit from sur-
> rounding circumstances.
> (b) In recognising the 'tino rangatiratanga' of their lands, the Crown
> acknowledged the right of the Maori people for as long as they wished, to hold
> their lands in accordance with long-standing custom on a tribal and commu-
> nal basis. (Waitangi Tribunal 1987: 149, para 11.11.4)

A subsequent report by the Waitangi Tribunal also disengaged tino
rangatiratanga from any claim to separate sovereignty, restricting it
instead to 'tribal self-management on lines similar to what we understand
by local government' (Waitangi Tribunal 1995: 13) – a decision that
many say is narrow and restrictive. In short, the relationship between rangatiratanga and sovereignty is complex and multi-textured, and that puts
the onus on disentangling the issue over who controls what.

Principles and Philosophy

Tino rangatiratanga resists simple definition since it is an intangible that cannot be seen or touched, much like power or sovereignty. Only the exercise of tino rangatiratanga provides tangible evidence of its existence. As well, its meaning has evolved over time and varies with place, although differences in meaning may be more contextual rather than categorical (Durie 1997). Instead of a 'thing' with definable properties, tino rangatiratanga may be better seen as a process by which this attribute is applied after the fact. With those caveats in mind, we prefer a definition inspired by the writings of the American First Nation's scholar, Kirke Kickingbird: tino rangatiratanga is the supreme power from which all specific powers related to self-determination are based and derive their legitimacy (Kickingbird 1984).

More specifically, tino rangatiratanga refers to those indigenous rights to self-determination that Maori possess by virtue of their status as original occupants ('tangata whenua'), confirmed by Article 2 of the Treaty. Rangatiratanga rights do more than redress historical grievances; in addition to 'catch-up justice', they also establish patterns of belonging that contest Crown sovereignty, yet privilege Maori as essentially autonomous and self-determining political communities. As the epitome of power, strictly speaking, tino rangatiratanga is not interchangeable with sovereignty or self-determination (Walker 1995b). Tino rangatiratanga serves as a precursor of Maori sovereignty; it also provides the basis for, derives from, is contingent on, and is strengthened by claims to self-determination.

What are the constituent features of tino rangatiratanga? One of the more articulate expressions is drawn from a discussion paper by Mason Durie entitled 'Tino Rangatiratanga: Maori Self-determination', at an executive meaning of the Maori Congress in May of 1995. Tino rangatiratanga is analysed from different perspectives, including:

- its expression in Maori society;
- its compatibility with current constitutional arrangements within Maoridom;
- its status within a national Maori body politic; and
- its role in strengthening formal structures and improving relationships with the Crown.

Three principles are intrinsic to tino rangatiratanga. First, Nga Matatini Maori – the principle of Maori diversity. Maori are organised into a variety of traditional and non-traditional bodies, each of which is legitimate in its own right and deserves protection of its integrity.

Second, Whakakotahi – the principle of Maori unity. Despite diversity in affiliations and structures, there remains a cohesive core based on a shared sense of belonging and common destiny. Strength in numbers may also result from a unified base.

Third, Mana Motuhake Maori – the principle of autonomy and control. The single unifying aspiration under tino rangatiratanga is that of autonomy, that is, the right to take control of their destiny and resources through control of the decision-making policy process.

Taken together, tino rangatiratanga is about self-determination. With its sense of Maori ownership and active control over the future at both hapu/iwi and national levels, tino rangatiratanga symbolises a Maori right to exercise authority within a Maori constitutional framework.

In separate publications, Mason Durie equates tino rangatiratanga with self-determination over internal jurisdictions (Durie 1995; 1998). According to Durie, tino rangatiratanga prevails at the level of mana whenua in that it implies tribal control of resources as well as iwi rights to negotiate directly with the Crown for grievance resolution. It also must prevail at the mana tangata level by acknowledging recognition of Maori rights to organise according to a range of social and political groupings, from hapu and iwi to urban authorities and national bodies. More specifically, Durie continues, tino rangatiratanga is about the development of Maori policy by Maori as part of the special covenant with the Crown, together with assumptions of Maori responsibility over Maori affairs at iwi, hapu and national levels. Four additional elements round out tino rangatiratanga: mana wairua (the spiritual element that pervades all aspects of Maori life and organisation); mana ariki (the authority of chiefs to lead and guide their own people and other peoples); mana whenua/mana rangatira (the authority of iwi to secure ownership and exercise control over land and resources); and mana tangata (the right of all Maori, both individually and collectively, to determine policies and control over destiny without unnecessary dependence on governments). From this, tino rangatiratanga would be supported by three structural components of a Maori constitutional framework: namely, mana a iwi (hapu and iwi), mana a tangata (Maori community interests) and mana Maori (national Maori representation). Taken together, rangatiratanga rights constitute a level of Maori sovereignty that incorporates a separate power base with parallel institutions for reformulating Maori–Crown relations.

In brief, then, tino rangatiratanga is closely aligned with the principles and practices of indigeneity as discourse and transformation. Just as indigeneity constitutes a politicised ideology that privileges original occupancy as a basis for engagement and entitlement, so too does tino rangatiratanga pose a political challenge by the tangata whenua over prevailing distributions of power and resources. Tino rangatiratanga asserts the primacy of Maori rights of sovereignty not in the sense of separation or secession. Innovative patterns of belonging are invoked that privilege Maori values and rights as foundations for establishing a new constitutional order that acknowledges hapu, iwi and whanau as fundamentally autonomous political communities that are sovereign yet share sovereignty. Moreover, tino rangatiratanga was neither created by the Treaty nor bestowed by the Crown. Its pre-existence by virtue of Maori occupancy rights (tangata whenua) and reaffirmation in the Treaty of Waitangi only requires appropriate structures for its expression as principle and practice. In seeking to advance Maori indigenous rights, tino rangatiratanga is unmistakably Maori in spirit and style. Tino rangatiratanga is equally committed to building bridges by working together in a spirit of constructive engagement.

Tino Rangatiratanga in Practice

It is one thing to talk about tino rangatiratanga as a principle, and quite another to demonstrate its manifestation as practical activity. Is tino rangatiratanga solely a philosophical concept or can it be practised? Where should one look for evidence of tino rangatiratanga? In whose body should tino rangatiratanga be vested? Are there signs that New Zealand society has adapted to Maori demands for the acknowledgement of their customary rights?

In response to Maori political agitation and the build-up to the national sesquicentennial celebrations of 1990, New Zealand society has struggled to come to grips with its colonial past. Contemporary Maori demands for the recognition of their sovereignty surfaced publicly on 6 February 1971 at the annual formal celebration of the signing of the Treaty of Waitangi. From that time the movement has been constant, relentless and increasing in intensity and sophistication. In 1975 the *Treaty of Waitangi Act* allowed Maori to make claims against the Crown for current breaches of the Treaty of Waitangi; a decade later this act was amended to allow claims retrospective to 1840 to be lodged with the Waitangi Tribunal. As a result of this act there have been some landmark decisions such as the *Maori Language Act 1987*, which made Te Reo Maori an official language of New Zealand. In May 1995, the Waikato-Tainui peoples received $170 million as compensation from the government for lands confiscated by the Crown in the nineteenth century. This compensation, received through Treaty settlements, has created economic power for tribes which in turn has fortified Tainui-defined development growth (Mahuta 1996). Such developments have given substance to the notion of tino rangatiratanga at national and tribal levels. The language act constitutes an acknowledgement of Maori rangatiratanga; the Tainui Settlement and Ngai Tahu Settlement of 1998 are an expression of tribal rangatiratanga.

Evidence suggests that recognition of tino rangatiratanga is becoming socially acceptable in certain spheres of society. One of the earlier signs of shared sovereignty in practice took place within the Anglican Church of New Zealand. In 1990 it adopted a constitution that gave to the Maori and Pacific Island components of the church equal status to that of the dominant Pakeha component of the church. The constitution recognises each component, which it describes as tikanga, as autonomous:

> AND WHEREAS (12) the principles of partnership and bicultural development require the Church to: a) organise its affairs within each of the tikanga (social organisations, language, laws principles and procedures) of each partner. (Anglican Church 1990: 10)

It goes on further to state that each tikanga 'has power to structure and organise itself in such a manner as it shall from time to time determine' (Anglican Church 1990: 42). Additional signs include developments in the sports world where the rugby league's premier international competition, the 1998 World Cup, hosted a New Zealand Maori team in addition to the New Zealand national team (*Christchurch Press*, 10 June 1997).

These events are but random examples of changing perceptions among Pakeha, yet they could not have occurred without a significant shift in popular opinion. Formal political representation is yet another place to locate an expression of tino rangatiratanga, and the outcomes of the first MMP election in 1996 have been profound for Maori. Currently the five Maori MPs who occupy the Maori seats hold the balance of power. Other Maori MPs, especially those in the coalition government, enhance this position but the actual power lies with occupants of the Maori seats. For the first time Maori MPs wield real political power rather than delegated or negotiated power, at the highest levels of cabinet decision-making rather than on the margins. It could be argued that the status of Maori parliamentary representation has simply caught up with the actual position of Maori in New Zealand society. All political parties that seek power must interact with the Maori constituency and not just have a token Maori representation or relegate Maori to an advisory capacity. Maori have gravitated to the centre of political power without the abolition of the Maori seats, that is, on Maori terms and not as a product of expediency or assimilation. Increased Maori parliamentary representation under the new MMP system reflects an integrationist (or 'institutional') model of tino rangatiratanga that revolves around participation in the established parliamentary system. To be sure, the ultimate power under an integrationalist model still resides with the Pakeha majority who, if united in opposition to Maori initiatives, could prevent Maori political representation from having any effective say. Yet this line of thinking needs to be tempered by the fact that unilateral rejection of Maori political aspirations becomes less and less of an option as Maori become politically and economically stronger (Maaka and Fleras 1998).

More substantial expressions of tino rangatiratanga have taken place as a result of the Fisheries Settlement (Cheyne *et al.* 1997). Polarised views and shades of differing opinions on how tino rangatiratanga should translate into tangible ownership rights are being played out in the very public and hotly contested arena of 'who gets what'. After more than seven years of lobbying, Maori negotiators brokered a deal with the government for a settlement on treaty rights on off-shore fishing. The settlement was formalised under the *Treaty of Waitangi (Fisheries Claims) Settlement Act 1992*, which effectively gave Maori interests control over 23 per cent of the national off-shore fisheries, a substantial asset consisting of 57 000 tonnes of fish quota, and $30 million in cash. The actual settlement pivoted around the Sealords Deal. Sealords were the largest private fishing enterprise in New Zealand and the government financed a joint-venture acquisition of Sealord Products Ltd to purchase a half interest in the company for the Maori. In return, the Maori had to renounce all future fishery litigation against the Crown as part of the full and final settlement of all Maori claims to commercial fishing rights. The deal was negotiated by a small group of prominent Maori leaders who, over the period of the settlement process, became the Treaty of Waitangi Fisheries Commission (Te Ohu Kaimoana, TOKM). TOKM's role is to manage the asset until a system of allocation to Maori can be devised.

The settlement was unique in that it was a pan-Maori solution to a multi-tribal claim. But as the move to develop allocation models suggests, there was never any intention that the settlement remain a Maori asset. It was always going to be allocated out to sectional interests, the tribes that constitute Maoridom. The fishing settlement process caused and continues to elicit vigorous and often acrimonious public debate. The debates are many and multilayered, and those considered here are the ones surrounding the allocation models only. It is this area of debate that best illustrates conflicting views on tino rangatiratanga.

The first debate to surface was among the tribal groups and involved criteria for distribution – coastline versus population base. Coastal tribes advocated that allocation of the assets should be made in proportion to the amount of coastline contained in a tribal territory. Inland tribes, on the other hand, endorsed a pattern of distribution in proportion to the size of the tribe. There was to be no compromise in the debate and the government threatened to pre-empt TOKM and unilaterally impose a solution. On 17 April 1997 TOKM announced that 60 per cent of the assets were to be allocated on the basis of coastline and 40 per cent on the basis of population. The matter is far from settled, with at least one dissatisfied major tribe considering taking the matter to court.

As this debate was going on, a third party appeared and demanded inclusion in the allocation of assets. A combination of urban Maori Authorities from Auckland, Wellington and Christchurch have made claims for a share of the fisheries assets, namely a percentage of the money, not fishing quota. When TOKM rejected their claim, the matter went to court. On 30 April 1996 the Court of Appeal ruled in favour of the urban groups. The tribal groups responded by taking the matter to the Privy Council in London, which overturned the Court of Appeal's decision and asked that the case be returned to New Zealand to redefine the concept of iwi. At the High Court hearing in Auckland on 4 August 1998, Justice B. J. Paterson found that the urban groups were not 'iwi' for the purposes of allocation. As of August 1999 the issue is before the Court of Appeal. The situation has not altered since, with TOKM supported by tribal groups steadfastly refusing to negotiate with urban groups on the grounds that the assets are iwi-owned. Even proposals at the Annual General Meeting of the TOKM on 26 July 1997 to set aside $20 million in trust for urban Maori proved unacceptable.

The fisheries debate illustrates that tino rangatiratanga is contestable and is being redefined internally with changes to Maori social circumstances. The treaty claims and settlement processes in spite of several 'Maori' settlements, such as the *Maori Language Act*, have put tribes at the fore. Tribal groups remain at the forefront of the Treaty claims process and tribal formations have gained ascendancy in public awareness, especially in the wake of various iwi-development policies. Most Maori leaders do not recognise any other type of tino rangatiratanga. In an interview on sovereignty the Tainui leader Sir Robert Mahuta puts it very succinctly: 'To us Maori sovereignty is Kingitanga. Full stop' (Melbourne 1995: 144). Another well-known tribal leader, Sir Tipene O'Regan, also endorses tribal self-determination as the basis for tribes controlling assets in their own rohe (territory) (Melbourne 1995: 156). The underlying premise argued by Maori leaders has been that the chiefs signed the Treaty on behalf of their tribes, not on behalf of all Maori; therefore, tino rangatiratanga can only be expressed through tribal affiliation. Still, the fisheries claim, both in its settlement and allocation debate, has opened the way for more expansive definitions of tino rangatiratanga. With TOKM ceding 40 per cent of the allocation to the 'population'-based argument, the decision has signalled the negotiability of the 'one tribe, one territory' basis of tino rangatiratanga.

Maori parliamentary representation and the fisheries settlement demonstrate two mutually interrelated but analytically distinct expressions of tino rangatiratanga. Much of the controversy revolves around the dichotomous situation of defining tino rangatiratanga in terms of Maori rights or in terms of tribal first nations rights. In contrast to Australia, Canada and the US where a broad range of diverse indigenous groups exists, in New Zealand there exists but one: Maori. The notion of Maori as a collectivity is a post-contact social construct. Before colonisation Maori saw themselves solely as tribal peoples. While there was a considerable range of tribal and regional 'diversity', there was a clearly identifiable cultural homogeneity, expressed in a commonality of language and customary practice. In a letter to the settlers of Hawkes Bay, a chief from Ngati Kahungunu expressed it this way: 'Just as you are all English, though one is a Bishop, one is a Governor and another is a soldier and another is a settler so we are all one, Maori is my name' (Kawepo 1860: 5).

As a result of this history there are two ethnicities, namely, a tribal ethnicity and an all-inclusive Maori ethnicity. What needs to be kept in mind when considering tino rangatiratanga as a social reality as opposed to a political philosophy is that the two ethnicities coexist symbiotically and in a state of tension with each other.

Re-engaging with Indigeneity

Settler dominions such as Canada, Australia and Aotearoa are in the process of decolonisation. Yet structures of internal colonialism continue to tarnish the process of postcolonising from within (Bennett & Blundell 1995). Expansion of a unilaterally imposed economic paradigm has had the effect of co-opting indigenous peoples into a capitalist mode of production that is little more than an 'imprisoned internal exile' beyond the control of indigenous peoples (Frideres 1999). References to postcolonial renewal and reform notwithstanding, white settler dominions remain suspicious of any fundamental restructuring, preferring instead to depoliticise indigeneity by throwing money at the problem in the hope it will go away. Citizenship remains rooted in the espousal of universal individual rights rather than in recognition of indigeneity as a pre-existing right. Entitlement patterns are defined on the basis of formal equality before the law, in effect confirming liberal values that what we have in common is more important than what divides us, that what we accomplish as individuals is more significant as a basis for reward or evaluation than membership in a particular group, and that the content of our character rather than the colour of skin should serve as the basis for judgement. Diversity is tolerated, but only to the extent that everyone is different in the same way. Inasmuch as the intent is to simply rearrange the deck furniture without altering the floor plan of even a sinking ship, political agenda tend to focus on appearances rather than substance.

By contrast, indigenous peoples are seeking innovative patterns of entitlement and engagement in the hope of securing a new kind of belonging in which legitimacy is vested in indigenous models of self-determination. The challenge in dislodging the deeply ingrained cultural assumptions of white settler dominions will be formidable. As Renwick notes:

> They have to think of Maori not as a minority – the largest and the most important one but still a minority – but as tangata whenua, the original peoples of the land, and of themselves as later arrivals. They have to think of tribes and tribal forms of organisation not as relics of the past but as vital, contemporary expressions of personal and group identity. They have to understand that Maoridom is a form of society in which the ultimate authority – it's hard not to call it sovereignty – resides not in the nation-state but among many descent groups, all of them autonomous. They have to understand that rangatiratanga is the expression of that autonomy and, furthermore, that, although tribal groups cooperate and make common cause, they always retain their ultimate right to make their own decisions and, if that is the decision, to go it alone. Pakeha have, in short, to imagine a very different political model. (Renwick 1993: 40)

Ascendancy of indigeneity has catapulted to the forefront in reshaping the postcolonial society-building project (Fleras and Elliott 1992). In the space of one generation, indigenous peoples have moved from the margins to the centre of national stages, once the cost of exclusion from society proved detrimental. Still it remains to be seen whether innovative patterns of working through differences can be incorporated in contexts where state sovereignty is normally thought to be indivisible and unitary. Equally intriguing will be the extent to which political authorities can accommodate indigenous claims to sovereignty as a basis for allocating scarce resources. Reference to indigenous sovereignty as shared yet separate rarely extends to complete separation; by the same token, it rejects a multicultural desire to celebrate diversity and achieve institutional equality. Advocated instead are patterns of belonging that accentuate a sovereignty without secession involving models of relative yet relational autonomy in non-coercive contexts. No less critical is the reconstitutionalisation of the first principles that govern indigenous peoples–state relations. As distinct communities of a political nature, indigenous peoples are seeking to establish a post-sovereign political order in societies that historically denied or excluded indigeneity. Yet inclusion into nationhood is pivotal, without necessarily buying into the trappings of a fully fledged administrative unit known as a state. As Henry Reynolds (1996) points out, statehood may not be essential for cultural survival in the modern world; however, a sense of nationhood most certainly is in establishing living and lived-in realities.

Society-building is a complex and arduous undertaking at the best of times, and fraught with contradiction or conflict at the worst. Even more formidable is the postcolonising of white settler dominions when sovereignty is openly contested. Clear breaks with the past are ideal, but difficult to implement because of competing discourses and vested interests (Weaver 1991). Indigenous people–state relations are imbued with an air of ambivalence as colonialist paradigms grind up against postcolonial realities. Colonialist paradigms refuse to graciously exit since indigenous demands interfere with a host of deeply embedded privileges, power and values. Indigenous paradigms may be gathering momentum but confront powerful vested and national interests that remain resolutely opposed to power-sharing on a people-to-people basis, each autonomous in jurisdiction yet sharing in state sovereignty (Canada, Royal Commission on Aboriginal Peoples 1996a, b). Instead of a paradigm shift we are left with a paradigm 'muddle' of messy proportions in which the old and new coexist uneasily (Rotman 1997). Such a state of uncertainty and expediency is likely to persist until conventional thinking accepts a commitment to white settler dominions as an engagement between two consenting majorities, both of whom are sovereign in their own right, yet inextricably interlocked as partners in jointly exploring postcolonising possibilities.

PART II

Identity

CHAPTER 6

Paths Toward a Mohawk Nation: Narratives of Citizenship and Nationhood in Kahnawake

Audra Simpson

Political Theory and the Problem of Indigenous Nationhood

Once remarkable for their distance from matters indigenous, political theorists are now considering the political and historical issues of native people within their recent works on constitutionalism, citizenship and multiculturalism. The philosophical turn to matters indigenous has its history in the larger literature of liberal rights theory – theories that seek to understand, in philosophical terms, the reasons why certain injustices prevail. True to that earlier work, the more recent literature represents a point of convergence for challenges to and strengths of 'the just society' or the 'political good'. The question that drives much of this work is as normative as it is obvious: how may a society operate in a just manner without considering the claims of native people and other cultural groups?

Within Canada, the consideration of questions posed by 'aboriginality', a mode of arguing and defending one's collective identity based on a temporal relationship to the land, posed such a challenge to the state and to those that theorise the state.[1] Once coupled with well-publicised inquiries into residential school abuses and land claims, the strident nationalism of native peoples turned within political thinking into a deep, subterranean and theoretical movement for reconciliation. This philosophical movement attempted to move toward a space for dialogue, with the philosophy itself an enabling device for the development of new and more substantive conversations between previously silent peoples. It is hoped that from this conversation will come the construction of better and more just institutional practices. More than anything, perhaps, it is hoped that within this social space of listening and talking – one that may be characterised in its barest form, as one of possibility – some of the violence, suffering, glory and guilt of colonialism that blankets contemporary Canadian society may finally be shorn away.

Whether or not these philosophical desires can be fulfilled depends on what the future holds. However, it is of some benefit to light upon one of the important works in this new literature to appreciate the process that is now underway. James Tully's *Strange Multiplicity* (1995) is paramount among those philosophical works that seek to move us toward a political field that is predicated upon a praxis of listening. Articulated to the crisis in native–settler relations, his work attempts to enable a meaningful conversation through a copious historical and philosophical reflection upon constitutionalism. With this rethinking and refashioning of a key philosophical and political textual practice within the west, Tully reveals to us the ways in which its obtuse and 'hidden' languages have served to dominate women, national minorities and native people. In revealing these languages to us, it is hoped that the 'difference' of Indians (or others) may be listened to and understood in substantive and meaningful ways.

Strange Multiplicity is clearly articulated to the problems between Indians and the state (along with other 'minority' or subaltern peoples), and as such Tully's historical and decolonising approach to philosophical texts and history is complemented by other works and approaches to similar problems. Will Kymlicka's recent empirical examination of the multiculturalism policy in Canada (1998a) offers another reflection upon problems within the state. Although diverging in method (Kymlicka's work is remarkably sociological rather than historical), both are united in their commitment to 'difference' as the critical matter within their ruminations. And with difference, there is a dependence upon the notion of 'culture' to contain and then convey its content.

A question attaches itself to these works: if 'culture' is the matter of difference, then how is one to listen to and understand the particular 'difference' of indigenous peoples and their *particular* nationhoods? Both 'aboriginality' and nationhood are constituted (and constitutive of) political postures, experiences and discourses and these processes are inextricably joined to culture. As they are joined to culture they are articulated through the apparatii of history, power and experience. The very notion of an *indigenous* nationhood, which demarcates identity and seizes tradition in ways that may be antagonistic to the encompassing frame of the state, may be simply unintelligible to the western and/or imperial ear. Or is it not?

In this chapter, I take up the question of indigenous nationhood by examining 'membership' or citizenship-formation within Kahnawake, a Mohawk reserve community in Canada. In recent years Kahnawake has been involved in the development of a custom code that is based on lineage, rather than race, to determine who its members or citizens should be. This new code, which has yet to be ratified, is the result of a community consultation process that seeks to move Kahnawake away from the criterion of 'blood quantum' to a more cultural and kinship-based model

of descent. The 'blood quantum' years span 1984 to the present, and marks one of the many moments in Kahnawake's political history when the community spoke directly and obliquely to the tutelage of the state. 'Blood' appeared in this conversation as a means not only of excluding others, but of defining the self, of choosing among political alternatives and visions for that definition, and for maintaining control over the means of determining that process. I will provide some of the context that led to this important period in the community's history. Recent works in this area have emphasised the fractured 'nature' of the debate over membership criteria, the ways in which this speaks or does not speak to western citizenship theory, and the ways in which the community unsettles the individualism inherent in western liberal theory of Taylor and Kymlicka (Dickson-Gilmore 1999a; Paine 1999). Both are important to understanding the ways in which institutional practices affect political membership within communities, but both would be well served by a discussion of the very lived cultural process of citizenship formation in the context of a nation-in-being. Before taking up the specificity of Kahnawake's citizenship and the voices that convey this issue, however, I want to take up some very elemental questions that attach themselves to the notion of indigenous nationhood.

Indigenous Nationhood

What is it about indigenous peoples and their experiences that may constitute them as nations rather than as peoples? Were they not 'tribes' just a short time ago? Is this use of 'nationhood' in political circles and mainstream media a symbolic and semantic indulgence? Or is it some form of historical residue, a marker of colonialism's simultaneous beginning, end or continued life? Is 'indigenous nationhood' merely a perversion of signs and simultaneity rather than a set of concrete political objectives that are attached to collective experience? Is the notion of an Indian or indigenous nationhood merely a vagary of colonialism's living consciousness? Is its use in Canada among Indian peoples and Canadian intellectuals a curious case of appeasement? Is it an innocuous form of tolerance that precludes or sidesteps serious conversations and settlements regarding land?

As a concept and a practice, indigenous nationhood is not an exercise in liberal appeasement nor an exercise in indigenous cultural invention.[2] In this, particular indigenous peoples – such as those of the Iroquois Confederacy (the Seneca, Cayuga, Oneida, Onondaga, Mohawk and Tuscarora nations) – have a long and well-documented historical self-consciousness and recognition as peoples that constituted themselves and were thus constituted by others as 'nations'. The self-consciousness and recognition (albeit historical and strangulated) of the nationhood that the Iroquois enjoys is not only a matter of consciousness and oral history, it is one of a great documented history.[3] Within that history we find the trappings of European forms of nationhood: a past that is replete with treaties, diplomacy, procedure and political structure. And as with other indigenous peoples, this documented and experiential history lives within the present (Simpson 1998; 1999), and informs the particular consciousness and attitude of Iroquois people toward each other, toward other Indian peoples and toward the state.

In spite of the historically documented and thus, some would argue, epistemologically *convenient* case of Iroquois governmental practice, there is a more important argument to be made regarding indigenous nationhood, political and cultural theory, and the need for some talking and listening between the two. In order to contribute to such a conversation, the overarching argument regarding nationhood that will be pursued here is that, much like the nationhood of western states (which we will take to be the analytic norm and proceed to problematise), the nationhood of indigenous peoples is made from the bare parts of consciousness and history. However, unlike the nationhood of western states, the nationhood of indigenous peoples has been bifurcated and disassembled with global processes of colonisation. Thus their nationhood enjoys a diversity of forms and experiences, but because of invasion, conquest and settlement, is necessarily one that is spatially within that of another dominating society. So if theorists are to consider and take seriously the 'matter' of difference they must pick up where Tully has left off. They must continue to rethink the history and the vocabulary that is constitutive of their own society and its relationship with others. As well, they must continue to consider the grey areas of history and vocabulary that indigenous peoples share with them. But their reflections and ruminations upon difference, upon culture, and upon a 'good' within theory must be brought into the same analytic frame of its referents.

Here, I examine the sociality and narrativity that constitutes indigenous nationhood in order to achieve larger, more theoretical aims. The question pursued is the manner in which indigenous nationhood is understood, practised and narrated by its own people. The data for this 'practice' resides with the Mohawks of Kahnawake and their *everyday* nationalism. In taking up this everyday nationalism I am interested in illustrating the ways in which nationhood is constructed around several axes, but most importantly, the way that nationalism (and thus, the sense and style of nationhood) is localised around the critical axis of 'membership' or citizenship within their community. This question of membership, of what the criteria shall be for obtaining, maintaining and exercising rights within the community (not the Canadian state) has opened up internal conversations and contests over the very content of identity, of just 'who' a Mohawk is, and in this, what a Mohawk 'should be'. Discussions and debates surrounding the criteria over membership in the community point to the many ways in which indigenous peoples (and perhaps other non-standard/non-western nations) negotiate and construct their own boundaries around self, community and rights, the ways in which they investigate and enact what their vision of the 'ideal citizen' should be according to their own historical and epistemological experience.

In placing indigenous nationhood within the social and political space that has been cleared by activism, war and the ruminations of recent philosophical works, this case study of Kahnawake offers narratives of nationhood that speak from 'the ground up'. However, I will work from 'theory down' in order to appreciate the ways in which experience and the words that convey that experience converge in narrative. I will first contextualise Kahnawake's nationhood by reference to some anthropological and sociological theories of nationalism and nationhood. Nationalism energises and animates nationhood and, as such, requires some reflection in the context of the indigenous and the day-to-day; two overlapping arenas of social life that enjoy no critical attention in the literature of the anthropology of native peoples or theories of indigenous politics and power. I will then wed this body of theory to narratives with the method of 'radical empiricism' put forward by the anthropologist Michael Jackson. Jackson's anthropological method has heretofore unexplored analytical and *political* potential within indigenous and political study. As a stream within the anthropology of experience, his notions may be brought to bear on the kind of philosophy of listening that Tully and others are trying to bring into the literature of political theory. As well, these notions may be put to work in order to enable, in some very modest ways, a desired conversation between Indians and others. This conversation on the important issues of politics, history and power in settler societies is one that we all await. In these ways Jackson's methodological ruminations may offer us some direction toward the larger project of reconfiguring the relationships of power that characterise native–state relations, at the very least, in text. I will cover this necessary literary terrain by way of some anthropological and sociological theories of nationalism and nationhood to appreciate the ways in which there is agreement and disagreement between theory and lived practice as it relates to Kahnawake's history and narratives.

Achieving a 'Listening State' or a State that Listens: Recasting Nationalism and Nationhood

What is the 'stuff', then, of indigenous nationhood?

The nationalism of Kahnawake is a cultural articulation that occurs along the seams of colonialism in Canada, following the structural 'traces' of the initial colonial encounter between settlers and Indians. We find within the methods of domination that are the colonial legacy the practice of enframing Indian lives through the assumption of authority over personal agency. As well, we witness the forced cultural transformation of native culture through the bounding of people and bounding of space. These efforts at boundedness are represented in the creation of reserves and the *Indian Act*, instruments of colonial control that are now fundamental in the construction and maintenance of the Mohawk nation, as it is expressed in Kahnawake.

Mohawk nationalism, as it is expressed in Kahnawake, is replete then with colonial ironies. Mixing parts, it draws from Iroquois teachings, from the ancestral and immediate past, and from the neocolonial present. The nationalist project in Kahnawake is a hybrid form in its impetus and expression, and therefore transcends any understanding of its impetus or focus as 'resistance' to the Canadian state (or the American state). Rather, it appears on one level to be about maintaining for *Kahnawakero:non* ('People of Kahnawake') what they have in the present, while guaranteeing a space for them in their future.[4] This nationalism, like many others, necessarily privileges the past and looks to an uncertain future in a dialogue with the state that is by no means exhaustively defined by that state (Wilmsen and McAllister 1996).

In carrying a consciousness of themselves as members of a nation that pre-dates Canada and the US, *the contemporary* among Mohawks is conjoined to the postmodern, the colonial and pre-colonial – to an indigenous Iroquois past and present. Here, *culture* is both a self-conscious, deliberate and politically expedient formulation and a lived, and implicit, rather than contemplated, phenomenon. *The nation*, similarly, is a collectively self-conscious, deliberate and politically expedient formulation and a lived phenomenon. Both constitute a terrain of consensus, disagreement, discord and hopeful contemplation that connects the categorical 'Mohawk' to the individual, their family and the extension of their family to a living entity: their nation.

In this context, as in any, 'the nation' receives its analytic particularities in the process and the place that it is articulated through. In other words, if it is industrial England that defines those processes under discussion, 'the nation' will be positioned and defined in just that context. Hence, the nation will exhibit the characteristics of industrialisation, of concomitant alienation from the means of production, and is understood as a form of social organisation that is arrived at through the false consciousness of its people. 'The nation', then, will be something observable and assertive, arrived at through an often bloody patrolling of clearly established and yet shifting boundaries. But more importantly (anthropologically rather than journalistically), *the nation* is a product of a mystified process called 'nationalism'. Nationalism is the means to an end – the end being the formation of 'the nation' and its political enclosure, 'statehood'. Toward an understanding of this process Ernest Gellner devised a model for nationalism where the conditions of modernity create the consciousness that would lead one to 'nation'. The nation, he tells us, emerges from a marriage between the modern industrial division of labour and the Protestant work ethos (Gellner 1983: 39–42).

Fundamental for a Gellnerian theorisation of nationalism, then, are material conditions and global processes that restrain us from an understanding of nationalism as an awakening of dormant collectivities (an image that is key in some nationalist rhetoric) toward a more contingent and planned project. Of this Gellner elaborates:

> Nations as a natural, God-given way of classifying men, as an inherent though long-delayed political destiny, are a myth; nationalism, which sometimes takes pre-existing cultures and turns them into nations, sometimes invents them, and often obliterates pre-existing cultures: *that* is a reality . . . Those who are its historic agents know not what they do, but that is another matter. (Gellner 1983: 48–9)

Here, Gellner has taken the core complex of nationalism – self, identity and history – and treated the constituents as matters of manipulation for the historic agents of nationalism. These agents are 'nationalists', culture brokers who steward people forward in their creative use of the past to meet the pressing and collective needs of the present. Gellner's analysis is a solid sociological accounting of the conditions that beget nationhood, but dismisses or elides the collection of meanings (through event, history and present interaction) that distil into the consciousness of nationhood in a people. Nationalism is more than an attribute of modernity or a fall-out from agrarian society; it is a process that is wedded to culture and must be treated so in analysis. I argue later that nationalism is a consciousness that is not limited to industrial or post-industrial society. Analytically, it is nested in the experience of statehood in Europe, which serves at once to prove the perspectivist and historically constructed nature of theory, and at the same time limit its use in analysis to other western or western-influenced societies. I concur with Gellner that nationalism is, for analysts, a political theory of legitimacy (Gellner 1983: 1), but as a theory nationalism should be extended to the aspirations and actions of those collectivities that do not fit the template – those that are non-western, economically integrated and at times, appear to be politically dominated.

Nationalism is exhibited and expressed by collectivities that do not fit Gellner's model. Among other non-western people, but central to the discussion at hand, are the experiences of native peoples in Canada.

Much of the public culture of native peoples in Canada has been stridently, remarkably assertive on matters of territory, jurisdiction, boundaries and selfhood – demanding an understanding of their collective behaviour and aspirations as nationalist.[5] They must be recentred in nationalist terms, as these are the terms (for some native peoples and not for others) that are their own.

It is from the point of extending nationalism to other peoples that we move away from Gellner to Benedict Anderson. Anderson takes nationalism a step further than Gellner, bringing it into the arena of cognition and creation, an exercise that serves to take nationalism out of Europe (and the preconditions of industrialism) and into other cultural spaces. For Anderson, nationalism is an imaginative process that leads to the construction of what he calls a 'cultural artefact' – the nation. The nation, Anderson concludes neatly, is 'an imagined political community – and imagined as both inherently limited and sovereign' (Anderson 1991: 6). By privileging the imagination rather than the salience of boundaries, Anderson opens up 'the nation' to diaspora and other transnational collectivities, and in doing so he centres the nationalist not as a clueless and stigmatised inventor or myth-maker, but as an agent actively involved in its production of self and its people. From here, Anderson critiques the logic that leads us to a juxtaposition of 'authentic' and 'false' nations in Gellner's model. He argues that political communities are not to be distinguished by their 'falsity'/'genuineness' (or degree of nationness) but rather by the *style* of their imaginings – by their nationalism (6).

Anderson brings us away from the restraints of industrialism through an emphasis on the cognitive dimension of nationalism. However, as with Gellner, he nests his discussion in the experiences of Europe, replacing the Protestant Ethos and industrialism with similar attributes of modernity: the novel and the newspaper (25). Each, he argues by taking up Walter Benjamin, is responsible for representing the kind of imagined community that is the nation, thereby shaping the style and the tenor of nationalism. Anderson assigns nationalism to a particular space in time, 'a simultaneity of past and future in an instantaneous present' (24), thus explaining the effervescence and naturalness of nation as something that always was.

'Boundaries' are implicit within this discussion of political legitimation as a subject of nationalist energy, as they are an elemental means of separating people from one another, and producing personal and collective identity. Like the people they identify and demarcate from others, boundaries must be situated within 'the contemporary'. The contemporary may be understood as modernity, radical modernity, postmodernity and postcolonialism – all signifying similar processes in different places. These processes may be understood as industrialism, alienation, the collapse of face-to-face interaction and, in simpler, Bhabhian terms, 'newness'. Nationalism emerges out of this newness as it has both the veneer of timelessness itself and strikes us with its assertions. In appreciating its simultaneous newness and timelessness, we may be able to locate its impetus and examine the style that it takes – along rhetorical, artistic, political or other culturally expressive lines.

Gellner and Anderson form some of the terrain of nationalism by mapping out causality: the reasons why, in historical and philosophical terms, people start to assert themselves in certain ways. They share the perspective of nationalism as a theory of political legitimacy and at the same time as a western phenomenon with its roots in hierarchy and industrialisation. Here, nationalism is a means to an end, and that end is statehood. These are important points in the discussion of nationalism as a collective endeavour – as a means to something – but must nationalism always point to statehood? Is the end of statehood something that all nations share? Is it possible for peoples – and here I am thinking of encapsulated communities such as reserves and meaningful but dispersed associations such as 'the diaspora' – to behave as nations do and not desire, at the end of their cultural labouring, statehood? Perhaps the desire may be for an abstraction – a principle, such as sovereignty, for moral victory, or simply for *respect*.

We will continue this discussion then, with residual issues in Gellner and Anderson and take up the importance that they place on state structure, a key institutional form in the era of modernity. We will take from them the insight that state structure is essential for the production of identity and nationalism. However, we will examine the state for its role in boundary making and identity construction rather than as a level of social organisation that groups pass through on their way to industrialisation.

Nationalism is shaped, then, by a relationship with the state. Nations, as many point out, exist both within states and without states. The state creates the image – Anderson's 're-presentation' of the essence of the nation, a process that is accelerated by rituals of the state such as national parades, coronations, museums and exhibitions, all of which communicate in some way what the essence of the nation is. More than simply suggesting through iconic imagery who its people are, the state has a crucial role in the classification and definition of those people through its monopoly over territorial boundaries and institutions. In this way, the state provides the inspiration as an institution of control and influence that suffuses nationalism (taken here as a sentiment and expression writ large of identity) with its energy.

How does nationalism apply in Canada today? What is the relationship between the state and the Indians in Canada – or, more specifically, Canada and the Mohawks of Kahnawake and their nationalist project? In holding a monopoly over administration, official governance and control

over public and 'official' culture (such as the Canadian Broadcasting
Corporation, museums etc.), 'the state' is what Brackette Williams calls 'a
context of analysis' (Williams 1989: 426), that is, directly related to the
processes of ethnogenesis and nationalism. The state is one frame in
which visibility is produced, creating the conditions under which difference becomes apparent, political aspirations articulated, and culture,
authenticity and tradition appear as politically expedient resources. By
framing what is official, the state creates conditions of either affiliation or
distance, association or disassociation. The affiliations arise from the
state's project of *homogenising heterogeneity*, 'the construction of myths of
homogeneity out of the realities of heterogeneity that characterise all
nation building' that all nations undertake (Williams 1989: 429). In this
context, Williams instructs us that:

> Seriously investigating the 'aura of descent' that surrounds ethnic group pro-
> duction requires detailed attention to how, in the conjunction of race-making
> as nation building and the invention of purity which it entails, blood becomes
> a synecdoche for all things cultural. (Williams 1989: 431)

This is not to say that the state is the only frame around which nationalism is found, or is the author in the local investigations and discussions
into the 'aura of descent'. Among the co-authors in these investigations
are narrative, experience and history. However, when articulating and
analysing indigenous nationhood, we must account for and understand
the foreignness that embeds their aspirations – the machinery of settlement that has hardened into institutions of governance. The abstractions
of 'nationalism', 'nationhood' and 'the state' are departure points for
understanding these other frames of experience and identity.

Anthropology, Representation and Indians

I want to move from theories of nationalism and nationhood to anthropological practice into a discussion of what the 'culture' is that we all discuss, and what 'the matter' of the difference is that some wish to decipher.

Anthropology is the traditional framework for representing and interpreting the culture and politics of native people and, as such, has framed
understandings of both 'the indigenous' and their 'culture'. Some discussion of *representation* is thus in order before we can arrive at a point of
listening to this culture, as the narratives that we will listen to are, in their
barest form, *representations of experience*. But in order to listen to and
understand these processes we have to understand something of the history of knowing and writing culture in anthropology.

Much as it was in the past, anthropological discourse and practice is
still shaped by colonialism (Kuper 1996; Asad 1973; Said 1989). The field

however, has changed (Wafer 1996: 259–61); 'the expedition', 'the mission' and 'the colony' have been replaced by new structures and semantics. In the wake of settler rule, enter 'confederation', 'self-government' and 'the nation-state', each working in concert to name, to make sense of and to manage the geographies of colonial inheritance. With its power base reconfigured to accommodate the politics of decolonisation and globalisation, anthropology has not lost its purpose. More than merely maintaining a place in 'the field', the discipline is still committed to engagement with and exegesis on social life. The question that then confronts and confounds some contemporary anthropologists is how to execute their purpose now that their ship appears to have lost its moorings.

Once unaware of the power relations and contradictions implicit in conducting fieldwork in societies 'conquered by our own governments', anthropologists, for the most part, are now grappling with the history and politics that such a past has made for them. Their awareness of the incestuous relationship between colonisation, military power and knowledge production has been brought on in part by global, political and philosophical factors. Here decolonisation movements and literature (Césaire 1972; Fanon 1963), polemical and scholarly critique (Deloria 1969; Said 1978; Hymes 1969; Medicine 1971) as well as the conceptualisation of the discipline as a discourse, and the understanding that no discourse is value-free (Asad 1979; Foucault 1980) have fed into the radical reconstruction that is underway in anthropological literature. This reconstruction is marked by experimentation with form as well as the recasting of ethnography as cultural criticism (Marcus and Fischer 1986), calls for politically engaged and collaborative work (Biolsi and Zimmerman 1997: 17–18), 'rapprochement' or collaboration across disciplines (Cohn 1980) and the overall feeling, for some, of an ongoing 'crisis' (Said 1989: 205–6; Marcus and Fischer 1986: 7–16), or a spell of debilitating experimentation with passing fads and fashions (Salzman 1994: 35).

Much of contemporary anthropology, then, issues from a tension between objective and more subjective models of cultural analysis – the two models that are often invoked when explaining how anthropology 'should' be done, now that the ship appears to have lost its moorings. Working within this tension – one that is an ongoing and perhaps endless source of debate in the social sciences – Michael Jackson, in *Paths Toward a Clearing* (1988), removes us from the disagreements and directs us instead to a new space and method for anthropological inquiry. This space is cleared by Jackson's argument for a phenomenologically driven form of cultural analysis. Toward this end, he reminds us, first, that thought is a way into and through the world – that it is like a movement to a clearing. Taking up Adorno, he likens this movement to a 'human praxis' – a dialectic that carries us from one idea to the next, testing our

vocabulary against the exigencies of experience. This testing of vocabulary against the living of life carries one to 'a clearing' – a space not yet
specified by Jackson but one that may be understood in cultural and ultimately *political* terms. The political hues to Jackson's clearing here may
be interpreted as an opening into the poetics of possibility, of cultural
creation – a space within a world whose horizons are open, where Indian
people may be, finally, as we are.

   Jackson's central preoccupations in this text are those theories of
knowledge and power that should inform anthropological analysis. His
quarrel is with the 'scientific' tradition in anthropology that purports to
be objective and value-free, affording us the ultimate and absolute final-
ities of truth. This latter view of anthropology and its method has been
critiqued heavily by native and non-native scholars alike for making
objects of living people, their culture, their place and their way in the
world. In objectifying Indians and other anthropological subjects,
anthropological discourse has reproduced and, some have argued, perpetuated colonial relationships of power (Deloria 1969; Hymes 1969;
Asad 1973; Said 1978). Although Jackson's text is not prompted specifically by the politics of knowledge or the relationships of power that characterise the colonial legacy, his work offers some important channels for
students of culture and others who desire a way into the world that is different and perhaps more just than it was in the past. It is for this reason
that anthropology, colonialism and Michael Jackson serve as entry ways
into this discussion of contemporary Mohawk political praxis.

Mohawk Nationhood and Narrativity

Rather than focus his efforts on the style of anthropological discourse, as
some contemporary anthropologists have done (Crapanzano 1986; Clifford 1986), Jackson maps out instead a phenomenological approach to
writing culture that abandons the precepts of objectivity entirely and
engages instead the flux of lived experience. His way into experience is
'radical empiricism', a methodology that has as its unit of study the
'plenum of existence' in which all ideas and intellectual constructions
are grounded' (Jackson 1988: 3). For Jackson, radical empiricism will be
a method with which one will experience, interpret and write culture. As
such, Jackson's anthropological practice conjoins the intellectual ancestry of the discipline to the discursive practice of the subject as well as the
subjectivity of the analyst. In weaving these elements together in the
writing of culture, the understanding and 'way of being in the world' of
the anthropologist count as much as that of the subject, as each shapes
the other in the defining moments of their exchange. The result of such
an exchange produces renderings of social experience that lodge

'anthropological subjects' as active agents in the representation of their culture rather than static objects of scholarly contemplation.

There is much, then, in Jackson's work that Indians should be concerned with. In placing an overall premium on the dialectics of being – the currency of exchanges between people – Jackson's approach to culture and his methodological suggestions may deliver us from the necessary essentialisms that beset Indian people (and perhaps all former subject-peoples) in the representation of their culture.[6] As well, by engaging the flux of lived life, and having as its premise the untidiness and fluxist nature of culture, radical empiricism acknowledges the partiality and shifting nature of knowledge, a partiality that Abu-Lughod likens to 'standing on shifting ground' (1991: 142) – a perspective that embraces the politics of honesty (and humility). This promise offers cultural analysts and Indians a way out of the static and necessarily reified representations of identities and cultures that earlier approaches to cultural analysis demanded.

It is for that reason that I take radical empiricism toward the day-to-day politics of nationhood in Kahnawake. Although Jackson is not a Mohawk, nor is his work informed by the plenum of their existence within the nation-state of Canada, his particular attention to lived experience has much to offer contemporary studies of Mohawk nationhood. Jackson's arguments and suggestions bear on the particular concerns of contemporary anthropological practice – a practice beset by a 'crisis in representation' – by placing *experience* at the very centre of his analysis. But more importantly, perhaps, his analysis bears on this other *crisis in conversation* – issues pertaining to native–state relations, where the premium is on reconciling various solitudes and ways of being. Thus we have an alternative to the integrating, as Kymlicka would have it, 'minority nationalist' model of ethnic relations within a broader framework of the state, by listening in substantive ways to the voices and experiences within. Here is a philosophically and sensorially tuned encounter, one that attempts an understanding through listening, observing, entering into a conversation with one another through an attempt at engaging what was commonly misunderstood and misconstrued – *experience*. This centring of experience in analysis by Jackson resonates with native claims for sovereignty (if we may talk as well about exercising control over representations of native culture as well as control over native land) as much of our lives are lived with the knowledge that our experiences have simply not mattered much. And other experiences clearly have mattered more – witness canonical notions of history, literature and curricula. The marginalisation of certain experiences and narratives over others alone 'tells us' that there are some stories that simply matter more than others. If we were to argue, then, from a generic 'native' perspective we might say (and rather simply at that) that there are 'facts' that we own, knowledge that we share and, among these facts, that the land that we live on now is ours because (some of us believe that) we come from the earth. Furthermore, this land, which gave us our life and our subsistence and brought us into being, belongs by the miraculous interplay of history, luck, force, acquiescence and in some cases, outright battle, to outside people who claim it now as their own. This is a fact to us and is fiction to far too many others. We live then in a tension that must be resolved. Our questions are more immediate and more pressing perhaps than the philosophical and practice-oriented issues of Jackson, but there is resonance still.

It is because of these facts that we own, the history and knowledge that we share of this past, that *nationhood* is a terribly important concept for Indians and academics alike. It is the prism through which many Indians view their historical experiences, themselves and their aspirations and thought – 'nationhood' in the contemporary native landscape may be understood as a movement toward a clearing. It is a Herculean gesture away from the enframing efforts of the Canadian state, toward a place and a state of being that is our own. As with culture and the analytical approach that Jackson is arguing for, the culture and issues of native peoples can best be examined in terms of the lived experience of nationhood. In order to appreciate that experience, one must take account of the shared set of meanings that are negotiated through narrations – through the voices and structural conditions that constitute selfhood. In order to appreciate these representations, analysts must examine the words and stories that people share with each other; to the ways that Indians render their own experiences into being; how they represent themselves and their people *to each other.*

Kahnawake

This chapter is concerned with narrations of nationhood among contemporary Indians in Canada. My research centred on the volatile question of citizenship or 'membership' among Mohawks of Kahnawake. As a reserve community Kahnawake rests on land that is held in trust for the members of the community by the Canadian state (what is known as 'crown land'). It is through the provisions of the *Indian Act* that the Mohawks of Kahnawake, like those Indians belonging to other reserve communities in Canada, receive their right to reside on the 12 000 acres known as the Kahnawake Indian Reserve.[7] Their names appear on a federal registry of Indians in Canada as well as a band-controlled registry that accords them the rights of status Indians in Canada.[8]

As a reserve community of indigenous people within a settler society Kahnawake is surrounded symbolically and materially by the governmental structures and peoples that inhabit the political landscape of Canada. Situated in the southern part of the francophone province of Quebec, the municipalities that surround the community – St Constant, Delson and Chateauguay – are largely white and francophone communities. Montreal, a large multicultural city, is approximately ten minutes away from the community by vehicle. The proximity of non-native people to the community exacerbates a sense of urgency about the community's sovereignty and identity. Although Kahnawake has its own police force made up of community members and native people from other parts of Canada, the issue of policing and jurisdiction is a constant source of concern, with community members adamant that neither the provincial police force nor police forces from the surrounding areas have a right to enter the boundaries of the community unless invited.[9]

Although surrounded by seemingly foreign peoples with governmental structures that have legal claim to their land and the operations of their community, Kahnawake behave as other nations do and attempt, at every turn, to exercise authority and control over the affairs of the reserve. 'Behaving as other nations do' requires that *Kahnawakero:non* maintain a strong sense of themselves as a distinct people with rights and obligations that flow from their distinctiveness. To maintain a sense of themselves as a nation, *Kahnawakero:non* shape their historical and contemporary experiences through discursive practice – a practice that uses the key tropes of 'being Indian' and having 'rights'. These tropes are tied to social and cultural praxis by working in the service of identity construction and maintenance for Mohawk individuals – a process that not only signals to individuals the social ideal, but suffuses everyday life with a sense of nationhood.

'Talking' nationhood and being Indian are not recent predilections or cultural inventions for *Kahnawakero:non*. As part of the larger matrix of Iroquois experience in what is now the Northeastern US, the Mohawks of Kahnawake are splintered from one of the Six (formerly five) Nations Confederacy, the Iroquois or *Haudenosaunee* ('People of the Longhouse'). The *Haudenosaunee* are a confederated group of Indian nations that militarily dominated what is now the Northeastern US before contact. The people of Kahnawake, along with Mohawks in Akwesasne and Kanehsatake (two other Mohawk reserves in the Province of Quebec), share a history of participation in the Confederacy and use this experience to construct and maintain their collective identity as a distinct people within the larger political and social geographies of Canada and the US. *Kahnawakero:non* also draw from the Confederacy of the past to recreate alternative forms of religion and government in the contemporary era (this structure is known today in the community as 'the Longhouse').

Kahnawakero:non have a strong sense of themselves as a distinct nation that is based on their pre-contact political experience and their more recent interactions with the governments of settler societies in Canada and the US. This has been documented in anthropological and historical research (Voget 1951; Hauptman 1986), and has recently been the explicit focus of a contemporary study in political science (Alfred 1995). Although each of these works has documented or focused on structural or institutional elements of Mohawk and Iroquois consciousness of self and society, analysis of Kahnawake's nationhood thus far has not examined the critical role of discursive or cultural practice of community members in constructing their identity and sense of being in the world.

I focus here on discursive practice or 'what people say' to each other. The focus on discursive practice flows from the different premise that Mohawk nationhood is built upon. Ethnicity and structural inequality are often the starting points in analyses that examine nationalism. Rather than use these as an entangled premise for all cultural activity and arguing from there that ethnicity = ethnogenesis (and ethnogenesis = nationalism), I will examine Kahnawake nationalism through the words of those people who produce it. Towards this end I will not be focusing wholly upon interactions with external forces (a precondition for the creation of 'ethnic consciousness'), or ignoring these interactions altogether. By privileging the interactions that Mohawks are having with each other, rather than those that they have with the 'outside', I hope to return nationalism to the web of meanings that comprise culture – the plenum of experience, rather than ethnicity.

Citizenship, Blood and Belonging

Indian reserves in Canada have only had control over their membership lists since 1985, when the federal government returned the authority to determine band membership from Indian and Northern Affairs Canada to reserve communities. Membership in an Indian community carries rights and obligations to that community. Band members have the right to build a home on the reserve, reside on the reserve, vote in band council elections and have their social welfare managed by the band. In order to maintain their membership on the band list *Kahnawakero:non* are required since 1981 to 'marry in' (Alfred 1995: 163–77). 'Marrying in' means that in order to maintain their place on the list of members in the community, individuals are required to marry another person who has at least 50 per cent Indian blood.

The 50 per cent blood quantum is replete with problems within Kahnawake. These are problems that revolve around the dual axes of 'rights' and identity and are manifest as disagreements over what criteria should be used for the granting of membership, on who an Indian is and, more specifically, what a Mohawk is and should be. Questions that then confront *Kahnawakero:non* when contemplating membership include: what should be the criteria for determining membership? To whom should it be given? Should membership be given to the children of two Indian parents? To children with one parent? What if that parent had one white parent? Furthermore, how far in one's lineage should the Mohawk Council of Kahnawake go to calculate their quantum? Why even use blood when there are traditional Iroquois practices and options such as adoption and the clan system reckoning of descent? Should rights to membership be given to anyone who does not have a clan or a commitment to Mohawk culture and community?

These questions and the resulting discussions around membership speak from and to the historical experiences that shape Kahnawake's collective sense of self. Here we will find interactions with the Canadian state that provided *Kahnawakero:non* with an enduring sense of mistrust and concomitant enclosure. At the same time *Kahnawakero:non* have had friendships, marriages and alliances with non-natives that now make the matter of membership a politically and an emotionally loaded matter to contemplate, let alone adjudicate.

From here, both self and nation are braided into past experiences and stories of those experiences (Kerby 1991: 1; Bhabha 1990: 1–7; 1994: 7; Connerton 1989: 16–17). This past is tied to ways of seeing and being in the world that are not 'pure' – modes of being that enter both indigenous and 'statist' notions of being into a dialogue, producing the on-going, processual and syncretic culture that is used forcefully to construct and maintain one's self and nation.

Here I have the experience and narrations of *Kahnawakero:non* that speak directly and sometimes obliquely to the issue of membership, but most definitely to notions of 'being Indian' and 'having rights'.[10] We will go first to a bingo hall, where one person's presence and identity was contested in an indirect but forceful way by another community member. As well, we will go to a band council meeting, one of the monthly meetings of the elected council and community where the subject of membership was discussed. A text then from *Onkwarihwa'shon:'a*, a monthly newsletter that is distributed by the Mohawk Council of Kahnawake to update community members on internal matters, which will provide a direct linkage made by the elected council between law, membership and Mohawk sovereignty. Finally, we will return to a meeting of the elected council again as they share their platforms for the then-upcoming elections in July 1996. Using a radically empirical method, these narratives have been provided to 'revalidate the everyday life of ordinary people, to tell their stories in their own words' (Jackson 1996: 36).

The Super Bingo

It is the summer of 1993 and we are sitting at the end of a long table in the Super Bingo. The hall has yet to fill up and Daniel and Martha, who work at the bingo, are smoking cigarettes and we are talking. I am waiting to play and killing time with them. The bingo is divided into service and security employees. The service employees, with the exception of Robert and Daniel, are women. The security guards are all men and are mostly young. They carry walkie-talkies and look for cellular phones, food brought in against regulations and other offences. They seem more interested, however, in checking out the young women who work there. Their furtive glances to one another and the purple bruises on their necks (which are also against employee regulations) attest to romance, and we are trying to figure out which security and which service staff are involved. We are watching for these signifiers while recalling the contours and the taste of 'zeppoles' in Brooklyn and the future of David Dinkins after the upcoming mayoral elections in New York City. Our conversation is redirected, however, to one service employee because she (in her thirties) has just walked in and is wearing an almost-against-regulations white leotard. We joke about the 'crack' security team and whether they will be able to concentrate on their work.

A man came near our table and Daniel knows he is close by. He didn't want to turn his head so he asked Martha: 'Is that 135?' (the man's name, as far as I know it).

Martha exclaimed: 'Oh yes, it's that dirty, skinny son of a bitch – 30 per cent!'

Now we are looking at her, trying not to laugh, listening, stealing glances at each other – where did that come from?

'His mother wasn't Indian and his father was barely Indian, he is lucky if he is even 30 per cent! Look at him in that "Warriors" jacket – who the hell does he think he is?! He's not even an Indian and he's got his jacket on, walking around here like that.'

Daniel and I are laughing out loud now, oblivious to the hickeys, David Dinkins and 135 himself. We are 'rolling', so to speak, and Martha is just catching her breath, she is excited with her information and the effect it is having on us. She then pointed a jewelled finger at Daniel and then at me (now dabbing a mess of make-up from under my eyes) and she said: 'Don't worry, you two – I know your mother [points at Daniel] and I know your father [points at me] – and I know your halves are whole.'

We suddenly stopped laughing and Martha continued, unfazed. She continued with the details of '135's' allegedly dubious family tree. I don't think either of us started to worry until then.

Band Council Meeting

The Knights of Columbus Hall is almost full. Families are positioned in their usual seats; men are standing by the entrance to the hall with their hands in their pockets. People are smoking and drinking coffee out of styrofoam cups. The meeting has been going on for about half an hour. The chiefs are answering questions about membership.

'What are we going to do', one woman asks, 'with so and so? He is with that white woman and they have a child – aren't they supposed to leave? How come so and so had to leave and he gets to stay? They married after '81, he knew what he was getting in to; how come the Peacekeepers don't go to his house?'

One chief gets up and says, 'I know who you are talking about and he has been told. He knows he is supposed to leave, he has been asked to leave but we have to as a community let him know the Law [Mohawk Law on Membership].'

There are more questions now, about individuals and who they are with, about the Law itself and how it is applied. Some people are standing when they ask their questions and voices are raised several times.

One community member says something about Council members and one of the Chiefs says: 'I know that this affects each and every one of you, each of us has someone in their family . . . me too, I have family in the States and they married out and they have children. I tell them you can't come back here, you have to know that . . . so don't think I don't know.'

He sits down and somebody brings up a *Kahnawakero:non* who married a non-native man in 1983 and her legal case against the MCK. One of the chiefs stands up and elaborates on the case. A man standing at the back of the Knights says: 'We don't have anything in place to take care of those people [C-31s].[11] Who is gonna take care of them? If we had a Traditional government in place they would be taken care of, if we base things here on anything else but the *Kaienerakowa* then we will be racist.'[12]

A woman seated near the back of the hall reminded us: 'There was a 1979 mandate towards Traditional government. What happened to that? You know, there is no stigma on half-breeds whose fathers are Indian, but if you are a C-31 in this community you are stigmatised and nobody talks about that. Why don't you people [at the meeting] throw down *The National Enquirer* and read the *Indian Act*? It's all there, why we are in this mess. How can we deal with these contradictions?'

An older woman then stands up. She is sitting by the chiefs at the front of the Knights. She speaks in Mohawk, her voice is loud and she seems angry. Her voice is rising and I ask my auntie what she is saying. She shushes me.

The woman says in English, wagging her finger around: 'Did you ever see those white women come on the reserve and *ask* [her emphasis] if they could marry an Indian?! [The non-Indian women who married Indian men before 1981.] Should our women have to do that – have a paper saying if they are widowed or divorced?!' [In order to get rights to residency on the reserve C-31s have to prove to the MCK that they are widowed or divorced.]

The Grand Chief stands up and says that the Mohawk Law on Membership should be a *method* [his emphasis], not a code. He then says: 'If a traditional system is appropriate, then so be it.'

Onkwarihwa'shon:'a ('Our Affairs')

Racism. In recent times, we have been accused of outright racism whenever we made any attempt to deny certain rights to those who are simply not entitled to those rights in the first place. Here, it has to be very clearly stated that there is a big difference between being backed into a corner and being guilty of racism. However, the tricky part is that, despite any such difference, the question of who is entitled to what must still be answered in terms of who is actually Indian. The aspect of the debate on membership is fixated on the term 'blood quantum' . . . Yes, race is involved in the matter Native Rights [sic]. And yes, it becomes a matter of who is entitled to those rights, by virtue of the kind of blood running through their veins. However, it is NOT about who is the purer of the species. It is about wrongs done through five hundred years of history to an entire race of people. It is about not allowing this to go on any more, and it is about putting things right once and for all, before they get any worse and a whole race of people is eradicated. It is about justice, and if nothing else at all, it is about survival. Indeed, we have a long, long journey ahead of us, if we're ever going to get this mess cleaned up. At times, journeys can be agonising, and clean-ups can be as messy as the mess itself. In any case the Mohawk Council of Kahnawake and the Membership Committee are duty-bound to follow the wishes of the Mohawk People of Kahnawake, and no-one else. In this, I can only ask that our own people contribute in any way they can, to the setting straight of the membership issue, and that for once, non-Native powers honor their part of the Two Row Wampum Treaty and stop meddling in our affairs.[13] *Nia:wen* (thank you). (Chief Allen Paul 1995: 5–6)

Candidates Night

It is Candidates Night and I am sitting with my auntie, some cousins and my cousin's wife in the Knights of Columbus. We are a little jittery because a family member is running for Council. We got to the Knights early and worked on his platform, feverishly jotting ideas on index cards while his wife scolded him for waiting until the last minute to prepare his speech. The meeting begins with all but four of the candidates present.

A name is randomly selected by the moderator of the evening and the platforms begin.

The first candidate is a man in his thirties. This is his second time running for Council and he is very prepared. He has a text that he reads from and an obviously rehearsed platform. He lost the last election by 40 votes and seems likely to win next week. He weaves the importance of education into his platform and shares his experience of having to borrow money and fundraise in order to go to school in the States. I make a note to myself to vote for him next week. The platforms continue with most candidates going over their allotted ten minutes. One talked about land, another talked about his past, another talked about reform and another talked about the curbs. I was tired, taking notes the whole time, my eyes bleary from cigarette smoke and I was losing the taste in my mouth because of too much coffee.

It was Sak's turn. He walked to the mike and raised his hand, '*Kwe Kwe*,' he bellowed, and smiled while waving to the audience. I jolted upright. Much to my surprise, he started to sing a song in Mohawk to the people. The words, although unknown to me, were sung to the *very* recognisable tune by Hank Williams, 'Hey Good Looking, What'cha got Cooking?' Everybody started laughing, looking at him, glancing at each other – what was he doing, what was he saying? Without giving us time to talk to each other he started his platform. He had no paper, no index cards and no unifying thread that I could identify at the time. He was telling stories, talking about language and the need to speak Mohawk: 'Why don't our people even try to speak their language, I mean, really try? It is not enough to tell your children "*satien*" [sit down!] or "*tohsa*" [stop it!]; *make full sentences*, for heaven's sake! I speak to young people and I say "*Kwe Kwe*" and you know what they say back to me? They say "Hi" [at this point he did an imitation of an uptight and affronted person, curled up his arms a little and screwed up his face into displeasure] and then they run away from me. Don't you want your children to be able to speak in *full sentences*? How come these Chinese who come here speak their language to their children and their children speak two languages? How come they can do it and we can't do it? They even come to Kahnawake and speak *our language*.' He now starts speaking Mohawk with a Mandarin accent – maybe alluding to the co-owners of Way Ta Le, a Chinese restaurant and take-out that opened on the reserve – he milks it more because everyone is laughing. I am thinking he is like Charlie Chaplin and an ironworker all in one.

And then he said, out of the blue: 'I don't like blood quantum, you could live on the Farm [farmland off Highway 120 going towards St Constant, remote in relation to 'Town' which is more central, where the main highway and two iron crosses are] your entire life and then come into

Town and people say "*Kwa*! Who's that?! I don't know him!'" He continues: 'Then next thing you know, he is listed at 47 per cent because
nobody knows his face . . . Being an Indian isn't whose band number is
lower [does an imitation of someone bragging in a whiny voice, 'My band
number is lower than your band number'], or how many beads you put
in your ears – it's your ancestry . . . *I could tell you a story about membership
that would break your heart, but I won't.*'

Sak sings more songs, and speaks in Mohawk. People are laughing and
I'm laughing too. I stop taking notes. I am listening to him and watching
him. He is imitating us – he is making fun – and in doing so, he is teaching us what being Mohawk *is*. He is holding up a mirror to us and we are
laughing at ourselves.

Post-candidates Night: the Phone Call

My good friend is in Albany, New York, working at the Iroquois Indian
Museum. He called me after the meeting and we are talking about the
platforms. He wanted to know what they said. He wants to know who, if
anybody, said anything about education. I tell him what he wants to know
and we agree that it is a good thing that there are so many young people
running.

'We need some young blood in there,' he says, and I agree. I tell him
about Sak's song and his platform. We are laughing at the platform and
at me trying to imitate Sak imitating everyone else. My friend says that it's
so good that he is running for Council because he will really push language. Sak was a Mohawk language teacher and we like him for this. I ask
my friend why Sak said that there was a story about membership that
would break our hearts. Does he know what Sak meant by that? Does he
know that story?

He answered: 'Don't you know about his family?' And then he told me
the story. Now I know.

This paper began with an argument and ended with a story. It was this
argument: that political theory desires a conversation with Indians, that
this conversation is something that might make Canada a better place to
be. This conversation, we might all agree, should be predicated on listening, and so it was to the problematic of indigenous nationhood, an
Indian means of expression, that we turned. We looked then at anthropology and its structural antecedents to arrive, some might say strangely,
at a place where we could listen to indigenous voices that speak, walk and
talk the stuff of nationhood. It was argued that anthropology is shaped
still by colonialism – that the geo-political relationships that gave it purpose, shaped its language and gave it some authority have changed, but

the impetus for research has remained the same. Anthropology remains committed to social engagement and exegesis on that engagement. The effects of conquest, however, are now woven into its preoccupations and discourse. Much of the production of text in the discipline is therefore articulated to the concomitant 'crisis' in representation – the question of how anthropologists are to speak *about* people without speaking *for* people – how the discipline is to manage its information and its identity in the face of movements for native sovereignty at the level of scholarly representation. The result of this dialectic between anthropology and local life has created an anthropological praxis that is punctuated by introspection, reflexivity, revision, creativity, nervousness and, at times, reactionary discourses. The discussion of these issues brought us to Kahnawake and these stories – stories that are laced together with hopes and desires for control and authority over life – in a naming and management of the issues that are our colonial inheritance.

The point of sharing these narratives was to contribute something to this conversation, to press into play the usefulness of a radically empirical method when considering contemporary culture and nationhood. As well, to share the interior frontiers of Mohawk nationhood, to step upon the terrain of agreement, discord and hopeful contemplation that unites *Kahnawakero:non* in their search for a way through the mass of contradictions that one interlocutor at a community meeting referred to. The intricacies of these stories – the names that *Kahnawakero:non* have for each other, the categories that they place on each other's being – may be lost on you, but that is fine. You have here a sense that rights and contemporary Indian identity are enmeshed – that they are tied to stories and these stories are tied to ourselves. These narratives illustrate that Mohawk nationhood is shaped through what people say to each other, by what they say about each other – they illustrate how 'place' in the world is staked out and guarded through the defining moments of shared experience and the words that then give shape to this experience.

Leaving the Knights of Columbus again, and only for a moment, I want to return once again to political theory, to anthropology, to Jackson, and ask if this praxis that he talks about – the traffic from one concept to another, one emotion to another – can this ever be a directed, and yet miraculously neutral, innocent and value-free process? Can we ever go into our own reserves and political meetings and report on these events? Can we take into account the multiplicity of intentions that inform individual and social action and our own experience of it all and then suddenly, by some miracle, disengage? Is it possible for us to move across the terrain of knowledge production free from the constraints of specificity, locality and experience? And, is it possible to listen to each other in a substantive and meaningful way, as Tully and others are trying to do?

Can we liken the thinking and living of life mapped out by Jackson to the path of Kahnawake's debates over membership? Each is a process that tests individual knowledge, emotion and vocabulary against the exigencies of the present. Each is informed by the desire for a future that is in some ways better than the one we left behind. Indeed, I think that we can. Are Kahnawake's attempts at finding a way back into the world – to find a clearing – an objective and value-free affair? Can we liken their attempts to find this clearing, much like the social and cultural analysis of the past, to shots that are fired into a universe of abstractions by a remarkably dispassionate marksman? Occurring at the intersection of experience and cognition, *thought*, like nationhood, is a process, and as such is shaped from social interactions, sensorial deposits as well as personal and collective desires. It is not objective, nor is it a random praxis. Like the marksman and the community members in Kahnawake, you too will take shots that are shaped by these lessons: memory, forgetting, the sense and specificity of life and those around you. In these ways the marksman and the Mohawk stand on common ground with us. He is like us – he squares himself on the ground that he stands on, he takes aim and he fires. We watch the shot cut through the sky until it fades into sudden dissolution – we listen for a response from somewhere out there. He looks to the ground. We wait together for an answer.

CHAPTER 7

(De)Constructing the Politics of Indigeneity

Manuhuia Barcham

These Māori today
are not Māori any more
I don't know what they are
*Apirana Taylor, 'Feelings
and memories of a
Kuia' (Taylor 1989)*

One could easily be forgiven, in light of the apparent success of programs of reconciliation and rapprochement between indigenous
peoples and settler governments in recent years, for thinking that the
worst of the colonial legacy has been put behind us, and that – apart
from the occasional deviation along the way – all that remained was
mainly a matter of fine-tuning strategies of implementation. Recent
struggles over the allocation of pre-settlement Treaty assets and over the
validity of emergent forms of indigenous organisational form in New
Zealand have, however, brought this utopian view into question. The
tensions leading to the emergence of these struggles can be traced to
fundamental disagreements over issues of identity and authenticity,
including the questioning of who and what constitutes an 'authentic'
indigenous subject, and debate over the forms and configuration that
'legitimate' indigenous institutions can take. Indigenous–settler relations are thus an ongoing dynamic, with many issues still remaining to
be resolved, the most important of which at this point in time appears
to be the problematisation of indigenous identity.[1] These problems of
'indigenous identity' are, in turn, symptomatic of a more fundamental
deficiency in current theories and praxis of indigenous rights: the
recognition of difference only in terms of the maintenance of prior
identity. In their rush to accommodate the notion of indigenous rights

– and its associated 'politics of difference' – theorists and practitioners alike have created and reified an ahistorical idealisation of the indigenous self whereby the constitution of oneself as an 'authentic' indigenous self has been conflated with specific ahistorical assumptions concerning the nature of indigeneity, a process intricately linked to the continued subordination of difference to identity.[2]

The prioritisation of identity over difference leads to the necessarily synchronic predication that bodies (be they concrete or abstract, singular or plural) exist in an ahistorical essentialism wherein reality is collapsed into a timeless present such that what *is* now is the same as what *was*, which in turn is the same as what *will be*, thereby effectively excluding any chance of recognising notions of social transformation and change. The inability of current political and judicial frameworks to recognise the legitimacy of difference not predicated upon the maintenance of a prior identity (Patton 1995a; 1995b) has meant that the implementation of official frameworks for the recognition of indigenous rights in New Zealand has led to the exclusion and delegitimisation of associational forms of Māori organisation. The atemporality of such official recognitions of difference has led to the reification of certain neo-traditional Māori organisational forms to a privileged position wherein they have come to constitute *the* definitional means by which Māori are identified as 'authentically' indigenous. While this process has led to the creation of a voice for 'authentic' indigenous claims, it has also led to the coterminous silencing of the 'inauthentic' (Griffiths 1994) and the alienation of many Māori people whose identity is shaped more by the aftermath of colonialism and their disadvantaged position in New Zealand society than in terms of a tradition-orientated model of 'authentic' identity. The prioritisation of identity over difference has led to the creation of an existential dichotomy of *being* and *non-being* that has effectively excluded recognition of the dynamic process of *becoming*. There is thus an urgent need for theorists and practitioners of indigenous rights to come to terms with the continued subordination of difference to notions of identity, both in order to resolve the practical tensions inherent in the current process, and to enable theories and policies to emerge that take seriously the fact that cultures and societies necessarily change over time, providing a firmer ontological foundation for a 'politics of difference'. This chapter argues that this new foundation can, ironically, be found within the very body of work known best for its anti-foundationalism – poststructuralism. In doing so I challenge the validity of political theory that speaks in terms of abstract rights without recognition, or regard to, the fact of the continually changing nature of the specific, situated experiences of those individuals and groups whose plight led to the creation of those very same transcendental principles.

Theorising Difference: Temporal Anomalies

There is a long tradition in Western thought – from Platonic notions of immanence through to Kantian concepts of transcendental idealism – wherein identity is prioritised over difference. The genesis for this tradition emerged from an attempt to escape the paradoxical situation that, while the identity of any given thing is dependent upon its differences from other things, the existence of those differences themselves is in turn dependent upon the possession of an identity by those things as particular things. In overcoming this paradox, Western thought has, particularly since the Enlightenment, taken identity as the definitional element of the relationship. Difference was placed in a position of subordination to identity. This subordination, however, has led to problems in more recent times, as various minority groups attempt to assert their right to difference. The ensuing problems associated with the subordination of difference to identity are two-fold.

The first complication arises from the fact that the atemporality of difference predicated on the maintenance of a prior identity implicitly, and perhaps unintentionally, reduces group identity to a dichotomy of '*being*' or '*non-being*', thereby effectively excluding recognition of the possibility of '*becoming*'. The prioritisation of identity leads to the construction of an ideal of community that fails to recognise the possibilities of alternative forms of community identity. This static notion of community then precludes the right of communities to undergo historical change. The inability of these theories to take into account changes in both the discursive outlines and changing substantive institutional and organisational forms that groups take over time leads to the second complication. In the transference of ideas of group identity to the level of policy implementation, an operational 'politics of difference' based on this atemporal dichotomy of *being/ non-being* may lead – through the synchronic reification of community – to the exclusion and associated increase in levels of oppression among the very groups that the 'politics of difference' were created to assist. The prioritisation of identity over difference thus acts to restrict the possible forms that identity can take, as identification becomes a process structured around the recognition of fixed selves – wherein lived existence is devalued as subordinate to the idea of an ahistorical ideal of community – a process therefore effectively limiting the capacity of these theories to truly recognise difference.

The practical problems associated with atemporal conceptions of difference are no more apparent than in the field of indigenous rights, a field where academic and policy-orientated definitions of Māori and other Fourth World peoples are, more often than not, derived from notions of indigeneity contingent upon the possession of 'authentic'

cultural norms and traditions. It is with regard to these predicated conceptions of indigeneity that the problem lies, as these 'facts' are intricately linked to the conceptualisation of identity as a state – an action
that has, in turn, led to the creation of an implicit belief among many
that the adaptation of an indigenous minority to social change necessarily lessens the indigenous character of that minority.[3] The implications of
this are profound, for the majority of theoretical and empirical work on
Fourth World peoples is predicated on this timeless, essentialised conception of indigeneity, yet the diachronic nature of human institutions
undermines its foundation. The apparent contradiction between the
postmodern acceptance of the contingent nature of modern identities
and subjectivities and the essentialised basis to claims of indigeneity is an
example of the manifold tensions underlying the current discourse on
indigenous rights. Indigeneity is taken as a 'natural' and unproblematic
category where in reality it is, as are all identities, socially constructed
and historically contingent.[4] Indigenous rights are thus generally seen as
being dependent upon an ahistorical, hence synchronic, basis. Problems
arise, however, when this interpretation of indigeneity is used as the basis
for policy creation, as has been the case in New Zealand.

   While recognition by the New Zealand government of the validity of
the principle of *tino rangatiratanga* (indigenous rights)[5] has resulted in the
implementation of a wide variety of policies and legislative instruments –
an endeavour that has acted to empower many – it has also led to an
unfortunate polarisation of Māori society between those who argue that
the traditional institutions of iwi (the tribe) are the only 'true' institutional bases of Māori identity, and those who argue that the diverse social
circumstances that characterise modern Māori means that not all Māori
aspirations can now be found totally within tribal agendas. Tensions
inherent within this ideological division have culminated in recent years
in legal battles over the allocation of pre-settlement Treaty assets and the
continuing controversy over the funding opportunities available to non-
iwi Māori organisations. While at a superficial level these struggles are
often dismissed as merely altercations over funding, a close reading of
these disputes reveals a much deeper problem at work. The effective delegitimisation of non-iwi groups can therefore be read as an example of the
practical problems inherent in the privileging of identity over difference.

Indigenous Rights and the Iwi-isation of Māori Society

The 1980s saw a period of considerable change in New Zealand government policy towards Māori. Policy then was characterised both by the
more formal recognition of the basis for indigenous rights in New
Zealand and the accompanying re-interpretation of these indigenous

rights as constituting a Treaty-based partnership between the Crown and iwi, an action that effectively excluded and delegitimised other forms of Māori community. Thus, while the government accepted that the positive recognition of difference was the basis of claims by Māori for indigenous rights, they nonetheless based this recognition upon the maintenance of earlier institutional and organisational identities. Government reports released during this period thus outlined the government's new policy position as being that *rangatiratanga* (indigenous rights) was to be exercised through iwi (Minister of Maori Affairs 1989), and that increased focus was to be placed upon iwi as the major player in Māori economic development (Minister of Maori Affairs 1990) as they were seen by the Government as constituting part of an unbroken line of cultural continuance as the legitimate receptacle of current Māori voices. The empowerment of indigenous rights in New Zealand has meant that indigeneity and indigenous identity there, as in North America, become subsumed under the rubric of the 'tribe', wherein membership of a tribe has become the 'foundation for the assertion of individual and group rights to land, services, or exemptions guaranteed by treaty or legislation' (Cornell 1988: 41).[6]

New Zealand government policy has played a pivotal role in the iwi-isation of Māori society as the conflation of Māori society with the institution of iwi was given legislative force through the codification in law of a number of specific legislative acts throughout the 1980s. One of the most important pieces of government legislation in this iwi-isation of Māori society was the *Treaty of Waitangi Amendment Act (1985)*. While the Act empowered Māori by allowing claims under the Treaty of Waitangi to be backdated to 1840, its implementation also meant that the tribal groups, territories and institutional forms acknowledged by the law were those that existed in 1840. This legislative Act thus played an important part in defining modern iwi as the legitimate descendants of Māori society in opposition to the perceived 'inauthenticity' of modern associational forms of Māori institutional organisation. Similarly, the passing of the *Runanga Iwi Act* (1990) meant that Iwi became strongly centralised in order to pass stringent government accountability standards.[7] And although the *Runanga Iwi Act* was repealed the same year it was passed, its legacy of iwi with a strong centralised structure remained. The passing of these various Acts to empower Māori through the recognition of their status as indigenous peoples meant, however, that by the beginning of the 1990s the New Zealand government had reached the conclusion that only traditional kin-based iwi were their Treaty partners, thereby creating a paradoxical process whereby the Crown construed the Treaty against 'Māori who are not organised in traditional tribal groupings, while at the same time acknowledging that such people have Treaty rights' (Waitangi

Tribunal 1998: 210). In the 1990s difficulties have arisen because more
than 80 per cent of Māori live in urban areas and for many of them, iwi
affiliation no longer plays an important part in their day-to-day lives
(Maaka 1997; Metge 1964).[8]

The Challenge of Urban Māori

Māori society is generally perceived as being traditionally organised
along a framework of kin-based descent groups. This 'traditional' organisation consists of three major social classificatory units: whānau (immediate and extended family), hapū (clan) and iwi (confederation of
hapū). This standard model of 'authentic' Māori socio-political organisation, from which iwi have (re)gained their current status is, however,
constructed largely on the basis of ethnographic data collected more
than a century after initial contact and which was in turn dependent
upon the ahistorical and objectivist assumptions common at the end of
the nineteenth century (Meijl 1994: 317; Webster 1975). These social
units were not completely discrete groups: the lines between them were
blurred and amorphous, with their size and functions varying widely
from region to region (Walker 1989: 35–52). The transformation of
Māori organisational forms and traditions from a pre-bureaucratic situation of Heraclitian flux to one of neo-Parmenidean stasis and ahistoric-
ity began from the very first point of contact with the west, wherein
records were kept of customs of the newly discovered peoples. Tribal territories and groups were later further crystallised and frozen in legislative space through their recording and subsequent reification in the
proceedings of the Native Land Court in the late nineteenth and early
twentieth centuries. This process was further compounded by the work
of various European scholars at the turn of the nineteenth century, such
as Elsdon Best and Percy Smith, who were hoping to salvage ethnographic histories of Māori traditions for the future, in their belief that the
spread of European modernity would lead to the gradual extinction and
disappearance of these customs. Certain Māori elite, such as Sir Apirana
Ngata and Sir Peter Buck, also played a key part in this process of temporal freezing with their concern to collect records of 'traditional' Māori
life at the turn of the century to demonstrate that these traditions were
eternally essential for Māori identities – past, present and future (Meijl
1996: 329–30). Māori traditions and organisational forms were thus
objectified and reconstituted in a timeless asynchronicity.

Iwi institutions can therefore be said to be no more authentic than
other forms of Māori associational organisation, a historical fact highlighted by Angela Ballara (1998) who demonstrated in a well-researched

book that hapū were the primary political and economic organisations of pre-European Māori society. Ballara asserted that the notion of iwi as an active political body wielding tribal sovereignty was a comparatively modern phenomenon that was not at all in keeping with the historical reality of the decline of the political power of Māori kin-based organisational forms from the point of colonisation onwards. Following the signing of the Treaty of Waitangi, the loss of their military power in the 1860s, and an unsuccessful attempt to establish a separate parliament, iwi and hapū found themselves at the end of the nineteenth century facing an ever-decreasing power base (Maaka 1997: 3).[9] Throughout most of the twentieth century iwi were thus relatively weak politically, and more a cultural institution than a political one.[10] The massive migration of Māori to the cities in search of jobs in the years following World War II further compounded the decreasing importance of traditional kin-based organisations to the everyday life of the majority of Māori.[11] Throughout this period, however, Māori maintained a distinct group identity, even in the face of the radical social restructuring that the shift to the urban environment entailed, and the need to create their own support networks in the absence of support from traditional social networks. The situation presented by urbanisation was thus the catalyst for the development of new forms of social institutions and organisational norms for Māori (Walker 1995a: 501).[12] It has been argued that urban Māori have been able to reconcile their new urban environment with the attachments of their past, with neither being to the exclusion of the other (Barcham 1998). However, the emergence of these strong urban Māori institutions has been at odds with official government interpretation of the ways in which indigenous rights will be exercised, due to the fact that the legislative environment up to this point in time has asserted that Treaty rights, apart from those of equal citizenship, are valid only for iwi – an assumption due to atemporal perceptions of difference that have manifested themselves in prejudicial funding decisions in favour of 'authentic' kin-based Māori organisations and against 'inauthentic' associational forms of Māori organisation.

Two recent disputes between Iwi Māori, the Crown and non-Iwi Māori demonstrate the practical problems inherent in approaching the recognition of difference in an atemporal manner. These two cases over the allocation of social welfare spending and the allocation of pre-settlement Treaty fishery assets illustrate the ways in which the practical implementation of policies of indigenous empowerment based on this atemporal recognition of difference have led to the exclusion of large numbers of the very people they were supposed to help, through the inability of this current framework to address notions of social change and transformation.

Social Welfare Spending and the 'Te Whānau o Waipareira' Trust

In accord with the New Zealand government's official policy of bi-culturalism, the government's Central Funding Agency (CFA) developed
protocols in the late 1980s and early 1990s for consultation with 'iwi'
(whom they defined as traditional kin-based tribal groups) over social
welfare funding decisions in recognition of their *rangatiratanga* – which
they, as a part of the institution of the Crown, were sworn to uphold.
Problems arose when certain Māori organisations who did not fit the
restrictive legislative criterion of an iwi, yet who felt they were entitled to
funding opportunities as Māori, were denied funding. One of these
organisations denied funding, the 'Te Whānau o Waipareira Trust' – a
non-iwi based organisation run by and for Māori in West Auckland –
argued that the CFA had established inappropriate policies and funding
procedures for meeting the needs of the Māori population of West Auckland because of the absence of any negotiation and consultation with
them – the representative body of West Auckland Māori. This absence of
negotiation and consultation, the Te Whānau o Waipareira Trust argued,
demonstrated that the Crown was not properly serving Māori interests in
West Auckland. Dissatisfied with their treatment by the CFA, the Trust
took their claim to the Waitangi Tribunal for arbitration.[13]

The Te Whānau o Waipareira Trust claimed that they possessed rights
under the Treaty of Waitangi as a Māori group exercising *rangatiratanga*.
The members of the Trust did not claim to be an iwi – defined as a 'traditional' tribal body – as it was not kin-based and did not possess a customary territory over which it exercised *mana whenua* (suzerainty),
although it did claim to be an iwi if this term was defined merely as 'a
people'. The Trust based its claim instead on the argument that its existence, and the community that it represented in its present form, were
the result of the efforts of West Auckland Māori over the last fifty years to
manage their affairs in a Māori way in an urban environment. The Trust
claimed to have gained the mandate to represent the non-tribal population of Māori in the West Auckland area through the operation of non-
tribal marae, and through annual general meetings which made the trust
fully accountable to the community.[14] Thus, the Trust argued, the non-
tribal Māori community of West Auckland had come together to exercise
rangatiratanga for its own purposes, and as the communities' chosen
institutional body, the Trust exercised 'a mandate in respect of a community of Māori who have come together for the purpose of maintaining
cultural integrity in an urban environment' (Waitangi Tribunal 1998:
14).

In contrast to the case put forward by the Trust, the Crown argued, on
behalf of the CFA, that the Trust was not an 'iwi' as the agency under-

stood the term, and therefore not considered a Treaty partner of the Crown, and so not entitled to consultation or special consideration. This argument was based upon the official stance of the CFA that (for the purposes of the *Children, Young Persons, and Their Families Act 1989* at least) only traditional kin-based groupings of Māori were in Treaty partnership with the Crown (Waitangi Tribunal 1998: 5). The Te Whānau o Waipareira Trust was disqualified under the *Children, Young Persons, and Their Families Act 1989* from being treated as an 'iwi social service' because it was not kin-based, and was only able to be treated as a charitable trust for funding purposes and not as a Treaty partner. The Crown thus explicitly denied the Trust recognition as the legitimate representatives of the Māori community of West Auckland.

This restrictive interpretation by the New Zealand government of the recognition of difference, such that the recognition of indigenous rights was only accepted through the maintenance of prior identities, has resulted in the effective exclusion of one of the largest Māori organisations in the country from representation as a legitimate 'indigenous' institution. Moreover, this interpretative exclusion has the potential for even greater political, social and economic ramifications for the New Zealand Māori population, as hinted at in the massive amounts of monies now being made available in the treaty-settlement process.

Pre-settlement Treaty Fisheries Assets

In September 1992 the government signed a deal giving Māori $150 million worth of commercial fisheries assets and 20 per cent of future fisheries quota allocations. The deal allowed for the Waitangi Fisheries Commission to distribute $200 million worth of assets it held before the settlement to various Māori organisations. In return, Māori fishing rights as recognised under earlier fisheries legislation were to be wiped off. The Fisheries Commission held the view, however, that since the settlement was in exchange for fishing rights that belonged to iwi, the settlement could only go to iwi. It was up to iwi to decide how those assets were distributed.

Iwi groups also argued that since the fisheries assets were a Treaty-based property right they must therefore remain in iwi hands.[15] Non-iwi groups however, particularly urban based Māori organisations, claimed that all Māori have ownership rights through the Treaty of Waitangi and so should be free to choose to claim them however they wanted, and through the institutional and organisational forms they chose. The legal effort by these two groups has seen the iwi-based decision of the Treaty of Waitangi Fisheries Commission overturned by the Court of Appeal who ruled that the Sealord deal was intended to benefit all Māori, and that urban Māori were therefore entitled to a share of the cash and assets.

This decision itself was later overturned by a Privy Council ruling in early 1997 that the Appeal Court had gone beyond its mandate. The Privy Council ordered that the case be sent back to the New Zealand High Court to make a new ruling. In this new case the presiding judge, Justice Paterson, had to rule on two decisions: should Treaty assets go only to iwi? If the answer was yes, does iwi mean only traditional tribes?

The fundamental problem underlying this new case was whether or not iwi meant 'a people' or was defined merely as a specific 'traditional' form of Māori social institution. In a long and detailed decision, Justice Paterson ruled, following the wording of the *Māori Fisheries Act* (1989), as amended by the *Treaty of Waitangi (Fisheries Claims) Settlement Act 1992*, that all assets held by the Commission before the settlement date can only be allocated to iwi and/or bodies representing iwi. Justice Paterson further ruled that in terms of the allocation of these assets, only 'traditional' Māori tribes qualified as iwi (Paterson 1998: 82). This decision was then appealed, but in late October 1999, the New Zealand Court of Appeal upheld Justice Paterson's interpretation of iwi. The case of non-iwi Māori in New Zealand demonstrates that, while the recognition of difference is reconfiguring the space of politics, the atemporal basis of this recognition means that political repositioning is not necessarily a change for the better for many Māori.

Non-iwi Māori, specifically represented in the examples above by urban Māori, thus act to destabilise the currently accepted bases of indigeneity. While Māori embody a plurality of self – with their composite selves positioned simultaneously along multiple social axes – the importance of the interplay of these multiple and shifting identities has been ignored in the recognition of atemporal difference through the reification of indigeneity to an ideal of immutability. Claims of the inauthenticity of 'urban' indigenous subjects are often linked to the notion of special rights available to indigenous people; rights that some argue that 'urban' individuals have lost. The realisation must be made, however, that recent changes in the shape and form of indigenous identities do not necessarily signal the demise of their indigeneity. Instead, it should be viewed as the signal of a transition of indigenous society toward a dynamic phase of growth and reawakening – a dynamic act of decolonisation from within. The problem, however, lies in accommodating transformations of indigenous society without losing the distinctiveness of indigenous culture. For, as Roger Maaka has cogently noted:

> minority indigenous peoples in post-colonial situations struggle to balance a desire to modernise their cultures while retaining those institutions from the past which foster and perpetuate their distinctive identity. (Maaka 1993: 213)

The problems faced by Māori in the exclusion of various forms of indigenous institutional organisation by the implementation of policies designed to empower indigenous rights act to demonstrate the very real problems of exclusion that the implementation of policies constructed upon an atemporal recognition of difference make manifest, while simultaneously highlighting the theoretical deficit in current work on minority rights and group identity. The problem facing us, then, is how to construct a theory of difference that is not dependent on the subordination of identity to difference, and hence able to adequately take account of notions of change. The genesis of this answer, I argue, can be found within the broad body of work commonly known as poststructuralism.[16]

Poststructuralism and a New 'Politics of Difference'

Western metaphysics has a long history of structuring reality in terms of dichotomies and binary oppositions. These binary pairs are not generally regarded, however, as representing two equal terms, for while the first term is usually defined positively, the second is customarily defined negatively as the absence of the first. The dominant term defines the terrain of the other, placing the second term within a position of subordination. In the case of New Zealand, non-iwi Māori have been defined negatively in terms of the (presumed) authenticity of iwi Māori. Derridean deconstruction can be seen to provide a way to escape this trap of logocentrism.

The definition of Māori identity and culture that has gained currency in the iwi-isation of Māori society relies implicitly on a colonial chimera of race and innate cultural and linguistic knowledge that virtually ignores the realities of the lived experiences of the majority of Māori, in favour of a small minority group who speak Māori natively and are knowledgeable about what is assumed to be 'traditional' culture (Webster 1989: 35). This view is mistaken for a number of reasons. First, iwi never were the organisational level at which kin-based Māori communities had operated to deliver what would be classed as social and welfare services (Ballara 1998). Secondly, pre-contact Māori communal forms had ebbed and flowed across historical landscapes, constantly shifting their definitions over time (Ballara 1998; Webster 1975). Thirdly, because of the traumatic experiences of colonisation and urbanisation, many Māori no longer identify with iwi; their identity is currently shaped more by their disadvantaged position in New Zealand society than by interaction with 'traditional' frameworks, yet no-one can deny their Māori-ness, as their physical characteristics and day-to-day interactions confirm their Māori identity. In New Zealand, the representation of Māori difference has thus led to Māori identity entering a hyper-real state in which the organisational model chosen to represent Māori identity – iwi – has become a simulacrum, a copy of a copy, more real than the reality it supposedly represents (Baudrillard 1983). Representation has thus been conflated with the thing-in-itself. Representation, however, is always indeterminate because the definition of what is represented must necessarily be constituted on the basis of difference between what is being represented and everything else (Baudrillard 1981; 1983). Similarly, Derrida's notion of *différance* suggests that meaning can never come to rest on an absolute presence, as its determinate specification is deferred from one substantive linguistic interpretation to another, ever-changing and ever-moving. Thus, wherein '*différance* is also the element of the *same* (to be distinguished from the original)' (Derrida 1981: 9) difference can never be established before definition – it is forever postponed.

Representation of Māori difference has thus assumed a clear distinction between the 'indigenous' and the 'non-indigenous'. Reflection on poststructural notions of *becoming*, however, leads to the erasure of the foundations of this distinction. Organisations such as the Te Whānau o Waipareira Trust are not indigenous in that they do not possess the definitional legislative and organisational elements associated with representations of 'indigeneity', yet they are not in themselves 'not indigenous'. Non-iwi Māori, specifically urban Māori, thus collapse into contemporaneity – spatio-temporal oppositions such as indigenous and non-indigenous, modern and traditional, through their occupancy of the indeterminate third space of '*becoming*'. While each of these terms is constitutive of the whole, none is on its own complete: they are immanent to each other. It is this creation of a space of '*becoming*', wherein neither notion of identity nor difference is prioritised over the other, that opens up the possibility of cultural identity that entertains difference without the assumption of a temporal hierarchy. So, while some have claimed that the infinite sliding of the Derridean signifier means that poststructuralism collapses reality into a constantly shifting, nihilistic state of chaotic flux (Graff 1983), I see this shifting characteristic of Derridean *play* as a strength.

The supposed need, in theoretical and practical terms, to define and to determine the boundaries of bodies (be they concrete or abstract, singular or plural) led to the emergence of the very problem of synchronic reification bedevilling current indigenous rights discourse. The need to specify and determine in precise terms was the genesis for the exclusion of bodies that refused (in passive or active terms) to fit within boundaries so defined. Just as Heisenberg's Uncertainty Principle argues that we cannot ever precisely know both the position and momentum of a particle, so poststructuralism shows us we can never fully know the determinate characteristics of a body. Instead, 'the map is open and connectable in all its dimensions; it is detachable, reversible, adapted to any kind of mounting, reworked by an individual, group, or social formation'

(Deleuze and Guattari 1987: 25). We can therefore do away with the impossible dream of precisely defining existence, and instead embrace the indeterminacy in which Derridean *play*, while not celebrated, is at least recognised. In any discourse of identity is always present the danger that identities will be dogmatised into some naturalistic or immutable essence that could in turn lead to the generation of destructive resentments and fears; for while all identities are formed through difference, all identities are simultaneously threatened by these same differences. These destructive impulses can, however, be held at bay by a politics of mutual challenge and disruption in which we are constantly reminded of the contingent nature of our identities. The success of this politics in turn depends on the successful permeation of all involved with a 'culture of genealogy' that helps us to recognise the contingent and contestable nature of our identities (Connolly 1991: 64–8). The recognition of the necessary contingency of identity allows for the emergence of an ethical sensibility wherein accounts of morality that do not accept this inevitable contingency merely for the sake of efficient government are contested (Connolly 1998). In the public policy field, for example, the use of periodic reviews, and the official recognition of the legitimacy of the process of self-definition in the construction of official policies, would approximate the degree of self-reflexivity that this approach endorses, and thereby allow for the creation of policies that engage with, rather than suppress, difference. We should thus not 'speak of a dualism between two kinds of "things", but of a multiplicity of dimensions, of lines and directions in the heart of an assemblage' (Deleuze and Parnet 1987: 133).

In practical and theoretical terms we cannot, nor should not, do away with representation; instead we should modify its praxis through the inclusion of the realisation of its necessarily contingent nature. While the short-term costs of such an indeterminate self-reflexivity may be high, the long-term gains of a temporally sensitive basis for recognising and accommodating difference will far outweigh these earlier costs. In addressing the idea of indigenous rights we should appeal not to an atemporal and juridically (pre)conceived subject, but focus on the realisation that the subject of rights is not a juridical subject; rather it is a subject formed out of specific processes and sites of struggle (Ivison 1998). We should look to the processes that shape our lives, rather than the organisations that represent us, for guidance on how to construct a more ontologically sound politics of difference. The ruling by the Waitangi Tribunal on the case presented by the Te Whānau o Waipareira Trust is a promising practical example of this process.

Prospects for a New Beginning

It is a commonly acknowledged fact that the Treaty partnership in New
Zealand arose out of the transferral of the Māori right of governance
(*kawanatanga*) to the Crown, in exchange for the promise of the Crown
to protect Māori *rangatiratanga*. With respect to this, the Te Whānau o
Waipareira Trust argued that: 'The adoption of an exclusive Iwi paradigm . . . is to deny that Māori can be Māori outside that paradigm and
to deny treaty rights to Māori who do not fit within it' (Waitangi Tribunal
1998: 163), and that while 'kinship and descent provide ready-made networks of relationships among Māori . . . it is rangatiratanga that determines which of those relationships have current significance' (214).

   In response to these arguments, the Waitangi Tribunal found that *rangatiratanga* lay with Māori people, not with some specific institutional or
organisational form such as the tribe. The Tribunal went on to conclude
that while devolution itself had not been detrimental to the Treaty relationship between Māori and the Crown, the restricting of the devolution
to tribal authorities had been. In ruling on the Waipareira claim, the Waitangi Tribunal therefore found that the Te Whānau o Waipareira Trust
was established to address the results of the Crown's Treaty breaches and
to reconstruct traditional Māori structures and patterns in an urban context, and therefore should be considered as a legitimate Treaty partner
representing the West Auckland Māori community. The Tribunal thus
found that the Trust exercised *rangatiratanga* on behalf of a Māori community in West Auckland.[17] In accord with this finding, the Tribunal recommended that the government should aim to apply the principles of
the Treaty of Waitangi to protect the *rangatiratanga* of all Māori in contemporary situations, kin-based or not, where evidence points to the
exercise of *rangatiratanga; as iwi, while being modern descendants of earlier
forms of kin-based Māori institutional form, did not provide a complete explanation of Māori identity*. Arguing that Māori perform best when the principles of *rangatiratanga* are maintained, when a community is empowered
to determine its own needs and resolve its problems in its own ways (Waitangi Tribunal 1998: 236), the Tribunal suggested that section 396 of the
Children, Young Persons, and Their Families Act 1989 be amended by substi-
tuting the term 'Māori social service' for the term 'Iwi social service'.
The release of the *Te Whānau o Waipareira Report* therefore sent a clear signal to the New Zealand government that Māori are the Crown's Treaty
partner, not iwi, hapū or whānau.

'Aboriginality' and 'indigeneity' were originally constructed to acknowledge a specific form of difference and to overcome certain forms of
discrimination. The problem remains, however, of 'continually recon-

structing a previously absent general identity, while devising strategies that accommodate the diverse Aboriginal identities associated with place and region' (Stokes 1997: 170). I have argued that the prioritisation of identity over difference has led to the synchronic reification of identity in the case of indigenous New Zealanders. Also, any engagement with notions of indigeneity must take seriously the realisation that indigenous cultures and societies necessarily change over time – a realisation enabled by the embracing of poststructuralist notions of *différance* and *play*.

In practical terms, the realisation that the institutional forms through which indigenous cultures manifest themselves necessarily change over time would lead to the recognition that new urban-based indigenous social institutions are not any more or less authentic than older forms of kin-based social institutions, as both can act as appropriate mechanisms for the recognition and exercise of indigenous rights. When institutional structures are set up to force people to fit into prescribed tribal divisions, old values concerning respect and notions of inclusiveness are put at risk. The spirit of Māori society lies not in its organisational structures, but in the ongoing, dynamic relationships between its members. If this realisation is not made soon, then the institutional structures and practices which were constructed to empower indigenous peoples such as Māori may end up ultimately destroying the very cultures they were meant to protect. It is time, both in theory and in practice, to accommodate the diachronic nature of indigenous social institutions and relationships in order to avoid the possibility of the continuation of the case wherein:

> Aboriginality in European eyes is reduced to the immediately observable and the primitive. Where manifest aboriginality in these terms does not exist, people are perceived as empty vessels, drained of their content by European contact, and capable only of echoing the loud noises from European society. (Chase 1981: 24)

As the world continues to change at an exponential rate there is an ever greater need for the theorising of indigenous culture and society to catch up with the events of the 'real' world, a world in which the dynamic character of Māori, and other Fourth World cultures, has never been lost. For only when the realisation is made that identity is not a state but a dynamic process can the Fourth World be said to have been truly decolonised.

CHAPTER 8

On Display for its Aesthetic Beauty: How Western Institutions Fabricate Knowledge about Aboriginal Cultural Heritage

Sonia Smallacombe

Aboriginal art and culture have become a key focus of Australian national identity and now represent a core part of what is distinctive about Australia. Unfortunately, these cultural symbols are used without recognition of their source or displayed in a way that offends indigenous peoples. Consequently, there is growing concern among Aboriginal and Torres Strait Islander peoples that appropriation of our culture by the wider community fails to benefit the communities that have ownership of the artistic and cultural symbols.

The protection of indigenous peoples' intellectual and cultural property rights has become a major concern for the world's indigenous population. In recent years the rise in interest in indigenous groups has led to a greater demand for indigenous cultural products. Until a few years ago the idea that indigenous peoples 'owned' our own intellectual and cultural property did not exist as such property was seen to belong to anthropologists and museums who preserved and studied indigenous groups 'to add to western knowledge' (Marcus 1990: 4). Indigenous peoples are concerned that any unauthorised use and reproduction of our cultural material, particularly secret or sacred items, may result in its disclosure to individuals who are not authorised to know or view such material.

There is a general feeling among indigenous groups that most museum legislation in Australia has a tendency to focus on the anthropological and scientific significance of indigenous cultural products rather than on their cultural and spiritual meaning to indigenous peoples (Janke 1998: 14). This was evident during my visit to the Royal Museum of Scotland in Edinburgh in 1996, where I had the opportunity to meet museum staff who were keen to show me the Aboriginal and Torres Strait Islander collection. In the basement storeroom I was shown an amazingly large collection of cultural products such as the usual boomerangs, spears and shields. According to their tags they had been taken from many areas around Australia, including the area known as the Port Phillip district, dating back to the 1890s. Later, I walked around the public area of the museum and, to my shock and horror, an Aboriginal sacred item was on full public display. I was told the item was displayed for its 'aesthetic beauty'. This experience has led me to believe that the cultural significance of cultural products and their connections with the living communities from where they originate have little or no relevance to museum staff or people who visit them.

Exclusion of Australia's Indigenous Population

The idea that indigenous cultures can 'add to western knowledge' provides a clue as to why there is such an interest in indigenous peoples. It raises the issue of whether this anthropological view still remains within the minds of the dominant culture and furthermore raises the question of whether there is a grand plan to appropriate and consume the 'primitive'. Or, alternatively, are people beginning to appreciate and accept aspects of indigenous cultures in the same way that indigenous peoples themselves view their own cultures?

Indigenous Australian cultural products were in demand long before the 1788 invasion. In the north of Australia, Macassan fishermen and Aboriginal peoples developed trading relationships long before Captain Cook claimed this country for the British crown. The first known incident of looting took place in 1623, when European explorer Jan Cartenz stole ethnographic items from a Cape York beach after shooting the Aboriginal owners (Mulvaney 1985: 87). During the nineteenth and early twentieth centuries, Aboriginal and Torres Strait Islander cultural products and ancestral remains were robbed from Aboriginal graves and left the colonies in large quantities. They either have found their way into private collections or are used as government gifts or museum exchanges.

In 1925 Pope Pius XI organised a missionary exhibition to applaud missionary work in the non-western world. About 100 000 items were sent to the exhibition and only half were returned. The remaining items were subsequently placed in the new Vatican museum, which opened in Rome in 1927. The museum would, according to the Pope, demonstrate that the 'dawn of faith among the infidel of today can be compared to the dawn of faith which . . . illuminated pagan Rome' (Greenfield 1989: 10). Included among the 1925 exhibits were cultural property from Papua New Guinea and over 200 Aboriginal materials that were sent by missionaries in Australia. The Vatican's portrayal of indigenous cultures as heathens was a justification for imposing Christianity on indigenous populations.

Australia was founded on the popular and political (mis)conception of nineteenth-century social Darwinism that asserted the natural superiority of the 'white race' underlying British colonial expansion. This ideology justified the violence, dispossession and incarceration of Australia's indigenous population, as it was deemed necessary to clear the way for the 'white nation'. Not surprisingly, Aboriginal and Torres Strait Islander peoples were effectively excluded from the emerging nation not only through our displacement and confinement to reserves and mission stations and our inferior legal status, but also through the nation's collective amnesia, which systematically removed us from the images and language of the new nation. Aboriginal and Torres Strait Islander peoples were constructed as 'the Other' in that our placement outside the nation and outside humanity was due to our supposed 'primitiveness' and our inevitable demise in accordance with social Darwinism.

Aboriginal and Torres Strait Islander cultures have often been portrayed 'as fragile, finely balanced, irretrievably shattered through contact with whites'. The protection policies introduced by the various state and federal governments in the late 1800s and early 1900s generated a morbid fascination with an 'exotic culture doomed to extinction' (Pettman 1988: 3). As part of the fascination with 'the Other', indigenous Australians were taken to Europe 'as the living spoils of European plunder' (Langton 1994: 13–14) and displayed as entertainment in circuses, vaudeville tent shows, sideshows and carnivals. Not surprisingly, the showcasing of Aboriginal and Torres Strait Islander peoples and our cultures to the outside world did not diminish the underlying motivation to exclude indigenous peoples from participating in the Australian nation.

Since the 1970s indigenous issues have remained distinct from 'multicultural affairs' but have been incorporated into the state's notion of cultural pluralism. As a result, Aboriginal and Torres Strait Islander peoples have been relegated to the rhetorical status of 'First Australians', and aspects of our art and culture are appropriated to play a prominent role in constructing the spirit of the Australian nation. The use of Aboriginal designs in the construction of the Australian nation is prominent not only in the main entrance to Parliament House, but also within the tourist industry. Aboriginal designs appear on T-shirts, wine bottles, Qantas jets, as logos for major companies and advertisements for Australian events. This demand has generated an enormous output of indigenous art, film, video, music, literature and performing art, and will no doubt reach its peak in the forthcoming 'Aboriginal-flavoured' Sydney Olympics in 2000 (Janke 1996: 13). The significance attached to the use of Aboriginal designs raises serious questions as to whether there is a genuine desire on the part of the Australian nation to change the present social, economic and political position of indigenous Australians or if it is simply about incorporating and containing us within the 'culture' areas of Australian society.

The incorporation of Aboriginal and Torres Strait Islander cultures into Australian identity was evident in 1996 when Governor-General Bill Hayden used his final Australia Day speech to advance the view that the power of indigenous art could be harnessed to uncover 'enduring spiritual truths' about national identity. He stated:

> Aboriginal creativity has taken its place as a major influence in our national consciousness. We're receptive to what Aboriginal artists, dancers, writers and performers have to say. In a very real sense they are helping to reshape our own concept of self and of country – of the way we see and feel things as Australian – and as others see us. (Rothwell 1996: 1)

It is interesting that any mention of Australia's indigenous population is restricted to the area of 'culture' and 'national identity'. While intending to be complimentary, Hayden's speech reinforces the view that only certain aspects of indigenous culture are acceptable to the Australian nation.

Hayden's speech also gives the impression that the distinctive cultural practices of indigenous peoples continue to be a source of wonder for non-indigenous audiences. The hunger for the 'exotic', 'primitive' and 'the unknown', which is part of the fascination of 'the Other', is very much evident in Australian society. This observation was made by Djon Mundine, an Aboriginal art expert, who pointed out that gallery owners and curators often refuse to see classical indigenous art such as bark painting, sculptures and dot paintings in a contemporary sense. The idea that the category 'Aboriginal' or 'the Other' is a fixed position is also obvious as Mundine stated that these same gallery owners and curators do not accept non-classical, urban-based contemporary art as 'true' or 'authentic' indigenous art (Langton 1994: 13–14). The perception of Aboriginal art as 'authentic' or the product of the 'noble savage', untouched by 'civilisation', is out of step with reality, particularly with regard to the conditions in which such artwork is produced. Another primary concern is that while some non-Aboriginal art commentators see links between urban Aboriginal art and black artists in Europe and America, there is still a fear of entering into critical debate because the work of urban Aboriginal artists is intensely political (Gray 1996: 25).

Aboriginality

The colonial construction and definition of Aboriginal cultural heritage is part of the wider creation of a particular form of knowledge about Aboriginal and Torres Strait Islander peoples. The construction of Aboriginality occurs at a number of levels: in the work of researchers or those who write about Aboriginal people, which is often based on their assumptions of the 'authentic Aborigine', and through power relationships of domination and subordination that are manifest between Aboriginal and white Australians.

Throughout the twentieth century the discipline of anthropology has determined how Aboriginal and Torres Strait Islander peoples were to be perceived by the government and Australian society at large. Distinctions were made between Aboriginal people living in the remote areas who were destined to 'die out', but at the same time were the 'authentic Aborigines', and Aboriginal people living in urban areas, particularly in the south-east of Australia, who were somehow 'less Aboriginal' and thought to have 'lost their culture'. This anthropological construction of Aboriginality has been extremely powerful and is very much evident in legislative and political thought today. Such a construction is continually reinforced because a majority of Australians only occasionally interact directly with Aboriginal and Torres Strait Islander people, and therefore rely on the accounts of 'expert commentators'. These commentators, who still rely on anthropological constructions, are often found in academia where they create Aboriginal Australia for the majority of non-Aboriginal Australians. As a consequence, in every academic discipline, the representations of Aboriginal people have occurred without any reference to the voices of Aboriginal people (Harris 1996: 29; Anderson 1993: 24).

Western Constructions of Cultural Heritage

In the past, knowledge about Aboriginal and Torres Strait Islander sites, art and cultural property was classified as 'western scientific' discourse and appropriated as the property of white academics to enhance their careers. A small group of academics, consisting mainly of archaeologists and anthropologists, lobbied for legislation (to protect Aboriginal heritage) that was introduced in all Australian states in the late 1960s and 1970s. This lobby group did not have any input from or the support of Aboriginal people. Archaeologists were preoccupied in protecting their sites from indiscriminate destruction and from unscientific, amateur and destructive research. These sites were considered to have important heritage and scientific value, and rock-art sites were seen in terms of their aesthetic and public value. They were often compared in quality with, and held up as rivalling those of, Europe, which were highly valued as part of the European cultural and archaeological tradition. Not surprisingly, white academics ignored the connections and relationships between these cultural sites and the living Aboriginal communities, particularly in the south-east of Australia, because of the belief that there were no 'real' Aboriginal people left in this part of the country (Sullivan 1985: 141).

Cultural heritage is a western construct that focuses generally on material culture and subjective judgements about what is historically, artistically and 'archaeologically' significant. Because cultural heritage is a collective right and not adequately protected by common law doctrines in Australia, any form of protection must come from specifically designed legislation that has to be sensitively interpreted by the courts. Advocates of common law argue there is the opportunity for creative development of common law doctrine, which has been demonstrated through the acceptance of the existence of 'native title' by the High Court of Australia. The recognition of 'native title' is seen to represent a general recognition of Aboriginal cultural heritage as well as having the potential to protect particular sites through land claims (Puri 1993: 159; Gray 1993: 10–11). The current management of cultural heritage is integrally related to issues of property and environmental law that relate both to real property such as land, and to chattels such as cultural property (*Laws of Australia: Aborigines* 1995: 7–11). Therefore cultural heritage, as a western construct, enshrines European archaeological and scientific values and, as such, protects Aboriginal cultural heritage on that basis.

The concept of Aboriginal and Torres Strait Islander cultural heritage is based on the political and economic autonomy of European colonisation and its domination. As previously stated, there was little involvement by indigenous Australians themselves (*Laws of Australia: Aborigines* 1995: 7; Boer 1991: 88). Mick Dodson, the former Aboriginal and Torres Strait Islander Social Justice Commissioner, has this to say about the way western society views indigenous cultures:

> Our values have been filtered through the values of others. What has been considered worthy of protection has usually been on the basis of its scientific, historic, aesthetic or sheer curiosity value. Current laws and policy are still largely shaped by this cultural distortion and fail to extend protection in terms which are defined by our perspective. (International Alliance of Indigenous-Tribal Peoples of the Tropical Forests and International Work Group for Indigenous Affairs 1996: 78)

Conflicts between Western and Indigenous Concepts of Cultural Heritage

Dominant colonial ideologies are inherent in Australian institutions, which is reflected in the difficulty the latter have in understanding the experiences of many marginalised groups. The Kumarangk/Hindmarsh Island bridge affair is an example. The fact that indigenous knowledge systems give power to women is incomprehensible to Anglo-Australian institutions because of the assumption that Aboriginal women's knowledge holds little value in their own society, in the same way as women's knowledge does within most western societies. The devaluation of

Aboriginal women's knowledge was highlighted by the South Australian Government's Royal Commission, which sought not only to question the validity, but to denigrate the religious practices of a group of Aboriginal women (Bin-Sallik 1996: 207). My reference to the Kumarangk/Hindmarsh affair is not about the Ngarrindjeri women's business of which I have no knowledge, but about the way that debates about Aboriginal cultural knowledge take place within a dominant colonial discourse.[1] As a result, indigenous rights to intellectual and cultural property go unrecognised, despite the application of the *Aboriginal and Torres Strait Islander Heritage Protection Act 1984* (Cth), designed specifically to protect areas and objects that are of particular cultural significance to Aboriginal and Torres Strait Islander peoples.

For many Australians, the spiritual and political beliefs of Aboriginal and Torres Strait Islander peoples in regard to cultural heritage are difficult to comprehend because they are outside the political and economic realm of colonialism. Many Australians believe there is only one law, British law, operating in this country, which holds that all Aboriginal spiritual beliefs are 'no more than fairytales'. The contempt toward Aboriginal beliefs was evident when a former Coalition front-bencher, Ian McLachlan, questioned the validity of the Ngarrindjeri women's claim to sacred sites within the area of the proposed Kumarangk/Hindmarsh Island bridge. He stated it was ridiculous that fewer than thirty-five women could be the custodians of sacred spiritual beliefs and asked 'why can't other Australians be told the [secret] stories that Aboriginal people has miraculously managed to pass on to generation to generation' (Chamberlin 1995: 6). McLachlan's criticism, supported by the South Australian government, developers and members of the public, including some sections of the Ngarrindjeri community, has resulted in bitter conflict that has never been satisfactorily resolved.

McLachlan's intention to invade the secrecy of women's business was evident in March 1995, when it was revealed in Parliament that he had a copy of the secret material regarding Ngarrindjeri women's business, and that it had been photocopied in his office. What transpired was that an entire box of materials destined for the then Minister for Aboriginal Affairs Robert Tickner's office had mistakenly been delivered to McLachlan's office, and a male staff member had photocopied its contents and sent copies to interested parties. Subsequently, McLachlan was forced to resign from the Opposition front bench, admitting he had inadvertently misled Parliament when he claimed that the envelopes (consisting of material that his staff had photocopied) were not sealed or marked 'secret' or 'confidential' (*Aboriginal Law Bulletin* 1996: 22). What is unpalatable about this issue is that the fact that McLachlan had violated the sensitivities of a group of Aboriginal women appeared to be of no major concern for any of the Members of Parliament.

It would seem that Australians have not learned any of the lessons from the controversial debates of 1991 when Aboriginal peoples opposed the proposal by BHP to mine Coronation Hill in the Northern Territory. In this case, the Jawoyn people, the traditional owners, opposed mining on their land because Coronation Hill is located within an important place called Bulajang, or Sickness Country. This area is connected with Bula, a major creation figure that would wreak havoc if disturbed. According to a Jawoyn elder, if Bula were awakened, 'the whole country would shake, everyone going to die; bullock, white man, black man' (*Land Rights News* 1989: 2, 16; Chamberlin 1995: 6). Bula quickly became the object of ridicule and the Jawoyn people were further exploited by the mining industry when they paraded, before the media, some twenty-five relatively junior Aboriginal people who wanted jobs at the proposed new mine site.

The Jawoyn people were successful in their bid to stop mining because of support from the then Prime Minister, Bob Hawke, who broke ranks with most colleagues and carried Cabinet to ban mining on Coronation Hill. Prime Minister Hawke defended his decision by raising the issue of why whites (Anglo-Australians) should be so presumptuous as to question Aboriginal beliefs 'simply because they are outside the intellectual framework with which we are comfortable'. He went on to say 'it would be just as preposterous, in my judgment, for spokespersons for the Aboriginal people to question the Christian mysteries' (Chamberlin 1995: 6).

Many Australians, particularly developers, are contemptuous of Aboriginal and Torres Strait Islander spiritual beliefs. It can be argued, however, that there are various levels of contempt operating, and this can be seen in the differences between Coronation Hill and Kumarangk/Hindmarsh Island. The differences are based on gender and concepts of Aboriginality. Coronation Hill is located in the remote areas of the Northern Territory and it is the Jawoyn men who have knowledge of the stories – women are forbidden from knowing the details. The Jawoyn men also fit the common stereotypes that most Australians hold about 'traditional' Aboriginal people. In contrast, it is the Ngarrindjeri women who are the custodians of the sacred sites at Kumarangk/Hindmarsh Island. Further, Kumarangk/Hindmarsh Island is situated in the rural districts of South Australia, where the indigenous population were dispossessed of their lands in the 1850s when they were removed to nearby Port McLeay Mission (Tehan 1996: 12). It would seem that many Australians are willing to entertain the idea that Aboriginal men living in the remote north would be able to retain their spiritual beliefs. At the same time, they are dismissive of the idea that Aboriginal women in the rural and urban south possess spiritual beliefs, especially after having had exposure to western forms of knowledge. In other words, the Jawoyn elders portrayed in the media coverage fit within the colonial ideals of patriarchy and representations of the 'authentic' Aboriginal person, while the Ngarrindjeri women of 'mixed ancestry' are at variance with this representation.

In the Kumarangk/Hindmarsh Island case, the western legal and political institutions were called upon to balance the interests of developers and the Ngarrindjeri claimants. In performing this task, the interests of the developers were clearly definable and hence there was the compulsion to find a clear concept of 'heritage'. However, the Kumarangk/Hindmarsh Island case brought out the widely differing views of the Ngarrindjeri peoples as well as the differences between the experts arrayed on the opposing sides of the case. While the often conflicting views of witnesses and experts are commonplace in western legal institutions, and the courtroom has the function of balancing these interests, this case was highly controversial. The wider context of the dispute involved the place of indigenous peoples within the Australian state and the demands of western institutions to establish what is clearly impossible; that is, the one 'true' version of the religious beliefs and cultural system of the Ngarrindjeri peoples.

The categorising of indigenous cultural knowledge, including religious beliefs, to the heritage of humankind relegates this important issue to western concepts of heritage. Consequently, while the western legal system may find ways to deal with disputes over buildings, objects and environmental heritage, and experts may be able to verify authentic provenance, there is an assumption that disputes involving indigenous 'heritage' (cultural values) can also be resolved by the same processes. Western concepts of heritage are based on the construction of hierarchies and classifications that are imposed, through the colonising process, on the knowledge and cultural systems of indigenous peoples, thus rendering them subordinate to western systems. For example, the idea that Ngarrindjeri people may possess a religious belief system comparable to western religious beliefs was never acknowledged by the legal system. It is therefore hardly surprising that there has not been a satisfactory legal solution to the Kumarangk/Hindmarsh Island case.

The debates around ownership of the past and the demands for the return of cultural property, including ancestral remains, affect national and international laws and conventions. At the core of the debates is the privileging of western 'science' above all else. The generalised model of western science is based on control, technical rationality, order, discipline and measurement (Davis 1996: 2). Science and its technologies have been important tools of colonisation, and employed extensively in measuring, surveying, medically dissecting, classifying and controlling indigenous peoples. It is often assumed that science is objective and value-free, and the exclusive domain of non-indigenous populations. Consequently, indigenous peoples and their knowledge systems are subordinated to western science. The idea that indigenous knowledge could be regarded as indigenous 'science' is viewed with some scepticism by some academics, even though 'science' is designated as 'knowledge' (Davis 1996: 2).

Attempts by Aboriginal and Torres Strait Islander people to protect their cultural property through land rights claims, to ask western institutions to return indigenous cultural property, or to assert custodianship over sites have been met with incredulity, resentment and denigration of these claims. As illustrated previously, in Australia, there has been a general lack of recognition toward indigenous cultural heritage. Further, any indigenous feelings and connections toward our own heritage have not been accepted as legitimate. As a result, white academics have been able to operate in a vacuum that enables them to provide Eurocentric interpretations and fabrications of indigenous intellectual and cultural property that harms and insults us (Davis 1996: 144–47).

Disputes surrounding the demand for recognition and respect of indigenous peoples' cultural practices and the appropriation of indigenous cultures are contentious, and emotionally and politically charged. What seems to be at the core of these disputes is that western perceptions have, to a large degree, failed to recognise that indigenous conceptual systems have their own internal logic and rationality, which are not always translatable into the dominant western legal and political system. This is particularly evident in the policy-making areas, where western terminology and concepts are imposed as a way to define, categorise and evaluate concepts in indigenous societies. Such action often serves to legitimate the interests of the existing legal and economic system of the state, denying, misrepresenting or fabricating the concepts or categories of indigenous peoples. As a result, colonialism is perpetuated, because indigenous systems are subjugated to a lesser order within the dominant framework.

The intellectual and cultural property of indigenous Australians provides the foundation of our personal identity and ancestral anchorage. It offers a distinctive world view that outsiders can rarely grasp. When our knowledge is fabricated by outsiders, a wedge is thrust between the object and its meaning and, as a result, the world view and cultural matrix of our societies are attacked. Protecting our cultural property and knowledge systems from exploitation has become part of our agenda. However, it cannot become a question of how to fit indigenous culture and knowledge systems into western legal and conceptual frameworks, but that our systems and concepts should guide the debates. It is when we decide how we define our knowledge and cultural property rights that we may be able to protect ourselves from the exploitation and fabrication of our culture that is widespread in our communities today. This may also enable us to control and challenge the myths regarding our Aboriginality. As indigenous peoples, we need the protection and the right to say 'no' to commercialisation, exploitation, misuse and abuse of our cultural resources. If we choose to commercialise, donate or share our knowledge, then our interests need to be protected, and we must also be compensated where exploitation has occurred (Greaves 1996: 2).

CHAPTER 9

On the Plurality of Interests:
Aboriginal Self-government
and Land Rights

John Bern and Susan Dodds

In this chapter, we examine some concerns about the way in which recognition of Aboriginal self-determination or self-government within Australia is significantly shaped by legislative and other institutional forces that frame Aboriginal claims. We also examine some problems in identifying national or group interests independent of these external influences.

Debate about Indigenous Self-government,
Self-determination and Land Rights

A number of models for indigenous people's self-government have been advanced within Australia. One recurring concern is how indigenous self-government and representation should be structured, given the array of goals that self-government is supposed to meet, and the diversity of Aboriginal communities. For example, should self-determination be understood in terms of a bi- or tri-national confederation, made up of the non-indigenous nation, the Aboriginal nation and the Islander nation? Or should it be realised much more locally and pluralistically, to reflect the vast array of indigenous peoples and traditions within Australia?

Henry Reynolds has suggested that self-determination be understood as a 'single Aboriginal nation'. This brings together the political force of Aboriginal or Torres Strait Islander solidarity with a notion of a geographically diffuse nation (Reynolds 1996). A limitation of this model is that the moral force of the self-government of a people becomes diluted because the nation in question is composed of a large number of smaller groups with distinct languages, histories and cultural practices. Local or regionally focused approaches to self-government may be more promising, although their success may depend on the national political will to support greater Aboriginal and Torres Strait Islander self-government, given the small indigenous populations involved.[1] Michael Mansell's approach to indigenous self-government, by contrast, highlights the importance of local Aboriginal control over the government of communities (Mansell 1994). Delegates from those communities would come together under the umbrella of the Aboriginal nation. The interests of local communities are given centrality, without loss of the political force of indigenous identity within a broader Aboriginal nation. Each approach that may be considered, however, involves a different balancing and shifting of the various goals that are hoped to be achieved by greater political autonomy.

One potential source of tension between indigenous peoples is the absence of a compelling model of political representation. What form of representation of Aboriginal groups will best capture both the diverse institutions and values of Aboriginal cultures and the democratic demand for non-discriminatory, effective representation? Further, any move towards recognising group-specific entitlements – including rights of self-government – involves some discrimination among possible beneficiaries of such rights, including discrimination among indigenous people. In the area of native title, for example, regulatory mechanisms for determining recognition of native title holders or traditional owners can lead to tensions within Aboriginal communities seeking greater self-government, between communities, and between communities and regional bodies such as land councils.

The formal recognition of indigenous entitlements to land contributes to at least two goals: first, recognition of distinct indigenous interests in land (that is, interests based on prior occupation and culturally specified rights and responsibilities), and second, enhanced self-determination of indigenous groups. In arguing for the particular rights of indigenous peoples to land or other resources, contemporary political theorists must use conceptions of group identity to pick out those who can claim these group-specific rights. Further, mechanisms for identifying the interests of the groups which are to be protected or promoted by recognition of indigenous rights to land must be articulated. For example, should the relevant groups be identified in terms of location – who lives, or has lived, on or near the land in question? Or in terms of their relation to each other and their collective, spiritual connection with the land? Or in terms of who uses the land for subsistence and/or farming? Or by some combination?

These different ways of carving out the scope of the group entitled to make land claims will not always pick out the same set of people. Some Aboriginal people who have been long separated from their land may retain relations with a local family group but may not necessarily have

knowledge of spiritual or other connections with the land.[2] Children of
the stolen generations, taken from their Aboriginal families, may not
even know of their Aboriginal descent (*Bringing Them Home* 1997: 296–301,
419–20). Finally, recognition of land rights may promote or protect an
array of interests in land; these may reflect the (sometimes overlapping)
difference in interests held by different groups within particular Aboriginal communities. In other words, there are questions of the appropriate
representation of indigenous identity and of indigenous peoples' interests.

Within a single Aboriginal community there may be those:

• who have special spiritual responsibilities with regard to the land
  and/or sites on the land;
• who wish to see the community gain greater control over their own use
  and control of the land to achieve greater economic independence;
• who wish to have their historic claim to the land and their subsequent
  unjust dispossession formally recognised; and
• who use the land to hunt and to gather food in a traditional manner,
  and wish to have continued access to the land for those purposes.

Political theorists, arguing for greater recognition of indigenous interests, frequently focus on the differences between indigenous and non-
indigenous interests, downplaying or ignoring any differences between
and among indigenous groups and interests. This apparent dichotomy
between indigenous and non-indigenous interests can serve to mask the
diversity of interests that indigenous people have, silence debate among
indigenous peoples, and/or support arguments against greater self-
determination.

In this chapter, we focus on internal community effects and illustrate
this by outlining some of the different kinds of interests in land one
group of Aboriginal people may have. We examine the ways in which the
various Australian regulatory structures for recognising Aboriginal interests in land may fail to recognise that diversity of Aboriginal interests and
the plural bases for those interests.

The assumption of a single, coherent set of indigenous interests may
exclude indigenous people from debate in a way that reduces their self-
determination. Regulatory mechanisms for recognition of land interests
may, paradoxically, fail to recognise certain kinds of interests in land. In
particular, the emphasis on continuity of physical association in the
Native Title Act, and on descent and spiritual responsibility in the *Aboriginal Land Rights (NT) Act*, discriminates against people whose historical
associations are post-contact, and those who retain an affinity to their
traditional territory but not a physical presence. If the goals of greater

recognition of indigenous land rights include enhanced self-determination, it is important that the legal and political mechanisms used to provide for that recognition do not frustrate genuine self-determination.[3]

The *Aboriginal Land Rights (NT) Act* sets out criteria for people to be
recognised as traditional owners and for making claims to the traditional
ownership of certain types of land in the Northern Territory. Land claims
brought under this Act and challenges to it have framed much of the
debate about rights of traditional ownership in that jurisdiction. We discuss
certain aspects of the land claims of people living in the Roper River region
to draw out the diversity of interests that an Aboriginal group may hold
with regard to an area of land. We also look at the ways in which the regulatory mechanisms shape and privilege some kinds of interests over others.

Contemporary Group-specific Entitlement Accounts
in Political Theory

Iris Young (Young 1990) and James Tully (Tully 1995; 1997) have argued
for pluralistic approaches to political institutions and for formal recognition of group-based entitlements to enhance self-determination within
contemporary states. Will Kymlicka (Kymlicka 1995) has argued for a
recognition of cultural pluralism within a single set of state institutions as
a way of acknowledging the potential for disadvantage where pluralism is
denied, and the value of cultural membership for individuals' life-plans.
In order to advocate political pluralism in the functioning and shape of
political institutions, or to advocate recognition of cultural pluralism
within the state, theorists need to be alive to the ways in which political
and regulatory institutions shape the interests of groups within the state
and shape the boundaries of those groups. If legislation identifies some
set of interests as *the* recognised interests of a group, it gives priority to
those interests over other interests which members of the group may
have. Similarly, if a regulatory mechanism recognises one set of people
within a group as *the* legitimate authority for pronouncing the interests
of the group, it gives the voice of those people stronger claims to recognition than those of others within the group.

Tully on Nations and Negotiation

In his arguments concerning indigenous self-government in Canada,
James Tully's pluralism takes the form of plural political institutions
within a confederation of distinct nations: those institutions of the First
Nations of Canada, those institutions of the Métis nation and those institutions of the Canadian nation. In the realm of land rights Tully argues
for proper recognition of the distinct and pre-existing set of relations

with land enjoyed by indigenous peoples before expropriation, and the need to avoid seventeenth to nineteenth-century cultural biases in understanding both the nature of indigenous nations and the systems of property characteristic of those nations (Tully 1994).

In doing so he uses a framework of three conventions: recognition, continuity and consent. Proper recognition is recognition by all Canadians of the diverse nations to which indigenous people belong as well as the non-indigenous nation. It is also recognition of the continuity of the nations, their traditions and law – that is, their on-going existence and significance. Further, it is recognition of the democratic norm shared by indigenous and non-indigenous people of consent to those things that affect each group in a society (Tully 1995: 116). As such, the kind of pluralism Tully advocates is a pluralism of national institutions and structures as federated within one over-arching, plural, Canadian confederation.

One benefit of this approach is that it shifts the discussion of land rights from a debate about distributive justice *within* a set of supposedly shared state institutions to a debate about justice *between* nations. Between these nations the three conventions are then applied to frame negotiation and debate, and to carve out the scope for group-specific rights of self-government. In the Australian context, however, it is unlikely that this federalist approach is available, given the general absence of a history of treaties or recognition of pre-contact Aboriginal sovereignty before the 1992 *Mabo* decision.

In lifting the debate to the level of relations between nations, and arguing for greater self-government of the affairs of each nation by the nation, there is a risk of homogenising the diversity within each nation. Tully uses a concept of sovereignty that he envisages as a move away from one understood as absolute authority over a uniform polity:

> Sovereignty in this non-absolute sense means the authority of a culturally diverse people or association of peoples to govern themselves by their own laws and ways free from external subordination. (Tully 1995: 195)

While Tully envisages a range of cross-cutting interests, especially as these relate to the specific interests of indigenous women, it is unclear how his approach protects members of each nation from *internal* subordination or exclusion from the political institutions (Tully 1997: 30; 1995: 193). For example, what are the criteria for membership in one or another nation, and who sets those criteria? How are representatives of each nation determined, and which interests are the *central*, 'defining' interests of each nation?

Tully's answer appears to be that each nation should determine these for themselves. However, the construction of each is going to be shaped by the institutions of the wider state and the specific set of interests that the nations view as central at the time of negotiation for the federation. Tully argues that 'the condition of democracy must be met' and that Aboriginal governments must be answerable in a manner appropriate to their way (Tully 1995: 193). It is difficult to see, within his account, how the basic institutions are constituted to *ensure* that the interests of all are given a voice, or how self-definition is to be achieved, given the influence of external structures.[4]

Young on Groups and Special Representation

Iris Young's pluralism takes the form of recognising group-based differences within the state and the need for special representation of oppressed groups in order to give those groups a political voice. Her goal is justice understood, not simply as just distribution, but more as the development of 'institutional conditions necessary for the development and exercise of individual capacities and collective communication and co-operation' (Young 1990: 39). Specific representation of oppressed groups ensures effective democracy (Young 1990: 184). Oppressed groups have been silenced in democratic debate because they have relatively fewer of the opportunities to shape debate and to be heard that dominant groups have historically enjoyed. For Young, groups are neither aggregates of individuals nor associations of chosen members. Rather, to be a member of a group is to find one's identity as (partly) constructed by one's membership of a group (for example, woman, Jew, Native American, black). While one can attempt to reject or reinforce one's group membership, it is not usually something separable from who one is – it constitutes an aspect of one's identity. As Young puts it:

> A social group is a collective of people who have affinity with one another because of a set of practices or way of life; they differentiate themselves from or are differentiated by at least one other group according to these social forms. (Young 1990: 186)

For Young, an oppressed group is one whose members suffer disadvantage relative to others as the result of the institutions and structures of the state (not limited to those which are intended to cause disadvantage). As such, oppressed groups are subject to systemic constraints, constituted by the state's institutions (Young 1990: 41–3).

Young argues that within representative bodies, oppressed groups ought to have special representation rights, at least in those areas that specifically affect those oppressed groups. This special representation is aimed at ensuring a democratic voice for oppressed groups so that they can shape the institutions that affect their lives:

The principle of group representation applies to all such democratised publics. It should apply, for example, to decision making bodies formed by oppressed groups that aim to develop policy proposals for a heterogenous public. Oppressed groups within these groups should have specific representation in such autonomous forums. The Black caucus should give specific representation to women, for example, and the women's caucus to Blacks. (Young 1990: 197)

But what of people within a social group whose interests and ways of life *within the group* are shaped by their role or status within the group? Must they count as oppressed by or within the group for their interests to merit special representation? Are their specific interests certain to be represented by the group?

Most social groups contain heterogeneous mixes of people. Groups are made up of subgroups whose membership in the subgroup may be constituted by the nature of the wider group: within a diverse community there will be different roles for different people. Some subgroups may be oppressed relative to the wider group in some areas (for example, indigenous women who are members of a women's representative body), but other subgroups may not be oppressed simply by virtue of their membership of the subgroup (for example, Aboriginal elders or those who live in town rather than on the mission) but they may nonetheless have distinct interests from those which are dominant in the wider group.

How are these interests to be recognised? Two things need to be acknowledged properly. First, representative bodies of indigenous people are geared toward some aspect of self-determination or of negotiation with the wider state. To a certain extent, then, the agenda is set from the outside and that agenda will often set criteria for identifying which kinds of interests are given priority and which members of the group are representatives of the group's interests.

Secondly, there may be a diversity of interests within a group that are not so much opposed to one another as they are to all aspects of the rich complexity of a shared way of life. As such, it is not a case of an oppressed subgroup's interest against the interests of the wider group but, rather, an array of partially overlapping but different interests that, together, form the full array of group interests. That full array of interests may not be heard or recognised by a regulatory mechanism that seeks out *one kind* of group interest.

Kymlicka and State Recognition of Cultural Pluralism

In *Multicultural Citizenship*, Will Kymlicka seeks formal recognition of the plurality of cultural memberships within a single set of state institutions. Kymlicka argues that the liberal commitment to equality and individual pursuit of the good demand institutional recognition of some group-based rights and protections. Employing the liberal democratic ideal of self-determination, Kymlicka challenges the claimed neutrality of liberalism and overturns much of the orthodoxy about liberal citizenship. He argues on two fronts, both of which attempt to reconcile ideals of universal citizenship with political recognition of cultural difference. Kymlicka challenges the view that liberalism is inherently atomistic, insisting that cultural membership and cultural participation are necessary conditions of each individual's pursuit of the good life. In a pluralistic democratic society, individuals whose cultural identification is associated with a minority culture will, in the absence of special protections, be disadvantaged in the pursuit of their conception of the good, relative to members of dominant majority cultures. Concern to protect the equal rights of each to the pursuit of the good grounds three kinds of rights that recognise difference between groups in a state, by protecting the group from the actions of other groups: polyethnic rights, which protect cultural practices while enhancing inclusion in civic life; group-specific rights of self-government; and special group representation rights (Kymlicka 1995: 37–8).

Of particular relevance to our concerns here is Kymlicka's argument for recognition of the threat posed by forced inclusion in the state to the continuation of some cultural groups. He argues for greater political autonomy for forcibly annexed groups through indigenous group-specific representation rights or rights of self-determination within state borders. These may be necessary for indigenous national groups to have the same freedom to pursue their preferred cultural life and conception of the good that members of the dominant cultural groups enjoy by virtue of their shared linguistic, cultural, spiritual and institutional history. Kymlicka maintains that there are circumstances in which indigenous groups should be granted regional political and legal self-determination, not just legal ownership of (parts of) their historical territories. In rare cases, secession and full self-government rights may be the only means of protecting rights to cultural identity (Kymlicka 1995: 173–92).

While Kymlicka provides a strong defence of cultural membership and the need for differential rights within a single state to protect the cultural participation and identity of members of minority cultural groups, his discussion stays within liberalism because it is based on formal justice, equality of participation in cultural life, and removal of disadvantage. He does not argue for indigenous autonomy and land rights on the basis of historical injustice alone. Reference to historical injustice, including forced state membership, provides the *causal* explanation for the current disadvantage. It is not an independent ground for differential rights. Kymlicka argues that historic treaties provide some evidence of what those indigenous people who took part in the treaty had agreed to at the time of the treaty, and that this is a reason to maintain the status and benefits granted to indigenous people in treaties. He does not appear to argue, however, that unjust historic dispossession or invasion is an independent basis for indigenous group-specific rights *within the state*. Rather, it is a ground for secession, as the group never agreed to federate with the colonisers (Kymlicka 1995: 116–20). For most national minorities, however, secession comes at a very high cost; for indigenous peoples, secession may be equivalent to abandoning demands against the state for justice and compensation as recognition of prior occupation.

There are some problems in attempting to apply Kymlicka's approach to the issues surrounding the Australian land rights debates. First, although the relative disadvantage of Aboriginal people is a legitimate ground for some land rights claims, Kymlicka's approach cannot recognise specific indigenous interests which can be advanced through land rights, but which are not grounded in disadvantage or recognised features of cultural membership.

Second, there is no clear answer to the question of how group-specific representation rights are to be identified, given they appear to simply reflect 'indigenous interests', although it is the dominant culture that determines which interests are indigenous interests and, at the same time, the recognition of group-specific representation rights themselves shape indigenous interests and cultural membership.

Third, disadvantage and cultural membership form the basis for *different* group-specific rights and/or will identify potential claimants for such rights differently. Indigenous identity will be constituted depending on whether the focus for group-specific rights is relative disadvantage or cultural membership. A disadvantage basis for rights might well broaden the scope of indigenous identity by broadening the range of people who are entitled to claim group-based rights, while a focus on the preservation of cultural pluralism and cultural membership might justify rights that limit the potential claimants of indigenous identity and the group-specific rights attached to that identity. It is unclear if Kymlicka's approach can take account of the dynamic aspect of these ascriptions of rights and rights claimants.

Tully, Young and Kymlicka each seek to develop mechanisms for enhancing indigenous peoples' self-determination. However, we have raised a number of questions about how differences between group members are to be given adequate hearing within an indigenous group seeking to achieve self-determination, given the role that outside institutions have in the construction of those interests. Tully invokes the idea of indigenous nationhood as the basis for self-determination without articulating the representative structures required to give all indigenous interests political voice. Young provides an account of representation for minority groups, but one that is unable to recognise internal group differences except where they are structured within oppressive relationships. Kymlicka's focus on the significance of disadvantage and cultural membership for individual citizens limits his ability to respond to historical injustice against indigenous groups; his approach to the grounding of group-specific rights expands the problems of recognising indigenous peoples and indigenous interests.

Must we accept that the only interests that can be properly recognised are those associated with elite or dominant members of the group, as defined by external institutions and structures, or those of subgroups, acknowledged to be oppressed or disadvantaged within the group? How can indigenous peoples' self-determination resist the external constitution of their interests and the singularity of this constitution?

One of the virtues of the *Mabo* native title decision was that it did *not* specify a unique set of rights of native title. Native title rights are to be specified by reference to local Aboriginal law (*Mabo and Others* v. *Queensland* (No. 2) (1992)). However, *within* particular communities, there may be a number of different, overlapping and sometimes inconsistent sets of interests in the land at issue. As indicated earlier, these interests may include: the spiritual/cultural significance of the particular land or parts of that land; the opportunity to exercise a degree of community self-determination over an area of land; the opportunity to use the land for increased community self-sufficiency; the opportunity to negotiate mining rights over the land to provide the community with income, infrastructure and services; recognition of distinct bases for the group's ownership of the land or recognition of individual ownership of the land. While there is no conceptual difficulty with attempts to realise some of these different interests simultaneously, it is important to assess if legislation and policies concerning indigenous rights to land are framed so they *can* recognise the diversity of interests in land and their relations to the different ways of identifying potential claimants.

Clearly the self-determination of indigenous people requires that it be *indigenous* people who identify and articulate indigenous interests. However, political theorists and all those pursuing an ideal of indigenous self-determination as the route to Aboriginal justice should be alert to two general problems of articulating group interests and group-based rights grounded in those interests. First, institutional structures which are designed to hear claims of interests privilege *certain kinds* of interests and, second, these institutional structures can define who, of the indigenous people, are those recognised as entitled to these group-based rights. That is, there may be no way of identifying the pre-existing or independent interests of any group, including Aboriginal groups, because the very institutions that recognise those interests already shape – even constitute – those interests. As such, institutional responses to the injustices borne by indigenous people should be treated warily and, at least sometimes, with resistance to the ways in which these responses constitute indigenous interests.

How Institutional and Regulatory Structures Shape and Identify Interests

As applied to Australia, the issues we raise are best approached through concrete practices of Aboriginal self-government and control of land rather than the more abstract notion of Aboriginal sovereignty. The framework of Aboriginal claims to land is set by government legislation. In the case of the *Aboriginal Land Rights (NT) Act* (1976 and after) and the *Native Title Act* (both before and after the 1998 amendment), the testing of a claim sets different interests in opposition to each other. This is shaped by the dichotomy of indigenous and non-indigenous interests. The effects are many, but one we shall focus on here is the propensity to write out any diversity within the indigenous interests or, alternatively, to construct these in destructive and disintegrative modes. While there is a strong political imperative to provide a unified voice in arguing for a land claim, we argue that in seeking to find that single voice, important interests may be silenced, or at least muffled.

Land Rights and Governance

Contemporary land rights claims focus political as well as economic and cultural demands. Claims to land have two main facets that highlight the dual (not to say contradictory) nature of Aboriginal self-government claims. On the one hand, each claim is an expression of parochial property rights, while on the other, each is an instance of the more abstract claim for the recognition of Aboriginal sovereignty. The Northern Territory legislation gives primacy to the former. The importance of spiritual affiliation and a site/group-based tradition for land claim success not only favours narrow local interests, but may also pit site-anchored kinship groups against otherwise constituted residential groups in the same locality.

Already, the right to decide priorities and determine their implementation on the major issues of land rights, health, education and the forms and processes of the institutions themselves are formulated and decided upon at state or national levels, namely *Mabo*, *Wik*, federal, state and territory land rights legislation. On the whole, management of these affairs is in the hands of state/territory and commonwealth governments. However, there are significant Aboriginal-controlled extra-local organisations. The most notable are the regional land councils, but there are other significant ones. The commencement of the Aboriginal and Torres Strait Islander Commission (ATSIC) in 1990 was seen by some as extending this development and providing a basis for the national integration so far absent. Nonetheless, the land councils and ATSIC depend on state, territory or federal legislation. They are, in effect, derivative rights of self-government.

The specifically Aboriginal polity is constituted, through the *Aboriginal Land Rights (NT) Act*, within three main domains in the Northern Territory: the land councils, the local communities and the kinship/language-related groups. In the context of the *Aboriginal Land Rights (NT) Act*, however, each of these groups has its form mediated through the criteria of the Act. Only the last of these polities claims its origins in traditional societies of the past. Local communities are more complex, but in their sedentary present they are largely based on pastoral containment and/or government/mission institutions. The land councils are established under commonwealth government statute. Any concept of Aboriginal autonomy is necessarily limited by state or territory and commonwealth sovereignty, welfare and fiscal dependence and the absence of treaty obligations. In the Northern Territory a significant proportion of the Aboriginal population has certain rights and entitlements through the *Aboriginal Land Rights (NT) Act*, which, arguably, gives its beneficiaries, collectively, a status in the society that contains elements of self-government.

The land councils of the Northern Territory are established under the *Aboriginal Land Rights (NT) Act*. Their statutory functions relate to Aboriginal land and land that may be subject to a land claim. The areas of competence include access to the land, management schemes, protection of sacred sites, lodging land claims on behalf of Aboriginal people, and negotiating mining and other uses of Aboriginal land by non-owners. In these matters they are the buffer between Aboriginal groups and outside interests, many of which have major economic and political as well as social significance.

The two principal land councils also play an important coordinating role in the formulation and presentation of Aboriginal peoples' political claims at both Territory and national levels. They are among the central lobbying bodies for the representation of Aboriginal views. While the basis for their activity is Aboriginal land interests, these are so pervasive in their social, economic and political effects as to involve the land councils in the maintenance and development of a very wide spectrum of affairs affecting Aboriginal peoples' social and political lives. These range from national policy in relation to mining and national parks to many aspects of community decision-making and management, including conflict management and distribution of resources.

Land councils have two overlapping constituencies within their charter. On the one hand, they represent and must consult with traditional owners of the lands within their jurisdiction, while on the other, Council members are elected by and from the local communities. These two groups generally overlap, but are rarely identical. The *Aboriginal Land Rights (NT) Act* defines traditional Aboriginal owners as a local descent group of Aboriginals who:

> (a) have common spiritual affiliations to a site on the land, being affiliations that place the group under a primary spiritual responsibility for that site and for the land; and
> (b) are entitled by Aboriginal tradition to forage as of right over that land . . .
> (*Aboriginal Land Rights [NT] Act* 1976 (REPA028) Consolidated to No. 75/1987)

Traditional owners are language/place/kinship groups whose property rights over particular territories are recognised through the *Aboriginal Land Rights (NT) Act* and are grounded in their spiritual responsibilities. The structure of local communities, on the other hand, is variable and ranges from small family groups to rural towns with indigenous populations of over a thousand people. This overlap can and has become a source of conflict, particularly where the recognised traditional owners of an area are not the same group as the residents of the local community within that area. The most persistent of these conflicts has occurred where the Aboriginal leadership of the local community is not made up of the traditional owners of the land on which their town is situated.

Broader regional indigenous geographical and language group interests do exist and have an impact on the political scene. The Yolngu-speaking people of north-east Arnhem Land and the Pitjantjatjara people of the Western Desert are two such groupings that have been successful in representing themselves as specific interest groups in the wider political arena. The Tiwi of Bathurst and Melville Islands and the Groote Eylanders each have their own land council. So far, only these few strong language and geographical groupings have been able to organise effectively above the level of the local community. However, even here, the bases of organisation is kin/language/spiritual associations, though a broader integrity has been maintained, at least partly, as a result of particular historical and geographical circumstances.[5] In the case of the Yolngu and Pitjantjatjara, Australian political control has been recent and was applied under a regime having a relatively benign impact. In the case of the Tiwi and Groote Eylanders there is also the insular island location and subjugation to a single mission authority in the pre-citizenship period.

Interests that are poorly accommodated within the Northern Territory *Aboriginal Land Rights Act*'s structure are those distinguished by age, gender, rural/urban location, individuals and class. Women, in particular, are marginalised through the emphasis on traditional male spiritual attachments. There are circumstances where male authority has broken down and only adult women have the coherence to represent the community and manage its affairs. In these cases they do so as the (temporary) holders of those male-focused traditions.

The *Aboriginal Land Rights (NT) Act* is one of the key institutions that has shaped Aboriginal self-determination and identity in the Northern Territory. The recognised interests of Aboriginal groups is at times constituted in ways that may cause tensions within those groups. While some could be addressed by giving internally oppressed subgroups greater voice, as Young argues, the core of the problem lies in the ways in which the regulatory structures for recognising Aboriginal land rights constitute Aboriginal land interests.

Roper River Land Tenure

We present here aspects of decision-making concerns among the Ngalagan and related people of the Katherine and Gulf District of the Northern Territory to illustrate the ways in which Aboriginal interests can conflict in the arena of land rights claims and the benefits that may flow from such rights. We argue that some of these differences are shaped externally, through the *Aboriginal Land Rights (NT) Act*, the functioning of the Aboriginal land commissioner under that Act, and the administration of decisions flowing from the granting of a land claim.

During the 1980s the land tenure system of the people of the middle and lower Roper River area in the Northern Territory has been the subject of investigation in four land claims under the *Aboriginal Land Rights (NT) Act* (Aboriginal Land Commissioner 1981; 1982; 1985; 1988). In each of these cases the Aboriginal land commissioner made different findings concerning the constitution of the group of traditional owners of the land in question. The land commissioner needed to deliberate on three key issues in deciding the constitution of the groups to be awarded traditional ownership under the Act. They are that the group constituted a *local descent group* who have *common spiritual affiliations to a site on the land*, and that these affiliations place the group under a *primary spiritual responsibility for that site and for the land*. The differences we are concerned with here arise from difficulties in reconciling these three elements.[6] There is potential in each to arrive at a more or less inclusive result.

In the 1982 claim to the Roper Bar Police Reserve, the land commissioner, after finding that a broadly based local group formed the Local Descent Group, found that the mingirringgi (those people related through their father and father's father) alone were the traditional owners (Aboriginal Land Commissioner 1982: 7). It is important to note that in his report on Roper Bar, the Commissioner (Justice Toohey) leaned toward the inclusion of junggayi (those related through their mother and father's mother).[7] However, in the end, the Commissioner was swayed by the claimants' assertions of the differences in the roles of the two categories with regard to responsibilities for sites and the land (Aboriginal Land Commissioner 1982: 12–14). In a land claim on behalf of a related group in the same year, to the former Cox River pastoral lease, another Land Commissioner (Justice Kearney) found that mingir-ringgi, junggayi and darlnyin (the last being related through their mother's mother) together formed both the local descent group and the traditional owners. The Mataranka Land Claim, heard in 1986, includes country associated with many of the people participating in the Roper Bar land claim. The finding of the Land Commissioner (Justice Maurice) in that case was consistent with the findings in the Cox River land claim: that mingirringgi, junggayi and darlnyin together formed both the local descent group and the traditional owners.

The discrepancy between the findings as to the composition of traditional owners has outcomes in the politics of the indigenous communities in that region. The recent history of relations between the people identified as traditional owners in the Roper Bar land claim and the predominantly indigenous community at Ngukurr township (population circa 900) is pertinent here. Ngukurr is only a few kilometres down river from Roper Bar. A significant number of the Roper Bar traditional owners live there and most of the rest of the community are closely related to them. Part of the town is a sacred site on the totemic path identified with one of the traditional owner groups at Roper Bar. The traditional owners have, at times, used this to press their rights within the town as against the rights of the wider community and its elected local government. For example, they were successful, using their traditional owner status, in gaining the right to receive rents for the lease of the local general store.

Traditional ownership status and the rights that flow from it have been challenged on a variety of grounds from within the local community, including that the traditional owner group should include the junggayi and darlnyin, as well as the mingirringgi. This view gained strength in the light of other land claim results. For the Ngukurr community leadership, it was a better fit with the practices of responsibility and for the general range of social relations. It was also the position adopted by the community in negotiations with outside interests over various commercial agreements, such as mining exploration, rights of way and so on (Bern 1989: 165–76).

There was another type of disagreement concerning the very efficacy of the local descent group, whether exclusively or inclusively structured. This is a complex matter, for those arguing against the primacy of the descent group accept the importance of kinship, co-residence, long-term association and ties to the land, while rejecting the singular importance of descent. The main points of division within the region have often been articulated in terms of this issue. This dispute is fraught with difficulties as there has been extensive intermarriage and long-term co-residence among the disputants on each side. The Ngukurr community, including the Roper Bar traditional owners and their local descent groups, has resided in the area for much of this century and has developed a strong attachment to the place in traditional and other historical ways, including common spiritual attachments and responsibilities. The argument from these critics is for an inclusive ownership regime based on the Ngukurr community, which gives due regard to the range of particular interests, but primacy to none of them. The view is one that might be consistent with the aspirations of local self-government.

The foci of these differences are not contained locally. The Northern Land Council, charged with responsibility to administer the Act, has obligations to local descent groups and local communities. Such obligations have the capacity to put the Council in contradictory positions, and thus an object for attack by the perceived disadvantaged parties. A section of the Ngukurr community leadership regarded the Northern Land Council as bound to support the local descent group and sought support from other quarters. The Northern Territory government, aiming to counter land council influence in indigenous communities, has devised and supported its own local governance model through the Community Government Scheme. While this model places weight on local community identity under the *NT Local Government Act*, it does so without a significant devolution of control to the community. Territory government support for the primacy of present-day local ties also includes support for smaller, regionally based breakaway land councils, including one based on the town of Ngukurr (Bern 1989; 1990).

In examining the workings of the *Aboriginal Land Rights (NT) Act* in its application to the Roper Bar traditional owners and the Ngukurr community, we have shown some of the ways in which the Northern Territory land rights regime constructs both Aboriginal interests in land and those who have authority to represent those interests. Land interests not reflected in the legislation can be overlooked and undervalued. As such, the legislation is limited in its ability to recognise the array of Aboriginal interests in land and to provide for genuine Aboriginal self-government. Those who view land rights legislation as a vehicle for recognition of Aboriginal interests and autonomy should be concerned to examine if it is possible to create legislation that does not construct Aboriginal interests externally and can be sensitive to the diversity of Aboriginal concerns.

To make sense of arguments about representative recognition of group differences within complex societies, the diversity of interests within the group must be properly recognised. At the same time, there must be recognition of the ways in which regulatory structures shape and privilege interests. It may turn out to be impossible to express, in the abstract, what interests an Aboriginal group or community has as all group interests are partly constituted by the internal and external institutions to which the group is responding at a particular time.

Our argument and conclusions connect directly with positions raised in other parts of this book. Our concerns about the constitution of identity being mediated by current and historical external institutions and laws echo Audra Simpson's account of the internal and external debates about Mohawk identity in her chapter. There she highlights both the political force to be found in the language of indigenous nationhood and the social costs of using cultural identity criteria that have been heavily shaped by historical legislative regimes (*The Indian Act*). Sonia Smallacombe's critique of the ways in which Aboriginal culture is constituted by the dominant culture in Australia and by the dominant culture's understanding of 'cultural heritage' connects directly with our discussion of the ways in which the *Aboriginal Land Rights (NT) Act* constitutes both who traditional owners are and the scope of indigenous interests to be realised through land rights. And Manuhuia Barcham's account of the shifting nature of Maori identity and social institutions in the context of wider social changes connects with our concerns about the construction of indigenous identity and the ways in which indigenous interests are sometimes treated as historical constants. Barcham draws attention to the problems of recognising what is distinctive about Maori culture while acknowledging the changing, 'evolutionary' notion of social relations and institutions.

Our conclusions about the interdependence of identity, interests and state institutions are not unique to Aboriginal self-determination, but are endemic to all approaches to democratic representation. Thus, rather than assuming that all Aboriginal interests can be articulated in the abstract, it is worth examining critically the institutional structures which shape Aboriginal interests and which can silence the diversity of Aboriginal concerns. This might be done by addressing the construction of Aboriginal concerns at a more concrete level. To do so would involve treating all institutional attempts to recognise Aboriginal interests as open to ongoing negotiation, in light of what Aboriginal constituencies find to be the limitations of the institutional mechanism to respond to their articulated concerns. At the same time there is a need for on-going internal debate and examination by Aboriginal constituencies of the impact of the institutional mechanisms on their various interests. Those constituencies will be able to articulate their resistance to having the group's interests constituted externally.

PART III

Democracy

CHAPTER 10

The Liberal Image of the Nation

William E. Connolly

My aspirations in this chapter are, first, to consider the adverse effects on Aboriginal peoples of the pursuit of the nation in liberal states; second, to undercut the claim that the liberal nation provides a necessary condition of civilisation and democracy; and, third, to sketch elements in an ethos of engagement that enables democratic governance, scrambles the nation and opens up new possibilities of negotiation and improvisation between minorities of several types.

The *Elementary Latin Dictionary* says that *nation* means 'a birth, origin', also 'a breed, stock, kind, species, race, tribe' and 'race of people'. The *OED* seconds this, saying that in early European uses race or stock was primary to the idea of nation, while in later usage a people formed through a common history takes on more salience. These two definitions may be connected. It is not that the image of the nation is always that of a race occupying the same territory. Sometimes the imagination of national unity is grounded in race; but at other times, when a common constitution, language, religion or set of memories is invoked as the mode of unity, the *degree of unity* projected into each element is drawn from the imagination of race. So even when race does not provide the explicit *basis* of the nation it symbolises the degree of *unity* to be embodied in the other principles of nationhood. This subterranean connection explains how, when the going gets tough for the nation, invocations of racial unity often return to shore up its pursuit. And, as we shall see, the irreducible instability of the national imaginary means that the going often gets tough for the nation.

This double connection between the imagination of race and the image of the nation exposes a problem. For today, race is widely held to be a fable rather than the exemplar of national unity to which other dimensions of national unity might refer when their degree of unity is being gauged. Even Ernst Renan, the nineteenth-century idealist of the nation, agreed that race could no longer provide the exemplar: 'The truth is that no race is pure, and . . . to base politics on ethnographic analysis is tantamount to basing it on chimera' (Renan 1995: 148). But if race loses its role as exemplar of natural unity, what is the model to which the drive to national unity might refer? I suspect there is none. The terms identity, commonality, unity and sameness which shape the very imagination of the nation lack both a close definition and a stable model to emulate.

The nation is experienced by many as an imperative that must be achieved if cultural belonging is be secure, or if public morality is to be intact, or if democratic governance is to be possible, or if sovereignty is to be stable. But the nation is also an imagination of unity or wholeness that has never been actualised. That is the paradox of the nation: it never simply exists in the present; it is always represented as something from the past that has been lost or something projected into the future yet to be realised. At any particular moment between past and future it either fades into the background of cultural imagination or is invoked as a lack that must be filled by some desperate means or other. As both imperative and lack the nation creates a reserve of cultural energy to be activated when things become difficult in any domain of life. Its absence is invoked, then, to explain the inefficacy of the state, or the insufficiency of moral life, or the troubles of the economy, or the need to discipline selective constituencies. But the imperative of the nation is not exactly like other absent imperatives. For the historical standard of its realisation is bound up with the idea of race in one or both of the ways adumbrated above. The absence of the nation, then, becomes an acute experience when things are going wrong in any domain, and its historical association with a unity grounded somehow or other in race sets up a particular set of constituencies to be treated as the source of the defect.

It is not only that the nation is a dangerous chimera. But liberalism is more implicated in nostalgia for this chimera than many liberals tend to acknowledge. A shift in the relation between liberalism and the nation could have salutary effects on the political improvisation of new relations between Aboriginal peoples and the rest of the territorial state.

The Tocqueville Model of Nationhood

Alexis de Tocqueville is generally treated as one who celebrated pluralism, locality and federation in nineteenth-century America while worrying that majority tyranny will destroy this combination by giving too much power to the state. That reading is correct. But it also misses the national imaginary in which these themes are set. It does so because most of Tocqueville's interpreters participate in his imagination of the nation, for Tocqueville sets a minimal state within a dense territorial nation. The dictates of the nation must be branded into the instincts and mores of the people for Tocquevillian democracy to function well. Tocqueville:

> What keeps a great number of citizens under the same government is much less a reasoned desire to remain united than the *instinctive* and, in a sense, *involuntary accord* which springs from *like feelings and similar opinions*; only when certain men consider a great many questions from the *same* point of view and have the *same* opinions on a great many subjects and when the *same* events give rise to like thoughts and impressions is there a society. Although there are many sects among the Anglo-Americans, they all look at religion from the *same point of view*. (Tocqueville 1966: 373)

For a democratic civilisation to flourish, two fundamental accords must be burned into the instincts of the territorial people. First, they must concur instinctively on the fundaments of Christianity and its role as authoritative source of public morality. Second, they must till the soil agriculturally rather than roam over its surface like 'nomads'. Tocqueville knows that nomads wandered over America before Europeans arrived. But because they, at least as *he* represents them, differ from the settlers on these two fundamental points, they cannot be included within the American civilisation. Atheists, whose restless and unstable minds also remind Tocqueville of the nomads, form an internal constituency that must be marginalised in public life. Let's set Tocqueville's characterisation of the internal nomads aside here, even though it is pertinent to note that the definition of a foreign threat to the integrity of the nation almost always solicits identification of an internal constituency posing corollary dangers of its own. It is not quite that Tocqueville first has an image of the American territorial nation and then notes that there are people on the land who depart from it. Rather, it is more that his identification of the nomads already there helps him to define a couple of elements they lack and he deems essential to the unity of the American nation. Consider a sample of Tocqueville's utterances:

> These vast wilderness were not completely unvisited by man; for centuries some nomads had lived under the dark forests of the meadows of the prairies
> . . .
>   The Indians occupied but did not possess the land. It is by agriculture that man wins the soil . . .
>   North America was only inhabited by wandering tribes who had not thought of exploiting the natural wealth of the soil. One could still properly call North America an empty continent, a deserted land waiting for inhabitants . . . In this condition ['watery solitudes', 'limitless fields never yet turned by the plowshare'] it offers itself not to the isolated, ignorant, and barbarous man of the first ages, but to man who has already mastered the most important secrets of nature, united to his fellows, and taught by the experience of fifty centuries. (Tocqueville 1966: 27, 30, 280)

Tocqueville weaves Christianity, morality, agriculture and the mastery over nature into the territory of American democracy. In doing so, he generates an image of the nation that requires the displacement of nomads already there. You wonder what he would say today, for instance, about the contemporary capitalist form that is now nomadic in finance, trade, management, communication and travel and has left agriculture in the Tocquevillian sense far behind. Perhaps he would adjust his image of the nation to encompass this development. Or perhaps he would join those on the Christian Right who invoke his name today to re-nationalise the state in every other respect while supporting the conversion of agri-culture into agri-business.

But in the nineteenth century Tocqueville found agriculture and Christianity to be closely intercoded, and thought both were essential to a public morality conducive to democracy. It is the internal connection between agriculture, Christianity, public morality and nationhood that propels this democratic moralist to accede to massive violence against Amerindians. Put another way, the democratic nation does embody morality of peace and justice in itself, but the territorial formation of the moral nation unfortunately requires massive violence against the nomads who preceded its formation. Such a violence is to be regretted and construed as unfortunate. Tocqueville takes no pleasure at all in vio-lence. He is not a bellicose nationalist. But because a nation of agricul-ture and Christianity sets two key conditions of possibility for moral liberty, violence against Amerindians is not opposed by Tocqueville as intrinsically immoral or repudiated as undemocratic.

The Liberal Image

John Stuart Mill is a little too close for comfort to Tocqueville. Mill hon-ours individuality, tolerance and the agitation of public opinion by cre-ative minorities. But he also endorses an image of civilisation, progress and nationhood in which the shape and limits of the first three disposi-tions are set.

Civilisation, for Mill, is an advanced mode of living and governance. Generally growing out of a Christian culture, it equips people with the discipline, character, disposition to regular obedience and appreciation for rule of law necessary to representative government. The world is made up, for the most part, of 'peoples', but not all 'peoples' are equally susceptible to the civilising process:

> Nothing but foreign force would induce a tribe of North American Indians to submit to the restraints of a regular and civilised government. The same might be said, though somewhat less absolutely, of the barbarians who overran the

Roman Empire. It required centuries of time, and an entire change of circumstances, to discipline them into regular obedience even to their own leaders, when not actually serving under their own banner. (Mill 1958: 6)

Mill does not follow Tocqueville in legitimating as necessary the holocaust against Amerindians. But the trace of such a sentiment might hover over the first sentence. Civilisation is something given to 'peoples', one people at a time, over 'centuries of time'. A long, slow, progressive process of discipline forges a people into a civilisation capable of regular obedience, 'forbearance', respect for law and a streak of independence. While Mill is a secularist, his secularism is set in the hegemony of the Christendom from which it emerges. Thus the 'most melancholy cases in history' are those peoples who advanced civilisation to a certain point and then proved incapable of continuing its advance:

The Egyptian hierarchy, the paternal despotism in China, were very fit instruments for carrying those nations up to the point of civilisation they attained. But having reached that point, they were brought to a halt through want of mental liberty and individuality. (Mill 1958: 35)

What in Judaism, and then in Christianity, prepares a people to become a civilised, democratic nation? The Jews had 'an absolute monarch and hierarch'. But the counter 'order of prophets' provided a creative minority which, through its very ethical energy and political dissidence, kept pushing the nation to a higher level of achievement (Mill 1958: 34). Restrained conflict between the priests and the prophets installed an 'antagonism of influences which is the only real security for continued progress' (Mill 1958: 34). Christianity continues this creative antagonism of influences within the nation. Creative minorities in each monotheistic people provide critical impulses that propel the nation toward 'further improvement'. It is very pertinent to note, then, that a 'creative minority' for Mill is typically a constituency *above* the general run of people culturally, morally and educationally, but it is *part of the people* in its major ethnic, linguistic, religious and moral heritage.[1] The prophets and intellectuals Mill invokes to advance civilisation belong to the 'people' or the 'nation' they agitate. There is a cartoon with two well-dressed wall-street financiers walking down the street. One says, 'John Stuart Mill taught that the happiness of the individual is paramount. He didn't name names, but I suspect that you and I are the sort of the individuals he had in mind.' Mill's conception of minority shows both how this cartoon is off the mark and how close it is to the mark it misses.

According to Mill, we live for the most part in a world of territorial nations already there. Mill's territorial maps are two-dimensional and national rather than three-dimensional and, well, rhizomatic. For when you incorporate diversities and struggles from the past onto the territorial map of the present the history of violence upon which the project of territorial nationalisation is based becomes very visible. But when you reduce the three-dimensional map to the two dimensions of longitude and latitude, that history easily becomes buried under the Millian idea of a pre-existing world of peoples. In the film 'The Man Who Fell to Earth', David Bowie, the guy who drops in, sees the shadows and feels traces of pain from past violences as he walks over the ground of Texas. Such a temporal sensitivity, embodied in Bowie as the return of Jesus to Texas, can be debilitating to humans if it overwhelms all other experience. But Millian liberalism needs to incorporate a dose of it into its territorial maps. For, as the example of creative minorities suggests, only a particular type of territorial nation nurtures the growth of freedom and individuality. This means the boundaries of liberal individuality, rights and justice are set in advance by the parameters of the liberal nation. It is this latent theme within liberalism that makes it so difficult for many defenders of liberal freedom to negotiate new forms of property, freedom and rights involving patterns of land use and ownership at odds with the image of the nation with which they begin.

This connection between the liberal nation and the shape of the individuality not only encourages liberals to misread the past violences upon which construction of a nation is based, it also sets the stage for later struggles within liberalism itself over the limits to diversity in the liberal state. Today, protectionist liberals, insisting upon the priority of the nation during a time when its realisation meets with even more obstacles than heretofore, dismiss as 'special rights' any constituency claims not already grounded in the nineteenth-century image of the liberal nation. They thus marginalise the claims of indigenous peoples, gays and atheists from the start. Meanwhile, more generous liberals, inspired by liberal impulses that exceed the liberal image of the nation, seek to extend rights into new domains. But they seldom rethink the image of the nation in which they participate as they do so. This latter combination, as we shall see, thins liberalism out. It simultaneously opens up space for new rights and invites the charge that the liberal expansion of rights thins out the public resources a political culture needs to sustain itself. Since the generous liberals do not actively explore a positive model of democratic politics that transcends the image of the nation, such charges place them in a defensive position. They have no vibrant, positive image with which to counter when it is said that they have 'weakened' the nation or 'depleted its moral centre'. They can only sink defensively into a proceduralism or 'deliberative democracy' of one sort or another that eventually lends further credibility to the charges levelled against them.

An intercoded vocabulary of civilisation, progress, peoples, nations and races is prominent in *Considerations on Representative Government*. Mill, who views the world through the eyes of a recent administrative officer for Indian Affairs (1856–58) and a potential tourist, supposes the world of his time to be divided already and for the most part into territorially separate peoples. He speaks, in various inflections, of '*a race* who have been trained in energy and courage', of how foreign rulers can sometimes be 'of the greatest advantage to *a people*', of 'uncivilised *races* . . . averse to continuous labor of an exacting kind', of '*a rude people*', of 'the form of government which is most effectual for carrying *a people* through the next stage of progress' and of 'a hundred other infirmities or shortcomings in *a people* . . . which might disqualify them from making the best use of representative government' (Mill 1958: 59, 59, 32, 24, 7, 63 respectively). It is only because the Millian world already comes equipped with territorial peoples that representative government can hope to consolidate itself on a few spots on the earth. Both the generosity and the limits of the Millian vision express this fantastic imaginary. Thus: 'Where the sentiment of nationality exists in any force there is a *prima facie* case for uniting all of the members of the nationality under the same government' (Mill 1958: 230).

But what *is* a people or a nation to Mill? 'A portion of mankind', Mill says, 'may be said to constitute a nationality if they are *united* among themselves by *common* sympathies which do not exist between themselves and others'. It is this unity and commonality that makes them 'desire to be under the same government' (Mill 1958: 229, my emphasis). Notice how much weight the indeterminate ideas of unity and commonality are asked to bear. The uncertainty in these heavy ideas becomes even more conspicuous when you notice how often they are invoked without elaboration. Listen to their invocation again, then, even as Mill explains how numerous the *sources* of nationhood might be:

> Sometimes it is the effect of *identity* of race and descent. *Community* of language and *community* of religion greatly contribute to it. Geographical limits are one of its causes. But the strongest of all is *identity* of political antecedents: the possession of a *national* history and consequent *community* of recollections; *collective* pride and humiliation, pleasure and regret, connected with the *same* incidents in the past. (Mill 1958: 229)

Three points here. First, Mill invokes the language of commonality, identity, community, sameness and collective to imagine nationality, but he never explains how tight, centred or close identity must be to be identity. It is this combination of indispensability and uncertainty that sets the nation up as something to be remembered but never known, pursued but always absent, absent but never eliminable as measure and imperative.

Second, and closely connected, Mill says that sameness of race, religion or language may not each always be crucial to the unity of the nation, for its unity may be drawn from other sources. But the examples he actually gives of nationalities as advanced states, of peoples ill-prepared to become democratic states and of dispersed populations unprepared for statehood are very often delineated by some mixture of race, language and religion.

Third, Mill employs the nation to explain political rule by a state, but he also refers to a long period of political rule on the same territory to explain the formation of a nation. This appears most dramatically when he uses the phrase 'national history' to help explain how a nation comes into being. His rendering of the temporal dimension of nationhood does not discriminate carefully enough (for me) between two possibilities: a series of interactions between diverse constituencies on several registers (for example, ethnicity, religion, first language, gender performance, sexuality, relation to the land, the moral source honoured the most etc.) forming an ethos of engagement across lines of difference on the same territory; and a series of interactions that becomes consolidated into a territorial nation united by the correspondences Mill lists.

In the first model, you have a diversity of religious faiths, gender practices and so on, informed by an ethos of engagement; on the second you have pluralism along one or two dimensions, with unity on the others. The first is what you might call multi-dimensional (or rhizomatic) pluralism; the second national pluralism. And Mill does not sufficiently distinguish between them. His emphasis upon identity in religion, language and memory is not vigorously complicated by reference to political forces of pluralisation that might:

- expose violences built into the pursuit of these historical identities;
- mark the contemporary violences upon which they continue to rest;
- open up dominant constituencies to come to terms more robustly with the historically contingent, shifting and uncertain character of the unity they represent themselves to embody; or
- probe critically the unexamined idea of unity itself so that subterranean diversities, pluralities and hybridities already circulating through it might be drawn upon to inspire another image of the democratic state.

The dominant tendency in Mill's orientation to the nation can be condensed into a sentence: 'For the preceding reasons, it is in general a necessary condition of free institutions that the boundaries of governments should coincide in the main with those of nationalities' (Mill 1958: 232). But there is another strain in Mill's thinking, already intimated by the clauses 'in general' and 'in the main'. It emerges most sharply when Mill bumps into 'parts even of Europe', in which the territorial conditions of nationhood are absent:

The population of Hungary is composed of Magyars, Slovaks, Croats, Serbs, Romanians and, in some districts, Germans, so mixed up as to be incapable of local separation; and there is no course open to them but to make a virtue of necessity and reconcile themselves to living together under equal rights and laws (Mill 1958: 233). Mill imagines that 'Hungary' is an exceptional case rather than a dramatic exemplification of the typical case – his vision of liberal representative government pushes him in that direction. But then Mill notices that several 'nations' have a majority population punctuated by significant minorities on the same territory. There are the Basque in Spain and France, 'the Welshman or the Scottish Highlander' and so forth. What can a liberal do in these cases? Mill says:

> Whatever really tends to the admixture of nationalities and the blending together of their attributes and peculiarities in a common union is a benefit to the human race. Not by extinguishing types, of which, in these cases, sufficient examples are sure to remain, *but by softening their extreme form and filling up the intervals between them.* (Mill 1958: 234, my emphasis)

One tendency in this formulation is to pursue a politics of blending and assimilation. But the formulation – expressing a tension between Mill's general image of a world of pre-existing territorial peoples and his secondary recognition of several places that do not fit the image – can also be inflected in a different direction. If you connect the idea of 'not extinguishing types' to that of 'filling up the intervals' with multiple differences that increase the number of constituencies by creating points of connection between them you move to the edge of a multi-dimensional conception of pluralism. If Mill were to recognise 'Hungary' as an extreme case that reveals how most politically organised territories are in fact 'so mixed up as not to be capable of local separation', he would be encouraged to ask more carefully why some territories are able to negotiate multi-dimensional diversity effectively while others are not. He might then be pressed to transfigure his image of national democracy into a network model of pluralism informed by a generous ethos of engagement between the parties involved.

A multi-dimensional pluralist culture contains several religious orientations, ethnicities, orientations to gender experience, modes of sensual affiliation, final sources of moral guidance, modes of property use and so forth. So there is, first, a plurality of dimensions, and, second, considerable diversity within each dimension. Wherever multi-dimensional plurality already exists on a politically organised territory, democracy either becomes grounded in negotiation of an ethos of engagement between multiple constituencies honouring different moral sources or it degenerates into majoritarian suppression of minorities. There are no other options, really, except civil war, cultural war or cultural gridlock. The multiplication of differences across several dimensions itself creates one of the pressures for each constituency to promote lines of connection to others. The best way to displace the liberal image of the nation, then, is to enact a multi-dimensional pluralism in which the attempt by any single constituency to claim that it embodies in itself the essential virtues of the nation is stymied by multiple constituencies banding together to resist the outrageous presumptiveness of that claim. Multi-dimensional pluralism sets a necessary but insufficient condition of non-national democracy. What else is needed?

An Ethos of Engagement

The liberal image of the nation is ruled by the idea that a layered centre is crucial to three collective goods: to a sense of *belonging* to something larger than self, church, job and family; to an indispensable logic of political *communication*; and to the possibility of collective *enactment* of general policies by democratic means. The idea is that belonging, communication and enactment are possible only when each passes through the vital centre of the nation.

Contemporary revisions of the Millian image of the nation are advanced by secular theorists such as Rawls and Habermas. They retain the idea of an indispensable centre, but then, because they are generous souls, they respond to each newly recognised evil of enforced religious conformity, racial purity, Aboriginal displacement, linguistic uniformity and compulsory heterosexuality by pulling more elements of cultural life out of the centre. The centre now becomes reduced to a practice of justice, or adherence to a written constitution, or a set of procedures, or a model of public deliberation, or some combination thereof. Such strategies to secularise the nation do not seem entirely wrong to me. They are just misleading and radically insufficient.

To cling to the logic of the nation while shucking off its religious, ethnic, gender and sensual *core* is to present yourself to its virulent defenders as an unreliable and weak advocate of the centre you purport to support. So whenever people encounter both uncertainty at the centre and the insufficiency of proceduralism, the vacated centre now becomes the compelling site to revitalise through occupation. The black hole at the centre is then occupied by a bellicose constituency which insists on restoring the vital essence of the nation. The instability of the centre is now covered over by the narcissistic self-representations of those who occupy it. To the extent such a drive succeeds, every other interest, faith and moral orientation now becomes a minority to be tolerated or corrected by the self-proclaimed occupants of the centre. The national culture becomes one with an unmarked constituency at the centre, surrounded by various minorities whose space to manoeuvre depends increasingly upon the level of tolerance or intolerance felt by the unmarked constituency. These minorities – sometimes numerous enough to be a numerical majority – are now set up to become objects of vilification, discipline, regulation and violence when things go wrong anywhere in the state.

Liberal nationalists protect the image of a national centre by subtracting each ugly element from it. But the logic of subtraction they follow not only creates a shallow centre and places them on the defensive politically, it also discourages them from experimenting with another model that unites cultural density with cultural diversity. I pursue, then, a counter-image of a dense, rhizomatic political culture that draws selective sustenance from the secondary strain in Mill's thinking. In this image no cultural constituency sits at the centre surrounded by diverse minorities. Nor does proceduralism provide a sufficient basis of communication, belonging and public enactment. Rather, the public culture of the territorial state itself becomes pluralised. The image of a tolerant or intolerant public centre now inclines toward the regulative ideal of a public culture itself populated by several zones of plurality, with each zone containing a range of diversities in it. You now live in a world of multiple minorities with no dominant cultural majority around which they are ranged. Each minority brings large pieces of its particular orientation with it into public contests and negotiations, depending upon the issues raised. The 'unity' of the public sphere is now replaced by an ethos of engagement between multiple constituencies drawn from multiple sources.

The key to such a transition involves a glacial shift in the governing model of public morality. In Tocqueville, and to some extent in Mill, the image of nationhood is bound to the idea that a people must share the same final source of morality if civilisation and governance are to flourish. Morality and nationhood are interwoven so that each becomes a precondition of the other. But today it is important to the viability of public ethics itself to insist that no single religious or philosophical source of public morality has established itself as universal and uncontestable.[2] If and as a variety of constituencies come to accept this condition of possibility for generous political engagement the pursuit of a single source of morality to which all give obeisance dissolves into negotiation of an ethos of engagement between multiple constituencies honouring different moral sources.

There are already expressions and glimmers of such an ethos of engagement in several places, even though the image of the nation tends either to blur these forces or to treat them as lacks and defects to overcome. Its further elaboration is retarded by political theorists who are enraptured by the democratic nation, by philosophers and priests who persist in claiming that their particular religious or secular moral source is so firm or necessary that all others must consent to it, by media talking

heads who invoke simple models of public virtue, by nervous constituencies which sanctify themselves by purporting to occupy the absent
centre of the nation, and by numerous gentle souls who are wary of the
previous orientations but not yet been engaged by an alternative model
of public life strong enough to challenge them.

But when each constituency, first, honours the moral source that
inspires it, second, acknowledges the contestability of the source it hon-
ours the most, and, third, addresses the history of violences enacted to
universalise the source it honours, conditions become ripe to negotiate
an ethos of engagement between and across constituencies. Where such
an ethos is fashioned, attachment across the space of distance insinuates
forbearance into strife and generosity into interdependence. The culture remains dense, but that density is now forged through numerous
lines of connection across multiple lines of difference. It becomes a rhizomatic or networked density rather than a national density in which
each connection must pass through a national centre. Now it may no
longer seem that the essence of the nation is jeopardised if, for instance,
multiple orientations to land and property are improvised on the same
territorial space. Sharp lines of division between individual and communal rights or individual and collective ownership may become susceptible
to pluralisation through renegotiation.

The most important thing stalling the formation of multi-dimensional
pluralism grounded in a generous ethos of engagement is persistence of
the political instinct that a dense, free and effective political life requires
the production of a national culture. One obstacle to the correction of
that mistake is the current reduction of the terms of public debate to two
alternatives: a debate between transcendental narcissists who insist upon
occupying the vital centre themselves, and defensive liberal secularists
who pretend that proceduralism (or one of its surrogates) can suffice to
govern public life. I think both of these perspectives are mistaken and
need to be challenged by a third possibility: a thick public culture of multi-
dimensional pluralism well oiled by an ethos of engagement between
diverse constituents who reciprocally relinquish the narcissistic demand
to occupy the national centre.

When multi-dimensional pluralism is informed by a generous ethos of
engagement it is false to say that there is no possibility of collective action
through the state. Rather, several constituencies now have a lot to go on
in building general assemblages for particular purposes. Indeed, a generous ethos of engagement defeats the single most powerful source of
stalemate or fragmentation in the state. For the most virulent cultural
war occurs when contending partisans struggle over the right to occupy
the authoritative centre of the nation. Disaggregating the imperative of
the nation does not suffice to stymie drives by particular constituencies

to occupy the vacancy at its centre. But to the extent such an ethos becomes installed it prepares a variety of constituencies to band together in opposition whenever such a hostile take-over is attempted.

But isn't this just too convenient to be true? Doesn't a rhizomatic, non-national democracy require much more? Might not the debate over procedures become too intense in multi-dimensional pluralism? Or isn't the contemporary radicalisation of divisions too intense to render such a rhizomatic image viable? Perhaps. But by giving preliminary voice to a positive counter-image, it becomes possible to explore new modes of political improvisation without falling right into the black hole of the nation. For the above objections are introduced to restore pursuit of the national chimera when in fact the impossible drive to nationhood has itself helped to promote the most severe racial divisions and economic inequalities.

Now, were such a pluralised ethos to become prominent, it could be said to reoccupy the old centre. And it would produce a new set of limits and exclusions, limiting, for instance, the expansionary impulses of constituencies which are discontented unless they embody the authoritative centre. This formal equivalence issues in a predictable charge: 'Connolly, you presuppose, what you protest against.' Or: 'You cannot avoid the language of unity and identity even as you attack it' etc. The point is not to deny these formal(istic) rejoinders. It is, rather, to explore how the ethos fostered by a *pluralised* we both supports a dense public culture and keeps open the possibility of improvising new settlements as new constituencies come into being. For you never reach a point at which the politics of pluralisation is over. The crucial thing is not, as reductionists insist, that both imaginaries set limits and encounter closures. Everybody understands that elementary point. It is that under contemporary conditions of political being, the limits of multi-dimensional pluralism speak more profoundly to the political need for peaceful coexistence between interdependent constituencies than the limits set by the models of the regular individual, secular proceduralism, or the nation.

Such changes in the grain and fibre of politics are no more or less imaginable today than the *modus vivendi* of secular liberalism was in several Christian nations a few centuries ago. That *modus vivendi* provides an inspiration of sorts, even if it has now become insufficient. For its terms were only vaguely imagined before its consolidation; and it curtailed destructive civil wars while opening up cultural space to *negotiate* a new public ethos. We urgently need new improvisations today, those that rework received representations of majority rule, minorities, progress, dissent, rights, sympathy, property, tolerance, secularism and creative dissidence. The eventual shape of such a complex can only be glimpsed, partly because it must emerge through negotiation between multiple constituencies relieved of the necessity of conforming those negotiations to an impossible image of the nation.

Consider an example that speaks to the contemporary politics between 'settler' states and the indigenous populations displaced by them. Before the advent of capitalism, the idea of acquiring mining or oil rights over land farmed by others was absent. But today oil and mining companies can acquire mining rights to land owned in other respects by farmers. In a capitalist state new forms of property are constantly emerging and new divisions often arise within the property form. Thus, to take another example, the privately incorporated, non-profit university provides a legal forum of governance over property that modifies the typical practices of individual or corporate ownership. So does the apartment collective. If people yell about inalienable property rights whenever the question of distinctive forms of governance over lands previously wrested from Aboriginal peoples comes up, they might be pressed to consider these examples of creativity in the property form. And they might be encouraged to come to terms with the fact that such creativity in the past has been reserved mostly for those who already control economic resources. Tocqueville, for example, suspected the American nation would fall apart if it moved away from an agricultural economy, and that served as one of his two major reasons to rule the 'nomads' out of the democratic civilisation. But now the progeny of these nomads are being ruled out because their practices are, well, considered to be too agricultural and not sufficiently in tune with new forms of advanced capitalism. It is fascinating to recall that Tocqueville worried about the future effects of 'new manufacturing aristocracy' on the property form. But he did not take this assault against agriculture to require the exclusion of that aristocracy.

To recall that property practices in contemporary capitalist states were not themselves ordained by a national imaginary that preceded them is to release the mind to legitimise forms of land governance that speak more generously to claims indigenous peoples have to the places wrested from their ancestors by force and trickery. Today new land practices must be forged in generously defined areas, and the negotiations must take into account the violence through which control over the lands was previously wrested from people still inhabiting them. When large tracts of land are set aside for Aboriginal governance, other use rights within those domains can be acquired only through negotiation with the governing board involved. Now mining, grazing and oil interests are obligated to negotiate with indigenous occupants to gain selective access to these resources. Entering into such agreements allows the governing board to set conditions of use, acquire capital for communal use and protect the integrity of the land practices they cherish most. Properly organised, such modes of governance can enable indigenous peoples to overturn the pretence to be stationary peoples with unchangeable ancient customs and to sustain relations to the land that expresses the spirituality they honour the most.

The history of interactions between settlers and indigenous peoples is important here. For while the idea of the nation, with its ineliminable racial overtones, has been a primary concept through which indigenous peoples have been marginalised by populations of European descent, it is also one through which indigenous peoples have forged counter-identities within settler societies. The history of adverse treatment itself generates special rights for indigenous peoples. It can also encourage descendants of settlers to think more creatively about elements in their traditions that exceed capitalist conceptions of property and connect affirmatively to indigenous practices. The ideas of 'place', 'land' and, particularly, 'earth' provide promising possibilities here. Today, for instance, an increasing number of people in settler societies such as Australia, Canada, New Zealand and the US identify the earth as simultaneously a vibrant source of life, a resource exceeding our possible knowledge and mastery of it, and a fragile planet to be nurtured and protected as a source of sustenance and creative evolution. While multidimensional pluralism operates to displace the nation, the earth now emerges as a transcendent place upon which to relocate those guttural experiences of identification traditionally reserved to the nation.

Consider the irony. In 1968 *Apollo 8* sent back pictures of a vivid blue planet suspended in the middle of the solar system, a stunning, bright sphere unlike any other planet observable from the earth itself. This picture, taken from a site beyond the earth, underlines how unique the earth is by comparison to other planets so far encountered. The others can't even hold water, while the fine balance the earth maintains between evaporation and precipitation is sustained to a considerable degree by the behaviour of *life* on the planet.[3]

Today states and corporations collide and collude to jeopardise balances favourable to life. But the image of the planet returned to us by *Apollo 8* and the experience of the earth nurtured by indigenous peoples might today enter into a promising assemblage. An assemblage in which divergent, yet overlapping, commitments to nurture the earth/planet set new limits to conceptions of property, mastery and nationhood previously promulgated by capitalist states. An assemblage in which an ethos of multi-dimensional pluralism is set in a general commitment (drawn from multiple sources) to protect the earth/planet in which we are set.

It is because this general commitment is drawn from multiple sources that it has a chance to gain a more secure foothold in contemporary culture. Of course, the obstacles are severe and the chances of success are limited. Everyone knows that. But the stakes are also high. And, again,

the irony of the late-modern age is that part of the inspiration to acknowledge new limits and modes of connection comes from enterprises originally conceived to transcend them.

I present these ideas as premonitions. Premonitions of how creative
extrapolations from already existing forms of property governance in
capitalist states might generate modes of land use, governance and
respect for the earth appropriate to the contemporary conditions of
both indigenous peoples and the new nomads of the space age. In a non-
national, rhizomatic state it is possible to pluralise modes of land identification as well as the experience of cultural identity. These two objectives
are in fact interwoven to the extent that respect for the earth emerges
from both traditional and late-modern experiences. The specific shape
such settlements might assume can only emerge through good faith
negotiations as Aboriginal peoples achieve full rights of participation in
a culture of multi-dimensional pluralism.

The formation of a post-national ethos of engagement cannot be
willed into place. The political momentum for it might emerge from a
historical conjunction between the moral exhaustion of nationalising
constituencies, the sense of shame felt by others over the history of violence against indigenous peoples in the name of the nation, the energi-
sation of yet others seeking to pluralise the public culture, and a few
propitious court decisions that press stalemated constituencies to negotiate under new conditions. To prepare ourselves for the possibility of
such a conjunction it is wise to rethink the relations between liberalism,
diversity, the imagination of the nation and our connections to the earth.

CHAPTER 11

Minority Claims under Two Conceptions of Democracy

Philip Pettit

There are two different conceptions of democracy – two conceptions of what it is for government to be controlled by the people – and my aim here is to consider the likely fate of special minority claims under each of these. A thin conception of democracy equates it with popular electoral control of government; a richer conception equates it with what I shall describe as electoral-cum-contestatory control. I argue that only the richer conception of democracy is hospitable to special minority claims, and that it ought to appeal, therefore, to those who think that it is important to establish such claims on a firm institutional basis.

Special minority claims come in various forms. They include rights that might reasonably be granted to minority nations such as the Québécois in Canada, or indigenous, Aboriginal peoples in Australia and North America. And they include rights that minority, immigrant groups can reasonably claim against a government that represents a distinct, mainstream culture. The rights in question range from exemptions from certain mainstream laws and regulations to claims on public support for minority languages and cultural practices; and from rights of special representation in parliament to rights of collective landholding and limited self-government (Kymlicka 1995: chapter 2).

Special minority rights serve to protect certain minorities in the way various general rights may also do: for example, rights of free speech, association and movement. What makes them special – what distinguishes them from such general, protective rights – is that they are group-differentiated or group-specific, as Will Kymlicka (1995: 46) puts it. They are accorded on the basis of group identity or group membership; they are special to the minorities in question. Some are collectively exercised by those groups – for example, in the manner of a right to self-government – while others are exercised not by the groups as such, but by their individual members: an example would be the right of a male Sikh to wear his traditional head-dress, and not a safety helmet, while riding a motorcycle. But whether they be rights of groups or individuals, the common feature is that they are exclusive to the minorities they favour.

In the first part of this chapter, I outline the electoral conception of democracy and show why it is not particularly hospitable to special minority claims. In the next I introduce the electoral-cum-contestatory conception. And in the third I indicate why this two-dimensional conception of democracy naturally makes room for the possibility of special minority claims.

I have argued elsewhere in support of the two-dimensional conception of democracy. One argument in its favour is that only such a conception promises to protect the freedom of citizens, in the neo-Roman republican sense of freedom: that is, in the sense in which freedom means not living in subjection to arbitrary power, private or public (Pettit 1997; 1999). And another, so I maintain, is that it gives a satisfactory interpretation to the idea that government should be guided by all and only the common perceived interests of the people (Pettit 2000). I have nothing more to say in this chapter, however, on the republican defence of two-dimensional democracy, and will only sketch the other defence. My principal aim is not to defend the two-dimensional conception but to show that it does much better than the standard, one-dimensional view in accommodating the possibility of special minority claims.

Neither will I have much to say on the detail of the minority claims that might be established under such a democracy. The two-dimensional conception of democracy does have implications on this front, as should become clear, but I will not pursue them here. Thus I will not be commenting on the debate between different theorists like Will Kymlicka and Chandran Kukathas (1997a); nor shall I be annotating the more radical perspective for which Jim Tully looks (Tully 1995).

The Electoral Conception of Democracy and Minority Claims

What is there in common to those systems of government that we would be happy to describe as democratic (Przeworksi 1999)? We would expect any democracy worthy of the name to allow for the periodic, popular election of certain authorities: at the least, the legislators. We would expect the periods between elections not to be very long and we would expect the elections to be popular in the sense that all competent adults would have electoral standing and be able to make their voting decisions without undue pressure. This pattern of usage does not tie down the word 'democracy' in any very determinate way but it still points us toward some minimal assumptions that we spontaneously make about any system we would be happy to describe in that term; it points us toward a conception of democracy that informs our ordinary speech. I describe this as the electoral conception of democracy.

Regimenting that conception a little, we can break it down into three principles:

- government is elected by the people on a periodic basis: certain key government authorities are elected by the people at intervals of not more than a stipulated, generally agreeable minimum;
- the people enjoy full and equal electoral standing: no-one is excluded without generally agreed good reason to do with age, competence or incarceration, for example, from standing or voting or speaking out in such elections; there is no systematic intimidation brought to bear on those who stand or vote or speak out; and no-one's vote is weighted more heavily than anyone else's, except where there is generally agreed good reason – say, to do with ensuring regional representation or maintaining a federal system – for such a weighting;
- the people are collectively sovereign: subject to the constraint of promoting people's equal electoral standing, the rules under which government authorities are elected and act are subject to determination or amendment either by the collective people directly – say, in a referendum – or by their elected representatives.

This conception may not apply fully in every system that is generally recognised as democratic; it may be that there are small departures from one or other of the principles. But the principles are certainly going to be approximated, I think, by any system of government that makes a persuasive claim to be described as democratic. The electoral conception of democracy that they represent is a widely applicable, real-world notion of what democracy involves; it is no utopian dream. Some will say, of course, that a democratic system needs to involve more than just the electoral elements described, but I will come to that misgiving in the next section when I introduce the richer electoral-cum-contestatory conception.

The question with which we must now deal is this. How plausible are special minority claims going to look in the light of the pure, electoral conception of democracy? What I want to point out is that they are not going to have much plausibility if they are viewed in that light alone.

Some will object that special minority rights, as envisaged here, do not treat all citizens equally and that they offend to that extent against the second principle in the electoral conception. But I think that that is a relatively minor problem. The more serious issue is that special minority rights appear to conflict with the third – the sovereignty of the people.

The less serious equality problem can be raised for a range of rights that most of us find unproblematic, such as the right of the mentally handicapped to special educational and informational provision; the right of those with renal failure to dialysis treatment; and the right of those who live in remote areas to the special resources necessary for providing them with services that are standard in cities and towns. In the case of these latter rights, we think that while their implementation may provide unequal treatment for people, it still treats people as equals (Dworkin 1978). While their implementation only benefits people in certain conditions, the rights can still be represented as general in character: each has the right, should the conditions in question apply to them, to receive the treatment offered.

It is clearly going to be possible to maintain a similar line with special minority rights, or at least with any plausible examples of such rights. If they are justifiable, then special minority rights presumably accrue to people or groups on the grounds of their having certain needs that the state should try to help them meet. In that case the claims can each be represented as a general right that everyone or every group has: the right, should the individual or group suffer the need in question, to be treated in the manner required by the minority right. Kymlicka provides one candidate for the need that underlies such minority rights when he argues that a liberal democracy should be committed to everyone's enjoying a certain kind of personal autonomy; that if people are each to enjoy this autonomy, then their local culture must provide them with a robust framework and perspective from which to make their choices; and that if a liberal democracy is to cater for this general need on the part of the members of minority cultures, then it will often have to grant them special rights (Kymlicka 1995).

But the really serious problem with special minority rights, as I said, is not that they offend against the second, equality principle; it is rather that they conflict with the third principle of the sovereignty of the collective people. The problem here is that if we embrace the need for special minority rights then we appear to say that the sovereignty of the people should be restricted in a way that is inconsistent with that principle.

There is an obvious contrast in this regard between special minority rights and the sorts of rights that we canvassed in discussing cases of handicap, renal failure and rural isolation. There is no reason to think that these latter rights would not be acceptable to a majority: after all, anyone may have a handicapped child or grandchild; anyone may suffer renal failure; and anyone may find themselves forced to move to the country. Insisting that a legal–political system ought to incorporate such rights, then, will not mean adopting a posture where one puts the sovereignty of the people, as encoded in democratic institutions, into question. For all that the insistence suggests, one may happily accept that sovereignty; one may believe that majority will ought to prevail. The argument may simply be that this is the path that the people and their representatives – in effect, the majority – ought to take in making policy.

But insisting that a legal–political system ought to incorporate certain special minority rights is rather different. It comes from a policy of protecting minorities against 'economic and political decisions made by the majority' on the grounds, for example, that 'They could be outbid or outvoted on resources and policies that are crucial to the survival of their societal cultures' (Kymlicka 1995: 109). It means arguing that whatever the majority wants, certain rights should still be accorded to minorities; and so it means suggesting that the sovereignty of the people is not sacrosanct. Special minority rights are inherently countermajoritarian in character.

This aspect raises a problem for providing a democratically robust vindication of special minority rights: that is, a vindication that we might expect to be able to uphold in a fair and open discussion that is structured by a shared commitment to democracy. Any democratically robust vindication must be able to show that the tension between special minority rights and the democratic sovereignty principle is not a straight-out inconsistency. And it is not clear that this can be done under the electoral conception of democracy.

The problem can be appreciated by the contrast between special minority rights and the countermajoritarian rights that are generally countenanced in contemporary political and constitutional practice. These are those general rights – say, of freedom of speech, association, movement and the like – that are invoked as protections that everyone enjoys, not just against individual others, but even against majority, political will. Some have argued that we have to accept that such rights are opposed to democracy and recognise that democracy is not the be all and end all (Riker 1982), while others have countered that the authority of the rights derives from a democratic will that has supported them at critical, constitutional moments (Ackerman 1991). But the striking thing about such rights – or at least many such rights – is that even if we do not find an electoral origin for them, they still can be justified in terms that the electoral conception of democracy itself provides.

Such a justification is outlined by those authors who argue that while the general rights in question are indeed countermajoritarian – while they do constrain the electoral will – they are essential for the functioning of electoral democracy. Thus Stephen Holmes argues in this spirit that any feasible mode of democratisation that does not place an impossible burden on public decision-making will have to take issues of private life off the public agenda and give people the rights associated with negative liberty (Holmes 1995: 206). And Jürgen Habermas urges that a proper, deliberative form of democracy is bound to give such rights to the citizenry, since they are a *sine qua non* of deliberative participation in government: they are as essential to the working of such a democracy as the rights associated with equal electoral standing (Habermas 1996: 142).

According to this style of argument, regular countermajoritarian rights cannot be overridden by electoral will without the very prospect of an electoral democracy disappearing. There cannot be a rule of majority will, such as the electoral conception of democracy envisages, unless – paradoxically – majority will operates within the countermajoritarian constraints of those rights. Like the constraints of grammar on ordinary speech, these constraints on electoral democracy make possible the very activity that they regulate.

Unlike general countermajoritarian constraints, however – and unlike the rights associated with equal electoral standing – special minority rights cannot be defended on the grounds of being themselves essential to democracy. So long as we think of democracy in the image of the electoral conception, we must see special minority rights as countermajoritarian constraints that are themselves unnecessary to the working of democracy and that are visited upon democracy from outside. And this means that it will be difficult to uphold such rights in a discussion where the guiding framework is the electoral conception of democracy. The rights may have a powerful moral appeal but they will not be democratically robust. They will be open to the charge of representing a form of special pleading that is inconsistent with letting democracy run its natural course.

The Electoral-cum-Constestatory Conception of Democracy

At the most abstract level where no one will disagree, the concept of democracy is that of a system under which the people control government. The electoral assumptions presented in the last section offer a particular interpretation of what this involves: a particular conception of democracy. Here, I try to make the case for a richer, two-dimensional conception of the sort of system that would best answer to the abstract concept. Under this conception, a democracy must certainly have an electoral dimension, but this has to be complemented by a second, contestatory dimension.

My introduction to the richer conception of democracy will be in three stages. I argue, first, that a second dimension is needed if government is to be brought properly under the people's control; second, that an extra dimension of control is available and even partially implemented in current institutional structures; and third, that these observations point us towards a two-dimensional conception of the democratic ideal.

A Second Democratic Dimension is Needed

Democracy is a system under which the process of government – the process of public decision-making – is subject to popular control. By almost all accounts, the guiding idea is that unless the governors are controlled in this way by the governed, then the relevant interests of the governed – however they are interpreted – need not be taken into account and respected. Unless government is controlled by the people, so the rationale goes, there is no guarantee that government will be for the people: there is no guarantee that it will advance the relevant interests of the governed.

The relevant interests of the governed are not their special or sectional interests, but rather, their shared or common interests. If a community has no common interests – in defence, security, health or education, for example, or provision against emergency need – then there is no obvious case for unifying it under a single government. Assuming that a government is desirable, then, that government ought to take its guidance from the common interests of its people.

But how to define such common interests? The argument I make can abstract from any particular answer to this question but it may be useful if I indicate the sort of approach that I favour. A certain good will represent a common interest of a population, as I see things, just so far as cooperatively avowable considerations support its collective provision (Pettit 2000). Cooperatively avowable considerations are those considerations such that were the members of the population holding discussions about what they ought to cooperate in collectively providing, then they could not be dismissed as irrelevant (Elster 1986; Habermas 1984; 1989). They are those considerations to which no participant in a cooperative scheme could deny relevance or weight under ordinary standards of conversational practice. They are not selfish or sectional considerations, for example, nor considerations that some parties to the discussion would see as calls for special treatment and, in particular, as calls that they had no particular reason to heed.

If the rationale of democracy is to force government to take its guidance from people's common interests, then this has an immediate implication for how democracy should be organised. It means that democracy should incorporate institutions that give salience and standing to all common interests, and that democracy should incorporate institutions that reduce or eliminate the influence of other interests: say, interests that are particular to certain individuals or groups within the community.

Institutions of the first sort would guard against the possibility of certain common interests not getting articulated or empowered. They would reduce 'false negatives': that is, the non-identification of certain common interests. Institutions of the second would guard against the possibility of inappropriate interests affecting what government does. They would reduce 'false positives': that is, the misidentification of certain interests as common interests. Institutions of the first sort would police the social world in such a way that a community of interest is established among people. Institutions of the second kind would police it in such a way that no individual or group has a lesser place within that community: each counts for one, and none for more than one. Institutions of the first sort would promote democratic effectiveness; institutions of the second would promote democratic equality.

Electoral institutions of the kind that satisfy the principles presented in the last section may be expected to do as well as any institutions can be expected to do in identifying and empowering candidates for the status of common interests. They allow individuals and groups of individuals to come forward with policy proposals about what is purportedly in the common interest, they ensure that such proposals will be submitted to public examination and discussion, and they enable the people to determine, on the basis of majority vote, whether a given policy program will be selected or not. The process is fallible and subject to corrupting pressures, but it promises to do better than almost any conceivable alternative, making it likely that all common interests are recognised and that 'false negatives' are avoided. Or so at least I am happy to concede here.

But electoral institutions are unlikely to work as successfully on the second democratic front. They are unlikely to do as well in ensuring that only common interests will be recognised and empowered, and that 'false positives' will be avoided. They may serve to weed out the intrusion of foreign interests into the agenda of policy-making. But they may allow the interest of a majority to be represented as a common interest, given reliance on majority voting. And, even more importantly, they may allow all sorts of special interests to have an impact on the way policies are specified and implemented in the course of day-to-day government. Electoral institutions are vulnerable both to majoritarian and to manipulative control. They do not do enough to ensure that only common interests have an influence on government and that no individual or group gets privileged access to power.

This observation suggests that democracy should encompass more than electoral institutions. Not only should there be electoral institutions that serve, however imperfectly, to give salience and standing to what are allegedly common interests, there should be institutions in place that try to guard against interests masquerading as common interests and, more generally, against interests having an impact on how government is conducted. Democracy needs a second, non-electoral dimension.

A Second Democratic Dimension is Available

There are two distinct ways in which any process can be controlled and, in particular, in which the people might be given control over government. Consider the process whereby the content of a newspaper or magazine is determined. One way of controlling this process is through the contribution of authors who write the different columns. The other way is by the monitoring of the editors who object to certain passages and make suggestions for revisions. The authorial mode of control exists so far as there are always authors at the origin of the text that presents itself for publication. The editorial mode of control exists so far as there are editors who stand poised, ready to intervene and initiate changes in the event that the text does not satisfy them. The authorial mode of control is essentially causal or generative: the authors determine the input to the process. The editorial mode of control is essentially selectional: the editors only allow text that satisfies them to survive that process.

The most striking thing about the electoral conception of democracy, as encoded in the principles presented, is that it mainly seeks to give the people an authorial form of control over the process of public decision-making. And the authorial control it gives the people is very limited. Only the majority have a say on any issue; there is always a defeated minority. Except in the case of referenda, the majority do not themselves generate the laws and other regulations that will rule in public life. They merely select those who will oversee and orchestrate the authorial process.

But once we see the possibility of editorial as well as authorial control, then the limitations of popular authorship ought to raise the question of whether we cannot enhance democracy – enhance people's control over government – by making provisions for something analogous to editorial control. Can we see a way to ensure that the common people are able to stand over the process of public decision-making, ready to intervene in the event of what they see as objectionable decisions coming under consideration or being implemented? In particular, can we see a way to ensure this sort of control, short of going to the unworkable extreme of giving everyone a veto on public decisions? I believe we can.

Imagine you are the editor of a newspaper and you want to exercise your control to effect a general result. What steps might you take? One obvious step would be to make clear that if you are unhappy with some text that is presented for publication then you will see that it is changed to suit your line. You may be able to do this peremptorily, as in the case of most contemporary newspaper editors. Or you may have the power to refer your objection to an editorial board: a board, presumably, that supports your general line and that can be expected to uphold any reasonable objection.

But it might not be a very effective way of promoting your editorial control just to rely on your right to object to any text presented for publication. You could be swamped, for example, by unsatisfactory texts so that your task would become almost impossible. There are two other steps, therefore, that you would do well to contemplate as well: these involve putting in *ex ante* controls, and not just relying on *ex post* objection.

The first *ex ante* step would be to present your authors with guidelines on your editorial policy, or to enunciate constraints on how text is cleared before it comes for your inspection, and to make clear to them that you are likely to object to anything that breaches those guidelines or constraints. You may not make yourself the judge of whether a breach has occurred; you need only assert the right to refer any alleged breach to the editorial board for adjudication. But in either case this first step ought to reduce the need for resorting to *ex post* objection; it ought to allow your editorial control to run on smoother paths.

The other *ex ante* step that you could take to establish your regime is to insist that if authors are worried about whether they may be breaching editorial policy, or if they are writing in an area where such policy is particularly important or at risk, then they should follow certain routines. In particular, they should consult with you or with certain parties that you designate as your agents in consultation.

I spell out the steps that you might take to establish editorial control over a newspaper because they point us to steps whereby the governed in a democracy might establish a second, non-electoral form of control over government. The first *ex ante* measure, corresponding to the editorial guidelines and constraints, would involve the imposition of restrictions, formal or informal, on how government can act. Examples of potential constraints are various: the recognition of restrictions on the ends that government can legitimately pursue, such as the principle that only acts harmful to others should be criminalised by government. The institutionalisation of rule-of-law conditions that any legislation must satisfy. The requirement that those who support a law, or impose any government decision, give a deliberative justification of the line taken. The separation of judicial from executive and legislative power. The introduction of a bicameral structure that requires legislation to be endorsed by different sorts of representative bodies. The appointment of certain statutory officers and bodies – officers like an Auditor General, an Electoral Commissioner, a Director of Public Prosecutions, a Central Bank Director – who must be involved in the making of certain decisions. And of course the endorsement of a constitution, or a bill of rights, or a set of laws or conventions that enjoy a certain entrenched status.

The second *ex ante* measure would be to insist that at least in certain areas government should put out its proposed initiatives for public consultation, and seek to ascertain the opinions of those of the public generally and in particular of those likely to be affected by a proposed decision. A government might consult the public without a commitment to take the consultation seriously, but this danger can be reduced by requiring the government to place submissions on the public record and to take account of the points made in its own justification of what it eventually does.

Is there also an *ex post* measure, corresponding to the editor's power of objection, that might be taken to empower the interests of the governed? Many institutional provisions fall into this category: the possibility of seeking judicial review of government legislation. The possibility of seeking administrative review of government decisions (Cane 1996). The possibility of appealing to an ombudsman against such decisions or of triggering an internal review of some sort. And the informal possibilities of attracting the interest of an opposition party or a parliamentary committee, or the attention and criticism of the media or of some relevant social movement.

Two-dimensional Democracy

It should be clear that the second dimension that democracy properly requires has a good chance of being advanced by the editorial measures briefly reviewed. The provisions outlined all represent ways in which it may be possible for different groups among the governed to be reassured that they are protected in some measure against unequal treatment. If the *ex ante* and *ex post* measures can be suitably designed, then they should help to ensure that when the elected government makes decisions, it doesn't systematically neglect the ways in which those decisions impact negatively on certain people. They should help to ensure that government treats the governed as equals – that only the common interests of the governed shape government policy – even as it makes decisions that will be more welcome in some quarters than in others.

This is not the place to review the likely effectiveness of these different measures, or to explore the ways in which they might be strengthened and supplemented (Waldron 1999). The only point that we need to register is that there are institutions imaginable, there are indeed institutions in existence, that promise to give people a power of contesting what government does that parallels their collective power to determine who shall be in government. The measures serve a number of contestatory purposes: they render contestation less likely to be needed; they make clear the bases on which contestation can occur; and they serve to implement contestation, whether in or after the period of decision-making.

If it is desirable and feasible to give democracy a second, contestatory dimension, then we should extend the principles outlined in the first section to characterise an enriched, electoral-cum-contestatory conception of the democratic ideal. There are four principles that the conception would seem to require. The first two principles are as before; the third, which introduces the contestatory element, is new; and the last is amended to give recognition to that novel element:

- government is elected by the people on a periodic basis: certain key government authorities are elected by the people at intervals of not more than a stipulated, generally agreeable minimum;
- the people enjoy full and equal electoral standing: no-one is excluded without generally agreed good reason to do with age, competence or incarceration, for example, from standing or voting or speaking out in such elections; there is no systematic intimidation brought to bear on those who stand or vote or speak out; and no-one's vote is weighted more heavily than anyone else's, except where there is generally agreed good reason – say, to do with ensuring regional representation or maintaining a federal system – for such a weighting;
- the people enjoy full and equal contestatory standing: there are a variety of measures in place whereby people, individually and collectively, can be reasonably well assured of being treated as equals in government decision-making; in particular, there are measures available whereby anyone who has doubts about being treated as equals can contest government decisions and have a reasonable level of confidence that discriminatory decisions will be reversed;
- the people are collectively sovereign: subject to the constraints of promoting people's equal electoral and contestatory standing, the rules under which government authorities are elected and act are subject to determination or amendment either by the collective people directly – say, in a referendum – or by their elected representatives.

The electoral conception of democracy outlined in the earlier set of principles is an intuitive ideal of democracy, even if it does not exactly correspond to any actual practice. The fact is, we would expect any democracy worthy of the name to approximate to the satisfaction of those principles.

I would say something similar is true of the enriched conception. While we are not in the habit of associating the abstract ideal of democracy – the abstract ideal of popular control of government – with matters to do with how government is constrained in its operations, few of us would be happy to apply the term 'democracy' to any regime that deprived people of contestatory standing. Imagine a regime in which government is entitled to legislate on any matter, no matter how personal; or where government is not required to formulate decisions in a rule-of-law manner and can act by name against certain individuals or groups; or where the executive or legislature controls judicial decision-making; or where there is no room whatsoever for consultation between elections with the populace; or where there is no possibility of appealing against government decision in any area. Few, if any, of us would feel comfortable about describing such a regime as 'democratic' in character; we would feel that the term was being abused.

That being so, I think we can be happy enough about taking the principles just given to characterise an intuitive conception of democracy and a conception that we would expect real-world democracies to approximate in some measure (Shapiro 1996). If there is any element of controversy in the proposal to characterise democracy in this electoral-cum-contestatory way, it comes of the fact that contestatory constraints on what a democratically elected government can do are often described as limitations on democracy, rather than aspects of a democratic regime. But this habit of speech ought not to inhibit us, particularly in view of the fact that the constraints in question can serve to give editorial control of government to ordinary people. On the contrary, I would say, we ought to seize upon the fact that while there is an obvious contrast between electoral and contestatory action, they both represent moments in the assertion of the interests of the governed: they represent ways in which the governed can hold the governors to account.

Minority Claims under the Electoral-cum-Contestatory Conception

It remains to show that whereas special minority rights are vulnerable under an electoral conception of democracy – they look like democratically unmotivated constraints on majority will – they are not similarly vulnerable under the enriched way of conceiving democracy. Let democracy be seen as involving two dimensions – one electoral, the other contestatory – and it becomes quite natural to think that in many circumstances it will require the recognition of special minority claims.

The model for how special minority claims might be established under the two-dimensional conception of democracy is provided by the way in which Habermas, Holmes and others try to establish the claims of certain general, minority-protecting rights under the purely electoral conception. They argue that unless majority will is constrained by those rights then, paradoxically, majoritarian, electoral democracy will not be able to function properly. I argue, in parallel, that unless special minority rights are put in place then in many circumstances electoral-cum-contestatory democracy will not be able to function properly either.

The circumstances that are likely to call for special minority rights are readily specified:

- there is a robust minority or set of minorities present in the population, where robustness means that the group is not unified just by a single issue; its unity comes of a common culture or creed or whatever;

- the minority or minorities in question have a common set of interests that can be jointly advanced for all members;
- those interests are at least partially distinctive: they conflict with the interests of people outside the group in question;
- those interests are vulnerable to collective, majoritarian decision-making: it is quite possible for a majority to support a line that is inimical to the group's interests, even as it advances interests that are shared in common by all;
- all of these things are a matter of common awareness in the society at large, particularly within the group. Almost everyone believes that almost everyone believes this. And so on, in this sense: at no level is there a general disbelief in the belief at the level below; it is not the case, for example, that almost everyone disbelieves in the belief mentioned in the last sentence. Almost everyone believes in the existence of a culturally distinctive, democratically vulnerable minority or set of minorities in the population that the state governs.

Where circumstances like these obtain, then members of the minority will naturally be sensitive to the question of how far their interests are going to be taken equally into account – of how far they are going to be treated as equals – in the process of democratic government. The contours of diversity will be so numerous, and some will run at such variance from the general landscape, that there will be a salient possibility that many government decisions are directed by majority interests, to the neglect and detriment of the minority.

If the overall state is to have any justification, then there must be certain substantive interests that are common to the minority and the majority cultures, and the state must serve to advance those interests. The common interests may include interests in defence, law and order, environmental soundness, economic prosperity; and we may assume that the electoral process can serve – at least as well as any feasible alternative – to identify and advance those interests. But given the cultural diversity that obtains, there will often be a question as to whether the state really treats minorities as equals in this process. There will be a question as to whether it is only such common interests that dictate government policy.

Under conditions of cultural diversity there is great scope for people not to be treated as equals by the state. In the monocultural state, you and I may have rival interests in matters to do with where an airport will be constructed, where a prison will be built and the like. But in the multicultural state, the room for rivalry of interests expands dramatically. You and your culture may have interests that conflict with mine across a spectrum that ranges from language to religion to symbolic practices; and from conventions of family life to habits of economic activity to the customs under which land is held and used. And if you and your culture are in the minority, then you have a very broad base for concern that you and yours will not be treated as equals in the exercise of public power. In a monocultural society the existence of an independent planning board may be sufficient to assure you that you were just unlucky to have a new airport or prison situated in your neighbourhood. But if conditions of cultural diversity obtain then it may take much stronger institutions of contestation to assure you that decisions you and your minority culture do not like are really just the product of bad luck.

The fact that a society is multicultural, then, means that the democratic state is going to have to take special steps to try and establish the equal and full contestatory power of those in minority groups. Otherwise the members of those groups will not be guaranteed of being treated as equals and of living in a proper, two-dimensional democracy. They will live under the thumb of those in the majority and the mainstream.

The only recourse in such a predicament is to require the recognition of minority claims of various sorts. The predicament may be more or less severe, but no matter what the level of severity, the obvious response will be to establish minority rights of a corresponding kind. I shall make the point by considering three possible levels of severity at which the multicultural challenge may arise.

Suppose that a minority culture is much respected in a society, and that while there is a rivalry of interests between its members and those in the mainstream, still it is a matter of more or less common awareness that no-one is likely to resent those interests being taken fully into account by government. In such a situation there might not be any need to restrict government formally in order to ensure that the minority members are treated as equals. It might be enough to establish the minimal right of those in the minority to be specifically consulted about legislation and decision-making, where appeal could be made – say, in an administrative appeals tribunal – against any decision taken without consultation, or in defiance of consultation.

But it does not take much imagination to recognise that in many cases the divergences between the minority and the majority will be so deep that a satisfactory response must involve something more besides. It may require not just that the minority have a right of consultation and appeal, but also that specific exemptions or provisions are made in their favour by the government. This sort of case will arise wherever the way things happen in the society, in particular the way government behaves, is almost bound to impact negatively on the minority, and where the only way in which the minority can be treated as equals is for them to receive special treatment of some kind.

There are many examples of where special minority treatment will be required. The society and the state tend to privilege the language of the majority, so there must be provision for furthering minority language and for making it possible to use that language in certain forums: say, in court hearings. The majority religion is naturally given recognition in the public holidays and in the public symbols adopted by the state, so there should be provision for the minority religion to be given some compensatory recognition and for minority members not to have majority practices thrust upon them. The majority culture is inevitably represented in the educational practices prevalent in the society, particularly in state-supported schools, so there ought to be provision for substitute, or supplementary, education in matters relating to the minority culture.

There is also a further level of severity at which multiculturalism may make a challenge for democracy: a level such that neither rights of consultation nor rights of special treatment will be sufficient to ensure that the minority are treated as equals by the state in which they are incorporated. In this situation the cleavage between the minority and the mainstream is so deep that the minority will not be assured of being treated as equals just because they must be consulted in the process of decision-making or just because the decisions taken must make special provisions in their favour. The cleavage is so deep that the only recourse possible is for the state to give over its decision-making powers on a range of issues that affect the minority to their own representatives and, as it will be, their own government.

The case where such special rights of minority self-government will be most plausible arises when a minority nation, in particular an indigenous one, is incorporated in a democratic state. Here the rivalry of interests may extend to differences in the significance accorded to land and tradition, in the view taken of the nature of landholding and group-membership, in the rules under which certain claims are adjudicated, and so on; it may extend beyond any limits envisaged in mainstream tradition (Tully 1995). Where the difference goes this deep, then it is hard to see how the members of such a minority could possibly think that they were treated as equals – quite apart from any issue of historical justice – unless they were given suitable powers of self-government in relation to the matters in question.

It is natural to speak of the radically distinct minority group envisaged in this third case as a nation that is separate from the majority nation; indeed I have already done so. After all, how can traditions come apart as radically as they are imagined without the minority constituting a distinct nation? But though the case involves two or indeed more nations, it is important that the rationale for minority self-government continues to derive from the need to give people equal contestatory standing within one and the same democratic system. If the case for minority self-government is made to derive from the distinctness of the nations as such, and not from the contestatory problems to which the distinctness gives rise, then it may be too strong for comfort. It may suggest that it is appropriate for the majority nation to present the minority with a dilemma: become a separate state (and suffer the consequences of living in our shadow) or join us on our terms, without any special recognition of your separateness.

These comments are meant only to be illustrative and I apologise for the sketchy nature of the examples. But my main claim, I hope, is clear. If we think that democracy requires a regime under which people have equal and full contestatory as well as electoral standing, then we should have no difficulty in seeing special minority claims as a natural part of the broad democratic package. We should have no hesitation about asserting that multicultural democracy is bound to make room for establishing such rights, whether at a minimal or at an intensive level.

To return to the themes of the first section, I think that this is an important claim to be able to defend. Special minority rights are inherently countermajoritarian in character and it is of the greatest importance to be able to show that that does not make them antidemocratic. The ideal of democracy is the guiding light in most contemporary political discussion – it is the one ideal that no-one ever questions – and special minority claims would be very fragile indeed if they were inconsistent with the democratic vision of a society where government is pursued in the interests of the governed. They are certainly inconsistent with a purely electoral conception of democracy. But, as I tried to show in the last section, most of us are committed to a richer, electoral-cum-contestatory conception. Far from being inconsistent with it, special minority rights will often be required under the richer conception: they will often present themselves as essential for the proper functioning of democracy.

CHAPTER 12

American Multiculturalism and the 'Nations Within'

Will Kymlicka

Like citizens in many other countries, Americans have been vigorously debating issues of multiculturalism for the last few years. But the debate in the US has a special importance because of the profound influence of American ideas around the world. This influence is greater than ever before now that the US is the world's only superpower. Moreover, American foundations and government agencies are among the leading funders of scholars, non-governmental organisations and research projects around the world, particularly on issues of ethnicity and democracy, and this inevitably encourages the tendency to view the US as the 'model' by which ethnic relations in other countries should be understood and assessed.

But the American debate about ethnic relations would be important even without this superpower status. For, as David Hollinger notes, the US has been a multi-ethnic democracy 'for a longer period of time than any of the comparably multi-ethnic societies [and] it has done so with a population more ethno-racially diverse' than most other democracies (Hollinger 1995: 140). So it is natural that other countries pay close attention to American models of ethnic relations. As a result, even those books which are written solely for 'my fellow Americans' are influential in international debates.

Unfortunately, I believe that the international influence of American debates has not been entirely a happy one. To be sure, it has been beneficial on some issues, but has been unhelpful on others, serving to exacerbate rather than remedy important injustices, particularly for indigenous peoples and other 'nations within'. I'll try to explain why.

American Multiculturalism

A wide range of views has been expressed in the American debate about multiculturalism, and I won't make any effort to summarise them here.

216

But I think we can see an emerging consensus, or at least a dominant paradigm, centred on the following three claims:

- that some or other form of multiculturalism is now unavoidable – 'we are all multiculturalists now', as Nathan Glazer puts it (Glazer 1997) – and that the interesting debate is not whether to adopt multiculturalism, but rather what kind of multiculturalism to adopt;
- that the appropriate form of multiculturalism must be fluid in its conception of groups and group boundaries (that is, it must accept that new groups may emerge, older groups may coalesce or disappear); voluntary in its conception of group affiliation (that is, it must accept that individuals should be free to decide whether and how to affiliate with their community of descent); and non-exclusive in its conception of group identity (that is, it must accept that being a member of one group does not preclude identification with another group, or with the larger American nation). Only such an open-ended, fluid and voluntary conception of multiculturalism fits with the fluid and open nature of American society, and its deep respect for individual freedom and choice;
- that the greatest challenge to creating such a fluid conception of multiculturalism remains the disadvantaged and stigmatised status of African-Americans. Being 'Black' is an ascribed identity that is very difficult for most African-Americans to escape or renounce. The child of a Greek-Arab mixed marriage can choose whether to think of himself or herself as a Greek-American or Arab-American or both or neither; the child of a Greek-Black mixed marriage will be seen by others as 'Black', whether or not that is how s/he wants to be seen (Waters 1990). Moreover, the result of this ascribed identity is a greater degree of social exclusion and segregation than for other ethnic groups (that is, Blacks are more likely to live in segregated neighbourhoods, attend segregated schools, pray in segregated churches and so on). The main challenge for American multiculturalism, therefore, is to reduce the ascriptive, stigmatising and segregating elements of 'Black' identity, so that being Black can come to resemble the open, voluntary and fluid nature of other ethnic identities in America.[1]

I will not dispute any of these three claims – on the contrary, I share them. However, I worry about the way in which they have typically been defended by American writers, and the influence these defences are having in other countries. The problem, from an international perspective, is that this open, fluid and voluntary conception of American multiculturalism is typically explained and defended *in contrast to minority nationalism*. That is, when American authors explain what a closed, static and involuntary conception of multiculturalism would look like, they typically point to cases of groups (like many indigenous peoples) which view themselves as 'nations within' and which mobilise along nationalist lines.

In the rest of this essay, I explain why I think this contrast is mistaken and unhelpful. I don't think that this contrast is helpful as a way of thinking about multiculturalism even within the US. My main concern, however, is with the influence of this argument abroad. I believe it is having a pernicious influence in other countries, inhibiting efforts to understand and accommodate the minority nationalisms they face, including the legitimate claims of indigenous peoples.

Hollinger's Postethnic America

I will take as my example the recent work of David Hollinger, whose *Postethnic America* is the most subtle and sophisticated proponent of the consensus view I discussed earlier (Hollinger 1995). Hollinger distinguishes two kinds of multiculturalism: a 'pluralist' model that treats groups as permanent and enduring, and as the subject of group rights; and a 'cosmopolitan' model that accepts shifting group boundaries, multiple affiliations and hybrid identities, which is based on individual rights. He summarises the distinction this way:

> pluralism respects inherited boundaries and locates individuals within one or another of a series of ethno-racial groups to be protected or preserved. Cosmopolitanism is more wary of traditional enclosures and favours voluntary affiliations. Cosmopolitanism promotes multiple identities, emphasises the dynamic and changing character of many groups, and is responsive to the potential for creating new cultural combinations. (Hollinger 1995: 3)

Hollinger strongly defends the latter cosmopolitan form – with its 'ideal according to which individuals decide how tightly or loosely they wish to affiliate with one or more communities of descent' (Hollinger 1995: 165) – while criticising the former. He argues that this cosmopolitan model has worked well for white European immigrants in the past, and that it continues to work well for more recent immigrants from Latin America, Africa and Asia. He recognises that it will be much more difficult to bring African-Americans (the descendants of the slaves, as distinct from new immigrants from Africa or the Caribbean) under this 'postethnic' umbrella. However, he insists that this is what most Blacks want, and what justice requires, and that it remains an achievable goal, although certain special measures may be required (for example, more targeted forms of affirmative action) (Hollinger 1996).

As I noted earlier, I share these basic views about the appropriate and desirable form of multiculturalism in the American context. But how do Hollinger's arguments apply to other countries? Consider my own country, Canada. There are two quite different forms of 'multiculturalism' in

Canada, corresponding to two different kinds of ethno-cultural groups. Like the US and Australia, Canada is a British settler society, formed by the union of former British colonies. In addition to the descendants of these British settlers, we have two kinds of ethno-cultural minorities.

First, we have those groups which emigrated as individuals or families to Canada after the British established their dominion. Until quite recently, these immigrants were expected to shed their distinctive heritage and assimilate almost entirely to existing British cultural norms (this was known as the 'Anglo-conformity model' of integrating immigrants). However, in the 1970s, the Canadian government rejected the assimilationist model of immigration, and instead adopted a more tolerant policy that accepts the public expression of immigrant ethnicity. This change was formalised in 1971 with the adoption of an official 'multiculturalism policy' by the federal government. The policy acknowledges the inevitability and desirability of the public expression of immigrant ethnicity, and makes a commitment to reform public institutions (for example, schools, hospitals, media) to accommodate the distinctive identities and practices of immigrant groups (so long as these do not violate the rights of others). However, this policy works alongside other policies (such as naturalisation policies, education policies), which encourage the long-term linguistic and institutional integration of immigrants into mainstream society.

Second, we have those groups which were on Canadian soil before the British arrived, and which were conquered or colonised by the British. These are the indigenous peoples, and the Québécois. These 'nations within' were originally self-governing, and like other conquered or colonised peoples around the world, have consistently fought to gain (or rather regain) their autonomy, so as to maintain themselves as separate and self-governing societies. They call themselves 'nations', and assert national rights. And indeed both the indigenous peoples and the Québécois do have substantial autonomy within Canada: the former through the system of self-governing Indian bands; the latter through the system of federalism.

In the Canadian context the term 'multiculturalism' is only used to refer to the first category. The federal multiculturalism policy concerns the accommodation of immigrant ethnicity. The accommodation of our 'nations within' is dealt with by other policies, under other government departments, and indeed under separate sections of the Canadian constitution. However, for the purposes of this paper, I will describe them as two forms of multiculturalism: one focused on immigrant ethnicity; the other on minority nationalism.

How does Hollinger's theory apply to the Canadian case? Some commentators have argued that both kinds of multiculturalism in Canada fall into Hollinger's 'pluralist' category, treating immigrant groups and national minorities as fixed and self-contained entities. However, on inspection, it is clear that the immigrant multiculturalism policy in Canada, in its intentions and consequences, is much closer to Hollinger's 'cosmopolitan' version. It explicitly treats ethno-cultural affiliation as voluntary, and encourages members of different ethnic groups to interact, to share their cultural heritage and to participate in common educational, economic, political and legal institutions. The long-term result of this approach has been a breaking down of the barriers between ethnic groups, including a significant increase over the last thirty years in rates of inter-ethnic friendships and inter-marriages – higher than in the US – and to the proliferation of shifting, multiple and hybridic identities.[2]

Like Hollinger, I think that the integration of immigrants into this fluid and hybridic form of multiculturalism is desirable, and indeed is quite a success story. And, like Hollinger, I think that this process can work not only for the older white immigrants from Europe, but also for newer Arab, Asian and Caribbean immigrants.

I wouldn't use the term 'cosmopolitan' to describe this form of multiculturalism, for reasons I will explain later. But I agree that it is a good model for thinking about the integration of immigrants groups, and I have defended it in Canada (where it is already fairly strongly entrenched) and in Europe (where it remains strongly resisted). So on this issue I think that Hollinger's account of a postethnic America is a good model for other countries. Countries such as Austria or Belgium could learn a great deal from the US about the successful integration of immigrants.

My worry, however, is about the applicability of this model to non-immigrant groups, and in particular to the 'nations within', that is, to those groups that have been conquered or colonised, like the Québécois or indigenous peoples in Canada. Hollinger never explicitly addresses the question of the rights of colonised or conquered peoples within liberal democracies, or the legitimacy of the forms of minority nationalism adopted by such groups. But it is fairly clear that he does not support minority nationalism.

For example, he says that his model rejects 'the notion of legally protected territorial enclaves for nationality groups' (Hollinger 1995: 91), and that pluralism differs from cosmopolitanism 'in the degree to which it endows with privilege particular groups, especially the communities that are well-established at whatever time the ideal of pluralism is invoked' (Hollinger 1995: 85). These passages implicitly reject the essence of minority nationalism in Canada or elsewhere. After all, the Québécois and indigenous peoples in Canada claim legally recognised rights of self-government over their traditional territories, and the justification for these claims is precisely that these societies were 'well-established' before

British dominion. Hollinger's theory implicitly seems to rule such nationalist claims out of court.

Hollinger is not just implicitly rejecting minority nationalism, he explicitly criticises it as well. For example, he describes Québécois nationalism as the extreme form of 'pluralist' multiculturalism, since it treats the Québécois as a permanent and enduring group, and as the bearer of group rights. Indeed, he says it is a form of 'ethnic nationalism' (Hollinger 1995: 134), which is logically equivalent to racial segregation in the US (131). And while he singles out the claims of stateless nations for criticism, his objections seem to apply to indigenous peoples as well, and one suspects that he views their national claims as forms of illiberal racism.

I think this is wrong, on several levels. First, Hollinger's views are out of step with the emerging practice of other Western democracies; second, they are out of step with the US's practice itself; and third; they are based on a misunderstanding of the nature of minority nationalism. I will discuss each of these problems in turn, and examine the impact they have had on the recognition of the claims of indigenous peoples and other 'nations within' around the world.

Accommodating Minority Nationalism

How have other Western democracies dealt with their 'nations within'? By 'nations within' (or 'national minorities'), I mean groups that formed complete and functioning societies on their historic homeland before being incorporated into a larger state. The incorporation of such national minorities has typically been involuntary, due to colonisation, conquest or the ceding of territory from one imperial power to another, but may also arise voluntarily, as a result of federation.

The category of national minorities (or what others call 'homeland minorities') includes indigenous peoples like the Inuit in Canada, Maori in New Zealand or Sami in Scandinavia, but also includes other incorporated national groups, like the Catalans in Spain, Scots in Britain or Québécois in Canada. These latter groups are sometimes called 'stateless nations' or 'ethno-national groups', to distinguish them from indigenous peoples.

There is no universally agreed criteria for distinguishing indigenous peoples from stateless nations, but one criteria concerns the role these groups played in the process of state-formation. As a rule, stateless nations were contenders but losers in the process of European state-formation, whereas indigenous peoples were entirely isolated from that process until very recently, and so retained a pre-modern way of life until well into this century. Stateless nations would have liked to form their own states, but lost in the struggle for political power, whereas indigenous peoples existed outside this system of European states. Within the western democracies, then, the Catalans, Basques, Puerto Ricans, Flemish, Scots, Welsh and Québécois are stateless nations, whereas the Sami, Greenlanders, Australian Aborigines, Maori, Inuit and American Indians are indigenous peoples.[3]

In most of the sociological literature on ethnic relations, and the international law literature on minority rights, these two categories of national minorities are discussed in isolation from each other. And of course there are many important differences between stateless nations and indigenous peoples, both in the nature of their cultural and social organisation and in the nature of their incorporation into larger states. However, I want to examine them together here for a variety of reasons.

First, there are important similarities in the ways both types of national minorities have responded to their incorporation into larger states. Stateless nations and indigenous peoples have typically sought to gain or regain their self-governing powers in their traditional territory to maintain themselves as separate and distinct societies alongside the majority.[4] That is, they have typically sought to maintain or enhance their political autonomy.

At the extreme, this may involve claims to outright secession, but more usually it involves some form of territorial autonomy. And they typically mobilise along nationalist lines, using the language of 'nationhood' to describe and justify these demands for self-government.

Both stateless nations and indigenous peoples reject any idea that they are simply 'minorities' within the larger political community, and insist instead that they form their own distinct and self-governing political community within the boundaries of the larger state.[5] As James Tully argues, the sort of relationship desired by indigenous peoples in Canada must be one based on the recognition of Aboriginal people as 'peoples' or 'nations'.[6]

This 'nation-to-nation' relationship is sought by most stateless nations and indigenous peoples around the world. While the ideology of nationalism has typically seen full-fledged independence as the 'normal' or 'natural' end-point, economic or demographic reasons may make this unfeasible for some national minorities, particularly for indigenous peoples. Moreover, the historical ideal of a fully sovereign state is increasingly obsolete in today's world of globalised economics and transnational institutions. Hence there is a growing interest among stateless nations and indigenous peoples in exploring other forms of self-government, such as federal or quasi-federal forms of regional autonomy. The precise nature of these arrangements will certainly differ for indigenous peoples and stateless nations, as I discuss later, but they raise some common challenges to the theory and practice of Western statehood.

Second, discussing indigenous peoples in isolation from other 'nations within' can reinforce the perception that they are somehow exotic and exceptional; of interest to a few specialists, perhaps, but not a central issue for political life and political theory in the modern world. If we examine stateless nations and indigenous peoples together, we can see that the problem of the 'nations within' is truly universal in scope, of enormous urgency and of staggering proportions. As Walker Connor notes, the list of countries affected by minority nationalism is global, and includes countries:

> in Africa (for example, Ethiopia), Asia (Sri Lanka), Eastern Europe (Romania), Western Europe (France), North America (Guatemala), South America (Guyana), and Oceania (New Zealand). The list includes countries that are old (United Kingdom) as well as new (Bangladesh), large (Indonesia) as well as small (Fiji), rich (Canada) as well as poor (Pakistan), authoritarian (Sudan) as well as democratic (Belgium), Marxist-Leninist (China) as well as militantly anti-Marxist (Turkey). The list also includes countries which are Buddhist (Burma), Christian (Spain), Moslem (Iran), Hindu (India), and Judaic (Israel). (Connor forthcoming)

These conflicts are not only pervasive, they are deadly serious. Ethnocultural conflict has become the main source of political violence around the world, and studies show that the single most important cause of these ethno-cultural conflicts is struggles between states and nations within, particularly over land and settlement policies (Gurr 1993). Given the ubiquity and severity of these conflicts, some scholars have called it the 'Third World War', which has 'produced millions of casualties and massive forced dislocations of [national minorities] who make up the majority of the world's refugees'.[7]

Put in this light, the problem of how states deal with 'nations within' is not a marginal issue: it is one of the key issues, perhaps even the central issue, for states in the twenty-first century.

How should liberal democracies respond to such minority nationalisms? In the rest of this section, I will examine the general trends in Western democracies toward greater recognition of minority nationalism, and then in the next section consider whether the US diverges from this general trend.

Historically, liberal democracies have tried to suppress minority nationalisms, often ruthlessly, whether advanced by stateless nations or indigenous peoples. At various points in the eighteenth and nineteenth centuries, for example, France banned the use of the Basque and Breton languages in schools or publications, and banned any political associations that aimed to promote minority nationalism. In the nineteenth-century Canada stripped the Québécois of their French-language rights and institutions, and redrew political boundaries so that the Québécois did not form a majority in any province.

Similar policies were adopted toward indigenous peoples. Canada and Australia prohibited the use of indigenous languages in schools and public institutions, and encouraged the massive settlement of indigenous lands. Canada also made it illegal for Aborigines to form political associations to promote their national claims.

All of these measures were intended to disempower national minorities and to eliminate any sense of their possessing a distinct national identity, justified partly on the grounds that minorities which viewed themselves as distinct 'nations' would be disloyal and potentially secessionist, and partly on the grounds that national minorities are 'backward' and 'uncivilised', and that their languages and cultures were not worthy of respect and protection.[8] But the attitude of liberal democracies toward minority nationalism has changed dramatically in this century. It is increasingly recognised that the suppression of minority nationalism was mistaken, for empirical and normative reasons. Empirically, the evidence shows that pressuring national minorities to integrate into the dominant national group simply will not work. Western states badly misjudged the durability of minority national identities. The character of a national identity (for example, the heroes, myths and traditional customs) can change quickly. But the identity itself – the sense of being a distinct nation, with its own national culture – is much more stable. Liberal democratic governments have, at times, used all the tools at their disposal to destroy the sense of separate identity among their national minorities, from the prohibition of tribal customs to the banning of minority-language schools. But despite centuries of legal discrimination, social prejudice and indifference, national minorities have maintained their sense of forming distinct nations with a desire for national autonomy.

As a result, when the state attacks a minority's sense of distinct nationhood, the result is often to promote rather than reduce the threat of disloyalty and secessionist movements. Indeed, recent surveys of ethno-nationalist conflict around the world show that self-government arrangements diminish the likelihood of violent conflict, while refusing or rescinding self-government rights is likely to escalate the level of conflict (Gurr 1993; Hannum 1990; Lapidoth 1996). In the experience of Western democracies, the best way to ensure the loyalty of national minorities has been to accept, not attack, their sense of distinct nationality.

This is a striking trend visible in most Western democracies containing national minorities. In the mid-nineteenth-century, Switzerland was the only democratic country with a federal system that enabled national minorities to be self-governing. Today, however, Switzerland has been joined by several other federal countries which grant extensive language rights and regional autonomy to their stateless nations. These include Canada, Spain, Belgium and the emerging federalism of Britain. Other western democracies have adopted quasi-federal forms of territorial autonomy, including Finland (for the Swedes of the Aaland Islands) and Italy (for the Germans in South Tyrol).[9]

We see the same trend with respect to indigenous peoples. After decades of assimilationist policies, virtually all western democracies containing indigenous peoples have shifted toward recognising the rights of indigenous self-government. Indigenous peoples have fought for, and increasingly won, respect for their land rights, and for their right to be self-governing on their lands. This is reflected in section 35 of the Canadian Constitution, in the formation of the Sami parliaments in the Scandinavian countries, the home rule provisions for Greenland and the new-found respect for the Treaty of Waitangi in New Zealand.

Unlike stateless nations, federalism has rarely been the mechanism for ensuring self-government for indigenous peoples. With few exceptions, indigenous peoples currently form a small minority even within their traditional territory, and no redrawing of the boundaries of federal sub-units would create a state, province or territory with an indigenous majority.[10] For most indigenous peoples, therefore, self-government is being achieved outside the federal system, typically through some system of reserved lands. Indigenous communities in several countries have been gaining (or more accurately, regaining) substantial powers over health, education, family law, policing, criminal justice and resource development in their reserved lands. They are becoming, in effect, a kind of 'federacy', to use Daniel Elazar's term, with a collection of powers that is carved out of both federal and provincial jurisdictions (Elazar 1987: 229).[11] As the term suggests, a 'federacy' has important analogies with federalism – in particular, both involve a territorial division of powers, and both involve an ideal of shared sovereignty and a partnership of peoples.

While the form of autonomy differs between stateless nations and indigenous peoples, the trend is the same. Throughout the west, the goal of eliminating minority national identities has been abandoned, and it is now accepted that both stateless nations and indigenous peoples will continue into the indefinite future to see themselves as distinct and self-governing nations within the larger state.[12]

There was a time when eliminating this sense of nationhood among national minorities was a realistic possibility. After all, France was more or less successful in integrating the Basques and Bretons (but not the Corsicans) into the majority French national group in the nineteenth century. But this is no longer a realistic possibility for western democracies. The evidence suggests that any national group that has survived into this century with its sense of national identity intact cannot be pressured into relinquishing its desire for national recognition and national autonomy. France was only successful in the nineteenth century because it employed a level of coercion against the Basques and Bretons which would be inconceivable now. And even where a similar level of coercion

has been employed in this century (for example, against some indigenous peoples), it has failed to eliminate the minority's national identity.
Few, if any, examples exist of recognised national groups in this century
accepting integration into another culture, even though many have
faced significant economic incentives and political pressures to do so. As
Anthony Smith notes, 'whenever and however a national identity is
forged, once established, it becomes immensely difficult, if not impossible (short of total genocide) to eradicate' (Smith 1993: 131).

So earlier attempts to suppress minority nationalism have been abandoned as unworkable and indeed counter-productive. But they have
also been rejected as morally indefensible. After all, on what basis can
liberal-democratic theory justify the suppression of minority nationalisms? National minorities typically want to regain powers and institutions that were unjustly taken from them, and they do so in order to be
able to live and work in their own language and culture, something
which the majority takes for granted.

For prudential and moral reasons, therefore, an increasing number of
Western democracies that contain national minorities accept that they
are 'multination' states rather than 'nation-states'. They accept that they
contain two or more nations within their borders, and recognise that
each constituent nation has an equally valid claim to the language rights
and self-government powers necessary to maintain itself as a distinct
societal culture. And this multinational character is often explicitly
affirmed in the country's constitution.

This shift is reflected not just at the domestic level, but in international law as well. The last decade has witnessed a remarkable shift in
international norms regarding both stateless nations and indigenous
peoples. The most striking development regarding indigenous peoples is
the Draft UN Declaration on the Rights of Indigenous Peoples, which is
working its way through the labyrinthine structure of the United
Nations.[13] But other international bodies, such as the Inter-American
Commission on Human Rights, have also helped to codify and implement emerging international norms regarding indigenous rights.[14]

We also see major developments regarding stateless nations. For example, the Organisation for Security and Cooperation in Europe adopted a
declaration on the Rights of National Minorities in 1991, and established
a High Commissioner on National Minorities in 1993. The UN has been
debating a Declaration on the Rights of Persons Belonging to National or
Ethnic, Religious and Linguistic Minorities (1993); and the Council of
Europe adopted a declaration on minority language rights in 1992 (the
European Charter for Regional or Minority Languages), and a Framework Convention on the Rights of National Minorities in 1995.

In short, there is a common trend to codify and strengthen the rights
of national minorities, although this has taken the form of two parallel

developments: one set of conventions and declarations concerning indigenous peoples, and another set of conventions and declarations concerning stateless nations. While often discussed separately, they clearly reflect a common trend toward rethinking the status of the 'nations within', accepting the legitimacy of minority nationalism and therefore acknowledging the enduring reality that we live in 'multination' states.

An increasing number of multination states are also recognising that these national rights are best protected through some form of federal or quasi-federal power-sharing which involves the creation of regional political units, controlled by the national minority, with substantial (and constitutionally protected) powers of self-government. What we see emerging within several western democracies, therefore, is a new form of 'multinational federalism' – that is, a model of the state as a federation of regionally concentrated peoples or nations, in which boundaries have been drawn, and powers distributed, in such a way as to ensure that each national group is able to maintain itself as a distinct and self-governing society.[15]

I believe this trend is one of the most important developments in western democracies in the twentieth century. We talk a lot (and rightly so) about the role of the extension of the franchise to women, the working class and racial and religious minorities in democratising western societies. But in its own way, this shift from suppressing to accommodating minority nationalisms has also played a vital role in consolidating and deepening democracy. Indeed, it is important to stress that these multination federations are, by any reasonable criteria, successful. They have not only managed the conflicts arising from their competing national identities in a peaceful and democratic way, but have also secured a high degree of economic prosperity and individual freedom for their citizens.[16] This is truly remarkable when one considers the immense power of nationalism in the twentieth century. Nationalism has torn apart colonial empires and Communist dictatorships, and redefined boundaries all over the world. As we've seen, the pervasive and violent conflicts between states and 'nations within' have been described as the Third World War. Yet democratic multination federations have succeeded in taming this conflict. Democratic federalism has domesticated and pacified nationalism, while respecting individual rights and freedoms. It is difficult to imagine any other political system that can make the same claim.

Minority Nationalism in the US

So Hollinger's critique of minority nationalism seems out of step with the emerging developments in other democracies. But we don't need to look too far abroad: his model doesn't apply to national minorities in the US.

By national minorities, I do not mean African-Americans, the descendants of slaves brought to America. Hollinger argues, and I agree, that
most Blacks in the US have never thought of themselves as a separate
nation, but rather have fought for inclusion into the American nation.
Whites have promised to make this possible, and it is time to make good
on this promise. Hollinger doesn't say much about how exactly this is to
be achieved, but I share his hope and belief that, with concerted efforts,
Blacks in the US can be brought into the postethnic society.

My concern, however, is with those colonised groups who *do* think of
themselves as 'nations within' – for example, Puerto Rico, the Chamoros
of Guam and American Indians. These are the paradigm cases of minority nationalism within the US. And in each of them, the American government has basically followed the same pattern we have seen in other
Western democracies.

In the nineteenth and early twentieth centuries several efforts were
made to suppress these minority nationalisms. For example, when the
US conquered Puerto Rico, it tried to replace Spanish-language schools
with English-language schools, and made it illegal to join political parties promoting independence. Similarly, Indian tribes endured a long
series of policies (for example, the Dawes Act) aimed at undermining
their traditional institutions, and at breaking open Indian lands for
colonising settlers.

Today, however, the situation is very different. These national minorities are now treated in effect as 'nations'. Political units have been created in such a way as to enable them to form a local majority, and to
exercise substantial rights of self-government on a territorial basis. They
all possess a distinct political status (for example, the 'Commonwealth'
of Puerto Rico; the 'domestic dependent nation' status of Indians) not
exercised by, or offered to, other territories or sub-units of the US.[17]

In short, there is no distinctively American way of dealing with minority nationalisms. The US has dealt with minority nationalisms in much
the same way other western democracies have: first by attempting to suppress them, then by accommodating them through various forms of
territorial self-government and special political status.

Hollinger says very little about these cases of minority nationalism in
the US. Nor is his book unique in this respect: national minorities are
also invisible in all the other best-selling books on American multiculturalism.[18] In one sense, this is understandable, since national minorities are relatively peripheral, both geographically and numerically, in the
American context. Yet they are important theoretically, because they represent the clearest cases where the US has confronted a minority nationalism. And with respect to these groups, the US is indeed a multination

state, a federation of distinct nations. The US treats these groups as permanent and enduring, and as the subject of group rights.

Is Postethnic Multiculturalism Incompatible with Minority Nationalism?

Why have liberal democracies shifted toward accommodating minority nationalisms if, as Hollinger claims, these nationalisms are 'ethnic nationalisms' based on the primacy of blood and descent, which operate on the same logic as racial segregation? The short answer is that Hollinger is simply wrong about the nature of these nationalist movements.

Consider Quebec. Quebec accepts immigrants from all over the world; it has roughly the same per capita rate of immigration as the US. Control over immigration is one of the powers Quebec nationalists have sought and gained, and the province administers its own immigration program, actively recruiting immigrants, most of whom are non-white. These immigrants are not only granted citizenship under relatively easy terms, but are encouraged by Quebec's own 'interculturalism' policy to interact with the members of other ethnic groups, to share their cultural heritage and to participate in common public institutions.

The result is just the sort of fluid hybridic multiculturalism within Quebec that Hollinger endorses. (Indeed, the level of acceptance of inter-racial marriage is considerably higher in Quebec than in the US.) Far from trying to preserve some sort of racial purity, Quebec nationalists are actively seeking people of other races and faiths to come join them, integrate with them, intermarry with them, and jointly help build a modern, pluralistic distinct society in Quebec.

Quebec is not unique in this. Consider Catalonia or Scotland, or indeed Puerto Rico. All of these minority nationalisms are 'postethnic' in Hollinger's sense, defining membership in terms of residence and participation in the national culture, not in terms of blood or descent.[19] To be sure, not all minority nationalisms are postethnic: Basque and Flemish nationalism both have a strong racialist component. Similarly, indigenous peoples differ in the extent to which they are defined in terms of race/descent. Some indigenous communities in the US and Canada have adopted 'blood quantum' membership rules; other communities denounce these rules as a violation of the traditional practices of indigenous peoples (which were generally open to the integration of outsiders). It also violates their self-understandings of themselves as 'nations' and 'cultures', rather than races.[20]

In short, the extent to which a particular form of minority nationalism is racialist or postethnic can only be determined by examining the facts,

not by conceptual fiat or armchair speculation. And the clear trend
throughout most western democracies is toward a more open and non-
racial definition of minority nationalism. In the case of Quebec, for
example, the overwhelming majority of Quebeckers forty years ago
believed that to be a true 'Québécois', one had to be descended from the
original French settlers; today, fewer than 20 per cent accept this view
(Crête and Zylberberg 1991).

Hollinger's argument here implicitly rests on a series of widely shared
myths and misconceptions about the nature of minority nationalism. It is
worth trying to make them more explicit, so I will identify four such common mistakes. Since these myths tend to be implicit, it is difficult to
determine to what extent a particular author adopts them, but I think
that one or more of these mistakes underlies many American discussions,
including Hollinger's.

First, there is a tendency in the literature to assume that the conflicts
raised by minority nationalisms within western democracies are conflicts
between a 'civic' (postethnic) nationalism promoted by the state, and an
'ethnic' (racialist) nationalism promoted by the national minority. In reality, however, in most western democracies, these conflicts are between two
competing forms of civic/postethnic nationalism.[21] Both state nationalism and minority nationalism are defined in postethnic, non-racial
terms.[22] And insofar as these are conflicts between two forms of postethnic nationalism, I can see no reason why liberals should automatically
privilege majority or state nationalism over minority nationalism.

Second, there is a tendency to assume that if the majority nation is not
defined in ethnic terms, but rather is a nation open to all regardless of
ethnic descent, then minority nationalisms become inherently unnecessary and pointless, except for those groups obsessed with racial purity.
For example, Rogers Brubaker claims that:

> it is difficult to assert a status as national minority in states such as the United
> States that do not have clear dominant ethno-cultural nations. If the nation
> that legitimates the state as a whole is not clearly an ethno-cultural nation but
> a political nation, open, in principle, to all, then the background condition
> against which the claim of national minority status makes sense is missing.
> (Brubaker 1996: 60, *n*. 6)

The examples of Puerto Rico in the US, Quebec in Canada, Scotland
in Britain, Corsica in France or of indigenous peoples throughout the
western world show that this analysis is deeply flawed. National minorities do not seek to maintain themselves as distinct societies because they
are excluded on ethnic grounds from membership in the dominant
nation. Rather, they mobilise as nations because they cherish their own
national identity and national institutions, and wish to maintain them

into the indefinite future. National minorities organise to defend their distinct society and culture whether or not they are eligible for inclusion in the dominant nation.

We cannot make any headway in understanding minority nationalism within western democracies unless we understand that it is not necessarily, or even typically, adopted as a compensation for exclusion from the majority nation. Rather, it is adopted because of an intrinsic commitment to the maintenance of the minority's own national identity, culture and institutions. Hence the fact that the majority nation is postethnic does nothing, in and of itself, to resolve or eliminate the claims of national minorities.

Third, there is a tendency to assume that minority nationalism is the extreme form of what Hollinger calls 'pluralist' multiculturalism (that is, based on a static, descent-based and exclusive conception of group identity and membership), and hence diametrically opposed to what he calls 'cosmopolitan' or 'postethnic' multiculturalism (where group identities and membership are fluid, hybridic and multiple). In reality, however, minority nationalism and cosmopolitan multiculturalism operate at different levels. Nationalism is a doctrine about the boundaries of political community, and about who possesses rights of self-government. Minority nationalists assert that as 'nations within', they have the same rights of self-government as the majority, and form their own self-governing political community. It is perfectly consistent with that view to insist that all nations – minority and majority – should be postethnic nations. This indeed is one way to understand the idea of *liberal* nationalism: liberal nationalism is the view that nations have rights of self-government, but that all nations, majority or minority, should be postethnic.

Minority nationalism need not, therefore, be the opposite of cosmopolitan multiculturalism. Insofar as it is guided by a liberal conception of nationhood, minority nationalism does not reject cosmopolitan multiculturalism. Rather it is a doctrine about the unit within which cosmopolitan multiculturalism should operate. Should cosmopolitan multiculturalism operate within Canada as a whole or Quebec? Within Spain as a whole or Catalonia? Within Britain as a whole or Scotland? Within the US as a whole, or Puerto Rico? In none of these cases is the debate about the merits of postethnic multiculturalism; nor is it a debate between 'civic' and 'ethnic' nationalism. All of these nations, majority and minority, share a postethnic model in Hollinger's sense. The debate is whether there is just one postethnic nation within the state, or more.

Hollinger's view seems to be that cosmopolitan multiculturalism should operate at the level of the state as a whole, not Puerto Rico, Quebec or Catalonia. But he offers no reasons (that I can see) for this preference, perhaps because he has never considered the possibility that minority nations can also promote and embody a postethnic form of nationalism.

One might think that there is an obvious reason to prefer the state as a whole over sub-state regions as the unit of multiculturalism: namely, freedom and choice is increased if fluid, hybridic multiculturalism operates at the largest possible level. But Hollinger himself rejects that argument. The logical consequence of that view is that cosmopolitan multiculturalism should operate at the level of the world. On such a view, states should have open borders, and put no obstacle to the mixing of peoples across state lines. This would be a genuinely 'cosmopolitan' form of multiculturalism.

Hollinger rejects that view on the grounds that Americans form a nation, cherish their national identity, and have a right to maintain it into the indefinite future (Hollinger 1998). That is, he treats Americans as a permanent and enduring group that exercises rights of self-government, and insists that his 'cosmopolitan' conception of multiculturalism operate within the stable and enduring boundaries of American nationhood. (In this respect, his preferred model of fluid multiculturalism would more accurately be called 'pan-American' than 'cosmopolitan'.) He denies that there is any contradiction in affirming a fluid and shifting form of multiculturalism within the stable and enduring boundaries of a nation.

I agree with Hollinger that 'the cosmopolitan element in multiculturalism is compatible with a strong affirmation of American nationality' (Hollinger 1995: 151). But it is also compatible with the strong affirmation of Puerto Rican nationality, or Québécois nationality, or Navajo nationality. If Hollinger thinks that Puerto Rican nationalism embodies the static and illiberal 'pluralist' model because it implies that multiculturalism should operate within the stable and enduring boundaries of a Puerto Rican nation, then so too is the American nationalism that Hollinger defends. Minority nationalism in Western democracies is no more inherently 'pluralist' than majority nationalism – they can both involve the same combination of fluid multiculturalism within stable national boundaries. And so there is no possible liberal justification that I can see for saying that Americans have a right to national existence, but not Puerto Ricans, Catalans or Québécois.

Finally, there is a tendency in the literature to conflate two separate claims. The first claim is that in order to be consistent with liberal values, nationalisms must be postethnic. I agree with this claim, and have defended it myself. It is one of the defining features of a liberal nationalism.[23] The second claim, however, is that a postethnic model of civic nationalism is inherently incompatible with the recognition of minority nationalism. This is conceptually mistaken, and inconsistent with the practice of most western democracies, including the US. As I see it, Hollinger and many other commentators have conflated these two very distinct claims.

Does it Matter?

But why does this matter? After all, minority nationalism is peripheral to the main debates in the US, and to Hollinger's argument. Indeed, he only refers to it in a few passing references in his book. These references may be misleading or inaccurate, but why make such a fuss about them?

I have focused on these passages because they are just one example of a much larger trend in post-war American thinking. American theorists and statesmen have consistently attacked minority nationalism, not only in their writings, but also in international forums (for instance, by opposing international efforts to codify the rights of national minorities and of indigenous peoples,[24] and by advising other countries not to accommodate minority nationalism).[25]

What explains this trend? One explanation, I think, is that American liberals have been deeply committed to the postethnic integration model for Blacks and for immigrants (a commitment I share). And for some reason, American writers have felt that the best way to defend this model for these groups is to say that it is the only acceptable model for *any* group. Rather than saying that Blacks and immigrants do not see themselves as distinct nations, and that minority nationalism is therefore inappropriate for such groups, American liberals say that minority nationalism is unacceptable in principle, even for those groups that do see themselves as nations.

I think it is a serious mistake, in theory and practice, to defend one group's claims by rendering invisible another group. I'm not saying that questions cannot be raised about the legitimacy of minority nationalism: not everyone will agree with my interpretation and defence of liberal forms of minority nationalism. But I do think that it is inappropriate to reject minority nationalism unless or until one has carefully studied the issues. For example, what does justice require for involuntarily incorporated national groups like the American Indians, Hispanics in Puerto Rico or Albanians in Kosovo? If minority nationalism is an unjustified response to such an involuntary incorporation, what is a legitimate response? These are difficult and complex questions. Rather than tackling these issues directly or in depth, however, post-war American writers have consistently rejected minority nationalism without any serious analysis.

But why think that any of this has had a pernicious influence on other countries? After all, Hollinger's book was written for a domestic audience, and the same is true of many other recent American books that make passing references to minority nationalism. Is there any reason to think that these references have affected how other countries deal with their ethnic relations?

I believe that American models of ethnic relations have indeed had a profound influence on other countries. Let me give two examples:

Canada and Eastern Europe. English-speaking Canadians have been heavily influenced by American models of liberalism, and one consequence of
this has been a reluctance to accord the Québécois the sort of public
recognition of their national identity they seek, which most other Western
democracies have given to their national minorities. I believe that the
influence of American liberalism has made it much more difficult to
come to an acceptable settlement with Quebec, even though, as I noted
earlier, the US itself was quite willing to extend this sort of national recognition to Puerto Rico.[26] If American writers had emphasised that it was a
part of the American practice (even if only a peripheral part) to accommodate minority nationalisms, then I am sure that Quebeckers today
would not be so perilously close to seceding from Canada.

Despite the ever-present threat of secession in Canada, the situation in
Eastern Europe is in many ways more serious. As the old saying goes, the
situation in Canada is critical, but not serious. For even if Quebec were
to secede, the result would probably be two relatively stable liberal
democracies in the northern half of the continent, instead of one. In
Eastern Europe, the inability to accommodate minority nationalism is a
threat, not just to existing boundaries, but to democracy itself, and to the
existence of a peaceful civil society. The inability remains the major
obstacle to democratisation in Eastern Europe. There is almost a direct
correlation between democratisation and minority nationalism: those
countries without significant minority nationalisms have democratised
successfully (Czech Republic, Hungary, Slovenia); those countries with
powerful minority nationalisms are having a much more difficult time
(Slovakia, Ukraine, Romania, Serbia, Macedonia).

And in this context, the influence of American models of ethnic relations has been distinctly unhelpful. You might wonder who in these
countries pays any attention to American liberals. In fact two groups pay
close attention to these American debates. First are the liberal intellectuals within these countries, who naturally look to American liberals for
guidance (a tendency reinforced by the fact that many of them receive
funding from American organisations). Liberals are thin on the ground
in most of these countries, and the influence of American liberalism has
been to marginalise them even further. Guided by American models,
these liberals have had little to say about the accommodation of minority nationalism, except to chant the mantra that the solution to ethnic
conflict is 'individual rights not group rights'. This is an unhelpful slogan
since it tells us nothing about how to resolve the issues raised by minority nationalism. The conflict in Kosovo, for example, centred on whether
political power should be centralised in Belgrade or whether the
regional government in Kosovo should have extensive autonomy. The

slogan 'individual rights not group rights' provides no guidance for understanding this conflict.[27]

The second group paying close attention is the majority nationalists. Nationalist governments in these countries have not only studied, but also largely adopted, the American rhetoric that a good liberal democracy should be a 'civic nation'. They adopt the language of liberal democracy and civic nationalism partly to impress foreign observers, but also for a more important reason: it provides an excuse to crush minority nationalism, and to strip national minorities of their separate public institutions and rights of self-government. We see this trend in Slovakia, Romania, Serbia and in Russia. You might be surprised to hear that majority nationalists in these countries adopt the language of civic nationalism, but they do. And they do so precisely *because* it legitimises policies that inhibit national minorities from expressing a distinct national identity or from demanding national rights.

What we see in many of these countries, therefore, is an unholy alliance of liberal intellectuals and majoritarian nationalists, both of whom invoke American models to justify rejecting the claims of national minorities. As I noted earlier, these attempts to suppress minority nationalism can only be achieved by extensive coercion, and the result has been to create fear among the minorities, to exacerbate inter-ethnic relations, and to strengthen authoritarian tendencies within both the majority and minority nationalist movements.

Americans are not the only culprits here. French liberals (who are also quite influential in some of these countries) are even worse in their denunciation of minority nationalism. And whereas pragmatic Americans have always been willing to qualify their principles when confronted with the reality of minority nationalism (such as in Puerto Rico), the French tend to take their principles very seriously, and so have been much less accommodating of minority nationalisms (for example, the Bretons, Basques, Corsicans).

Neither American nor French writers have endorsed or encouraged the adoption of coercive policies aimed at suppressing minority nationalism in Eastern Europe. They emphasise the necessity of peaceful dialogue and the maintenance of democracy and the rule of law. But these subtleties often get lost in the translation. What majority nationalist leaders like Milosevic hear is American and French liberals saying that a civic nation does not accord rights of self-government to national minorities. He hears that message because it is what he wants to hear.

I should emphasise that American foreign policy has often encouraged states to accept some minority claims. Indeed, the American government has used military force to press Serbia to accord autonomy to

Kosovo. But Milosevic sees this as hypocrisy. He sees it as yet another case of America trying to impose a settlement on weaker countries that it would never accept at home. After all, don't American liberals say that we should fight against ethnic minority nationalism and instead seek to build a single, shared civic nation within each state?

The American position on Kosovo isn't hypocrisy, since Americans have made a similar accommodation with their minority nationalisms in Puerto Rico, or American Indian tribes. Indeed, these accommodations are in many ways a good example to the world. Many countries could learn a great deal from the ongoing evolution of the 'domestic dependent nation' status of American Indian tribes.[28]

But the American position on Kosovo does contradict the official 'model' of American ethnic relations, and so it will be perceived as hypocrisy unless or until Americans emphasise that the accommodation of minority nationalism is a part of American democracy. I strongly believe that the transition to democracy in the multination states of Eastern Europe would have been smoother had this aspect of the American experience been emphasised by American writers and statesmen. If Americans want to understand and contribute to the resolution of ethnic conflict around the world, they need to understand better their own practices of minority rights. As Benjamin Schwarz puts it, in explaining why Americans misunderstand minority nationalism overseas, 'We get the world wrong because we get ourselves wrong' (Schwarz 1995: 58).

I am not suggesting that American theorists of multiculturalism put issues of minority nationalism at the front and centre of their theories; the situation of Blacks is, and should be, at the centre of American debates about multiculturalism. But I wish that, if only in a footnote or passing reference, Americans would admit that accommodating minority nationalism, far from being un-American, illiberal or undemocratic, is one (small) part of the American experience. In practice, the US has made important strides in securing justice for its 'nations within': it is time now to build this into our theoretical models of American multiculturalism.

CHAPTER 13

Hybrid Democracy:
Iroquois Federalism and the
Postcolonial Project

Iris Marion Young

On the eve of the bicentenary of the Constitution, the US Congress passed a resolution commemorating the influence of the Iroquois Confederacy on the founding institutions. A year later a New York state public school curriculum review panel recommended teaching that the Iroquois system of governance had an impact on the development of the institutions and practices of the state of New York and the US. These are noble and overdue gestures of recognition of Native Americans. It seems that most historians of the period, however, flatly reject the claim that Indian governance forms influenced the American Constitution. Critics of multiculturalism regularly point the finger at the Iroquois influence claim to demonstrate the mad excesses of the movement. No less a guardian of historical pedagogy than Nathan Glazer, however, asserts that teaching children that Indians contributed to the founding of American institutions may be a good thing even if scholars contest a claim to direct influence on the Constitution (Glazer 1997: 40). Clearly passions run high on this question, one that splinters American identity itself.

In this chapter I situate this debate in the postcolonial project. Anyone interested in justice today must face the project of undoing the legacies of colonialism. Understood as a project, postcoloniality does not name an epoch at which we have arrived, one where colonialism is in the past. On the contrary, precisely because the legacies of colonialism persist, progressive intellectuals and activists should take on the task of undoing their effects. The postcolonial project has an interpretive and institutional aspect. Institutionally, postcoloniality entails creating systems of global democratic governance that can meet the demands of the world's indigenous peoples for self-determination. Because the existing international system of nation-states cannot meet those demands, commitment to justice for indigenous peoples entails calling those state-systems into

question. In the last two sections of this essay I will review other reasons
for questioning the system of state sovereignty, and offer instead a model
of governance based on decentred diverse democratic federalism. This
institutional condition presupposes the interpretive aspect of the postcolonial project. Development of the institutional imagination and commitment to confront the colonial legacy depends partly on rereading the
history of modernity, democracy and the building of nation-states from
the point of view of colonised peoples considered as actors and not
merely as those acted upon (see Ivison 1997: 154–71). Drawing on the
methods of postcolonial interpretation offered by Homi Bhabha, particularly his notion of 'hybridity', I use the Iroquois influence debate to reread
some elements of the history of colonial and republican America for the
sake of our contemporary self-understanding. Among other things,
I find in this rereading an example of the interaction of distinct peoples
without sovereign borders that can help us imagine a post-sovereign
alternative to the existing states system.

Hybridising Historical Consciousness

Homi Bhabha suggests that narratives of national identity are predicated
on the obligation to forget the multi-dimensional cultural interaction
producing societies and institutions, especially in the colonialist interactions of European peoples with other peoples of the world:

> The anteriority of the nation, signified in the will to forget, entirely changes
> our understanding of the pastness of the past, and the synchronous present of
> the will to nationhood . . . To be obliged to forget – in the construction of the
> national present – is not a question of historical memory; it is the construc-
> tion of a discourse on society that *performs* the problem of totalising the people
> and unifying the national will. (Bhabha 1994: 161)

The postcolonial critic can confront colonial power's disavowal of its
situatedness and multiplicity by reinterpreting modern history as *hybrid*.
One story of world history describes a lineal progression where universal
values of liberty, democracy, technology and economic development born
in Western Europe spread around the world through the power and
knowledge of European nations. In this story the colonised peoples of the
world usually appear as objects of action, those upon whom the power
and influence of the west is exercised, usually for good, sometimes for ill.
While the story includes the encounter and conflict of cultures, it does
not depict the ideas, practices, institutions and events of the Europeans as
objects of and influenced by the subjectivity of the non-European Others.
    Understanding colonial history as hybrid, according to Bhabha,
means reversing the linearity of the official story, and allowing 'strategies

of subversion that turn the gaze of the discriminated back upon the eye
of power' (Bhabha 1994: 112). Events and institutions in any locale may
appear as products of cultural interaction where Europeans are as much
influenced as influencing, and the temporality and spatiality of action
themselves are multi-dimensional:

> If the effect of colonial power is seen to be the *production* of hybridisation
> rather than the noisy command of colonialist authority or the silent repression
> of native traditions, then an important change of perspective occurs. The
> ambivalence at the source of traditional discourses on authority enables a form
> of subversion, founded on the undecidability that turns the discursive condi-
> tions of dominance into the grounds of intervention.[1] (Bhabha 1994: 112)

The furnaces of modern national and empire building either absorb
cultural difference in their alchemy or expel them. A hybridising strategy
inserts the subjectivity of colonised people into the imperial narrative,
allowing the reflective emergence of a 'time lag' between the moment of
signification and its hearing. History becomes then not the narrative of a
single subject or national identity, but the encounter of cultural difference. Neither one nor the Other, the pluralised stories enact intersubjec-
tivity, subjects as relationally constituted, with an interactively constituted
world in between (Patton 1995b: 153–71). Among other things, this interpretive strategy upsets colonial dualities reiterated still today: self/Other,
inside/outside, civilised/savage, citizen/alien, modern/primitive.

Bhabha's ideas are inspired partly by a Lacanian theory of discourse
that I do not feel entirely competent to interpret or apply. I do not think
that I do his work violence, however, to carry a somewhat simplified version into a reflection on the interaction between indigenous peoples and
the thirteen British colonies in North America and the meaning of this
interaction for a postcolonial project that can do justice, among other
people, to the living descendants of North American indigenous people.
Hybridising the story of that relationship, as I see it, involves affirming
colonial North America as a terrain of interaction, constructing American subjectivity as ambiguous, and fashioning a relational understanding
of government jurisdictions. It could be argued that indigenous people
have always related colonial history as hybrid in this sense. That is one
reason to attend to indigenous voices in the effort to generalise a hybrid
story to Europeans and their descendants.

Iroquois–Colonial Interaction and the Influence Thesis

Several contemporary scholars have contributed to the argument that the
founders of the political institutions of the United States were influenced
by Native American ideas and institutions, including Jack Weatherford

(1988), Robert Venables (1992) and Jose Barriero (1988). I find the work of Donald Grinde and Bruce Johansen the most comprehensive, and rely primarily on it for an account of the relationship between British colonists and Native Americans. Their book, *Exemplar of Liberty* (1991), has been amply documented and the subject of serious criticism by other historians of the period.

Contact between Native peoples and British settlers in North America produced profound changes on both sides. Each group found the others strange, and they made war on each other often enough, but some members of both Native American and colonial groups also learned from and admired the strangers. Roger Williams, for example, learned several Indian languages and much about Indian culture and politics. Grinde and Johansen suggest that this knowledge contributed to Williams's design of the government of Rhode Island in the mid-seventeenth century. While conflict between Indians and colonists erupted repeatedly in the two centuries before the American revolution, the same epoch also saw widespread cooperation, trade and treaty negotiation. Colonists felt obliged to reach treaties with Indians about land and resource use, military alliance and other affairs because they recognised the Indians as well-organised self-governing peoples. Daily life activities were commonly governed by village councils and all group meetings. Many groups of North American Indians were organised into complex confederated governance systems, each of which might have included tens of thousands of people inhabiting and moving across vast unbounded territories.

Long before European settlers appeared at the shores of North America, five nations of the Iroquois – Mohawk, Oneida, Onondaga, Cayuga and Seneca – formed a federation that espoused peace and brotherhood, unity, balance of power, the natural rights of all people, impeachment and removal, and the sharing of resources. (The Tuscarora people joined the confederacy in the eighteenth century.) They developed an open set of decision-making practices that relied on deliberation, public opinion, checks and balances, and consensus.

People in any one of the federated groups might raise an issue to the confederacy, and then the Onondaga chiefs would meet to determine whether the issue should be considered by the Grand Council of the Confederacy. One of the chiefs operated as keeper of the council fire, with the power to call a council. Debate of an issue began with the Mohawk representatives. After they agreed on a position the issue was discussed by the Senecas, and then by the Oneida and Cayuga people. Once the Oneidas and Cayugas reached a position, the issue was discussed again by the Mohawks and the Senecas. Finally the issue was sent back to the Onondaga, who at this stage had power analogous to judicial review. They could raise objections to a proposal if they believed it was inconsistent with the Great Law of Peace. Iroquois principles included relative equality and participation. Male chiefs were chosen by women leaders, who also had the power to impeach and replace them. When issues were under discussion by the Grand Council the people in the separate regions and villages often engaged in public discussion and debate. The people could propose laws to the council on their own.

What *federalism* meant to the Iroquois, then, was an assumption of self-determination for the member nations at the same time as a commitment to procedural unity with the other five nations and the willingness to have any issue considered for federal decision making. Indian governance can be considered *democratic*, moreover, at least because of the following attributes: leaders were chosen on merit, although they usually came from designated families; they were expected to respond to public opinion, and in extreme cases could be impeached if they abused their power; issues and policy proposals could come from anywhere in the federation; decision-making relied on deliberation both within and among member nations and included mechanisms of review.

As I read it, Grinde and Johansen construct a broad and a narrow frame for a story of the hybrid constitution of American democracy. While it is not certain how much Americans knew of the details of Iroquois or other Indian governance systems, many did observe Indian meetings and had to adapt to Indian protocol in their trading or treaty negotiation. Some colonists and European visitors described the Indians as living without law because they lacked formally written principles and procedures, and they variously interpreted this as a sign of either backwardness or blissful freedom. Others, however, observed a complex government, and compared Indian oratorical powers to those of the Romans. Some admired the consultation, participation and search for consensus they observed in Indian decision-making bodies, and some saw in the Iroquois Confederacy the virtues of united strength that preserved a high level of local self-determination.

Grinde and Johansen argue that the agency and political intelligence of Indians had an impact not only on colonists, but also on some of those in the home European countries. Colonists and European visitors wrote detailed ethnographies and travelogues about diverse Indian peoples. While these may not have been terribly accurate in their descriptions of Indian institutions, they were influential in Europe. Some compared Iroquois and other Indian political practices to those of the Greeks, and commented on Indian statecraft and regard for individual autonomy. John Locke constructed his image of the state of nature partly with the lives of these native peoples in mind; that state is one without civil society, on Locke's account, but also one of natural liberty and the light of natural reason. Enlightenment fathers of modern constitutionalism and

democracy such as Montesquieu and Rousseau constructed their romanticised fantasies of Indian lives in their effort to promote ideas of liberty
and equality and criticise the corruption and subjection of European
societies. In 'Huron, or Pupil of Nature', for example, Voltaire, the pre-
revolutionary French republican, put a scathing critique of French aristocracy and hypocrisy into the mouth of a Huron leader. In the broad
frame of Grinde and Johansen's story, then, the Enlightenment political
philosophers that influenced the American founders to establish a
democratic republic were themselves conditioned by real and imagined
interaction with Native Americans.

Grinde and Johansen argue that independence-minded colonists
looked to Indian imagery and practices in their project of distancing their
loyalty from England and developing the symbols of patriotic American
loyalty. By the time of the American revolution, many British colonists had
only a distant feeling for England. By examining engravings and paintings, as well as records of patriotic societies, and written accounts of revolutionary meetings and rallies, Grinde and Johansen document the
significant degree to which the British colonists sought to construct an
American national identity through the use of Indian imagery.

The rebels of the Boston tea party dressed as Indians less in order to
disguise themselves, Grinde and Johansen argue, than to signify their
assertion of liberty. Pamphlets and banners during the revolutionary and
republican period repeatedly used images of Indians or symbols derived
from Indian visual art to signify American freedom, equality and democratic self-government. The famous snake of the New Hampshire flag is an
original Indian symbol, for example, as is the eagle grasping a cluster of
arrows that appears on the dollar bill of the US. Most conspicuous in this
story of Euro-American appropriation of Indian imagery, however, are
the Tammany societies. Founded as a secret brotherhood of revolutionary patriots, these clubs took their name from a Delaware leader. Their
'meetings' frequently consisted of Euro-Americans dressing as Indians,
singing songs and dancing in their own fashion 'as' Indians, and pledg-
ing their loyalty to the American republic. The Tammany societies continued as patriotic associations until well into the nineteenth century.

The story that Grinde and Johansen construct of an influence of the
Iroquois confederacy on the evolution of American political institutions
goes like this. The British colonists relied on the Indians' support in their
military confrontations with the French in the mid-eighteenth century.
At a treaty meeting in 1744 the Iroquois leader Canassteago recommended to the colonists that they form a federation of their governments, as the Iroquois people had done. An admirer of the Iroquois
people and their federation, Benjamin Franklin, published a report of
this meeting, including this speech, which was widely distributed. Ten

years later the Seneca leader Tryonoga, also called Hendrick, attended the conference in Albany where the British colonies drew up their first Plan of Union. Benjamin Franklin was one of the main designers of the Albany Plan.

While the Continental Congress sat in Philadelphia in 1775 and 1776, delegations of Iroquois came to observe and delegations of colonists went to meet with the Iroquois several times. The emerging Euro-American nation sought and received a pledge of neutrality from the Iroquois in their war with Britain. During many meetings the colonists discussed political and economic affairs with these and other Indian groups.

On Grinde and Johansen's account, the Articles of Confederacy which were adopted by the Continental Congress had an earlier iteration in the Albany Plan of Union, which in turn was influenced by the Iroquois Great Law of Peace. When they debated what provisions the new American Constitution should contain, the American revolutionaries discussed ideas of the Iroquois federation among others. John Adams, for example, included a discussion of Indian political institutions in his comprehensive survey of governments of the world. Adams urged the framers of the Constitution to study Indian governance systems thoroughly. Some speeches to the Continental Congress in the years leading up to the passage of the Constitution invoked Iroquois ideas and imagery. Thus Grinde and Johansen claim that the ideas and practices of Iroquois federalism had an indirect influence on the founding, as one of the many streams that flowed into the American democratic current.

Critics of the claim that American political institutions have a hybrid history focus almost exclusively on the claim that specific elements of the final American Constitution can be directly or indirectly traced to the Iroquois Great Law of Peace. These critics appear to take as the historical question whether some of the representatives to the Constitutional Congress have the structure or procedures of the Iroquois confederacy in mind when they debated the structures and procedures of the US. Whatever the founders knew of the Indian governance systems, they argue, this knowledge had next to nothing to do with their debates. Some who seemed to mention Iroquois institutions positively, such as John Adams, were on the losing side of the federalist debate. While Benjamin Franklin may have thought well of Iroquois political institutions and these may have influenced his writing of the Albany Plan of Union, that Plan was merely a military alliance, not the constitution of a government. The founders were most influenced by European ideas, including European models of federation. Much as I want to believe that American democracy is a hybrid product of European and Native American ideas, the broad consensus of historians of the period seems to be that the thesis has no basis (Tooker 1988; Levy P. 1996; Payne 1996).

In light of the strong disagreement over whether and how to assign influence of Native American governance systems in the formation of the American Constitution, it is surprising that the two sides appear to agree on so many other claims. There is little question, for example, that from the time of first settlement many Europeans had significant contact with Native Americans, learned much about their ways of life, and many admired as well as feared or loathed them. In many regions of North America, British and French settlers, along with African slaves, created a hybrid society from the complex encounter of very different cultures (White 1991).[2] Not an insignificant number of Europeans joined Indian groups over the course of the two centuries before the American founding, and not an insignificant number of Indians adopted European dress, language and ways of living, and some were educated in colonial or European institutions of higher learning. Colonists and British officials negotiated hundreds of treaties with Indian groups, evidence that the Europeans regarded Indians with a certain level of respect, even as in many cases they succeeded in manipulating the treaty process to their own advantage. One of the most adamant critics of the claim that the Iroquois federation influenced the American Constitution, Elisabeth Tooker, nevertheless agrees that at the time of seeking independence from England the colonists looked to images of Indians to help inspire commitment to independence and nation-building. Treaty and other diplomatic negotiations between colonies and Indians indicate that each regarded the other as distinct political formations, but unified sovereign states in the modern sense did not exist on the continent (Koenigsberger 1989; Tully 1995). Among other things, the founding of the US began the process of creating such a modern unified sovereign state, a process that spelled disaster for the Indians (Countryman 1996).

Most of the scholarly and journalistic reaction to work like that of Grinde and Johansen focuses on the truth or falsity of the Iroquois influence thesis. That focus, it seems to me, avoids the importance of the account Grinde and Johansen make, and the evidence they supply of the hybrid play of political ideas and symbols running between Native Americans and Europeans and colonists. From the perspective of a hybrid interpretation of colonial history, and for the purposes of the argument for a post-sovereignty global democratic polity that I will make later, I summarise the significance of work like that of Grinde and Johansen as follows. By proposing that Indians served for American revolutionaries as exemplars of liberty, Grinde and Johansen deconstruct the modern western discourse that positions the Native Americans as the excluded Other in comparison with which the Europeans confirmed their cultural superiority. On this hybrid interpretation, the Indians regard the Europeans as obsequious servants to distant lords and social conventions, while they know freedom. On this interpretation, Native Americans stand for an alternative to monarchist European structures, an alternative internalised in a plural European-American discourse.

Even if evidence does not support the claim that the Iroquois federation directly and specifically influenced the evolution of American government, the *question* of a relationship between the Iroquois government and the US government remains important for the way it hybridises the idea of democracy. Many people in European or European-settled countries implicitly and sometimes explicitly construct democracy as a specifically western value. In their struggle for independence and self-determination, some colonised and formerly colonised peoples of Africa and Asia themselves promulgate the claim that democracy is a specifically European set of institutions not appropriate to truly independent non-western states. If democracy means institutions of formal legislatures, elected by citizens in a multi-party competition, a system of administrative bureaucracies to apply the laws, and a system of courts to interpret and enforce them, then democracy is a specifically modern and western invention. But even the western lineage of democracy is not confined to this image. Athenian democracy, for example, for centuries romanticised as the most authentic of all democracies, fits this description in almost no respect. By asking the question, in what ways are the ideas and practices of American democracy similar to the governance system of the Iroquois federation, we pluralise our possible understandings of democracy. In today's search for new human possibilities of self-government, participation and societal cooperation, we ought to look to Indian governance practices, some of which have a living legacy in contemporary government institutions of indigenous North and South Americans, among other indigenous peoples. Nor is it absurd for new democracies in Africa to reflect on some traditional village practices as alternatives to modern western forms of democracy that offer resources for forging postcolonial African democracies (Wiredu 1997; Eze 1997). Iroquois institutions in particular valued deliberation, an orientation to collective problem-solving, and local self-governance in the context of a strong federation. Contemporary democratic theory is much occupied with each of these democratic values, and in the next section I will elaborate on the last. The project of rethinking democracy for a postcolonial age, I am suggesting, benefits from a hybrid vision of the history of societies and governments that refuses the traditional/modern, savage/ civilised dichotomies.

The Iroquois influence debate encourages a popular reinterpretation of European Americans as not only the agents of American history, but also as those in relation to whom Native Americans have acted. In this hybrid mode, we think of American society and identity as a product of the interaction of Native and European cultures; the very meaning of being American becomes decentred and relational. I shall argue that such a relational and decentred notion of subjectivity and polity contributes to reconceptualising self-determination and global governance.

The story of interaction between settlers and indigenous people in the mid- and late-eighteenth century in America, finally, provides a concrete image of federated and political interaction among distinctly identifying groups without the developed centralising and disciplinary institutions of the modern nation-state. While the postcolonial project does not advocate recreating such plural intercultural conditions, it can learn from them. Mid-eighteenth century America was the site of a bloody war of sovereign supremacy between two European states, France and England, affecting both Indians and colonists. In the midst of the conditions of war, however, the thirteen colonies negotiated interaction with each other and with diverse Indian governments. The Indian peoples had complex negotiated and federated interactions with one another as well.

The Great Law of Peace spelled out a complex set of rules for decision-making about those matters members of the federation thought concerned them all, such as war and peace or territorial dispute. These rules were designed in part to ensure the equality and continued autonomy of the federation members as they participated in the wider decisions. Other Indian peoples on the continent also thought of themselves as self-governing, and many participated in other federated relationships. At this time each of the thirteen colonies had their own system of governance; the seat of government of each was quite far from the others, and settlers outside the cities were quite dispersed. While colonists and Indians considered themselves as dwelling in distinct territories, there were no strict borders separating them. Instead, the places where jurisdiction was clear shaded into wider borderlands of common use and sometimes dispute. Colonial territories, moreover, might be 'within' Indian territories and vice versa. Some of the Lenni Lenape (or Delaware), for example, dwelt on either side of some of the settlements of the Commonwealth of Pennsylvania. So it was with the Seneca and the Pennsylvanians and the New Yorkers. Under these circumstances of territorial ambiguity, political autonomy, relative equality of power and interfusion, cooperative relations among the Indian groups, the colonial groups, and between Indians and colonial groups, when they existed, relied on dialogue and negotiation.

I do not wish to romanticise the relations among native peoples of this period, or between the native peoples and the European-descended settlers. Then, as now, there was plenty of violence, exploitation and corruption in inter-group affairs. The point is only to find in the past grounds for bracketing ossified assumptions about jurisdiction, governance and the relation of self-determining peoples. To the extent that indigenous peoples and other peoples who reject the state sovereignty model of government today live out this recollection in their current governance and intercultural relations, these grounds may also lie in the present.

Moral Challenges to Sovereignty

The postcolonial project begins after World War II, when one after another the international community of states recognised new sovereign states in the territories of former European colonies. The borders of many of these states were relatively arbitrarily drawn, often gathering peoples who considered themselves distinct under the rule of one state dominated by one of the groups. It can be argued that much of the violence on the Asian and African continents is traceable to this process of sovereign state creation. Ideals and practices of a global regime constituted by sovereign states, however, are coming under increasing normative and practical challenge.

As I discussed earlier, an institutional aspect of the postcolonial project consists in conceiving and bringing about a post-sovereignty global governance system. The legitimate claims of indigenous peoples today for self-determination cannot be fully met within the existing system of global governance that assumes the nation-state as the primary international actor. Consonant with these claims, we need to envision a more federated system of global governance with both stronger global regulation than currently exists and more regional and cultural autonomy. Before sketching some principles for such a global federated democracy, I will review some other reasons for challenging the principle of sovereignty in international affairs.

I distinguish the concept of sovereignty from that of *state* institutions. States are public authorities that regulate the activities of those within their jurisdictions through legal and administrative institutions backed by the power to sanction. While only states can be sovereign, they need not be, and many strong state institutions currently exist at a jurisdictional level smaller than sovereign states. State institutions are capable of being subject to review or overriding without losing their status as states. They can share jurisdiction with other states, and their jurisdiction need not encompass all the activities in a territory.

A *sovereign* state wields central and final authority over all the legal and political matters within a determinate and strictly bounded territory (Morris 1998; Pogge 1992).[3] Sovereignty entails a clear distinction between inside and outside. Within a sovereign state there are often partial and lesser governments and jurisdictions, but the sovereign government exercises a higher and final authority over them. The sovereignty of the state is partially constituted by the states outside it, moreover, who recognise it as a legitimate sovereign state. This recognition entails a principle of non-intervention; for a state to have final authority implies that no other state and no transnational body has the authority to interfere with the actions and policies of a sovereign state (Philpott 1995).

Some writers claim that states today no longer have sovereignty in the sense I define here, and perhaps never did. It is questionable if states today really exercise centrally coordinated power that is systematically connected over domains of government, and that they exercise it as a final authority. State power today, some claim, is in fact much more fragmentary and limited than the commitment to sovereignty would have one believe (Morris 1998). Whatever the factual situation of state powers, however, the *idea* of sovereignty still carries much weight among political leaders and scholars, both regarding the relation of states to internal organisation and jurisdictions, and international relations. Many today continue to believe that states *ought* to be sovereign, and that to the degree that their sovereignty is under challenge or in a process of fragmentation, that steps should be taken to reinforce a system of strong sovereign states. Others disagree, and promote either internal devolution or the external evolution of transnational authorities. I shall argue that a principle of state sovereignty lacks moral legitimacy, both regarding external and internal affairs.

External Challenges

Considerations of global justice call into question the legitimacy of claims by states that they alone have the right to attend to affairs within their borders and have no obligations to peoples outside their borders. Charles Beitz (1979), Thomas Pogge (1992) and Onora O'Neill (1996), among others, argue that there are no privileged grounds for limiting the scope of evaluations of justice to relations between people within nation-states. Moral evaluation of social relations in terms of justice and injustice apply wherever social institutions connect people in a causal web. To the extent that people assume the actions of distant others as background to their own, they stand with them in relations of justice. The scope and complexity of economic, communication and many other institutions in the world today constitute a sufficiently tight web of constraint and interdependence that we must speak of a global *society*.[4] Principles of justice apply to relations among persons, organisations and state institutions in diverse reaches of global society. These claims of justice constitute a double challenge to the moral boundaries of states. Agents outside of states have some claim to judge and regulate the activities of states over affairs within their jurisdictions, on the one hand; states and their members, on the other hand, have obligations to people outside their borders. Considerations of economic regulation, human rights intervention, environmental protection and migration are among those that raise profound issues of justice that challenge sovereignty in this double way.

The principle of sovereignty gives to states the right and power to regulate for the benefit of their own members. States ought positively to pursue economic gain for their own citizens at the expense of other people in the world if necessary, so long as they do not forcefully invade and conquer the territories of other sovereign states. They have the right to exclude persons from entry into their territory in order to preserve the privileged access their members have to resources and benefits there. States or their citizens owe no general obligation to others outside, whatever their needs or level of relative deprivation. Any efforts states or their members make to help needy people elsewhere in the world are supererogatory.

Several moral arguments can be offered against this view of the right of non-intervention in states' policies and their right to be indifferent to the circumstances of those outside their borders. Charles Beitz questions the moral right of states to keep for themselves all the benefits derived from the natural resources that happen to lie within their borders. Resources such as fertile land, economically valuable minerals and so on are by no means evenly distributed around the globe. Because the placement of resources is morally arbitrary, no state is entitled to treat them as its private property to be used only for its own benefit. Because certain resources are necessary for the productive capacity of all societies, they must be considered a global commons. Their use and the benefits of their use should thus be globally regulated under a cooperative framework of global justice (Beitz 1979).

The global resources argument is one example of a challenge to the sovereignty claim that outside agents have no claim to regulate the actions of states over activities that take place within their jurisdiction. The state of production, finance and communications in the world has evolved in such a way that many actions and policies internal to a state nevertheless sometimes have profound effects on others in the world. A moral challenge to a principle of non-intervention has come most obviously from environmental concerns. States' internal forestry policies, their kind and level of industrial pollution regulation, and similar policies, produce consequences for the air quality and climate of many outside their borders. Economic and communicative interdependence, moreover, generate certain international moral claims over other kinds of internal policies. Financial policies of the German or Japanese states, for example, can seriously affect the stability of many other economies. Such interdependencies as these call for some form of international regulatory scheme that aims for stable and just cooperation.

Many argue, furthermore, that current distributive inequality across
the globe raises questions of justice that require a globally enforced
redistributive regime. The fact that some peoples live in wasteful afflu-
ence while many more in other parts of the world suffer from serious
deprivation itself stands as prima facie grounds for global redistribu-
tion. But these facts of distributive inequality alone do not make a very
strong case for global economic regulation. More important is the history of dependence and exploitation between the now poor and now
rich regions of the world, and the continuance of institutional structures that perpetuate and even help enlarge global privilege and deprivation. Many scholars argue that the current wealth of Europe and
North America compared to societies of Africa, Latin America and
South Asia is due to a significant degree to the colonial relations among
these regions that looted for three centuries. While the poorer regions
of the world today are composed of independent states with the same formal sovereignty rights as any other states, many argue that the colonial
economic relations between North and South persist (Cardoso 1993).
The economies of the South depend on capital investment controlled
from the North, and most of the profits return to the North. Their work-
ers are often too poorly paid by multinationals or their local contractors
to feed their families, and farmers and miners of the South obtain very
unfavourable prices on a global resource market. Such deprivation has
forced most governments of the southern hemisphere into severe debt
to northern banks and to international finance agencies such as the
World Bank. This indebtedness severely restricts the effective sovereignty of southern states, because powerful financial institutions have
effective power to control their internal economic policies, all for the
sake of preserving the existing system of international trade and finance
and the benefits it brings primarily to some in the north.

The issue is not simply one of distributive inequality, that some people
in some parts of the world are seriously deprived while others in other
parts of the world live very well. Rather, the global institutional context
sets different regions in relations of dependence and exploitation with
others, and this institutional system reproduces and arguably widens the
distributive inequalities. Redress of unjust deprivation and regulation of
the global economy for the sake of promoting greater justice thus calls
for institutional change, and not merely a one-time or periodic transfer
of wealth from richer to poorer people.

In the absence of institutional change, many question the moral right
of states to limit immigration. According to Joseph Carens, for example,
excluding people from a relatively rich country, which people wish to
enter from elsewhere in order to better their lives, is little different from

the preservation of a feudal privilege. By the mechanism of immigration control, people whose privilege derives from birth are able to protect that privilege from encroachment by others who happen to have been born elsewhere (Carens 1987).

Internal Challenges

Internally, the idea of sovereignty entails that a state has ultimate authority to regulate all the activities taking place within a specific territorial jurisdiction. This often seems to mean, by implication, that the same form of law, regulation and administration ought to apply to all the peoples and locales within the territory. Both these aspects of internal sovereignty are morally questionable, however, because they do not sufficiently recognise and accommodate the rights and needs of national and cultural minorities. Political recognition for distinct peoples entails that they are able to practise their culture and that they can affirm their own public culture in which to express and affirm their distinctness. To the degree that peoples are distinct, moreover, they have prima facie rights of self-governance. These points entail that peoples who dwell with others within a wider polity nevertheless limit the sovereignty of that wider policy over their activities (Kymlicka 1995). The limitation of sovereign authority of a wider polity over groups and locales may vary in kind or degree, from local or group-based autonomy over nearly all affairs, to self-governance over only a small range of issues, such as family law or the management and use of particular resources. As those examples indicate, moreover, local self-determination may vary according to whether it is legislative or administrative or both. Despite the strong claims of most states to be sovereign over all the activities in a territory, the sovereign power of many states today is already limited or restricted in many ways that recognise or accommodate national, cultural and religious differences within their claimed jurisdictions (Levy J. 1997).

Many of these challenges come from indigenous peoples. Most of the world's indigenous peoples claim rights of self-determination against the states that claim sovereign authority over them. These claims are difficult or impossible for states organised in the existing states system to accommodate, because they involve claims about the rights to use land and resources, and the right to develop governance practices continuous with pre-colonial indigenous practices, which are often at odds with the more formal and bureaucratic governance systems of modern European law. The struggles of most indigenous peoples for culture rights and self-determination reveal asymmetries between the indigenous peoples' societies and the European societies that colonised them. This cultural and institutional clash continues to provoke many states to repress and oppress the indigenous people.

Despite unjust conquest and continued oppression, however, few indigenous peoples seek sovereignty for themselves in the sense of the formation of an independent, internationally recognised state with ultimate authority over all matters within a determinately bounded territory. Most indigenous peoples seek significantly greater and more secure self-determination within the framework of a wider polity (Polanco 1997). Most seek explicit recognition as distinct peoples by the states that claim to have jurisdiction over them, and wider terms of autonomy and negotiation with those states and with the other peoples living within those states. They claim or seek significant self-government rights, not only with respect to cultural issues, but with respect to land and access to resources. They claim to have rights to be distinct political entities with which other political entities, such as states, must negotiate agreements and over which they cannot simply impose their will and their law.

In their contribution to this volume, Roger Maaka and Augie Fleras detail one model of such indigenous self-determination in the context of a wider polity, which they refer to as 'soft' sovereignty. They explicitly eschew a notion of sovereignty as non-interference, and instead articulate a model of the relations of distinct peoples in which they engage with one another as equals on an ongoing basis.[5]

Indigenous peoples remain colonised peoples. Despite the locality of their claims, they have forged a global social movement that has achieved significant success since the 1980s in gaining recognition for the legitimacy of their claims. In some regions of the world they have had success in motivating some social and political changes to accommodate their needs and interests. Properly recognising the claims of indigenous peoples today, however, requires challenging the international system of sovereign states. Indigenous peoples worldwide have long been aware of the incompatibility of their claims to justice with the concept of state sovereignty that predominates in international relations. Especially in the last two decades they have organised across different parts of the world, and have succeeded, to some extent, in having the uniqueness of their claims recognised by international bodies such as the World Court or the UN. Their social movements have prompted some reforms in the policies of the states that claim to have jurisdiction over them. Despite these successes, many nation-states continue to repress indigenous movements. Their accommodation to indigenous demands for self-determination requires a degree of institutional change that most states are unwilling to allow, especially if other states in the international system are not doing so. Thus indigenous peoples' movements are both a source of ideas and action beyond the system of sovereign states, and at the same time show the limits of that system (Wilmer 1993).

Decentred Diverse Democratic Federalism

I have argued that the postcolonial project entails envisioning governance without sovereignty, partly because the predominant meaning of sovereignty cannot be kept in place, and justice also be done to indigenous people. With some others who question the sovereignty principle, I suggest that we draw some inspiration for an imagination of the future of global governance from the past before states as we know them had fully evolved. In particular, I have suggested that a revaluation of the meaning of Native American federated governance and the pre-state relations of colonists and Native Americans aids this project.[6]

While many share the criticisms of the system of sovereign states that I have summarised, they assume that we must continue to work within that system because we lack alternatives. To conclude, I sketch a vision of global governance with local self-determination that I call, in accordance with its major principles, *decentred diverse democratic federalism*. This vision should not be construed as the proposal for concrete institutional design, but rather as a set of principles that social movements and policy makers should keep in mind in their work. In articulating the vision I draw on the work of Gerald Frug, David Held and James Tully, among others.

A long-time advocate of increasing powers of local governance in the US, Gerald Frug points out that most concepts of decentralised democracy assume what he calls a centred subject. They assume that a unit of government, whether a state or a locale, is an independent, bounded jurisdiction with sole authority over matters in its purview. Most visions of decentralised democracy implicitly transfer the idea of sovereignty from nation-states to smaller units. Such a concept of the centred subject, however, is problematic at any level. Despite the interdependence I alluded to above, this concept of autonomy tries clearly to separate a realm of our business from an outside realm that is none of our business, and where outsiders should mind their own business and leave us alone.

Certain feminist and postcolonial theories question this 'sovereign self', and propose to substitute the notion of a relational self that recognises the constitution of selves by interaction with others and their interdependencies (Yeatman 1994; Nedelsky 1989; 1991). In the theory of a relational self, freedom or autonomy does not consist in separation and independence from others, or complete control over a self-regarding sphere of activity in which others have no right to interfere. Instead, a subject is autonomous if it has effective control over its own sphere of action and influence over the determination of the conditions of its action, either individually or with others in collective decision-making processes.

Frug proposes to extend this ideal of the relational self and the *decentred* subject to the empowerment of local government. Instead of assuming that decentralised units must be centred, bounded and separated from their neighbours in self-regarding and self-interested pursuit of local well-being, he proposes that more empowered localities should be understood as situated subjects. While locales or other units are or ought to be self-determining, at the same time we should recognise that the web of global, national and regional interactions draws all of us into relationships such that actions or events in one locale often have profound consequences for others, and that much about our local context is constituted by our relationship to those outside. While local and regional self-determination are important values, no jurisdiction ought to be sovereign. To reflect this, Frug calls for strong federated and negotiated regional governments in which local governments and their citizens directly participate (Frug 1999). I propose to extend this principle of federalism to the relationship between peoples at both regional and global levels.

The first element in a vision of global democracy, then, is local self-determination, but without sovereign borders. I take the claims of self-determination within the context of a wider polity made by many indigenous peoples as a model of what such local governance might mean. Regions, peoples, even non-governmental organisations, can each be thought of as having claims to self-determination, but none ought to be sovereign. This means rejecting a conception of self-governance as non-interference, clearly separating a realm of our business from a realm outside that is none of our business, and where those outside must keep out of our business. Whether at the level of individual persons, locales, local regions, nations or continents, self-determination subsidiarity decisions should be made and carried out at the most local level possible. Others have a right to make a claim to be party to a decision and its execution, or to review them, only if they can show that the issue and decision materially affect them. When issues and actions are thus mutually affecting, parties should make the decision together. Thus a principle of self-determination, as distinct from the principle of sovereignty, gives prima facie right of non-interference with participatory rights in collective decision-making in those many cases when the prima facie autonomy is justifiably overridden.

Thus with David Held, Thomas Pogge and others, I envision a principle of local self-determination enacted in the context of global governance structures (Held 1995). Both international distributive justice and self-determination would be better served by more global centralisation of some of the powers that supposedly sovereign states currently have, and at the same time more regional and local control at the level below that of current nation-states. While these may sound like contrary goals, the experience of some groups with the European union, for example, offers some grounds for thinking that more global regulation can enable more local control as compared with the current states system: locales can relate directly to global authorities in order to challenge and limit the ability of nation-states to control them. I imagine a global system of regulatory regimes to which locales, regions and states relate in a nested federated system. The global level of governance is 'thin', in the sense that it only lays down rather general principles with which all jurisdictions must comply. Interpretation and application of the principles, as well as any governance issues that do not come under the principles, are left to local jurisdictions. Public administration, according to this vision, is local and regional, which is to say that each locale has the power to decide for itself how it complies with the general regulatory principles.

My purpose is not to design global governance institutions, but only to set out and argue for a few principles of postcolonial governance. In that spirit, I envision at this 'thin' level of global governance seven kinds of issues about which moral respect and international justice would seem to call for a global regulatory regime: peace and security; environment; trade and finance; investment and capital utilisation; communications and transportation; human rights, including labour standards and welfare rights; citizenship; and the movement of peoples. Each of these issue areas already has an evolving regime of international law that could be built upon to create a global regime with greater enforcement strength and resources for carrying out its purpose. For the most part, however, states are the subject of what international regulation exists. An important aspect of decentring governance through global regulatory regimes would consist in making at least some of the activities of non-state organisations, such as indigenous groups, municipalities, corporations, nonprofit service associations and individuals, directly addressed in global regulation, with state, regional and local governments serving as the tools of implementation.

I do not envision a single sovereign government – a world state – that legislates regulation in these areas. I share with many others a fear and suspicion of the very idea of a single centralised government entity on a global scale. At a global level, more than any other, a principle of the separation of powers is vital. Thus I imagine that each regulatory regime has a functional jurisdiction legally separate from those of the others, each with its own regulative function. Each provides a thin set of general rules that specify ways that individuals, organisations and governments are obliged to take account of the interests and circumstances of one another. The visionary founders of the UN hoped that its institutions would evolve this way, and some of them would still have the potential to

256 IRIS MARION YOUNG

do so if they had the support of most of the world's governments and their people.

Held imagines global governance with nested levels of jurisdiction. Government would start with the presumption that an issue or conflict should be dealt with in locales or in associations not territorially based. If conflict is not resolved or if additional agents have a legitimate stake in the issue, then the governance structure would kick up to a more comprehensive level, and so on to a level of global judgement and regulation. Within such a nested set of governance relationships there would be no reason to eliminate that level of organisation now called the nation-state. The uniformity, centrality and final authority of that level, however, would be seriously altered. Decentred federalism allows sovereignty at no level. While there is a presumption of local or associational self-determination, outsiders have a right to claim that they are affected by a unit's or an agent's business, and problems and conflicts should be worked out through federated democratic negotiations and decision-making that create larger units.

With Held, I envision regimes of global federation as *democratic*. Some might regard this as the most far-fetched of all the elements in the vision. To the degree that more global coordination and negotiation occurs today transcending the level of existing states, most are deeply undemocratic. The growing global power of private corporations and financial institutions is explicitly undemocratic. The tribunals of international law have few channels of democratic accountability. Scholars and journalists bemoan the 'democratic deficit' they observe in the operations of today's most complex and thoroughly developed transnational governance body, the European Union. Most of its policies have been developed and implemented by a relatively small group of state-based elites, with little or no opportunity for the participation of ordinary citizens and locales (Pogge 1997). Especially because of the power and structure of the Security Council, the UN is not a democratic institution. Some might claim that at this level democratic participation and accountability is simply not possible.

Of course there are huge questions of institutional design for making decentred global federalism democratic, and I cannot begin to address those. At the level of vision, here are some things to bear in mind. First, one of the reasons to insist on localism, the devolution of sovereign authority onto more local units, is to promote democracy. Participation and citizenship are always enacted best at a local level. Democratic federated regimes of global regulation, however, do require institutions of representation and policy deliberation at levels far removed from the local. A global environmental regulatory decision-making body would not need to be any *more* removed from ordinary citizens than national legislatures currently are. For once we move beyond a local level, any polity – national, hemispheric or global – is an 'imagined community', whose interests and problems must be discursively constructed as involving everyone, because people do not have experience of most of the others in the polity. This problem is no greater for transnational and global regulation than it is for the existing nation-state. Institutions of representation must be constructed with mechanisms of popular and public accountability in regional and global regimes. Postcolonial possibilities of transportation and communication, finally, enable the formation of public spheres composed of active citizens in global civil society. By means of strong local organisation, ordinary citizens have organised knowledgeable and obstreperous civic publics around many major international treaty negotiations and policy conferences in the last decade.

With James Tully, finally, I envision decentred democratic global federalism as *diverse*. In *Strange Multiplicity*, Tully looks to pre-modern political and legal relations to fuel our imagination on alternative legal discourses and institutions (Tully 1995). As I have done earlier, he reflects on the hybrid moment of intercultural communication between indigenous peoples and Europeans on the North American continent before the emergence of nation-states. Aboriginal peoples were able to approach the European settlers to negotiate treaties and agreements in part because they had long histories of dealings with other Aboriginal peoples whom they recognised as distinct, and had institutions and practices for negotiating arrangements of cooperation and accommodation (as well as fierce institutions of war when they chose not to accommodate or cooperation broke down). Tully extrapolates three 'constitutional conventions' from this example of treaty constitutionalism, which he believes can be generalised as ideals for a postcolonial politics: mutual recognition, consent and continuity. Parties to negotiation on terms of cooperation and joint regulation must first mutually recognise one another as distinct but not closed political entities, with their own interests, modes of discourse and ways of looking at the world. In their negotiations they do not seek once and for all agreement on a general set of principles, but rather they seek to reach agreement on issues of distribution or institutional organisation on particular matters of contention or uncertainty. In the process of negotiated interaction they maintain continuity with their pasts, each party's distinctness is affirmed, they seek to maintain continuity with previous agreements, and to forge new links with new agreements that will have some lasting effect, though they are always also revisable by means of new negotiations.

Tully describes what emerges from such a process of interaction and negotiation among distinct groups as 'diverse federalism'. The local groups unite in federated arrangements that may be quite large and govern many aspects of societal life. As federated, however, they maintain

strong presumption of local or group-based self-governance. The federated relation to wider legal arrangements is diverse in several respects. A
polity in the mode of diverse federalism publicly recognises the diversity of
peoples, ways of life, modes of thinking and forms of self-government that
make it up. When units of the federated polity dialogue and negotiate
about matters of interactive or joint concern, they do not assume a single
common idiom of discussion, self or common premises – or a single common way of expressing themselves. Instead, they try to be open to the
diverse discourses and assumptions of one another in order to understand
how they are similar and how different. The relationships in which the
diverse units and groups stand to the federation, finally, are not necessarily uniform. Agreements and regulations may apply to different units in
different ways and degrees, or indeed, some may not apply at all.

   The postcolonial project entails, I have suggested, challenging the linearity of western history and recognising the history of both the colonisers and the colonised as hybrid. Most places, institutions and practices
are constituted through intercultural interaction without a bounded self.
Politically, the postcolonial project involves recognition of the claims of
indigenous peoples today for self-determination and challenging the
existing international system which by means of the institutions of state
sovereign preserves privileges for people in the north at the expense of
those in the south. I have sketched some ideas of decentred democratic
diverse federalism as a system of global governance with local self-
determination as an alternative to that states system.

Notes

1 Introduction

1 The historical material is now vast. For important recent discussions see Pagden 1982; 1995; Tuck 1999; Tully 1993, 1995; Connolly 1994; Arneil 1996; Said 1994; Chatterjee 1993; Cooper and Stoler 1997; Reynolds 1992, 1996; Walker 1987; Slattery 1987, 1991; Williams 1990, 1997; Canada, Royal Commission on Aboriginal Peoples 1996a.
2 For more discussion on the nature of western political theory in general see the essays in Vincent 1997.
3 There were significant strands of moral and political thought that resisted such assumptions. For a discussion of some of these strands and their limits, see Pagden 1995.
4 Note that Kymlicka has been criticised by some for being unwilling to impose liberal principles on groups like indigenous peoples; see, for example, Okin 1998.
5 See, for example, the Symposium on *Multicultural Citizenship* in *Contestations* 1997: 4, 1.
6 For a development of this claim see James Tully's chapter in this book and references therein. On the 'governmental' character of this aspect of the liberal state with regard to cultural minorities see Chatterjee 1993: 220–39.
7 See the important discussion by Slattery 1987: 745–78 especially at p. 748:

> So far as the doctrine of aboriginal rights is concerned, a native group that in the past lived mainly by hunting, fishing and gathering may now turn its lands to farming, ranching, tourism or mineral development.

See also *Delgamuukw* v. *British Columbia* (1997) 3 SCR 1010, especially Lamar CJ at paras 116–18, 123–24. The chapter by Barcham also touches on these issues.
8 There has been some debate over whether or not it is appropriate to italicise words in Māori. Our contributors take different stances on these issues. Given our desire to reflect, in part, the diversity and complexity of arguments concerning indigenous peoples' claims, we see no reason to impose a standard typographical practice where, in fact, one does not exist.

9 It has been argued on the grounds of liberal neutrality that the state has no business subsidising the cultural choices of individuals, but equally, has no business interfering with them. Hence there are no grounds for group rights, but individuals should be free to form or re-affirm their commitment to various kinds of associations (cultural or otherwise). See Kukathas 1997b.

2 Waitangi as Mystery of State: Consequences of the Ascription of Federative Capacity to the Māori

1 *Colonial Office memorandum CO 209/2*:409. Reference given by Paul McHugh in Kawharu 1989: 31, 57.
2 For Chief Justice Prendergast's judgment in the case *Wi Parata* v. *Bishop of Wellington 1877*, see Kawharu 1989: 110–13.
3 For a short statement of the view that this was a 'Declaration of Independence' intended to establish a Māori sovereign state and countered by the Treaty of Waitangi, see Durie 1998: 2–3. For the historical circumstances, with emphasis on the role of James Busby as resident on behalf of the Crown, see Orange 1987: 19–23.
4 For the enlargement of vocabulary from *rangatiratanga* into *mana*, see Durie 1998: 2–3. He uses the latter term to constitute the entire Māori world-view as a basis of identity and sovereignty. I continue to use *rangatiratanga* as a starting point for the non-Māori reader who is encountering the question.
5 The term 'contact' is a key one in Pacific historiography, denoting the moment at which the encounter between cultures began.
6 I owe much here to conversations with Mark Hickford at St Antony's College, Oxford.
7 See Windschuttle 1994 and the ensuing exchange in La Capra, Baswick & Leeson 1999: 709–11, alluding to the exchange between Peter Munz and Anne Salmond (Munz & Salmond 1994: 60ff).
8 For Locke on 'federative power', see *Second Treatise*, chapter 12, sections 143–48; it is mentioned last.
9 For a reconstitution of the Māori universe of *utu*, see Salmond 1997. The Māori cosmogony is set forth, and stated as the basis of cultural claim, in Durie 1998, and many other authors.
10 For questions about *pākehā* identity and history, and whether the word *pākehā* adequately ascribes them, see Sharp 1997: 64–9.
11 A meeting place where strangers are challenged, then recognised as guests, and where debate occurs among those qualified to take part in it.
12 The *waka* is the sailing vessel, single or double-hulled, in which Polynesians navigated the Pacific. The connotations of 'galley' make it a better English translation than 'canoe'. It is here used as a Māori translation of 'ship'. For *tau iwi* and its ambivalences, see Sharp 1997: 65–6.

3 The Struggles of Indigenous Peoples for and of Freedom

1 For the failure of Western political theorists to enter into a just dialogue with indigenous peoples and their political traditions, see Turner 1997. I am greatly indebted to this Anishnabai political philosopher for helping me to understand the shortcomings of Western political theory in relation to indigenous political theory, as well as the possibilities for a fair dialogue. See also Turner forthcoming.

2 The best introduction to how these two concepts are used by indigenous peoples is Turner 1997; forthcoming, and Alfred 1999a. I am greatly indebted to this Kanien'kehaka Mohawk political scientist for helping me to understand the system of internal colonisation and the two arts of resistance and freedom practised by indigenous peoples. See also Alfred 1995.

3 For a summary of the historical research on the four dimensions of colonisation over four historical periods in Canada, see Royal Commission on Aboriginal Peoples 1996a.

4 Accordingly, the techniques of government standardly have two objectives: to cope with the immediate situation in the short term and to move indigenous peoples towards extinguishment in the long run. See, for example, the four policies analysed by the Royal Commission 1996a: 245–604.

5 For a summary of historical research on the three strategies of extinguishing rights, see Royal Commission 1996a: 137–200, 245–604, and the subhead 'Legitimations of Internal Colonisation'.

6 For the strategies of assimilation and accommodation, see Armitage 1995; Royal Commission 1996a: 201–44, 245–604; Culhane 1998: 90–110; Warry 1998 and 'Legitimations of Internal Colonisation'.

7 For the concept of a 'word warrior', see Turner forthcoming, and the subhead 'Struggles for Freedom'. For a recent statement of indigenous sovereignty and self-determination, see Alfred 1999b.

8 The extensive research commissioned by the Canadian Royal Commission on Aboriginal Peoples from 1991 to 1996 is a good introduction to this field.

9 *Calder* et al. v. *AG BC* (1973), 34 DLR (3rd) 145 [1973] SCR 313: 156. For background, see Raunet 1996.

10 *Delgamuukw* v. *BC* [1997] 1 CNLR 14: 145. (Henceforth in text as Delgamuukw 1997.) For an analysis of *Delgamuukw*, to which I am greatly indebted, see McNeil 1998. For a broad textual and contextual analysis of the cases leading up to *Delgamuukw* in 1997, see Culhane 1998.

11 *R.* v. *Sparrow* [1990] DLR (4th): 404, cited in Asch 1999: 439.

12 The date the Court gives for the assertion of sovereignty over indigenous peoples and their lands is 1846, the year of the Treaty of Washington between the British Crown and the US in which the southern border of the colonies of British Columbia and Vancouver Island was settled between them. 'Settlement' is perhaps a misnomer as the immigrant settlements were resettlements on lands from which indigenous peoples had been removed (see Harris 1997). These resettlements covered a tiny portion of British Columbia and were nowhere near the Gitxsan and Wet'suwet'en territories. The indigenous population still outnumbered the non-indigenous population when the colony joined Canada in 1871 and their lands were transferred to the Crown in Canada without their consent. See the subhead 'Struggles for Freedom' for the rejection by the International Court of Justice of the Supreme Court's type of argument that settlement and recognition by another European power without the consent of indigenous peoples legitimates sovereignty.

13 *Delgamuukw* 1997: 114, 141. For the appeal to their 'distinctness' as 'aboriginals' as the sole basis of aboriginal rights in earlier judgments, see Asch 1999: 432, 436–37, 439. For the Court's rejection of any appeal to the general and universal rights of the Enlightenment as a source of aboriginal rights, see *Van der Peet* (1996) 137 DLR (4th): 289 (SCC): 300, cited in Asch 1999: 435, 439. Asch argues that this feature of the Court's judgments legitimates and continues the colonial status of indigenous peoples.

14 This is the main thesis of Asch 1999.
15 For these justifications, see Turner 1997; Williams 1990; Pagden 1995; Culhane 1998: 37–72 and Tully 1993: 58–99, 104. McNeil 1998: 11–12 comments:

> This sounds very much like a familiar justification for dispossessing Aboriginal peoples in the heyday of European colonialism in Eastern North America – agriculturists are superior to hunters and gatherers, and so can take their land. But Lamer CJ was not referring to the seventeenth and eighteenth centuries – he was talking about the present day, as justification for infringement only became relevant after Aboriginal rights were constitutionalized in 1982!

16 *Delgamuukw* 1997: 161. Lamer CJ is citing with approval an earlier case, *Gladstone*, para 73.
17 The Government of Canada, the Government of British Columbia and the Nisga'a Nation, *Nisga'a Final Agreement* (1998), Preamble, clauses 2, 3, 6, p.1. The Agreement was signed by the three parties on 4 August 1998 after twenty years of negotiation. The Nisga'a people ratified the Agreement by a vote of 61 per cent in a referendum and the people of British Columbia ratified it by a narrow majority vote in the provincial legislature. As of September 1999 the federal government has not ratified the Agreement. There are two court challenges to the Agreement that the self-government provisions violate the constitutional division of powers and that it violates the Charter rights of non-aboriginal citizens. One indigenous nation, the Gitanyow, claim that the original Nisga'a land claim includes part of their traditional territory. For an overview of the arguments *pro* and *contra*, see the articles in *British Columbian Studies* 1998–99. For the legal and historical background, see Foster 1998–99 and Raunet 1996.
18 See *Nisga'a* 1998: 31–158 (land and resources); pp. 159–95 (self-government and justice). For details of the land settlement, see Appendices.
19 See, for example, the 1989 submission of the Attorney General of Canada in defense of the earlier, lower-court challenge by the Gitxsan and Wet'suwet'en peoples for legal recognition of their rights to jurisdiction over their traditional territories. It states (cited in Asch 1999: 444, *n.* 29):

> The plaintiffs' claim to ownership and jurisdiction over all the lands in the claim area. The Attorney General of Canada responds: Ownership and jurisdiction constitute a claim to sovereignty. If the Plaintiffs ever had sovereignty, it was extinguished completely by the assertion of sovereignty by Great Britain.

20 Although the provincial government has heralded this treaty as a 'template' for the treaties now under negotiation with fifty other First Nations, most of the other First Nations have said that it is not a template. For a devastating criticism of the Agreement, and the modern treaty process in British Columbia more generally, as a strategy of assimilation, see Alfred 1995: 119–28.
21 For hinge propositions, see 'Struggles of Freedom' and note 42.
22 This starting point is a paraphrase of John Marshall, an early Chief Justice of the US, in *Worcester v. the State of Georgia* in 1832 (6 Peter's Reports, 515–97). The two-step procedure, international treaties and continuing sovereignty are also features of Marshall's famous argument. See Tully 1993: 117–27. This is incompatible with his earlier statement that indigenous nations are domestic and dependent, unless an indigenous nation has agreed to this status in international negotiations, but there is no evidence of this. For the limitations of

Marshall's use of the prior and continuing sovereignty argument, see Turner 1997. Another famous articulation of the prior and continuing sovereignty argument is the *Kaswentha* or Two Row Wampum model of treaty-making between free and coexisting peoples of the *Haudenosaunee* or Iroquois confederacy. See Tully 1993: 127–29 and Alfred 1999a: 52–3, 104, 113.

23 This fundamental principle has been upheld by the International Court of Justice in its *Advisory Opinion Concerning the Western Sahara* (1975). See note 28.

24 This understanding of treaties and of the Royal Proclamation of 1763, as international treaties among equal nations or peoples, is the way treaties are understood by indigenous peoples and it has gained considerable historical and normative support by Western scholars. See Burrows 1997; Venne 1997; Royal Commission on Aboriginal Peoples 1995a: 59–70; 1996b: 18:

> In entering into treaties with Indian nations in the past, the Crown recognized the nationhood of its treaty partners. Treaty making . . . represents an exercise of the governing and diplomatic powers of the nations involved to recognize and respect one another and to make commitments to a joint future. It does not imply that one nation is being made subject to the other.

25 See Royal Commission on Aboriginal Peoples 1996a: 675–96. That is, indigenous peoples are equal partners *with* Canada, not subordinate partners already *in* or *of* Canada. For the latter view, see Canadian Royal Commission 1993. There is a tension between these two views in the final Report of the Royal Commission. For a more detailed account of the former view, see Tully 1999. For an attempt to discuss the argument in the context of Australia, see Tully 1998.

26 For this conception of non-state and non-exclusive sovereignty, as 'popular' sovereignty or a 'free people', see Alfred 1999a: 54–72 and Turner 1997: 19–30. For a comprehensive account and pragmatic defence of this and the self-determination argument, based on a critical review of the extensive literature generated by the Royal Commission, see Murphy 1997. For a similar study for Australia, with more emphasis on the self-determination argument, see Strelein 1998. I am greatly indebted to these two excellent theses. See also the reconstruction and application of the prior and continuing sovereignty argument by Williams 1997.

27 See Murphy 1997; Strelein 1998; Venne 1998 and Macklem 1995 for the complementarity of the two arguments. When these two arguments are presented from an indigenous perspective, there is always in addition the reference to the special relation that indigenous peoples have to the lands they have occupied and identified with for millennia, a relation that is not captured by Western notions of private property or jurisdiction. For an introduction to this holistic understanding of being-in-the-world, see Alfred 1999a: 42–4; Royal Commission on Aboriginal Peoples 1996: 434–63 and Venne 1998: 122–28.

28 See Venne 1998: 68–106 for a careful survey of these documents and the major commentaries on them. Compare Murphy 1997: 116–51 and Strelein 1998: 54–86. Recall that the Supreme Court of Canada rejected an appeal to the universal right of self-determination as a ground of Aboriginal rights (see note 13).

29 International Court of Justice (1975) summarised in Venne 1998: 45–7. The Court continued this line of reasoning in *Case Concerning East Timor (Portugal v. Australia)* (1995). For the Supreme Court of Canada's use of the argument

of discovery and non-consent that the ICJ rejects in *Western Sahara* see note 12, and for the use by the Attorney General of Canada of an extinguishment argument that the IJC also rejects, see note 19.

30 See Venne 1998: 51–3, 92–4, 107–63 for the struggles over the Draft, and 205–28 for the Draft Declaration. The right of self-determination is asserted in Article 3 and qualified in Article 31.

31 Collective rights embodied in a claim to self-determination are seen as a threat to the sovereignty of the dominant state. This tension between indigenous self-determination and the state's assertion of [exclusive] sovereignty is a recurrent theme throughout this discussion [at the UN] as it is the basis of arguments against the recognition of a right of Indigenous peoples to self-determination (Strelein 1998: 55–6).

32 *Declaration on the Granting of Independence to Colonial Countries and Peoples* Resolution 1514 (XV) 14 December 1960, GA Official Records, 15th session, Suppl. no. 16. For the studies of four Special Rapporteurs see Venne 1998: 75–82, especially the study by Aureliu Cristescu, cited at 76.

33 *Declaration on the Granting of Independence to Colonial Countries and Peoples* Resolution 1514 (XV) 14 December 1960, GA Official Records, 15th session, Suppl. no. 16, 66, paras 6–7 together with Resolution 1541 (XV) GAOR 15th session, Suppl. no. 16, Principle IV, 29. See Strelein 1998: 59–60. This saltwater restriction on self-determination was introduced in 1960 in explicit opposition to the Belgium initiative to extend it to peoples, including indigenous peoples, within independent states.

34 'Any attempt aimed at the partial or total disruption of national unity and the territorial integrity of a country is incompatible with the purposes and principles of the Charter of the United Nations', *Declaration on the Granting of Independence to Colonial Countries and Peoples* Resolution 1514 (XV) 14 December 1960, GA Official Records, 15th session, Suppl. no. 16, 66, paras 6–7 together with Resolution 1541 (XV) GAOR 15th session, Suppl. no. 16, Principle IV, 29. This is reinforced by the *Declaration on Principles of International Law concerning Friendly Relations and Cooperation among States in accordance with the Charter of the United Nations*, GA Resolution 2625 (XXV) of 24 October 1970. See Venne 1998: 73–4; Strelein 1998: 59–61.

35 In addition to the references in note 25, see Venne 1998: 92, Strelein 1998: 16–33 and Moss 1995.

36 See Young forthcoming for a cogent theory of global democratic governance that recognises individuals, minorities, peoples and states, and her chapter in this volume.

37 *The Declaration on Friendly Relations*, para 1. See Strelein 1998: 60–2.

38 See Laden 1997; Murphy 1997 and Kymlicka 1995. Turner 1997: 1–30 and Murphy 1997: 59–74 argue that while Kymlicka's well-known theory protects indigenous peoples from assimilation, it preserves colonial accommodation.

39 This is a paraphrase of the rights of internal self-determination in the Draft Declaration on the rights of Indigenous Peoples, in Venne 1998: 205–28.

40 This distinction between internal and external self-determination reflects the way the right of self-determination has evolved within a framework of the territorial integrity of existing states. The Draft Declaration on the Rights of Indigenous Peoples accepts internal self-determination at Article 31.

41 This universal principle is endorsed by the Supreme Court of Canada in *Reference re Secession of Quebec*, file no. 25506, 1998.

42 For a detailed presentation of this argument with respect to Canada, see Tully forthcoming; for Australia, Strelein 1998; and in general, Young forthcoming.

4 Beyond Regret: Mabo's Implications for Australian Constitutionalism

My thanks to Bill Wagner for research assistance, and to Duncan Ivison, Garth Nettheim and Paul Patton for their comments on earlier versions of this manuscript.

Some of the more frequently mentioned cases have been abbreviated after their first mention in the text: *Delgamuukw* v. *British Columbia* (1997) 153 DLR (4th) 193 (SCC) becomes *Delgamuukw*; *Mabo* v. *Queensland (No. 2)* (1992) 107 ALR (HC) becomes *Mabo*; *Sparrow* v. *R* [1990] 1 SCR 1075 becomes *Sparrow*; *Ward* v. *Western Australia* (1998) 159 ALR 483 (FC) becomes *Ward*; *Wik Peoples* v. *Queensland* (1996) 141 ALR 129 (HC) becomes *Wik*; and *Yorta Yorta* v. *Victoria* [1998] 1606 FCA (18 December 1998) becomes *Yorta Yorta*.

1 *Mabo* v. *Queensland (No. 2)* (1992) 107 ALR 1.
2 *Wik Peoples* v. *Queensland* (1996) 141 ALR 129: 230.
3 This essay is a companion to Webber 1995a, which examined the process of moral reflection that underpinned the High Court's recognition of indigenous title.
4 For a discussion of Australian constitutional law as it affects indigenous people, see Clarke 1999.
5 This is the approach adopted in Brennan J's judgment in *Mabo* and implicitly followed by the great majority of subsequent commentators and judgments. See especially his discussion of the recognition and enforcement of native title by the ordinary courts at 42–5 of that decision:

> Native title is conceived as specific interests in land, which survive the assertion of sovereignty by the colonial power in much the same way that, under international law, rights held by private parties survive a change in sovereignty in the wholly non-Indigenous context. Indigenous title is enforceable before the general courts by the usual legal and equitable remedies. Its content is determined by the courts as a matter of fact, based on the customs and traditions of the people. The persistence of native title requires a measure of adjustment in the general property regime in order to take account of the title's continued presence, but the adjustment of rights and the enforcement of the interests is accomplished by the courts as an integral part of their adjudication of the common law.

Some commentators have criticised the confining of indigenous title to a purely private right, although they have generally conceded that that is the effect of the definition of native title in *Mabo*. See, for example, Grattan and McNamara 1999. Here, I argue that that limited conception of indigenous title (as a purely private right) is untenable, even on the terms laid down in *Mabo*.

6 *Mabo* 1992: 42. See also 65 and 83, *per* Deane and Gaudron JJ.
7 *Mabo* 1992: 44. See also 83, *per* Deane and Gaudron JJ.
8 In *Mabo* 1992: 20–1 and 51 (*per* Brennan J) and 57–8 (*per* Deane and Gaudron JJ), the High Court held, following the *Seas and Submerged Lands* case, *New South Wales* v. *Commonwealth* (1975) 135 CLR 337, that the sovereignty of the Australian state could not be questioned in proceedings before the courts of Australia. See also *Coe* v. *Commonwealth of Australia* (1993) 118 ALR 193 (HC) at 198–200 and, at an earlier stage of the development of the area, *Coe* v. *Commonwealth of Australia* (1979) 24 ALR 118 (HC). The recognition of that overarching sovereignty need not exclude a lesser right of self-government, however (although there are some comments that would suggest otherwise in the first *Coe* decision at 129 (*per* Gibbs J)). Within general Australian

constitutional doctrine, the division of governmental authority is not strange; sovereignty is undoubtedly divided at least between the Commonwealth and States, or perhaps vested in (or shared with) the Australian people, by virtue of their ability to amend the Constitution by referendum.

This is not the place to resolve all these conundrums of sovereignty. It is sufficient to note that the concept is a complex one, currently subject to substantial reconsideration, which may well have space for the recognition of significant indigenous rights to self-government. Regardless of whether such authority is recognised as a matter of constitutional right, native title necessarily presumes a measure of continued indigenous political autonomy.

9 For this reason, in its 1986 report, the Law Reform Commission rejected codification and court enforcement as ways of recognising Aboriginal customary laws (Law Reform Commission 1986: 87–8, 147).

10 Compare Noel Pearson's argument that native title is 'the recognition space between the common law and the Aboriginal law' in Pearson 1997.

11 *Cherokee Nation* v. *State of Georgia* (1831) 5 Peters 1 at 17 (US Supreme Court) *per* Marshall CJ. See also *Worcester* v. *State of Georgia* (1832) 6 Peters 515 at 556–60 (US Supreme Court).

12 This, it seems to me, is the best interpretation of the natural rights theory of Jean-Marie-Étienne Portalis, who, as *conseiller d'état* and *orateur du gouvernement*, was responsible for the provisions on ownership in the French Civil Code. See his speech, upon introducing the provisions before the Corps Législatif on 17 January 1804, in Locré 1827, vol. 8: 146–52. See also the discussion of Pufendorf in Tuck 1979: 160–61.

13 See, for example, *Mabo* 1992: 26–9. Locke, of course, used the indigenous people of North America as his chief exemplars of humanity in the state of nature (Locke 1986: 328). See also Tully 1993: 137.

14 See, for example, *Cooper* v. *Stuart* (1889) 14 App Cas 286 at 291; *Re Southern Rhodesia* [1919] AC 211 at 233–34.

15 Section 35 of the Constitution Act, 1982 protects 'aboriginal and treaty rights' from legislative impairment, subject to justification: see *Sparrow* v. *R* [1990] 1 SCR 1075 at 1109–11 and 1113–19. The Supreme Court of Canada has attempted to deal with the problem of how to define those rights by limiting 'aboriginal rights' to those activities that are 'an element of a practice, custom or tradition integral to the distinctive culture of the aboriginal group claiming the right' *Van der Peet* v. *R* (1996) 137 DLR (4th) 289 at 310 (SCC, *per* Lamer CJ). The application of this definition has been substantially limited, in *Delgamuukw* v. *British Columbia* (1997) 153 DLR (4th) 193 (SCC), by the conclusion that 'aboriginal title' itself is not subject to it. The definition has, however, been retained for other, lesser rights. The *Van der Peet* test has been fiercely criticised. See Borrows 1997.

16 See also Brennan 1995: 85–7; 197–200; Bern and Dodds in this volume. Coombs' principal concern is with those aspects of native title legislation that render indigenous land more easily alienable. Land rights legislation frequently allows the land to be dealt with in ways that would not have been possible before colonisation, may ratify past acts of dispossession, and may confer less protection against future dispossession than that accorded to non-indigenous interests. This has led some to suggest that the Australian legislation (especially the amendments to the *Native Title Act 1993* proposed and adopted in modified form under the Howard government) is discriminatory in its treatment of indigenous title (see, for example, Dodson 1997: 100ff; Clarke 1997: 22ff; Nettheim 1999: 564ff). Unlike Commonwealth legislation, Australian states' attempts to create arrangements for the control and man-

agement of indigenous title are subject to direct constraints imposed by the *Racial Discrimination Act 1975* (Cth): *Gerhardy* v. *Brown* (1985) 159 CLR 70 (in which South Australia's Pitjantjatjara *Land Rights Act 1981* was affirmed as a permissible 'special measure'); *Western Australia* v. *Commonwealth* (1995) 183 CLR 373 (in which the core of Western Australia's post-*Mabo* native title legislation was held to be invalid because of inconsistency with the *Racial Discrimination Act*).

17 *Mabo* 1992: 48–9 (*per* Brennan J) and 84 (*per* Deane and Gaudron JJ).

18 *Pareroultja* v. *Tickner* (1993) 117 ALR 206 at 214 (leave to appeal to the High Court was denied, but with the Court expressly declining to state whether the granting of land to a land trust would extinguish native title: *Pareroultja* v. *Tickner*, High Court of Australia, No. S156 of 1993, Transcript of Proceedings, 13 April 1994). In *Yanner* v *Eaton* [1999] HCA 53 at paras 76 and 77, Gummow J came to a similar conclusion by treating the issue as a question of merger of estates and applying equity's approach to find no merger had occurred.

19 For a useful review of the use of regional agreements in the first years of the regime, see Edmunds 1998. See also Yu in Yunupingu 1997: 168ff. The 1998 amendments to the *Native Title Act 1993* strengthened the capacity to resolve title issues by agreement, these particular amendments (unlike others in the 1998 package) having significant indigenous support. See Smith 1998.

20 *Wik* 1996. There is considerable anthropological literature on the appropriate claimant. For an especially thoughtful discussion, see Merlan 1996: 165.

21 *Mabo* 1992: 32–7 (*per* Brennan J).

22 See Gummow J's (one of the majority judges) careful discussion of the effect of native title's recognition on the interpretation of the statutes in *Wik* 1996: 232–34.

23 Compare, in the majority reasons, the reasons of Toohey J (*Wik* 1996: 186–87), Gummow J (*Wik* 1996: 234–37), and Kirby J (*Wik* 1996: 279ff), with those of Brennan CJ (*Wik* 1996: 154–59).

24 For a contrasting view, see Grattan and McNamara 1999, but note that they are talking about land law's feudal character in a manner very different from that here.

25 See also Slattery 1987: 744–45. Indeed, the cases on indigenous title at least implicitly acknowledge this, for they make clear that the specific rights of indigenous people *inter se* are determined by the law of the community concerned. See, for example, *Mabo* 1992: 44 (*per* Brennan J). The realisation that indigenous title is primarily about the recognition of the indigenous order, not the specific interests, may provide elements of a solution to the issue of group definition so ably presented (with intriguing proposals for resolution) by Sutton 1995a: 1.

26 See, for example, *Sparrow* 1990: 1119 (*per* Dickson CJ and La Forest J); *MacMillan Bloedel Ltd* v. *Mullin* 1985: 607 (BCCA, *per* Macfarlane JA); Canada, Royal Commission on Aboriginal Peoples 1996b: 561–62.

27 See *Delgamuukw* 1997: 228.

28 *Delgamuukw* 1997: 273. See also at 284 (*per* Laforest J).

29 Proposed sections 35.1ff of the Constitution Act, 1982, Charlottetown Accord, Draft Legal Text (9 October 1992), sections 29ff.

30 One wonderful example of this comes from the area north of Lakes Huron and Superior in the 1840s, when the Ojibways of the area responded to trespass by miners on their traditional lands by retaining a lawyer to press (with effect) their claims for a treaty, relying upon the provisions with respect to the alienation of Indian lands in the Royal Proclamation of 1763. Their

arguments resulted in the Robinson-Huron and Robinson-Superior Treaties of 1850 (Morrison 1994: 40–2, 47–69).

31 This is certainly true of the High Court judgments: *Mabo* 1992; *Wik* 1996. This is true even when, as in *Mabo*, the claim was originally brought by individuals for specified parcels of land. See also *Ward* v *Western Australia* [2000] FCA 191 at paras 203–6, where the court rejected an appeal based on precisely this ground. It has also generally been the case under the Northern Territory and Queensland legislative regimes (Sutton 1995a: 9–10).

32 *Ward* v *Western Australia* 1998: 529, 539–43, 638, 639. The vesting of the land in the entire community was affirmed on appeal; see *Ward* 2000: paras 200–2. The emphasis on negotiation is suggested by the terms used by Lee J both at relevant moments in his reasons (for example, *Ward* 1998: 533, 542) and by a passage he quotes from Lamer CJ's judgment in *Delgamuukw* (*Ward* 1998: 499; *Delgamuukw* 1997). The issue is not merely a lack of proof of the sub-groups' interest, for if this were the case, the Western Australian government would have won its argument that the lack of proof undermined proof of the people's title. Lee J dismissed this argument (at 533) by suggesting that it is the people's continuity as an organised society, rather than the continuity in descent of any of the subgroups, upon which title depends. This suggests that it is the indigenous societies' character as legal/political entities that is important to the establishment of indigenous title, not the continuity of any specific private rights to land. See also Lee J's comments at 542, when determining that native title is vested in the people rather than the subgroup:

> the community may be so organized that responsibility for, and, indeed, control of parts of the area occupied by the community may be exercised by sub-groups . . . but the traditional laws and customs which order the affairs of the sub-groups are the laws and customs of the community, not laws and customs of the sub-group.

33 See note 19.

34 For Coombs' remarks, see text accompanying note 16. See also Sullivan 1995: 97. The negotiations over the *Wik* amendments provided an occasion for severe misgivings as to the foundation on which indigenous title issues are resolved, not least because indigenous representatives were cut out of those negotiations. For criticisms, see Clarke 1997; Dodson 1997; Antonios 1998, especially Appendix 1. For defence, see Brennan 1998.

35 See Webber 1995a, which does not argue that moral reflection or arguments of justice operate unmediated in society (for that is clearly not the case), but nevertheless that they do operate, and sets out to chart the process of moral reflection that underlay *Mabo*.

36 See, for example, Markus 1996; Dodson 1997: 5–6.

37 See, for example, Kirby 1970–71.

38 But see Coombs 1994: 148 in which he argues, on the basis of the experience of the Waitangi Tribunal in New Zealand/Aotearoa, that context-sensitive adjudication may be better than 'political negotiations'.

39 Some constitutional rights also have this character. This is true, for example, of the right to schooling in minority official languages in Canada, found in section 23 of the *Constitution Act 1982*, where a range of potential means of implementation is acceptable: *Mahé* v. *Alberta* (1990) 68 DLR (4th) 69 (SCC) at 85ff. I suspect that the same is true of the guarantee of democratic institutions implicit in the Australian Constitution, especially that Constitution's stipulation (in section 24) that the members of the House of Representatives should be 'directly chosen by the people'. The High Court has been unwill-

ing to find that those provisions require a particular pattern of representation (in particular, 'one vote, one value'), especially given the apparent
acceptability yet potential variation of effective representation under the current Australian single transferable ballot system, a first-past-the-post system,
and various systems of proportional representation. Yet several judges say
that the scope for variation in representation may not be absolute, and that
extreme imbalance may not be permissible. This suggests the possibility of a
'framing norm' applying at a broad level of generality, compatible with a
broad range of variation in particular systems of representation. See the discussions in *AG Commonwealth; Ex rel McKinlay* v. *Commonwealth* (1975) 135
CLR 1 (especially *per* Stephen and Mason JJ) and *McGinty* v. *Western Australia*
(1996) 186 CLR 140.

40 See Bern and Dodds in this volume and Webber 1996: 275–76. The latter article specifically addresses issues posed by immigration. Indigenous peoples
raise additional considerations, although the general point with respect to
recognition remains the same.

41 The political role too had its antecedents, notably the extension of the Commonwealth franchise to all Aborigines in 1962 and the constitutional amendment of 1967, which permitted the counting of indigenous Australians in the
national census. See Chesterman and Galligan 1998.

42 See *Parliamentary Debates* 1996: 5975 (29 October) and *Parliamentary Debates*
1996: 6155 (30 October; John Howard); *Overview* 1997: 9–11; Blainey 1993:
11; Murray 1999: 222–25. See generally Attwood 1996a: 100–16.

43 The forced removal of Aboriginal children is one of the clearest examples
(but not the only example) of this. See *Bringing Them Home* 1997.

44 I explore justifications for such autonomy in Webber 1994: 219–22, 263–75,
and Webber 1993.

45 I give several examples of the distinctive framing of the issues, as against the
Canadian authorities, in Webber 1995a: 18–20.

46 See, for example, the implicit debate between Prime Minister Howard and
Patrick Dodson at the opening of the Australian Reconciliation Convention,
Overview 1997: 8–12. On 26 August 1999, the Commonwealth House of Representatives passed, on the Prime Minister's motion, a resolution that was
intended to go some way towards satisfying this demand. It acknowledged
'that the mistreatment of many indigenous Australians over a significant
period represents the most blemished chapter in our international history'
and expressed 'its deep and sincere regret that indigenous Australians suffered injustices under the practices of past generations' (*Parliamentary Debates*
1999: 9205ff [26 August]).

47 The phrase is that of Sir Owen Dixon, Australia's highly influential and long-
time Chief Justice of the High Court: 'Swearing In of Sir Owen Dixon as Chief
Justice' (1952) 85 CLR *xi* at *xiv*, although there is a real question whether
Dixon CJ himself had such a constrained conception of the judicial role (see
Gummow 1999: 73–4). For useful correctives of this assertion, as description
of how the courts have actually decided cases, see Zines 1997: chapter 17; Galligan 1987: 30–41.

48 See, for example, Myers 1986: 125–26.

49 There is a very good account of this phenomenon in Morrison 1994.

50 Of course, it is simplistic to paint the divide solely in indigenous/non-indige-
nous terms. The differences are also reflected within indigenous (and indeed
non-indigenous) communities. See, for example, the account of different
languages of justification in Macdonald 1997: 74–7. But the more general

point – about the tension between the traditionalist and voluntarist modes of justification – remains.

51 Thus, in what is otherwise a very fine article, Bain Attwood's concluding sentence is jarring:

> In political terms, [the solution to indigenous/non-indigenous relations] might reside in a new beginning for Australia, a republican moment in which Aborigines and settler Australians are offered the opportunity of joining and participating in a new polity on the basis of mutual recognition and respect, such that we might *all* be at home in this place. (Attwood 1996b: 116)

The aspiration is stirring, the need for a new approach important, but the republican language seems to me to be ill-chosen.

52 See, for example, the comments of Pat Dodson reported in Sullivan 1995: 99. Patton (1995a; 1995b) has argued from different philosophical foundations for a similar resistance to definitive conclusions.

53 Note that an attention to tradition need not be conservative, except in a weak sense. It does recognise that we define ourselves, and our current normative commitments, in relation to the past. Furthermore, the very fact that our normative arguments engage the past implies a measure of respect: we realise the need to take our past seriously, to understand it, and to define our own positions in relation to it. But that engagement is by no means uncritical. Even when we consciously follow past ways – when we draw, in a positive fashion, upon the past – we reflect upon the principles inherent in it, attempt to formulate and refine those principles, and inquire into their relationship to today. Moreover, there are times when our reflection leads to regret, and we define our present commitments in contradistinction to what went before. See Webber 1995a.

54 See, for example, the discussion of the dissolution and reconstitution of nations in the Great Lakes region of north-eastern North America during the seventeenth century in White 1991: 1–49.

55 See, for example, *Ward* 1998: 503 and 532ff, affirmed in *Ward* 2000 at paras 229–35 (where the possibility of adoption is expressly contemplated). In the Canadian context, see *Simon* v. *The Queen* (1985) 24 DLR (4th) 390 (SCC) at 406–7.

56 See Sturmer 1982: 69; Levitus 1991; Brennan 1995: 197–200. See also the report commissioned by the Commonwealth government (Reeves 1998).

57 See, for example, *Aboriginal Land Rights (Northern Territory) Act 1976* (Cth), sections 11 and 23.

58 Rowley 1970: 423; 422ff. See also Coombs 1982: 227; 1994: 137–38, 175. It is noteworthy that the Pitjantjatjara successfully pressed for a land rights regime that did not involve proof of individual interests, but rather placed the land under Pitjantjatjara control generally.

59 For a valuable discussion of these institutional dimensions, see Coombs 1994: 133ff. He also discusses the emergence of hybrid forms of administration at 27–8 and 48. See also Sullivan 1997; Sutton 1995b: 48; Suchet 1996.

6 Paths Toward a Mohawk Nation: Narratives of Citizenship and Nationhood in Kahnawake

This paper was presented at the Australian National University for the 'Indigenous Rights, Political Theory and the Reshaping of Institutions' conference in 1997. While there, the work profited from the suggestions and queries of many. It has also benefited from comments in the Canadian Anthropology Society meetings in 1998 as well as the Organization of American Historians meetings and the American Studies Association meetings in 1999. I am especially grateful to Duncan Ivison, Julie Cruikshank, Jean-Guy Goulet, Klaus Neumann, an external reviewer for CUP and others who engaged in substantial ways with the paper. Responsibility for the arguments and content therein resides with me.

1 'Aboriginality' enjoys more currency within anthropological literature than it does on the ground of day-to-day native political practice. It is nonetheless a somewhat useful concept and argument for linking 'rights' to temporality within the arena of political praxis. I will shortly argue that 'nationhood' is the more appropriate analytical framework for comprehending one native community within the context of Canada. 'Nationhood' may appear to be less strategic politically, but it reflects most accurately the historical experience and the politics of the Mohawks of Kahnawake. For further work on aboriginality in the context of Canada, see Levin 1993, and in the context of Australia, see Beckett 1988, Stokes 1997 and Tonkinson 1990.

2 A full review and discussion of the epistemological pitfalls (and arrogance) that surround the 'invention of tradition literature' is beyond the horizon of this essay. Suffice it to say that the underlying variable of authenticity creates this affection for and sets up the logic for 'invention' within analysis. This notion of authenticity (and its handmaid, tradition) frames culture in a fixed and an unmoving space in time. Authenticity then adds a certain value to this cultural moment. Assigning value and intentionality to these practices (or the rhetorics of tradition) is a deeply vexing practice for many. It is colonialism, and the claims that it commands in the contemporary, that sets such a premium on particular moments since past. And it is colonialism and its apparatii that place the 'burden of proof' for tradition, for culture and authenticity upon indigenous peoples. Povinelli 1999 argues that these practices set up a certain failure for indigenous claimants with the frame of juridical practice in Australia. Nonetheless, indigenous 'nationhood', which harnesses the past to the present through consciousness and discursive practice, should not be considered to be an invention in either its most opportunistic and non-constructionist sense, as is found in Keesing 1989, nor in its most nuanced sense, as found in Smith 1991. In the context of Kahnawake it is the marriage of consciousness and being. For an excellent summary of the invention debate and attendant textual issues please see Briggs 1996.

3 For a thorough discussion of the dynamics of the Confederacy see Richter 1992, Fenton 1998 and the special volume of *Recherches amérindiennes au québec*, 'Iroquois au présent du passé' (vol. 29, no. 2, 1999), devoted entirely to the history of the Iroquois.

4 Of the 'colonial ironies' that come to mind, one is the use of the *Indian Act* by contemporary elected councils to even determine membership within their communities at all. The *Indian Act* is a legislative instrument of colonial government that is rooted in Victorian notions of gender and civility. It enforced the protectionist and assimilative agenda of settlement but is ironically used by Indian governments to preserve and protect the contemporary Indian community today. This is not to say that the *Indian Act* is not recognised (and reviled) by some as an instrument of colonial governance. There are within Kahnawake institutional alternatives and counter-discourses to that of the elected council and the *Indian Act*. These alternatives offer 'tradition' as an alternative authority and institution for governance. For further

historical and ethnographic work in this area, please see Blanchard 1982, Jocks 1994, Dickson-Gilmore 1999b and Reid 1999. For a book-length argument in favour of returning to tradition from a perspective rooted in Kahnawake's history, see Alfred 1999a.

5 One need not look far for examples within contemporary expressive culture of native peoples in Canada. See McMaster and Martin 1992 and Kasprycki *et al.* 1998, two catalogues of curated exhibitions that dealt with the themes of contemporary culture, land, meaning and nationhood to native artists representing nations in Canada and the US. The first exhibition was prompted by concern over attempts at land expropriation and coercion by the Canadian government in Kanehsatake, Quebec (commonly known as 'The Oka Crisis') in the summer of 1990.

6 The representational tensions of text have 'real-life' equivalents in the living issues of native–State relations, tensions that are readable in the form of claims that are made upon the state. These claims — for land, for reparation and other forms of indemnity refer to a *past* of native-settler regime interactions that are expressed in the *present* by the critical notion of 'cultural difference'. This difference is premised more often than not upon a baseline of cultural wholeness, continuity and authenticity, of a static and deeply essentialist notion of identity and tradition. These claims, and the role that anthropologists occupy in their articulation and execution, illustrate both the anthropological and indigenous investment in 'tradition' in 'authenticity' and the power of these analytical concepts within the larger picture of justice and rights. It is in the convincing deployment of these concepts that may 'take' or may 'give' indigenous peoples their past and their rights that accrue to a particular past (Clifford 1988: 277–346; Campisi 1991; Whittaker 1994; Dominy 1995; Paine 1996; Mills 1994; Povinelli 1999).

7 The Mohawks of Kahnawake claim an additional 24 000 acres of land given to them in the form of a seignioral land grant in 1680. This grant is known as the 'Seigniory de Sault St Louis'.

8 'Band' is the terminology used in the *Indian Act* and is interchangeable with 'reserve'. In this context 'band list' should be understood as the community-controlled list of members, administered by the band council, or Mohawk Council of Kahnawake (MCK).

9 In 1995 the MCK signed a policing agreement with the provincial and federal governments that elicited two days of semi-violent protest within the community. The issues that energised the protest in 1995 trace back to the late 1970s. In 1979 the MCK fired their local police force, the Kahnawake Police, for failing to enforce their resolution to close two government-leased quarries on reserve. The Kahnawake Police refused to close the quarries for want of an outside court injunction. Once fired, another local police force, the Kahnawake Peacekeepers, was formed in its place. Later that year, two officers of the Quebec Police Force (QPF) came into the community and shot and killed David Cross in a botched arrest attempt (Beauvais 1985: 150–52). Coupled with the issues that surrounded the firing of the police force and the quarries, the racist hues to the Cross shooting strengthened the resolve of the Kahnawakero:non to have the Kahnawake Peacekeepers enforce the laws of the community and not outside governments. However, since 1979 the authority of the Peacekeepers was limited by their refusal to swear an oath of allegiance to the province of Quebec. In order to give them the authority that is required to issue fines and tickets with the backing of Quebec law, the MCK negotiated a tripartite policing agreement. As part of this agreement, outside

police were given limited jurisdiction in the community. Considering the difficult history just detailed, this was viewed as a concession to Quebec. Some community members, especially youth associated with the '207 Longhouse', found this an affront to Mohawk sovereignty. The two days of protest that followed the signing of the agreement involved young men defacing personal property of elected chiefs and councillors. I am grateful to Peter Thomas Sr for explaining the chronology of events in 1979.

10 These narratives cover the period of 1993 to 1996. They are direct reprints of notes taken at meetings or are textual reconstructions of certain moments that had passed without note-taking. All names have been changed to protect the identity and privacy of the speakers.

11 'C-31' is the label used to describe community members and their children who regained their Indian status when Bill C-31 was amended to the *Indian Act* in 1985. Aimed at redressing the patrilineal bias of the *Indian Act*, which retained the Indian status of Indian men who married non-Indian women (and passed on their status to children) and disenfranchised Indian women who married non-Indian men (and did not pass on their lost status to their children), Bill C-31 granted status to all those who had lost it due to out-marriage and previous enfranchisement to the Canadian state. Before 1951 Indians lost their status because of enfranchisement: this may have occurred because of service in the military, post-secondary education, voting or the individual sale of status for alcohol. At the same time as the federal government was enlarging the number of Indians on the federal registry, Bill C-31 expanded the power of band council governments to determine their own membership requirements for their communities. In the case of Kahnawake, the results have been a situation where rules were developed (such as *The Mohawk Law on Membership*) that appear to exclude specifically those people who the federal government now recognised as status Indians. For a thorough discussion of the *Indian Act* and Bill C-31 from a political science perspective see Cassidy and Bish 1989. For a perspective on Bill C-31 from those Indian women that fought at a grassroots level to have it passed into law see Silman 1987. With the exception of those women who are widowed or divorced, Kahnawake has refused to grant automatic re-admittance to anyone on the federal registry of Indians to the band list.

12 'The Great Law of Peace', understood by some anthropologists as the 'constitution' of the Iroquois. This is one basis for a traditional mode of governance for Iroquois people. The other is the *Gawi'io*, or 'Good Message of Handsome Lake'.

13 Or *Kaswentha*, a 1613 treaty between the Dutch and the Iroquois represented by a belt of purple and white wampum shells. There are rows of white wampum parallel to each other, with deep purple wampum between and around them. The purple represents the sea of life that each row shares. One row represents the Iroquois vessel and the other the European vessel. Although they share the same sea and sail alongside each other, they are separate: they should not touch or disturb each other or try to steer the other's vessel even though they must share the same space. Between the vessels are chains that connect them to each other. These are occasionally shined and maintained by one or the other vessel. The *Kaswentha* has great meaning to traditional and elected Council chiefs in Kahnawake as an enduring model of Indian–white relations that comes directly from Iroquois experience and history. The Two Row Wampum has also been incorporated into the Final Report of the Royal Commission on Aboriginal Peoples as a possible model

for government relations between Aboriginal people as self-governing nations and the Canadian state.

7 (De)Constructing the Politics of Indigeneity

1 The question of indigenous identity, of who is a 'real' Aborigine or Māori is central to recent conflicts over political and economic resources in Australia and New Zealand (Barcham 1998; Stokes 1997). For further work on the importance of indigenous identity to questions of indigenous rights, see the chapters by Simpson and Dodds and Bern in this volume.

2 A process through which indigenous peoples of the world are re-interpolated within a new spatio-temporal hierarchy of authenticity and legitimacy, sadly reminiscent of the hierarchies of domination characteristic of earlier periods of imperialism.

3 Some governments around the world have argued that land claims should only be given to indigenous groups that have maintained an 'authentic' culture. The Brazilian government, for example, has tried to reinterpret Indian land rights so that they only apply to 'real Indians' (Ramos 1994).

4 However, just as there may one day no longer exist a Māori or Kwakiutl culture and society as such – as the Roman or Lapita cultures and societies no longer exist – this should not deny the reality that their modern-day descendants should in no way be considered any less authentic. For just as the shifting and fluid nature of groups is not to deny their reality, so too neither should the contingent nature of identities act to deny their moral worth, or undermine claims of rights based upon those identities. Yet, in contrast to the members of western societies who are exempt from claims to authenticity due to the complexities and diversities of their histories and societies, 'proper natives are somehow assumed to represent their selves and their history, without distortion or residue' (Appadurai 1988: 37).

5 *Rangatiratanga* is derived from the root noun *rangatira. Rangatira* is often defined in older dictionaries as a chief or a person of noble breeding. More modern dictionaries similarly define *rangatira* as meaning a chief or a noble. Older dictionaries define *rangatiratanga* as evidence of breeding and greatness, while newer dictionaries translate it as sovereignty. The latter meaning is more in accord with modern parlance of the word. Gaining widespread popular acceptance in the 1970s and 1980s the term is now used to signify the basis of Māori rights to self-determination or empowerment. Thus while the term does not directly translate as 'indigenous rights', its modern usage as the basis for Māori rights does, however, lend itself to the inclusion of this sense of the word. The word should be interpreted in this sense throughout the remainder of the chapter. (The word *tino*, often found conjoined with the word in the phrase *tino rangatiratanga*, is a modifier that acts to intensify the meaning of the word following.)

6 Paul Patton (1995a; 1995b) has drawn attention to the operation of a similar dynamic in the Australian context. While the Mabo decision represented a rupture in previous ways of thinking about the place of notions such as difference, society and justice in Australia, the judgment itself was nevertheless based upon the understanding that the protection of newly recognised difference was dependent on the maintenance of a prior identity.

7 The *Runanga Iwi Act* (1990) was adopted to facilitate the devolution process through the establishment of iwi authorities capable of administering the

programs previously run by government departments. This process was to occur through the establishment of an Iwi Transition Agency which was to act as the conduit through which programs would be transferred from government to iwi control.

8 The 1996 Census showed that 26 per cent of all individuals who identified as being of Māori descent gave no iwi affiliation. The Census allowed for no reason to be given for this lack of iwi identification, so no differentiation can be made between individuals who were *unable* to identify with an iwi, or those who were *unwilling* to identify with an iwi.

9 Iwi experienced a short-lived resurgence in power with the recruitment of Māori soldiers for World War II along tribal lines. This resurgence was short-lived, as the returning soldiers settled at a variety of different locales around the country, including cities, in order to find work in the post-World War II era. This scattering of the serviceman prevented the regrowth of tribal sentiment gaining any political advantage.

10 In 1936 81 per cent of the Māori population lived in tribal areas, which, more often than not, were rural. In this rural environment, regardless of the dwindling political significance of these institutions, they still relied heavily on these traditional forms of social institution to provide meaning and structure to their day-to-day social interaction.

11 From 1939 to 1989 the rural–urban ratio of Māori switched from approximately 80:20 to approximately 20:80.

12 It is in support of ideas such as this, which led Professor Ranginui Walker to claim that the development of urban *marae* has been 'the most powerful cultural statement the Māori has made in modern times' (Walker 1987: 147).

13 The Waitangi Tribunal is a quasi-judicial body created by the New Zealand government to examine contemporary disputes stemming from the Treaty of Waitangi. The main function of the Tribunal is to inquire and make recommendations to the Crown for Māori claims or grievances relating to sections of the Treaty. The findings of the Tribunal, however, are only recommendations and have no binding force in law.

14 The lawyers for the Trust argued that the representative status of the Trust was an important aspect to the claim because if non-tribal West Auckland Māori are found to have rights under article 2, then those rights accrue to the *community* and the Trust claims to be the appropriate body to exercise those rights on behalf of the community.

15 This view can be challenged on the grounds that hapū, and not iwi, were the institutional bodies recognised by the Treaty of Waitangi. If, as some have argued, iwi are entitled to these rights as hapū are merely sub-sections of iwi, the argument can be made that since hapū were in turn made up of whanau and individuals, these monies should go to any institutional body that these individual descendants choose.

16 I am not alone in arguing that the work of the poststructuralists provides us with a convenient heuristic device with which to approach the notion of difference and its relation to concepts of identity. Paul Patton has, in consideration of the implementation of indigenous rights in Australia, argued that philosophies of poststructuralism contain within them the possibility for a 'politically open-ended space of possibilities of action, a space of becoming that allows for the non-self identical character of individual and collective agents' (1995a: 162).

17 Wherein *rangatiratanga* exists between a Māori community and its leadership it includes a set of reciprocal duties and responsibilities.

8 On Display for its Aesthetic Beauty: How Western Institutions Fabricate Knowledge about Aboriginal Cultural Heritage

1 The term 'business' is used by Aboriginal and Torres Strait Islander peoples to refer to any religious, sacred and secret knowledge or activities that pertain to specific sites or landmarks. 'Business' can also be associated in strict gender terms, so effectively 'women's business' excludes participation by men in the same way that 'men's business' excludes the participation of women.

9 On the Plurality of Interests: Aboriginal Self-government and Land Rights

1 In total, fewer than 2 per cent of the Australian population. The proportion is increasing through higher net birth rate than the general population, and through increases in the numbers of people identifying as Aboriginal.
2 The land councils and native title tribunals may tend, in practice, to use a fairly broad understanding of these ideas, but there is plenty of room for legalistic definitional debate.
3 See, for example, Martin and Finlayson 1996.
4 Although Tully 1997 acknowledges the overlapping interests between First Nations and non-Aboriginal Canadians, and the intercultural interests of the Métis, he appears to accept a view of the interests within either group as homogeneous, or at least equally open to articulation from within. See also Tully 1995: 176.
5 However, even groups with strong kin/language/site location ties such as the Torres Strait Islanders may find that the group can experience tensions in attempting to sort out land entitlements. See, for example, Sanders 1995.
6 This is discussed in some detail in Bern and Layton 1984.
7 On the specific issue of junggayi, see Bern and Larbalestier 1985.

10 The Liberal Image of the Nation

1

> It is not sufficiently considered how little there is in most men's ordinary life to give any largeness either to their conceptions or to their sentiments. Their work is a routine; not a labor of love, but of self-interest . . . neither the thing done nor the process of doing it introduces the mind to thoughts or feelings extending beyond individuals; if instructive books are within their reach, there is no stimulus to read them; and in most cases the individual lacks access to any person of cultivation. (Mill 1958: 53)

Mill, certainly, wanted to lift ordinary people out of the ruts and harsh routines of ordinary life. He thought that participation in governance was one way to do so, in combination with reforms in education and the distribution of income. I am with Mill on these last two points. I even agree that cultural elites can teach regular guys a thing or two on occasion, as long as the relation is sometimes understood to go the other way as well. I also suspect that the routines of Mill's life stopped him from thinking more creatively about the image of the nation. But the specific point of this quotation in this context is to bring out how prominent aristocratic, cultural constituencies are in the Millian conception of 'minority' and how concern for this minority plays such a major role in Mill's plans for proportional representation of minorities in representative government.

2 This theme is developed more extensively in Connolly 1999, particularly in chapter 6.

3 Even when the planet was crystallising into the earth a 'decisive reason why it was able to hold on to these volatile layers of melted comets was the emergence of living organisms which regulated crucial climatic conditions and kept them constant' (Norretranders 1998: 340).

12 American Multiculturalism and the 'Nations Within'

1 One reason why this is such a daunting challenge is the worry that some measures such as affirmative action, which are aimed at tackling the special burdens facing African-Americans, may perpetuate the problem by entrenching an ascriptive and stigmatising conception of Black identity.

2 For the evidence, see Kymlicka 1998a, chapter 1.

3 I should emphasise that this is just one criterion that has been used to distinguish indigenous peoples from stateless nations, and it doesn't cover all of the groups which claim the status of indigenous peoples. For example, the Crimean Tatars have recently asserted they are an indigenous people, although they were real contenders for state-formation, and hence are much closer to a stateless nation on my criterion. (Had the balance of power been a little different, Crimea might have been, or remained, a Tatar state, rather than a province of the Russian empire.) Partly in order to cover such cases, other criteria have sometimes been proposed to distinguish the two categories of national minorities, such as (a) that indigenous peoples exercised historical sovereignty whereas stateless nations did not; (b) that indigenous peoples lack a kin state, whereas stateless nations have kin states; (c) that indigenous peoples have a radical cultural or civilisational difference from the majority nation, whereas stateless nations typically are closer in culture. The first two of these proposed criteria are, I think, simply inaccurate, since many stateless nations have exercised historical sovereignty, and many lack a kin state (for example, Catalans, Scots). The third is more helpful, and is already implicit in the criteria I mentioned in the text: insofar as stateless nations and majority nations contended with each other in the process of state-formation, they tended to converge on certain cultural self-conceptions, and to share certain economic and social needs and influences. Indigenous peoples were not influenced in the same way by the pursuit of state formation. However, it would be a mistake, I think, to make radical civilisational difference a defining characteristic of indigenous peoples, since this has the potential for essentialising and freezing indigenous cultures, precluding them from adapting whatever they find most interesting or desirable in modern societies. For more on this, see Kymlicka 1999a.

4 This is a generalisation, not an iron rule. Some national minorities have become too decimated, dispossessed, dispersed or intermingled with settlers from other cultures for territorial autonomy to be a meaningful option. Ross Poole argues that the idea of territorial autonomy is more relevant for indigenous peoples in North America than in Australia, although he acknowledges this remains a source of ongoing controversy within the

Australian Aboriginal community itself, and that the territorial model is applicable to the Torres Strait Islanders (Poole 1998). It's also important to emphasise that even where indigenous peoples seek territorial autonomy, this will still involve substantial degrees of interdependence with the larger society. As Borrows puts it in the Canadian context, we need to think not only about 'Aboriginal control of Aboriginal affairs' but also 'Aboriginal control of Canadian affairs' if Aboriginals are to be truly self-determining (see Borrows 2000).

5 This is evident in the way both Aboriginals and Québécois reject the idea that their claims are covered by Canada's 'multiculturalism' policy, which focuses on issues of immigrant ethnicity. Similarly, the Maori in New Zealand deny that their claims are covered by New Zealand's immigrant multiculturalism policy.

6 See James Tully in this volume pp. 52–3. Parenthetically, I think that this nation-to-nation relationship is absent from the 'contestatory' and 'rhizomatic' models of democracy advanced by Philip Pettit and William Connolly respectively in their chapters of this volume. Whatever the merits of their theories for issues of cultural, religious and sexual diversity in general, I do not think that they can accommodate the specific needs and desires of 'nations within'.

7

> The Third World War has already begun. It began when new states tried to take over old nations . . . It began in 1948. Burma moved its army into the Karen and Shan nations and India started its military invasion of the Naga nation. The Third World War is now being fought on every continent except Antarctica. It has produced millions of casualties and massive forced dislocations of nation peoples who make up the majority of the world's refugees. It encompasses most of the peoples and groups who are accused of being terrorists. Each year it involves new areas, states and nations. (Nietschmann 1987: 1)

8 We are familiar with this sort of ethnocentric prejudice towards indigenous peoples, but it is important to remember that it has also been invoked against stateless nations. Recall John Stuart Mill's claim that:

> Experience proves it is possible for one nationality to merge and be absorbed in another: and when it was originally an inferior and more backward portion of the human race the absorption is greatly to its advantage. Nobody can suppose that it is not more beneficial to a Breton, or a Basque of French Navarre, to be brought into the current of the ideas and feelings of a highly civilised and cultivated people – to be a member of the French nationality, admitted on equal terms to all the privileges of French citizenship . . . than to sulk on his own rocks, the half-savage relic of past times, revolving in his own little mental orbit, without participation or interest in the general movement of the world. The same remark applies to the Welshman or the Scottish Highlander as members of the British nation. (Mill 1972: 395).

Mill also opposed the attempts of the Québécois to maintain a distinct francophone society in Canada, and encouraged their assimilation into the more 'civilised' English culture. Indeed, most nineteenth-century liberals and Marxists adopted the same denigrating attitude toward stateless nations as they did towards indigenous peoples. See Parekh 1994.

9 For a concise overview, see Minority Rights Group 1991.

10 In many countries it would have been possible to create a state or province dominated by an indigenous people in the nineteenth century, but given the massive influx of settlers since then, it is now virtually inconceivable. The one

important exception concerns the Inuit in the Canadian North. And indeed the boundaries of the Northwest Territories in Canada have just been redrawn so as to create an Inuit-majority unit within the federation, known as 'Nunavut'.

11 For the relation of Indian self-government to federalism in Canada, see Henderson 1994; Cassidy and Bish 1989; Long 1991; Elkins 1992.

12 France is perhaps the one major exception to this rule, which still refuses on principle to acknowledge the Corsicans as a national minority. I expect that even this bastion of Jacobin unitary statehood will eventually join the community of explicitly multi-nation democracies.

13 It was drafted by a UN Working Group on Indigenous Populations between 1985 and 1993, and approved by the UN Subcommission on the Protection of Minorities in 1994 (an independent body of experts), but still has several barriers to overcome before ratification by the UN General Assembly.

14 For a comprehensive overview of these developments in international law, see Anaya 1996.

15 For a more detailed description of the theory and practice of multinational federalism, see Kymlicka 1998a: chapter 10; Kymlicka and Raviot 1997.

16 There are important exceptions to this rule, most notably the violence in Northern Ireland and the Basque country. In response to the violence, Britain and Spain have passed laws restricting some civil rights. In this sense, the accommodation of minority nationalism has, in certain times and places, put definite strains on democracy. But it is obvious that the violence would have been worse, and the illiberal laws even more restrictive and long-standing, had the governments not moved toward greater accommodation of the nationalist sentiment. Had Spain or Britain persisted in trying to crush the minority's sense of nationhood, the result would be an almost permanent state of authoritarianism, like we see in Turkey as a result of its efforts to crush the Kurdish desire for national recognition.

17 For recent overviews of the rights and status of national minorities in the US, see (on Puerto Rico): Aleinikoff 1994; Martinez 1997; Portillo 1997; Rubinstein 1993; Barreto 1998. On American Indians, see O'Brien 1989; Prucha 1994. On Guam, see Statham 1998. For a more general survey, see O'Brien 1987.

18 For example, Lind 1995; Schlesinger 1992; Glazer 1997; Gitlin 1995.

19 See Shafir 1995. For what it's worth, if Hispanics or Blacks *were* to define themselves as self-governing nations within the US, then they too almost certainly would have to adopt a postethnic conception of national membership. After all, Hispanics are a complex amalgam of Europeans, Indians/mestizos, Blacks, with high rates of inter-marriage. And the same is true of Blacks.

20 In fact, the blood quantum rules were first introduced by the Federal governments in Canada and the US, against the wishes of the indigenous peoples themselves, as a way of limiting the amount of money federal governments would have to pay to the community. The continuing use of blood quantum rules was soundly criticised by the Canadian Royal Commission on Aboriginal Peoples, which argued that it was not only a violation of human rights, but also a violation of traditional Indian practices, and moreover was counter-productive to ensuring cultural survival. See Canada, Royal Commission on Aboriginal Peoples 1996b: 239. For an overview of the debate, see Dickson-Gilmore 1999a. For a partial defence of the practice of blood-quantum rules, see Alfred 1995: 163–75.

21 The term 'civic nationalism' is potentially confusing. It is often used to refer to the idea that membership in a liberal nation should be based solely on

adherence to political principles, and not in terms of participation in a particular national culture and language. Put this way, the idea of 'civic nationalism' is incoherent, and has no real-world referent. All nationalisms, even in the most liberal of states, have a cultural and linguistic component. In this essay, therefore, I am using 'civic' in a more restricted sense, simply as a synonym for 'postethnic' in Hollinger's sense, that is, where membership is open to all regardless of race, ethnicity or religion. For a more detailed discussion of the 'ethnic/civic' distinction, see Kymlicka 1999b: 131–40.

22 In many countries of Eastern Europe, by contrast, both sides to the conflict are forms of ethnic nationalism: state nationalism and minority nationalism are both defined in terms of ethnic descent. It is relatively rare to find a civic nationalism opposed to an ethnic nationalism: what we find are either civic v. civic conflicts or ethnic v. ethnic conflicts.

23 See Kymlicka forthcoming. While only postethnic forms of nationalism are consistent with liberal values this is not to say that liberal states have the right to impose such a liberal conception of group membership on indigenous peoples. From a liberal point of view, blood quantum rules are unfair, but the federal government may not have the legitimate jurisdiction to interfere with the decisions of self-governing indigenous communities on such issues. For more on this, see Kymlicka 1996.

24 For examples of US opposition to minority rights protection, see Van Dyke 1985: 194; O'Brien 1987: 276–80; McKean 1983: 70–1, 142–43; Sohn 1981: 272, 279.

25 For an example, see Hughes 1999: 3, 6. Hughes notes that American advisers in Russia discouraged the adoption of a multinational conception of federalism, which would give national recognition to the ethnic republics, in favour of a uni-national conception of federalism which denied any link between federalism and rights of self-government for national minorities. Fortunately, the Russians did not take this advice.

26 In a recent article, David Bromwich suggested that Charles Taylor's essay on 'Multiculturalism and the politics of recognition' is 'in some ways a Canadian sermon to Americans' (1995: 96). I think this is a misunderstanding. Taylor's lecture is better understood as a sermon to (Americanised) English-Canadians, and his argument is not that American-style liberalism is wrong for American society, where minority nationalism is peripheral, but rather that it is wrong for countries like Canada where minority nationalism is central to political life.

27 At best, it tells us nothing. At worst, it gets the wrong answer. Faced with a conflict between a majority seeking to centralise power in the state and a demand by a national minority for regional autonomy, many liberal commentators have assumed that the latter forms a kind of 'group right', and that liberals should therefore support the majoritarian nationalists who seek to centralise all power at a level where they dominate. It should be clear why this is not a just solution to the issue, but for a more detailed explanation of why decisions about the division of powers can lead to injustice, see Kymlicka 1998c.

28 For example, the Canadian Royal Commission on Aboriginal Peoples studied extensively the policing and judicial system run by the Navajo nation in the American southwest.

13 Hybrid Democracy: Iroquois Federalism and the Postcolonial Project

1 This strategy of reading modern world history as hybrid, where the colonised subjects act upon the colonisers as well as the reverse, should not be confined

to histories of the colonised places. Edward Said reads classic European texts as hybrid, internally related to the imperalised Others even as they celebrate European nationalisms (Said 1994).

2 See also Countryman 1996: 'If we accept that both slaves and Indians were important components of the colonial formation, neither a the-colonies-were-born-modern perspective nor a the-colonies-were-intrinsically-an-old-order-in-the-European-style perspective does justice to them' (350).

3 Definitions of sovereignty abound, but they vary only subtly. Morris defines it as: 'Sovereignty is the highest, final, and supreme political and legal authority (and power) within the territorially defined domain of a system of direct rule' (1998 166). Thomas Pogge (1992: 48–75) distinguishes degrees of sovereignty. For him, sovereignty is when an agent has unsupervised and irrevocable authority over another. Given this distinction, I am concerned with absolute sovereignty. I find it a bit puzzling that Pogge includes the condition that the decisions and laws of a sovereign power are *irrevocable*. This seems quite unreasonable, since in practice many states revoke or revise decisions previously made and no one considers this a challenge to their sovereignty. The condition should rather be put that a sovereign's decisions cannot be revoked or overridden by *another* authority.

4 Pogge 1992. Pogge distinguishes two approaches to social justice: an institutional and an interactional approach. Whereas the interactional approach focuses only on the actions of particular individuals as they affect identifiable persons, the institutional approach theories moral responsibility for the fact of others insofar as agents participate in institutions and practices that may or do harm them. An institutional approach as distinct from an interactional approach, he suggests, makes issues of international justice and moral responsibility with respect to distant strangers more visible. I make a similar distinction between a distributive approach to justice and an approach that focuses on the way institutions produce distributions (see Young 1990). Focusing on how structures and institutional relations produce distributive patterns, I suggest, makes a connected international society more visible and the relations of moral responsibilities of distant peoples within it.

5 In another paper I develop a model of relational self-determination interpreted as non-domination as distinct from non-interference; I derive this model from the way many indigenous movements talk about their aspirations, and I show how application of this interpretation of self-determination to relationships between non-indigenous and indigenous governments potentially opens ways to resolve conflicts less available under other interpretations of self-determination. See Young 1999.

6 John Pocock is no doubt correct to distinguish, in his essay in this volume, between confederacy, as intergovernmental relationships held together only by treaties, and federation, a relationship of self-governing entities with a more enduring and general set of procedures guiding their relations. Assuming this distinction the Iroquois were more of a confederacy than a federation, perhaps, though the Great Law of Peace could be interpreted as a general set of procedures. In any case, as Pocock points out, one of the points of the postcolonial project is to blur the distinction between these. The project aims to make relations between peoples who now understand themselves to be related to one another only through treaties more federated, and to make the relations between peoples within a given, existing state more like relations between treaty partners.

Bibliography

Aboriginal Land Commissioner (1981) *Limmen Bight Land Claim.* Canberra: AGPS.
—— (1982) *Yutpundji-Djindiwirritj (Roper Bar) Land Claim.* Canberra: AGPS.
—— (1985) *Cox River (Alawa-Ngandji) Land Claim.* Canberra: AGPS.
—— (1988) *Mataranka Land Claim.* Canberra: AGPS.
Aboriginal Law Bulletin (1996) 'Chronology of the Kumarangk/Hindmarsh Island affair', 3, 83 (September): 22.
Abu-Lughod, L. (1991) 'Writing against culture' in R. G. Fox (ed.), *Recapturing Anthropology: Working in the Present,* Santa Fe: School of American Studies Research Press.
Ackerman, B. (1991) *We the People (vol. 1): Foundations,* Cambridge, Mass.: Harvard University Press.
Aleinikoff, A. (1994) 'Puerto Rico and the Constitution: conundrums and prospects', *Constitutional Commentary,* 11: 15–43.
Alfred, G. R. (Taiaiake) (1995) *Heeding the Voices of our Ancestors: Kahnawake Mohawk Politics and the Rise of Native Nationalism,* Toronto; New York: Oxford University Press.
—— (1999a) *Peace, Power, Righteousness: An Indigenous Manifesto.* Oxford: Oxford University Press.
—— (1999b) '*Tewehià:rak* (We should remember)', Agenda Item 5, Working Group on Indigenous Populations, Sub-Commission on Prevention of Discrimination and Protection of Minorities, Commission on Human Rights, 17th session, 28 July.
Anaya, S. J. (1996) *Indigenous Peoples in International Law.* Oxford: Oxford University Press.
Anderson, B. (1991) *Imagined Communities: Reflections on the Origin and Spread of Nationalism,* London: Verso.
Anderson, I. (1993) 'Black suffering, white trash', *Arena,* June–July: 8.
Anglican Church (1990) *Constitution of the Anglican Church in Aotearoa, New Zealand, and Polynesia.*
Antonios, Z. (1998) *Native Title Report.* Sydney: Human Rights and Equal Opportunity Commission.
Appadurai, A. (1988) 'Putting hierarchy in its place', *Cultural Anthropology,* 3, 1: 36–49.

Archie, C. (1995) *Maori Sovereignty: Pakeha Perspectives*. Auckland: Hodder Moa Beckett.

Armitage, A. (1995) *Comparing the Policy of Aboriginal Assimilation in Australia, Canada and New Zealand*, Vancouver: University of British Columbia Press.

Arneil, B. (1996) *John Locke and America: The Defence of English Colonialism*. Oxford: Oxford University Press.

Asad, T. (ed.) (1973) *Anthropology and the Colonial Encounter*, New York: Ithaca Press and Humanities Press.

—— (1979) 'Anthropology and the Analysis of Ideology', *Man*, 14: 607–27.

Asch, M. (ed.) (1997) *Aboriginal and Treaty Rights in Canada*, Vancouver: University of British Columbia Press.

—— (1999) 'From "Calder" to "Van der Peet": Aboriginal Rights and Canadian Law, 1973–1996' in P. Havemann (ed.), *Indigenous Peoples' Rights in Australia, Canada, and New Zealand*. Oxford: Oxford University Press: pp. 428–46.

Attwood, B. (1996a) 'Introduction: The Past as Future: Aborigines, Australia and the (dis)course of History' and 'Mabo, Australia and the End of History' in B. Attwood (ed.), *In the Age of Mabo: History, Aborigines and Australia*. St Leonards: Allen & Unwin, pp. vii–xxxviii and 100–16.

—— (1996b) 'Making History, Imagining Aborigines and Australia' in T. Bonyhady and T. Griffiths (eds), *Prehistory to Politics: John Mulvaney, the Humanities and the Public Intellectual*. Carlton South: Melbourne University Press, pp. 98–116.

Awatere, D. (1984) *Maori Sovereignty*, Auckland: Broadsheets Publications.

Ballara, A. (1998) *Iwi: The Dynamics of Maori Tribal Organisation from c.1769 to c.1945*, Wellington: Victoria University Press.

Barcham, M. (1998) 'The Challenge of Urban Maori: Reconciling Conceptions of Indigeneity and Social Change', *Asia Pacific Viewpoint*, 39, 3: 303–14.

Barlow, C. (1996) *Tikanga Whakaaro: Key Concepts in Maori Culture*, Auckland: Oxford University Press.

Barreto, A. A. (1998) *Language, Elites and the State: Nationalism in Puerto Rico and Quebec*, Westport: Praeger.

Barriero, J. (ed.) (1988) *Indian Roots of American Democracy*, Ithaca: Akewkon/Cornell University Press.

Baudrillard, J. (1981) *For a Critique of the Political Economy of the Sign*, St Louis: Telos Press.

—— (1983) *Simulations*, New York: Semiotext(e).

Beauvais, J. (1985) *Kahnawake: A Mohawk Look at Canada and Adventures of Big John Canadian*, Kahnawake: Khanata Industries.

Beckett, J. (ed.) (1988) *Past and Present: The Construction of Aboriginality*, Canberra: Aboriginal Studies Press.

Beitz, C. (1979) *Political Theory and International Relations*, Princeton: Princeton University Press.

Belich, J. (1986) *The New Zealand Wars and the Victorian Interpretation of Racial Conflict*, Auckland: Oxford University Press.

—— (1989) *'I Shall Not Die': Titokowaru's War; New Zealand 1868–69*, Wellington: Allen & Unwin.

—— (1996) *Making Peoples: A History of the New Zealanders from Polynesian Settlement to the End of the Nineteenth Century*, Auckland: Allen Lane, the Penguin Press; Honolulu: University of Hawai'i Press.

Bennett, T. and Blundell, V. (1995) 'Introduction: First peoples', *Cultural Studies*, 9, 1: 1–10.

Bern, J. (1989) 'The Politics of a Small Northern Territory Town: A History of Managing Dependency' in P. Loveday and A. Webb (eds), *Small Towns in Northern Australia.* Darwin: ANU, NARU.

—— (1990) 'Community Management and Self-determination' in *Report to the House of Representatives Standing Committee on Aboriginal Affairs.* Canberra: AGPS.

—— and Larbalestier, J. (1985) 'Rival Constructions of Traditional Aboriginal Ownership in the Limmen Bight Land Claim', *Oceania*, 56, 1: 56–76.

—— and Layton, R. (1984) 'The Local Descent Group and the Division of Labour in the Cox River Land Claim' in L. R. Hiatt (ed.), *Aboriginal Landowners. Oceania* Monograph no. 27, Sydney.

Berndt, R. M. (ed.) (1982) *Aboriginal Sites, Rights and Resource Development.* Perth: University of Western Australia Press.

—— and Berndt, C.H. with Stanton, J. E. (1993). *A World That Was: The Yaraldi of the Murray River and the Lakes, South Australia.* Vancouver: UBC Press.

Bhabha, H. K. (1990) 'Introduction: Narrating the nation' in H. K. Bhabha (ed.), *Nation and Narration,* London: Routledge.

—— (1994) 'DissemiNation: Time, Narrative and the Margins of the Modern Nation'; 'Signs Taken for Wonders: Questions of Ambivalence and Authority under a Tree outside Delhi, May 1817' in *The Location of Culture,* London: Routledge: pp. 102–22, 139–70.

Bin-Sallik, M. (1996) 'Black witch hunt: white silence!', *Australian Feminist Studies*, 11, 24: 201–11.

Biolsi, T. and Zimmerman, L. J. (1997) *Indians and Anthropologists: Vine Deloria Jr. and the Critique of Anthropology,* Tucson: University of Arizona Press.

Blainey, G. (1993) 'Drawing Up a Balance Sheet of Our History', *Quadrant*, 37, 7–8: 10–15.

Blanchard, D. (1982) *Patterns of Tradition and Change: The Re-creation of Iroquois Culture at Kahnawake,* PhD Dissertation: University of Chicago.

Blythe, M. (1994) *Naming the Other: Images of the Maori in New Zealand Film and Television,* Metuchen, NJ: Scarecrow Press.

Boer, B. (1991) 'Sustaining the heritage' in M. Behrens and B. Tsamenyi (eds), *Environmental Law and Policy Workshop; Papers and Proceedings: Our Common Future,* Hobart: University of Tasmania Law School.

Boldt, M. (1993) *Surviving as Indians: The Challenge of Self-government.* Toronto: University of Toronto Press.

—— and Long, J. A. (1985) 'Tribal Traditions and European–Western Political Ideologies: The Dilemma of Canada's Native Indians' in M. Boldt and J. A. Long (eds), *The Quest for Justice: Aboriginal Peoples and Aboriginal Rights.* Toronto: University of Toronto Press: pp. 333–46.

Borrows, J. (1997a) 'The Trickster: Integral to a Distinctive Culture', *Constitutional Forum*, 8: 27.

—— (1997b) 'Wampum at Niagara: The Royal Proclamation, Canadian Legal History, and Self-government' in M. Asch (ed.), *Aboriginal and Treaty Rights in Canada.* Vancouver: University of British Columbia Press.

—— (2000) '"Landed" Citizenship: Narratives of Aboriginal Political Participation' in W. Kymlicka and W. Norman (eds), *Citizenship in Diverse Societies.* Oxford: Oxford University Press: pp. 326–42.

Brennan, F. (1995) *One Land, One Nation: Mabo – Towards 2001.* St Lucia: University of Queensland Press.

—— (1998) *The Wik Debate: Its Impact on Aborigines, Pastoralists and Miners.* Sydney: University of New South Wales Press.

Briggs, C. L. (1996) 'The Politics of Discursive Authority in Research on the "Invention of Tradition"', *Cultural Anthropology*, 11, 4: 435–69.

Bringing Them Home: Report of the Inquiry into the Forcible Removal of Aboriginal and Torres Strait Islander Children from their Families (1997) Sydney: Human Rights and Equal Opportunity Commission.

British Columbian Studies (1998–99) 120 (Winter).

Bromwich, D. (1995) 'Culturalism: The Euthanasia of Liberalism', *Dissent* (Winter): 89–102.

Brookfield, F. M. (1995) 'The Treaty of Waitangi, the Constitution and the Future', *British Review of New Zealand Studies*, 8: 3–21.

Brubaker, R. (1996) *Nationalism Reframed: Nationhood and the National Question in the New Europe*. Cambridge, Mass.: Cambridge University Press.

Campisi, J. (1991) *The Mashpee Indians: Tribe on Trial*, Syracuse: Syracuse University Press.

Canada, Royal Commission on Aboriginal Peoples (1993) *Partners in Confederation: Aboriginal Peoples, Self-government and the Constitution*, Ottawa: Minister of Supply and Services Canada.

—— (1995a) *Treaty-making in the Spirit of Co-existence*, Ottawa: Minister of Supply and Services Canada.

—— (1995b) *Aboriginal Self-government: Legal and Constitutional Issues*, Ottawa: Minister of Supply and Services Canada.

—— (1996a) *Looking Forward, Looking Back: Report of the Royal Commission on Aboriginal Peoples*, vol. 1, Ottawa: Minister of Supply and Services Canada.

—— (1996b) *Restructuring the Relationship: Report of the Royal Commission on Aboriginal Peoples*, vol. 2, Ottawa: Minister of Supply and Services Canada.

Cane, P. (1996) *An Introduction to Administrative Law*, third edn, Oxford: Oxford University Press.

Caney, S. (1999) 'Cosmopolitan Justice and Political Structures', paper presented at the Morrell Symposium on Sovereignty and Justice, September.

Cardoso, F. Henrique (1993) 'North–South Relations in the Present Context: A New Dependency?' in M. Carnoy *et al.* (eds), *The New Global Economy in the Information Age*, University Park: Pennsylvania State University Press: pp. 149–60.

Carens, J. (1987) 'Aliens and Citizens: The Case for Open Borders', *The Review of Politics*, 49: 251–73.

—— (1995) 'Citizenship and Aboriginal Self-government', paper prepared for the Royal Commission on Aboriginal Peoples.

Caselburg, John (ed.) (1975) *Maori is My Name: Historical Writings in Translation*. Dunedin: John McIndoe Ltd.

Cassidy, F. and Bish, R. L. (1989) *Indian Government: Its Meaning in Practice*. Lantzville: Oolichan Books.

Césaire, Aimé (1972) *Discourse on Colonialism*. New York: Monthly Review Press.

Chamberlin, P. (1995) 'Whites Out of Step in Clash over Native Lore', *Age*, 24 May.

Chartrand, L. A. H. Paul (1993) 'Aboriginal Self-government: The Two Sides of Legitimacy' in S. D. Phillips (ed.), *How Ottawa Spends: A More Democratic Canada...?* Ottawa: Carleton University Press: pp. 231–56.

—— (1996) 'Self-determination Without a Discrete Territorial Base?' in D. Clark and R. Williamson (eds), *Self-determination: International Perspectives*, London: Macmillan, pp. 211–34.

—— (1999) 'Aboriginal Peoples in Canada: Aspirations for Distributive Justice as Distinct Peoples' in P. Havemann (ed.), *Indigenous Peoples' Rights: In Australia, Canada and New Zealand*. Auckland: Oxford University Press: pp. 88–107.

Chase, A. (1981) 'Empty Vessels and Loud Noises: Views about Aboriginality Today' *Social Alternatives*, 2, 2: 23–7.

Chatterjee, P. (1993) *The Nation and its Fragments: Colonial and Postcolonial Histories*. Princeton: Princeton University Press.

Chesterman, J. and Galligan, B. (1998) *Citizens Without Rights: Aborigines and Australian Citizenship*. Melbourne: Cambridge University Press.

Cheyne, C., O'Brien, M. and Belgrave, M. (1997) *Social Policy in Aotearoa/New Zealand*. Auckland: Oxford University Press.

Clark, D. and Williams, R. (1996) *Self-determination in International Perspective*. Basingstoke: Macmillan Press.

Clarke, J. (1997). 'The Native Title Amendment Bill 1997: A Different Order of Uncertainty?' *Discussion Paper 144/97*. Canberra: Centre for Aboriginal Economic Policy Research.

—— (1999) '"Indigenous" People and Constitutional Law' in P. Hanks and D. Cass, *Australian Constitutional Law: Materials and Commentary*, sixth edn, Sydney: Butterworths: 50–112.

Clifford, J. (1986) 'On Ethnographic Allegory' in J. Clifford and G. E. Marcus (eds), *Writing Culture: The Politics and Poetics of Ethnography*. Berkeley: University of California Press.

—— (1988) *The Predicament of Culture: Twentieth-century Ethnography, Literature and Art*. Cambridge, Mass.: Harvard University Press.

—— and Marcus, G. E. (eds) (1986) *Writing Culture: The Politics and Poetics of Ethnography*. Berkeley: University of California Press.

Coates, K. (1996) 'International Perspectives on the New Zealand Government's Relationship with the Maori', in K. Coates and P. McHugh (eds), *Living Relationships, Kokiri Ngatahi: The Treaty of Waitangi in the New Millennium*. Wellington: Victoria University Press, 1998: pp. 18–65.

—— and McHugh, P. (eds) (1998) *Living Relationships, Kokiri Ngatahi: The Treaty of Waitangi in the New Millennium*. Wellington: Victoria University Press.

Cohn, B. (1980) 'History and Anthropology: The State of Play', *Comparative Studies in Society and History*, 22 (April): 198–221.

Colden, C. (1747) *The History of the Five Indian Nations of Canada*, London.

Connerton, P. (1989) *How Societies Remember*. Cambridge: Cambridge University Press.

Connolly, W. E. (1991) *Identity/Difference: Democratic Negotiations of Political Paradox*, Ithaca: Cornell University Press.

—— (1994) 'Tocqueville, Territory and Violence', *Theory Culture and Society*, 11 (winter): 19–40.

—— (1995) *The Ethos of Pluralization*. Minneapolis: University of Minnesota Press.

—— (1998) 'Beyond Good and Evil: The Ethical Sensibility of Michel Foucault' in J. Moss (ed.), *The Later Foucault*. London: Sage: pp. 108–28.

—— (1999) *Why I Am Not a Secularist*. Minneapolis: University of Minnesota Press.

Connor, W. (forthcoming) 'National Self-determination and Tomorrow's Political Map' in A. Cairns *et al.* (eds), *Citizenship, Diversity and Pluralism*. Montreal: McGill-Queen's University Press.

Coombs, H. C. (1982) 'On the Question of Government' in R. M. Berndt (ed.), *Aboriginal Sites, Rights and Resource Development*. Perth: University of Western Australia Press, pp. 227–32.

—— (1994) *Aboriginal Autonomy: Issues and Strategies*. Cambridge: Cambridge University Press.

Cooper, F. and Stoler, A. L. (eds) (1997) *Tensions of Empire: Colonial Cultures in a Bourgeois World*. Berkeley, California: University of California Press.

Cornell, S. (1988) 'The Transformation of Tribe: Organisation and Self-concept in Native American Ethnicities', *Ethnic and Racial Studies*, 11, 1: 27–47.

Council for Aboriginal Reconciliation (1997) *Overview: Proceedings of the Australian Reconciliation Convention: Book 1*. Kingston: Council for Aboriginal Reconciliation.

Countryman, E. (1996) 'Indians, the Colonial Order, and the Social Significance of the American Revolution', *William and Mary Quarterly*, 53, 2: pp. 342–62.

Crapanzano, V. (1986) 'Hermes Dilemma: The Masking of Subversion in Ethnographic Description' in J. Clifford and G. E. Marcus (eds), *Writing Culture: The Politics and Poetics of Ethnography*, Berkeley: University of California Press: pp. 51–76.

Crête, J. and Zylberberg, J. (1991) 'Une problématique floue: l'autoreprésentation du citoyen au Québec' in D. Colas *et al.* (eds), *Citoyenneté et nationalité: perspectives en France et au Québec*. Paris: Presses Universitaires de France.

Culhane, D. (1998) *The Pleasure of the Crown: Anthropology, Law and First Nations*. Burnaby, B.C.: Talon Books.

Daes, E. I. A. (1996) 'The Right of Indigenous Peoples to "Self-determination" in the Contemporary World Order' in D. Clark and R. Williamson (eds), *Self-determination: International Perspectives*. Basingstoke: Macmillan Press.

Davis, M. (1996) 'Competing Knowledges? Indigenous Knowledge Systems and Western Scientific Discourses', paper presented to Science and Other Knowledge Traditions Conference, James Cook University, Cairns, 23–7 August.

Deleuze, G. and Guattari, F. (1987) *A Thousand Plateaus: Capitalism and Schizophrenia*, trans. B. Massumi, Minneapolis: University of Minnesota Press.

—— and Parnet, C. (1987) *Dialogues*, trans. H. Tomlinson and B. Habberjam, New York: Columbia University Press.

Deloria, V. (1969) *Custer Died for Your Sins*. New York: MacMillan Co.

Derrida, J. (1981) *Positions*. Chicago: University of Chicago Press.

Dickson-Gilmore, E. J. (1999a) '*Iati-Onkwehonwe*: Blood Quantum, Membership and the Politics of Exclusion in Kahnawake', *Citizenship Studies*, 3, 1: 27–44.

—— (1999b) '"This is my history, I know who I am": History, Factionalist Competition, and the Assumption of Imposition in the Kahnawake Mohawk Nation', *Ethnohistory*, 46, 3: 429–50.

Dodson, M. (1994) 'The End in the Beginning: Re(de)fining Aboriginality' (the Wentworth Lecture), *Australian Aboriginal Studies*, 1: 2–14.

—— (1995) *Office of the Aboriginal and Torres Strait Islander Social Justice Commissioner: Third Annual Report*. Canberra: AGPS.

—— (1997) *Native Title Report – July 1996 to June 1997: Report of the Aboriginal and Torres Strait Islander Social Justice Commissioner to the Attorney-General as required by section 209 of the Native Title Act 1993*. Sydney: Human Rights and Equal Opportunity Commission.

Dominy, M. D. (1995) 'White Settler Assertions of Native Status', *American Ethnologist*, 22, 2: 358–74.

Doppelt, G. (1998) 'Is There a Multicultural Liberalism?' *Inquiry*, 41: 223–48.

Dudley, M. Kioni and Agard, K. Kealoha (1993) *A Call for Hawaiian Sovereignty*. Honolulu: Naa Kaane O Ka Malo Press.

Durie, M. H. (1995) 'Tino Rangatiratanga', *He Pukenga Korero*, 1, 1: 66–82.

—— (1997) 'Identity, Nationhood, and Implications for Practice in New Zealand', *New Zealand Journal of Psychology*, 26, 2: 32–8.

—— (1998) *Te Mana, Te Kawanatanga: The Politics of Maori Self-determination*. Auckland: Oxford University Press.

Dworkin, R. (1978) *Taking Rights Seriously*. London: Duckworth.

Edgeworth, B. (1994) 'Tenure, Allodialism and Indigenous Rights at Common Law: English, United States and Australian Land Law Compared after *Mabo* v. *Queensland*', *Anglo-American Law Review*, 23: 397–434.

Edmunds, M. (ed.) (1998) *Regional Agreements: Key Issues in Australia*, vols 1 and 2, Canberra: Australian Institute of Aboriginal and Torres Strait Islander Studies.

Elazar, D.J. (1987) *Exploring Federalism.* Tuscaloosa: University of Alabama Press.
Elkins, D. (1992) *Where Should the Majority Rule? Reflections on Non-territorial Provinces and Other Constitutional Proposals.* Edmonton, Alberta: Centre for Constitutional Studies, University of Alberta.
Elster, J. (1986) 'The Market and the Forum: Three Varieties of Political Theory' in J. Elser and A. Hillard (eds), *Foundations of Social Choice Theory.* Cambridge: Cambridge University Press: pp. 103–32.
Eze, E. Chukwudi (1997) 'Democracy or Consensus? A Response to Wiredu' in E. Chukwudi Eze (ed.), *Postcolonial African Philosophy: A Critical Reader.* Oxford: Blackwell Publishers.
Fanon, F. (1963) *The Wretched of the Earth.* New York: Grove Press.
Fay, B. (1996) *Contemporary Philosophy of Social Science.* Oxford: Blackwell.
Fenton, W. N. (1998) *The Great Law and the Longhouse: A Political History of the Iroquois Confederacy.* Norman: University of Oklahoma Press.
Ferguson, A. (1995) *An Essay on the History of Civil Society (1767),* ed. F. Oz-Salzberger, Cambridge, New York: Cambridge University Press.
Finlayson, J. and Jackson-Nakano, A. (eds) (1996) *Heritage and Native Title: Anthropological and Legal Perspectives.* Canberra: Australian Institute of Aboriginal and Torres Strait Islander Studies.
Fleras, A. (1992) 'Managing Aboriginality: Canadian Perspectives, International Lessons', paper presented to the Australian and New Zealand Association for Canadian Studies, Victoria University, Wellington, NZ, 6 December.
—— (1996) 'The Politics of Jurisdiction' in D. A. Long and O. Dickason (eds), *Visions of the Heart.* Toronto: Harcourt Brace: pp. 107–42.
—— (1999) 'Politicising Indigeneity: Ethno-politics in White Settler Dominions' in P. Havemann (ed.), *Indigenous Peoples' Rights in Australia, Canada, and New Zealand.* Auckland: Oxford University Press: pp. 187–234.
—— and Elliott, J. L. (1992) *The Nations Within: Aboriginal–State Relations in Canada, the United States, and New Zealand.* Toronto: Oxford University Press.
—— and Elliott, J. L. (1996) *Unequal Relations: An Introduction to Race, Ethnic, and Aboriginal Dynamics in Canada,* second edn, Scarborough: Prentice-Hall.
—— and Maaka, R. (1998) 'Rethinking Claims-making as Maori Affairs Policy', *He Pukenga Korero,* 3, 1: 35–51.
—— and Spoonley, P. (1999) *Recalling Aotearoa: Ethnic Relations and Indigenous Politics in New Zealand.* Auckland: Oxford University Press.
Foster, H. (1998–99) 'Honouring the Queen: A Legal and Historical Perspective on the Nisga'a Treaty', *British Columbian Studies,* 120 (Winter): 11–37.
Foucault, M. (1980) *Power/Knowledge: Selected Interviews and Other Writings 1972–1977.* New York: Pantheon Books.
—— (1998) 'What is Enlightenment?' in P. Rabinow (ed.), *Ethics, Subjectivity and Truth.* New York: New Press: pp. 303–20.
Frideres, J. (1999) 'Altered States: Federal Policy and Aboriginal Peoples' in P.S. Li (ed.), *Race and Ethnic Relations in Canada,* second edn, Toronto: Oxford University Press: pp. 116–47.
Frug, G. (1999) *City Making: Building Communities without Building Walls,* Princeton: Princeton University Press.
Galligan, B. (1987) *Politics of the High Court: A Study of the Judicial Branch of Government in Australia.* St Lucia: University of Queensland Press.
Gardiner, W. (1996) *Return to Sender: What Really Happened at the Fiscal Envelope Hui.* Auckland: Reed.
Gellner, E. (1983) *Nations and Nationalism.* Oxford: Blackwell.

Gitlin, T. (1995) *The Twilight of Common Dreams*. New York: Metropolitan.

Glazer, N. (1997) *We Are All Multiculturalists Now*. Cambridge, Mass.: Harvard University Press.

Government of Canada, the Government of British Columbia and the Nisga'a Nation (1998) *Nisga'a Final Agreement*. Victoria, B.C.: Ministry of Aboriginal Affairs.

Graff, G. (1983) 'The Pseudo-politics of Interpretation' in W. J. T. Mitchell (ed.), *The Politics of Interpretation*. Chicago: University of Chicago Press.

Grattan, S. and McNamara, L. (1999) 'The Common Law Construct of Native Title: A "re-feudalisation" of Australian land law', *Griffith Law Review*, 8: 50–85.

Gray, S. (1993) 'Wheeling, Dealing and Deconstruction: Aboriginal Art and Land Post-Mabo', *Aboriginal Law Bulletin*, 5: 11.

—— (1996) 'Black Enough? Urban and Non-traditional Aboriginal Art and Proposed Legislation Protection for Aboriginal Art', *Culture and Policy*, 7, 3: 25.

Greaves, T. (1996) 'Tribal rights' in S. Brush and D. Stabinsky (eds), *Valuing Local Knowledge: Indigenous People and Intellectual Property Rights*. Washington DC: Island Press.

Greenfield, J. (1989) *The Return of Cultural Treasures*. Cambridge: Cambridge University Press.

Griffiths, G. (1994) 'The Myth of Authenticity: Representation, Discourse and Social Practice' in C. Tiffin and A. Lawson (eds), *De-scribing Empire: Postcolonialism and Textuality*. London: Routledge: pp. 70–85.

Grinde, D. A. and Johansen, B. E. (1991) *Exemplar of Liberty: Native America and the Evolution of Democracy*. Los Angeles: UCLA American Indian Studies and UC Press.

Gummow, W. (1999) *Change and Continuity: Statute, Equity, and Federation*. Oxford, Oxford University Press.

Gurr, T. (1993) *Minorities at Risk: A Global View of Ethnopolitical Conflict*. Washington: Institute of Peace Press.

Habermas, J. (1984, 1989) *A Theory of Communicative Action*, 2 vols, Cambridge: Polity Press.

—— (1996) 'Postscript to *Between Facts and Norms*' in M. Deflem (ed.), *Habermas, Modernity and Law*. London: Sage: pp. 135–50.

Hannum, H. (1990) *Autonomy, Sovereignty, and Self-determination: The Adjudication of Conflicting Rights*. Philadelphia: University of Pennsylvania Press.

Hardimon, M. (1992) 'The Project of Reconciliation: Hegel's Social Philosophy', *Philosophy and Public Affairs*, 21: 165–95.

Hardin, R. (1995) *One for All: The Logic of Group Conflict*. Princeton: Princeton University Press.

Harris, C. (1997) *The Resettlement of British Columbia*. Vancouver: University of British Columbia Press.

Harris, M. (1996) 'Scientific and Cultural Vandalism', *Alternative Law Journal*, 21, 1 (February): 21.

Hauptman, L. M. (1986) *The Iroquois Struggle for Survival: World War II to Red Power*, Syracuse: Syracuse University Press.

Havemann, P. (ed.) (1999) *Indigenous Peoples' Rights in Australia, Canada, and New Zealand*. Auckland: Oxford University Press.

Held, D. (1995) *Democracy and the Global Order*. Cambridge: Polity Press.

Henare, Denise (1995) 'The Ka Awatea Report: Reflections on its Process and Visions' in M. Wilson and A. Yeatman (eds), *Justice and Identity: Antipodean Practices*. Wellington: Bridget Williams Books, pp. 44–61.

Henderson, J. Youngblood (1994) 'Empowering Treaty Federalism', *University of Saskatchewan Law Review*, 58, 2: 211–329.
Hiatt, L. R. (1989) 'Aboriginal Land Tenure and Contemporary Claims in Australia' in E. Wilmsen (ed.), *We are Here: Politics of Aboriginal Land Tenure*. Berkeley: University of California Press, pp. 99–117.
Hollinger, H. (1995) *Postethnic America: Beyond Multiculturalism*. New York: Basic Books.
—— (1996) 'Group Preferences, Cultural Diversity, and Social Democracy: Notes towards a Theory of Affirmative Action', *Representations*, 55: 31–40.
—— (1998) 'National Culture and Communities of Descent', *Reviews in American History* 26: 312–28.
Holmes, S. (1995) *Passions and Constraint: On the Theory of Liberal Democracy*. Chicago: University of Chicago Press.
Howitt, R. (1991), 'Aborigines and Gold Mining in Central Australia' in J. Connell and R. Howitt (eds), *Mining and Indigenous Peoples in Australasia*. Sydney: Sydney University Press, pp. 119–37.
Hughes, J. (1999) 'Institutional Responses to Separatism: Federalism and Transition to Democracy in Russia', presented to ASN Convention, New York.
Hutton, J. (1996) 'Rangatiratanga', *Outburst* (March): 5.
Hymes, D. (1969) *Reinventing Anthropology*. New York: Pantheon Books.
Ihimaera, Witi (ed.) (1995) *Visions Aotearoa: Kaupapa New Zealand*. Wellington: Bridget Williams Books.
International Alliance of Indigenous-Tribal Peoples of the Tropical Forests and International Work Group for Indigenous Affairs (IWGIA) (1996) *Indigenous Peoples, Forests, and Biodiversity*. London.
Ivison, D. (1997) 'Postcolonialism and Political Theory' in A. Vincent (ed.), *Political Theory: Tradition and Diversity*. Cambridge: Cambridge University Press: pp. 154–71.
—— (1998) 'The Disciplinary Moment: Foucault, Law and the Reinscription of Rights' in J. Moss (ed.), *The Later Foucault*. London: Sage: pp. 129–48.
—— (2000) 'Modus Vivendi Citizenship' in I. Hampsher-Monk and C. Mackinnon (eds), *The Demands of Citizenship*. London: Continuum.
Jackson, M. (1988) *Paths Toward a Clearing: Radical Empiricism and Ethnographic Inquiry*. Bloomington: Indiana University Press.
—— (1996) 'Introduction: Phenomenology, Radical Empiricism and Anthropological Critique' in M. Jackson (ed.), *Things as They Are: New Directions in Phenomenological Anthropology*. Bloomington: Indiana University Press: pp. 1–50.
Jackson, Moana (1995) 'Comment' in G. McLay (ed.), *Treaty Settlements: The Unfinished Business*. New Zealand: Institute of Advanced Legal Studies/Victoria University of Wellington Law Review.
—— (1997) 'The Maori View of the Law', paper presented at Canterbury University, June.
James Bay and Northern Quebec Agreement (1976) Quebec: Editeur Officiel du Québec.
Janke, T. (1996) 'Protecting Australian Indigenous Arts and Cultural Expression: A Matter of Legislative Reform or Cultural Policy?' *Culture and Policy*, 7,3: 15.
—— (1997) 'The Application of Copyright and Other Intellectual Property Laws to Aboriginal and Torres Strait Islander Cultural and Intellectual Property', *Art Antiquity and Law*, 2, 1 (March): 13.
—— (1998) 'Museums and Indigenous Cultural and Intellectual Property Rights', *Museum National*, August: 7.

Jennings, F. (1987) '"Pennsylvania Indians" and the Iroquois' in D. Richter and
    J. Merrell (eds), *Beyond the Covenant Chain: The Iroquois and Their Neighbors
    in Indian North America, 1600–1800*. Syracuse: Syracuse University Press:
    pp. 1–50.
Jocks, C. R. (1994) *Relationship Structures in Longhouse Tradition at Kahnawà:ke*.
    Ph.D. dissertation: University of California (Santa Barbara).
Johnston, P. M. G. (1994) 'Examining a State Relationship: "Legitimation" and
    Te Kohanga Reo', *Te Pua*, 3, 2: 22–34.
Jones, A., Marshall, J., Morris, K., Matthews, G., Smith, H. and Smith, L. Tuhiwai
    (1995) *Myths and Realities: Schooling in New Zealand*, second edn, Palmer-
    ston North: Dunmore Press.
Jull, P. and Craig, D. (1997) 'Reflections on Regional Agreements: Yesterday,
    Today, and Tomorrow, *Australian Indigenous Law Reporter*, 2, 4: 475–93.
Kaplan, W. (ed.) (1993) *Belonging: The Meaning and Sense of Citizenship in Canada*.
    Montreal and Kingston: McGill-Queen's University Press.
Kasprycki, S. S., Stambrau, D. I. and Roth, A. V. (eds) (1998) *IroquoisART: Visual
    Expressions of Contemporary Native American Artists*. Aldenstadt: ERNAS
    Monographs I.
Kawepo, R. (1860) 'Letter to the Settlers of Hawkes Bay. November' in J. Casel-
    berg (ed.) (1975) *Maori is My Name: Historical Maori Writings in Translation*.
    Dunedin: John McIndoe Ltd: pp. 82–4.
Kawharu, H. (ed.) (1989) *Waitangi: Maori and Pakeha Perspectives on the Treaty of
    Waitangi*. Auckland: Oxford University Press.
——— (1996) 'Rangatiratanga and Sovereignty by 2040', *He Pukenga Korero*, 1,2:
    11–15.
Keesing, R. (1989) 'Creating the Past: Custom and Identity in the Pacific', *Con-
    temporary Pacific*, 1: 19–42.
Kelsey, J. (1996) 'From Flagpoles to Pine Trees: Tino Rangatiratanga and Treaty
    Policy Today' in P. Spoonley, D. Pearson and C. McPherson (eds), *Nga
    Patai: Racism and Ethnic Relations in Aotearoa/New Zealand*. Palmerston
    North: Dunmore: pp. 108–30.
Kerby, A. P. (1991) *Narrative and the Self*. Bloomington: Indiana University Press.
Kickingbird, K. (1984) 'Indian Sovereignty: The American Experience' in Leroy
    Little Bear *et al.* (eds), *Pathways to Self-determination: Canadian Indians and
    the Canadian State*. Toronto: University of Toronto Press.
Kirby, R. (1970–71) 'Conciliation and Arbitration in Australia – Where the
    Emphasis?' *Federal Law Review*, 4: 1–29.
Koenigsberger, H. G. (1989) 'Composite States, Representative Institutions, and
    the American Revolution', *Historical Research*, 62: 135–53.
Krygier, M. (1986) 'Law as Tradition', *Law and Philosophy*, 5: 237–62.
——— (1988) 'The Traditionality of Statutes', *Ratio Juris*, 1: 20–39.
——— (1991) 'Thinking Like a Lawyer', *Poznan Studies in the Philosophy of the Sciences
    and the Humanities*, 23: 67–90.
——— (1997) *Between Fear and Hope: Hybrid Thoughts on Public Values*. Sydney: ABC
    Books.
Kukathas, C. (1992) 'Are There Any Cultural Rights?' *Political Theory*, 20: 105–39.
——— (1997a) 'Cultural toleration', *Nomos*, 39: 69–104.
——— (1997b) 'Liberalism, Multiculturalism and Oppresssion' in A. Vincent
    (ed.), *Political Theory: Tradition and Diversity*. Cambridge: Cambridge Uni-
    versity Press: pp. 132–53.
Kulchyski, P. (1995) 'Aboriginal Peoples and Hegemony in Canada', *Journal of
    Canadian Studies*, 30, 1: 60–8.

Kuper, A. (1996) *Anthropology and Anthropologists: The Modern British School.* London & New York: Routledge.

Kymlicka, W. (1989) *Liberalism, Community and Culture.* Oxford: Oxford University Press.

—— (1995) *Multicultural Citizenship.* Oxford: Oxford University Press.

—— (1996) 'Minority group rights: the good, the bad and the intolerable', *Dissent,* Summer: 22–30.

—— (1998a) *Finding Our Way: Rethinking Ethnocultural Relations in Canada.* Toronto: Oxford University Press .

—— (1998b) 'Is Federalism an Alternative to Secession?' in P. Lehning (ed.), *Theories of Secession.* London: Routledge: pp. 111–50.

—— (1998c) 'Human Rights and Ethno-cultural Justice', *Review of Constitutional Studies,* 4, 2: 213–38.

—— (1999a) 'Theorising Indigenous Rights', *University of Toronto Law Journal,* 49: 281–93.

—— (1999b) 'Misunderstanding Nationalism' in R. Beiner (ed.), *Theorising Nationalism.* Albany, NY: State University of New York Press: pp. 131–40.

—— (forthcoming) 'Ethnic Relations in Eastern Europe and Western Political Theory' in W. Kymlicka and M. Opalski (eds), *Can Liberal Pluralism be Exported?* Oxford: Oxford University Press.

—— and Raviot, J.-R. (1997) 'Living Together: International Aspects of Federal Systems', *Canadian Foreign Policy,* 5, 1: 1–50.

La Capra, D., Baswick, D. and Leeson, D. (1999) Discussion of Windschuttle (1994), *American Historical Review,* 104, 2: 709–11.

LaRusic, I. E. *et al.* (1979) 'Negotiating a Way of Life', report prepared for the Research Division, Policy, Research and Evaluation Group, Department of Indian and Northern Affairs, Canada, October.

Laden, A. (1997) *Constructing Shared Wills: Deliberative Liberalism and the Politics of Identity.* Ph.D. thesis, Harvard University.

Laitin, D. (1998) 'Liberal Theory and the Nation', *Political Theory,* 26: 221–36.

Land Rights News (1989) March.

Landmann, P. (1988) 'Co-management of Wildlife under the James Bay Treaty: the Hunting, Fishing and Trapping Coordinating Committee', unpublished MA thesis, Université Laval.

Langton, M. (1994) *Valuing Cultures: Recognising Indigenous Cultures as a Valued Part of Australian Heritage/Council for Aboriginal Reconciliation.* Canberra: AGPS.

—— (1997) 'Grandmothers' Law, Company Business and Succession in Changing Aboriginal Land Tenure Systems' in Yunupingu (1997): 84–116.

—— (1999) 'Estate of Mind' in P. Havemann (ed.), *Indigenous Peoples' Rights in Australia, Canada, and New Zealand.* Auckland: Oxford University Press: pp. 71–87.

Lapidoth, R. (1996) *Autonomy: Flexible Solutions to Ethnic Conflicts.* Washington: US Institute of Peace Press.

Law Reform Commission (1986) *Report no. 31: The Recognition of Aboriginal Customary Laws,* vol. 1, Canberra: AGPS.

Laws of Australia: Aborigines (1995) Melbourne: Law Book Company.

Levin, M. D. (ed.) (1993) *Ethnicity and Aboriginality: Case Studies in Ethnonationalism.* Toronto: University of Toronto Press.

Levitus, R. (1991) 'The Boundaries of Gagudju Association Membership: Anthropology, Law, and Public Policy' in J. Connell and R. Howitt (eds), *Mining and Indigenous Peoples in Australasia.* Sydney: Sydney University Press, pp. 153–68.

Levy, J. (1997) 'Classifying Cultural Rights' in I. Shapiro and W. Kymlicka (eds), *NOMOS XXXIX: Ethnicity and Group Rights*. New York: New York University Press: pp. 22–66.

Levy, P. A. (1996) 'Exemplars of Taking Liberties: The Iroquois Influence Thesis and the Problem of Evidence', *William and Mary Quarterly*, 51, 3: 588–620.

Lind, M. (1995) *The Next American Nation: The New Nationalism and the Fourth American Revolution*. New York: Free Press.

Linden, W. (1994) *Swiss Democracy*. New York: St Martin's Press.

Locke, J. (1986) *Two Treatises of Government*, ed. P. Laslett, New York: Cambridge University Press.

—— (1988) 'Second Treatise of Government' in P. Laslett (ed.), *Two Treatises of Government*. New York: Cambridge University Press.

Locré, (1827) *La Législation civile, commerciale et criminelle de la France.*

Long, J. A. (1991) 'Federalism and Ethnic Self-determination: Native Indians in Canada', *Journal of Commonwealth and Comparative Politics*, 29, 2: 192–211.

Maaka, R. C. A. (1993) 'Paeketanga – The World of the Aged' in P. G. Koopman-Boydman (ed.), *New Zealand's Ageing Society*. Wellington: Daphne Brasell.

—— (1994) 'The New Tribe: Conflicts and Continuities in the Social Organisation of Urban Maori', *Contemporary Pacific*, 6, 2: 311–36.

—— (1997) 'The Politics of Diaspora', paper given at the 'Treaty of Waitangi: Maori Political Representation Future Challenges' Conference.

—— and Fleras, A. (1997) 'Politicizing Property Rights: Tino Rangatiratanga as Constructive Engagement', *Sites*, 35 (Spring): 20–43.

—— and Fleras, A. (1998) 'Te Ara Motuhake: A Passage to Self-determination', paper presented at the Pacific Island Political Science Association conference, University of Canterbury, 7–11 December.

—— and Fleras, A. (1998–99) 'Reconceptualising Relationships: The Waitangi Tribunal', *International Policy Review*, 8: 78–91.

Macdonald, G. (1997) '"Recognition and Justice": The Traditional/Historical Contradiction in New South Wales' in D. E. Smith and J. Finlayson (eds), *Fighting Over Country: Anthropological Perspectives*. Canberra: Centre for Aboriginal Economic Policy Research: 65–82.

MacDuff, I. (1995) 'Resources, Rights and Recognition', *Cultural Survival Quarterly*, Fall: 30–2.

MacLaine, C. and Baxendale, M. (1991) *This Land is Our Land: The Mohawk revolt at Oka*. Montreal: Optimum Publishing.

McBryde, I. (ed.) (1985) *Who Owns the Past? Papers from the Annual Symposium of the Australian Academy of the Humanities*. Melbourne: Oxford University Press.

McHugh, P. (1991) *The Maori Magna Carta: New Zealand Law and the Treaty of Waitangi*. Auckland: Oxford University Press.

—— (1998) 'Aboriginal Identity and Relations: Models of State Practice and Law in North America and Australasia', paper presented at the Ministry of Justice, Wellington. Subsequently published in K. Coates and P. McHugh (eds), *Living Relationships, Kokiri Ngatahi: The Treaty of Waitangi in the New Millennium*. Wellington: Victoria University Press, 1998.

—— (1999) 'From Sovereignty Talk to Settlement Time' in P. Havemann (ed.), *Indigenous Peoples' Rights in Australia, Canada and New Zealand*. Auckland: Oxford University Press: pp. 447–67.

McKean, W. (1983) *Equality and Discrimination under International Law*. Oxford: Oxford University Press.

McMaster, G. and Martin, L.-A. (eds) (1992) *Indigena: Contemporary Native Perspectives*, Vancouver: Douglas & McIntyre.

McNeil, K. (1998) 'Defining Aboriginal Title in the 90s: Has the Supreme Court finally got it Right?' Twelfth Annual Robarts Lecture, York University, Toronto, 25 March.

Macklem, P. (1995) 'Normative Dimensions of the Right of Aboriginal Self-government' in Canadian Royal Commission, *Aboriginal Self-government: Legal and Constitutional Issues*. Ottawa: Minister of Supply and Services.

Maddock, K. (1984) 'Aboriginal Customary Law' in P. Hanks and B. Keon-Cohen (eds), *Aborigines and the Law*. St Leonards: Allen & Unwin, pp. 212–37.

Mahuta, R. T. K. (1996) 'Iwi Development and the Waikato-Tainui Experience' in P. Spoonley, D. Pearson and C. McPherson (eds) *Nga Patai. Racism and Ethnic Relations in Aotearoa/New Zealand*. Palmerston North: Dunmore Publishing.

Manderson, D. (1998) 'Unutterable Shame/Unuttered Guilt: Semantics, Aporia, and the Possibility of *Mabo*', *Law/Text/Culture*, 4: 234–44.

Mansell, M. (1994) 'Taking Control of Resources' in C. Fletcher (ed.), *Aboriginal Self-determination in Australia*. Canberra: Aboriginal Studies Press.

Marcus, G. E. and Fischer, M. M. J. (1986) *Anthropology as Cultural Critique: An Experimental Moment in the Human Sciences*. Chicago: University of Chicago Press.

Marcus, J. (1990) 'Anthropology, culture and post-modernity', *Social Analysis*, 27 (April): 3–16.

Markus, A. (1996) 'Between Mabo and a Hard Place: Race and the Contradictions of Conservatism' in B. Attwood (ed.), *In the Age of Mabo: History, Aborigines and Australia*, St Leonards, Allen & Unwin, pp. 88–99.

Martin, D. (1995) *Money, Business and Culture: Issues for Aboriginal Economic Policy*. Canberra: Centre for Aboriginal Economic Policy Research.

Martin, D. F. and Finlayson, J. D. (1996) *Linking accountability and Self-determination in Aboriginal Organisations*. Canberra: Centre for Aboriginal Economic and Policy Research, Discussion paper no. 116.

Martinez, R. B. (1997) 'Puerto Rico's Decolonization', *Foreign Affairs*, November: 100–14.

Mason, A. (1999) 'Political Community, Liberal-Nationalism and the Ethics of Assimilation', *Ethics*, 109: 261–86.

Mead, S. Moko (1997) *Landmarks, Bridges, and Visions: Aspects of Maori Culture – Essays by Sidney Moko Mead*. Wellington: Victoria University Press.

Medicine, B. (1971) 'The Anthropologist as the Indian's Image-maker', *The Indian Historian*, 4, 3: 27–9.

Meijl, T. van (1994) 'Maori Socio-political Organisation in Pre- and Proto-history', *Oceania* 65, 4: 304–22.

—— (1996) 'Historicising Maoritanga: Colonial Ethnography and the Reification of Maori Traditions', *Journal of the Polynesian Society*, 105, 3: 311–46.

Melbourne, H. (1995) *Maori Sovereignty: Maori Perspectives*. Auckland: Hodder Moa Beckett.

Merlan, F. (1996) 'Formulations of Claim and Title: A Comparative Discussion' in J. Finlayson and A. Jackson-Nakano (eds), *Heritage and Native Title: Anthropological and Legal Perspectives*. Canberra: AIATSIS.

Metge, J. (1964) *A New Maori Migration: Rural and Urban Relations in Northern New Zealand*. London: University of London; The Athlone Press.

Mill, J. S. (1958) *Considerations on Representative Government*, ed. C. V. Shields, New York: Liberal Arts Press.

—— (1972) 'Considerations on Representative Government' (1861), in H. B. Acton (ed.), *Utilitarianism: On Liberty, Considerations on Representative Government*. London: J. M. Dent & Sons.

Mills, A. (1994) *Eagle Down is Our Law: Witsuwit'en Law, Feasts and Land Claims.* Vancouver: University of British Columbia Press.

Minister of Māori Affairs (1989) *Te Urupare Rangapū: A Discussion Paper on Proposals for a New Partnership.* Wellington: Ministry of Maori Affairs.

—— (1990) *Ka Awatea: A Report on the Ministerial Planning Group.* Wellington: Ministry of Maori Affairs.

Minority Rights Group (1991) *Minorities and Autonomy in Western Europe,* revised edn, London: Minority Rights Group.

Mitchell, T. (1988) *Colonising Egypt.* Cambridge: Cambridge University Press.

Moody-Adams, M. (1997) *Fieldwork in Familiar Places: Morality, Culture and Philosophy.* Cambridge, Mass.: Harvard University Press.

Morris, C. (1998) *An Essay on the Modern State.* Cambridge: Cambridge University Press.

Morrison, J. (1994) 'The Robinson Treaties of 1850: A Case Study', unpublished report prepared for the Royal Commission on Aboriginal Peoples, 31 March: 40–2, 47–69.

Morse, B. W. (1992) *Comparative Assessment of Indigenous Peoples in Quebec, Canada, and Abroad: A report prepared for la Commission d'Ètude sur toute offre d'un nouveau partenariat de nature constitutionelle.* Ottawa, April.

Moss, W. (1995) 'Inuit perspectives on Treaty Rights and Governance' in Canadian Royal Commission, *Aboriginal Self-government: Legal and Constitutional Issues.* Ottawa: Minister of Supply and Services Canada.

Mulgan, R. (1989) *Maori, Pakeha, and Democracy.* Auckland: Oxford University Press.

Mulvaney, J. (1985) 'A Question of Values: Museum and Cultural Property' in I. McBryde (ed.), *Who Owns the Past? Papers from the Annual Symposium of the Australian Academy of the Humanities.* Melbourne: Oxford University Press.

Munz, P. and Salmond, A. (1994) Exchange of Letters, *New Zealand Journal of History* 28, 1: 60ff.

Murphy, M. (1997) *Nature, Culture and Authority: Multinational Democracies and the Politics of Pluralism.* Ph.D. thesis, McGill University.

Murray, L. (1999) *The Quality of Sprawl.* Sydney: Duffy & Snellgrove.

Myers, F. R. (1986) *Pintupi Country, Pintupi Self: Sentiment, Place, and Politics among Western Desert Aborigines.* Washington: Smithsonian Institution Press.

Nedelsky, J. (1989) 'Relational Autonomy', *Yale Journal of Law and Feminism,* 1, 1: 7–36.

—— (1991) 'Law, Boundaries and the Bounded Self' in R. Post (ed.), *Law and the Order of Culture.* Berkeley: University of California Press.

Nettheim, G. (1999) 'The Search for Certainty and the *Native Title Amendment Act 1998* [Cth]', *UNSW Law Journal,* 22: 564–84.

New Zealand Herald (1997) 'Pakeha Told Maori Law is Separate', 31 May.

Nietschmann, B. (1987) 'The Third World War: Militarization and Indigenous Peoples', *Cultural Survival Quarterly,* 11, 3: 1–16.

Nisga'a Final Agreement (1998) Victoria B.C.: Ministry of Aboriginal Affairs.

Norretranders, T. (1998) *The User Illusion,* trans. J. Sydenham, New York: Viking.

O'Brien, S. (1987) 'Cultural Rights in the United States: A Conflict of Values', *Law and Inequality Journal,* 5: 267–358.

—— (1989) *American Indian Tribal Governments.* Norman: University of Oklahoma Press.

O'Neill, O. (1996) *Toward Justice and Virtue.* Cambridge: Cambridge University Press.

O'Regan, T. (1994) 'Indigenous Governance: Country Study – New Zealand', paper prepared for the *Canadian Royal Commission on Aboriginal Peoples*, Ottawa: Minister of Supply and Services Canada.

Offe, C. (1997) 'Homogeneity and Constitutional Democracy', *Journal of Political Philosophy*, 6: 113–41.

Okin, S. M. (1998) 'Feminism and Multiculturalism: Some Tensions', *Ethics*, 108: 661–84.

Oliver, W. H. (1997) 'Pandora's Envelope: It's All about Power' in L. Edmond, H. Richetts and B. Sewell (eds), *Under Review: A Selection from New Zealand Books, 1991–1996*. Lincoln, NZ: Lincoln University Press.

Oman, N. (1997) *Sharing Horizons: A Paradigm for Political Accommodation in Inter-cultural Settings*. Ph.D. thesis, McGill University.

Onuf, N. G. (1991) 'Sovereignty: Outline of a Conceptual History', *Alternatives*, 16: 425–45.

Orange, C. (1987) *The Treaty of Waitangi*. Wellington: Allen & Unwin.

—— (1993) 'The Treaty of Waitangi: A Historical Overview', *Public Sector*, 11, 4: 2–6.

Overview: Proceedings of the Australian Reconciliation Convention: Book 1 (1997) Kingston: Council for Aboriginal Reconciliation.

Pagden, A. (1982) *The Fall of Natural Man*. Cambridge: Cambridge University Press.

—— (1995) *Lords of All the World: Ideologies of Empire in Spain, Britain and France c. 1500–c. 1800*. New Haven: Yale University Press .

Paine, R. (1996) 'In Chief Justice McEachern's shoes: Anthropology's Ineffectiveness in Court', *POLAR*, 19, 2: 59–70.

—— (1999) 'Aboriginality, Multiculturalism, and Liberal Rights Philosophy', *Ethnos*, 64, 3: 325–49.

Parata, H. (1994) 'Mainstreaming: A Maori Affairs Policy?' *Social Policy Journal of New Zealand*, 3 (December): 40–9.

Parekh, B. (1994) 'Decolonizing liberalism' in A. Shtromas (ed.), *The End of 'isms'? Reflections on the Fate of Ideological Politics after Communism's Collapse*. Oxford: Blackwell, pp. 85–103.

Parkinson, P. (1994) *Tradition and Change in Australian Law*. North Ryde: Law Book Company.

Patton, P. (1995a) 'Mabo, Freedom and the Politics of Difference', *Australian Journal of Political Science*, 30: 108–19.

—— (1995b) 'Post-structuralism and the Mabo Debate: Difference, Society and Justice' in M. Wilson and A. Yeatman (eds), *Justice and Identity: Antipodean Practices*. St Leonards: Allen & Unwin, pp. 153–71.

Paul, A. (1995) 'On Rights, Racism and Retribution: A Systematic Analysis of the Membership Issue', *Onkwarihwa'shon:'a*, 3 (15): 5–6.

Payne, S. B. Jr. (1996) 'The Iroquois League, the Articles of Confederation, and the Constitution', *William and Mary Quarterly*, 53, 3: 605–20.

Pearson, N. (1993) 'Reconciliation: To Be or Not To Be', *Aboriginal Law Bulletin*, 3: 14–17.

—— (1997) 'The Concept of Native Title at Common Law' in Yunupingu (1997): 150–62.

Pettit, P. (1997) *Republicanism: A Theory of Freedom and Government*. Oxford: Oxford University Press.

—— (1999) 'Republican Freedom and Contestatory Democratisation' in I. Shapiro and C. Hacker-Cordon (eds), *Democracy's Value*. Cambridge: Cambridge University Press: pp. 163–90.

—— (2000) 'Democracy, Electoral and Contestatory', *Nomos*, 42.

Pettman, J. (1988) 'Whose Country is it Anyway? Cultural Politics, Racism and the Construction of Being Australian', *Journal of Intercultural Studies*, 19, 1: 3.

Philpott, D. (1995) 'Sovereignty: An Introduction and Brief History', *Journal of International Affairs*, Winter, 2: 353–68.

Poata-Smith, Evan S. T. A. (1996) 'He Pokeke Uenuku i Tu Ai: The Evolution of Contemporary Maori Protest' in P. Spoonley, D. Pearson and C. McPherson (eds), *Nga Patai. Racism and Ethnic Relations in Aotearoa/New Zealand*. Palmerston North: Dunmore Publishing.

Pocock, J. G. A. (1992) 'Tangata whenua and Enlightenment Anthropology', *New Zealand Journal of History*, 24, 1: 28–53.

—— (1998) 'Law, Sovereignty and History in a Divided Culture: The Case of New Zealand and the Treaty of Waitangi', *McGill Law Journal*, 43: 481–506.

Pogge, T. (1992) 'Cosmopolitanism and Sovereignty', *Ethics*, 103, October: 48–75.

—— (1997) 'Creating Super-national Institutions Democratically: Reflections on the European Union's "democratic deficit"', *Journal of Political Philosophy*, 5, 2: 163–82.

Poirier, S. (1996) 'Negotiating Boundaries or When Itineraries Become Maps: Some Comments on the Native Title Legislation in the Gibson Desert (Australia)', paper presented to the Workshop on Negotiating Nationhood: An Intercultural Dialogue on Contemporary Native Issues, McGill University, Montreal, 6–7 December.

Polanco, H. Diaz (1997) *Indigenous Peoples in Latin America: The Quest for Self-determination*, trans. L. Rayas, Boulder: Westview.

Poole, R. (1998) 'Self-determination and Indigenous Peoples: National Liberation or Citizenship?' unpublished paper.

Portillo, M. Negron (1997) 'Puerto Rico: Surviving Colonialism and Nationalism' in F. Negron-Muntaner and R. Grossfoguel (eds), *Puerto Rican Jam: Essays on Culture and Politics*. Minneapolis: University of Minnesota Press: pp. 39–56.

Post, R. (forthcoming) 'Democratic Constitutionalism and Cultural Heterogeneity', *Australian Journal of Legal Philosophy*.

Povinelli, E. (1998) 'The State of Shame: Australian Multiculturalism and the Crisis of Indigenous Citizenship', *Critical Inquiry*, 24, 2: 575–610.

—— (1999) 'Settler Modernity and the Quest for an Indigenous Tradition', *Public Culture*, 11, 1: 19–48.

Pownall, T. (1993) *The Administration of the Colonies (1768): A Facsimile Reproduction*. Delmar, NY: Published for the John Carter Brown Library by Scholars' Facsims. and Reprints.

Prucha, F. P. (1994) *American Indian Treaties: The History of a Political Anomaly*. Berkeley: University of California Press.

Przeworksi, A. (1999) 'Minimalist Conception of Democracy: A Defense' in I. Shapiro and C. Hacker-Cordon (eds), *Democracy's Value*. Cambridge: Cambridge University Press: pp. 23–55.

Puri, K. (1993) 'Copyright Protection for Australian Aborigines in the light of Mabo' in M. A. Stephenson and S. Ratnapala (eds), *Mabo: A Judicial Revolution*. St Lucia: University of Queensland Press.

Ramos, A. R. (1994) 'The Hyperreal Indian', *Critique of Anthropology*, 14, 2: 153–71.

Raunet, D. (1996) *Without Surrender, Without Consent: A History of the Nisga'a Land Claims.* Vancouver: Douglas & MacIntyre.

Rawls, J. (1993) *Political Liberalism.* New York: Columbia University Press.

Reeves, J. (1998) *Building on Land Rights for the Next Generation: Report of the Review of the Aboriginal Land Rights (Northern Territory) Act 1976.* Canberra: AGPS.

Reid, G. F. trans. Christian Ruel (1999) 'Une malaise qui est encore présent: les origines du traditionalisme et de la division chez les *Kanien'kehaka* de Kahnawake au XXe siècle', *Recherches amérindiennes au québec,* 29, 2: 37–50.

Renan, E. (1995) 'What is a Nation?' in M. Chabour and M. R. Ishay (eds), *The Nationalist Reader.* New York: Humanities Press.

Renwick, W. (1993) 'Decolonizing Ourselves from Within', *British Review of New Zealand Studies,* 6: 29–60.

Renwick, W. (ed.) (1991) *Sovereignty and Indigenous Rights: The Treaty of Waitangi in International Contexts.* Wellington: Victoria University Press.

Reynolds, H. (1992) *The Law of the Land.* Ringwood: Penguin Books .

—— (1996) *Aboriginal Sovereignty: Three Nations, One Australia?* St Leonards: Allen & Unwin.

Richter, D. K. (1992) *The Ordeal of the Longhouse: The Peoples of the Iroquois League in the Era of European Colonization.* Chapel Hill: University of North Carolina Press.

Riker, W. (1982) *Liberalism against Populism.* San Francisco: W. H. Freeman and Co.

Rose, D. B. (1996) 'Histories and Rituals: Land Claims in the Territory' in B. Attwood (ed.), *In the Age of Mabo: History, Aborigines and Australia.* St Leonards: Allen & Unwin, pp. 35–53.

Rothwell, N. (1996) 'Whose Culture is it Anyway?', *The Weekend Review,* 30–1 March: 9.

Rotman, L. (1997) 'Creating a Still-Life Out of Dynamic Objects. Rights Reductionisms at the Supreme Court of Canada', *Alberta Law Review,* 36: 1–8.

Rowley, C. (1970) *Outcasts in White Australia.* Harmondsworth: Penguin.

Rubinstein, A. (1993) 'Is Statehood for Puerto Rico in the National Interest?' in *Depth: A Journal for Values and Public Policy,* spring: 87–99.

Said, E. W. (1978) *Orientalism.* New York: Vintage.

—— (1989) 'Representing the Colonized: Anthropology's Interlocutors', *Critical Inquiry,* 15: 205–25.

—— (1994) *Culture and Imperialism.* New York: Vintage.

Salee, D. (1995) 'Identities in Conflict: the aboriginal question and the politics of recognition in Quebec', *Racial and Ethnic Studies* 18, 2: 277–314.

—— and Coleman, W. D. (1997) 'The Challenges of the Quebec Question: Paradigm, Counter-paradigm, and...?' in W. Clement (ed.), *Understanding Canada.* Montreal/Kingston: McGill-Queen's University Press: pp. 277–314.

Salmond, A. (1997) *Between Worlds: Early Exchanges between Maori and Europeans, 1773–1815.* Honolulu: University of Hawai'i Press.

Salzman, P. C. (1994) 'The Lone Stranger in the Heart of Darkness' in R. Borofsky (ed.), *Assessing Cultural Anthropology.* Cambridge, Mass.: McGraw-Hill.

Sanders, W. (1995) 'Reshaping Governance in Torres Strait: The Torres Strait Regional Authority and Beyond', *Australian Journal of Political Science,* 30, 3: 500–24.

Schlesinger, A. M. (1992) *The Disuniting of America.* New York: Norton.

Schwarz, B. (1995) 'The Diversity Myth: America's Leading Export', *Atlantic Monthly,* May: 57–67.

Scott, C. (1996) 'Indigenous Self-determination and Decolonization of the International Imagination', *Human Rights Quarterly*, 18: 815–20.
Scott, J. (1990) *Domination and the Arts of Resistance*. New Haven: Yale University Press.
Sealy, L. (1962) 'Fiduciary Relationships', *Cambridge Law Journal*, 1962: 69–81.
Senior, C. (1998) 'The Yandicoogina Process: A Model for Negotiating Land Use Agreements', *Regional Agreements Paper no. 6, Native Title Research Unit*, Canberra: AIATSIS.
Shafir, G. (1995) *Immigrants and Nationalists: Ethnic Conflict and Accommodation in Catalonia, the Basque Country, Latvia and Estonia*. Albany: State University of New York.
Shapiro, I. (1996) *Democracy's Place*. Ithaca: Cornell University Press.
Sharp, A. (1997) *Justice and the Maori: The Philosophy and Practice of Maori claims in New Zealand since the 1970s*, second edn, Auckland: Oxford University Press.
Sharp, N. (1996) *No Ordinary Judgment: Mabo, The Murray Islanders' Land Case*. Canberra: Aboriginal Studies Press.
Silman, J. (1987) *Enough is Enough: Aboriginal Women Speak Out*. Toronto: Women's Press.
Simmons, A. J. (1995) 'Historical Rights and Fair Shares', *Law and Philosophy*, 14: 149–84.
Simpson, A. (1998) 'The Empire Laughs Back: Tradition, Power and Play in the Work of Shelley Niro and Ryan Rice' in S. S. Kasprycki, D. I. Stambrau and A. V. Roth (eds), *IroquoisART: Visual Expressions of Contemporary Native American Artists*, Aldenstadt: ERNAS Monographs 1.
—— (1999) 'Introduction: Au-delà de la tradition des études iroquoises traditionelles', trans. D. Legros, *Recherches amérindiennes au Québec*, 29, 2: 3–9.
Slattery, B. (1987) 'Understanding Aboriginal Rights', *Canadian Bar Review*, 66, 3: 727–83.
—— (1991) 'Aboriginal Sovereignty and Imperial Claims', *Osgoode Hall Law Journal*, 29, 4: 681–703.
Smith, A. (1991) 'The Nation: Invented, Imagined, Reconstructed', *Millennium: Journal of International Studies*, 20, 3: 353–68.
—— (1993) 'A Europe of Nations – or the Nation of Europe?', *Journal of Peace Research*, 30, 2: 129–35.
Smith, D. E. (1998) 'Indigenous Land Use Agreements: New Opportunities and Challenges under the Amended Native Title Act', *Regional Agreements Paper no 7, Native Title Research Unit*, Canberra: AIATSIS.
Smith, M. (1995) *Our Home or Native Land?* Victoria B.C.: Crown Western.
Smith, R. M. (1997) *Civic Ideals: Conflicting Visions of Citizenship in American History*. New Haven: Yale University Press.
Sohn, L. (1981) 'The Rights of Minorities' in L. Henkin (ed.), *The International Bill of Rights: The Covenant on Civil and Political Rights*. New York: Columbia University Press.
Spoonley, P. (1995) 'Constructing Ourselves: The Post-colonial Politics of Pakeha' in M. Wilson and A. Yeatman (eds), *Justice and Identity: Antipodean Practices*. Wellington: Bridget Wilson Books: pp. 96–115.
—— (1997) 'Migration and the Reconstruction of Citizenship in Late Twentieth-century Aotearoa', Immigration Research Network, published for the Asia–Pacific Migration Research Network, Albany, Auckland: Massey University.

——, Pearson, D. and McPherson, C. (eds) (1996) *Nga Patai: Racism and Ethnic Relations in Aotearoa/New Zealand.* Palmerston North: Dunmore.
Stasiulis, D. and Yuval-Davis, N. (1995) 'Introduction – Beyond Dichotomies: Gender, Race, Ethnicity, and Class in Settler Societies' in D. Stasiulis and N. Yuval-Davis (eds), *Unsettling Settler Societies.* Thousand Oaks: Sage.
Statham, R. (1998) 'US Citizenship Policy in the Pacific Territory of Guam', *Citizenship Studies*, 2, 1: 89–104.
Stea, D. and Wisner, B. (eds) (1984) 'The Fourth World: A Geography of Indigenous Struggles', *Antipodes: A Radical Journal of Geography*, 16, 2.
Stokes, G. (1997) 'Citizenship and Aboriginality: Two Conceptions of Identity in Aboriginal Political Thought' in G. Stokes (ed.), *The Politics of Identity in Australia.* Cambridge: Cambridge University Press: pp. 158–74.
Strelein, L. M. (1998) *Indigenous Self-determination Claims and the Common Law in Australia.* Ph.D. thesis, Australian National University.
Sturmer, J. von (1982) 'Aborigines in the Uranium Industry: toward self-management in the Alligator River region?' in R. M. Berndt (ed.), *Aboriginal Sites, Rights and Resource Development.* Perth: University of Western Australia Press, pp. 69–116.
Suchet, S. (1996) 'Nurturing Culture through Country: Resource Management Strategies and Aspirations of Local Landowning Families at Napranum', *Australian Geographical Studies*, 34: 200–15.
Sullivan, P. (1995) 'Problems of Mediation in the National Native Title Tribunal' in J. Fingleton and J. Finlayson (eds), *Anthropology in the Native Title Era.* Canberra: AIATSIS, pp. 97–103.
—— (1997) 'Dealing with Native Title Conflicts by Recognising Aboriginal Authority Systems' in D. E. Smith and J. Finlayson (eds), *Fighting Over Country: Anthropological Perspectives.* Canberra: Centre for Aboriginal Economic Policy Research, pp. 129–40.
Sullivan, S. (1985) 'The Custodians of Aboriginal Sites in Southeastern Australia' in I. McBryde (ed.), *Who Owns the Past? Papers from the Annual Symposium of the Australian Academy of the Humanities.* Melbourne: Oxford University Press.
Sutton, P. (1995a) 'Atomism versus Collectivism: The Problem of Group Definition in Native Title Cases' in J. Fingleton and J. Finlayson (eds), *Anthropology in the Native Title Era.* Canberra: AIATSIS, pp. 1–10.
——(1995b) *Country: Aboriginal Boundaries and Land Ownership in Australia.* Canberra: Aboriginal History Inc.
Tanner, A. (1979), *Bringing Home Animals: Religious Ideology and Mode of Production of the Mistassini Cree Hunters.* St John's: Institute of Social and Economic Research, Memorial University of Newfoundland.
Taylor, A. (1989) 'Feelings and Memories of a Kuia' in B. Gadd (ed.), *Pacific Voices: An Anthology of Māori and Pacific Writing.* Auckland: MacMillan.
Taylor, C. (1992) 'The Politics of Recognition' in A. Gutman (ed.), *Multiculturalism and "the politics of recognition".* Princeton: Princeton University Press.
Tehan, M. (1996) 'A Tale of Two Cultures, Hindmarsh Island Bridge: Protection Requires the Disclosure of Secrets', *Alternative Law Journal*, 21, 1: 7.
Tobias, J. L. (1991) 'Canada's Subjugation of the Plains Cree, 1879–1885' in J. R. Miller (ed.), *Sweet Promises: A Reader on Indian–White Relations.* Toronto: University of Toronto Press.
Tocqueville, A. de (1966) *Democracy in America*, two vols, trans. G. Lawrence, New York: Harper & Row.

Tonkinson, M. E. (1990) 'Is it in the Blood? Australian Aboriginal Identity' in J. Linnekin and L. Poyer (eds), *Cultural Identity and Ethnicity in the Pacific.* Honolulu: University of Hawaii Press: pp. 191–218.

Tooker, E. (1988) 'The United States Constitution and the Iroquois League', *Ethnohistory,* 35, 4: 305–36.

Tuck, R. (1979) *Natural Rights Theories: Their Origin and Development.* Cambridge: Cambridge University Press.

—— (1999) *The Rights of War and Peace: Political Thought and the International Order from Grotius to Kant.* Oxford: Oxford University Press.

Tully, J. (ed.) (1988) *Meaning and Context: Quentin Skinner and His Critics.* Cambridge: Polity Press.

—— (1993) 'Rediscovering America: The *Two Treatises* and Aboriginal Rights' in J. Tully, *An Approach to Political Philosophy: Locke in Contexts.* Cambridge: Cambridge University Press, pp. 137–216.

—— (1994) 'Aboriginal Property and Western Theory: Recovering a Middle Ground', *Social Philosophy and Policy,* 11, 2 (Summer): 153–80.

—— (1995) *Strange Multiplicity: Constitutionalism in an Age of Diversity.* Cambridge: Cambridge University Press.

—— (1997) 'A General Framework for the Nisga'a Treaty Negotiations and Agreement-in-Principle', *Submission to the Select Standing Committee on Aboriginal Issues* (3 December 1996; revised May 1997).

—— (1998) 'A Fair and Just Relationship', *Meanjin,* 57, 1: 146–67.

—— (1999) 'Aboriginal Peoples: Negotiating Reconciliation' in J. Bickerton and A.-G. Gagnon (eds), *Canadian Politics,* third edn, Toronto: Broadview Press.

—— (forthcoming) 'Freedom and Disclosure In Multinational Societies' in A.-G. Gagnon and J. Tully (eds), *Struggles for Recognition in Multinational Societies: The European Union, Spain, Belgium, United Kingdom and Canada in Comparative Perspective.* Cambridge: Cambridge University Press.

Turner, D. (1997) *This Is Not a Peace Pipe: Towards an Understanding of Aboriginal Sovereignty.* Ph.D. thesis, McGill University.

—— (forthcoming) 'Vision: Towards an Understanding of Aboriginal Sovereignty' in W. Norman and R. Beiner (eds), *Contemporary Canadian Political Philosophy,* Toronto: University of Toronto Press.

Van Dyke, V. (1985) *Human Rights, Ethnicity and Discrimination.* Westport: Greenwood Press.

Venables, R. W. (1992) 'American Indian Influences on the America of the Founding Fathers' in O. Lyons *et al.* (eds), *Exiled in the Land of the Free: Democracy, Indian Nations, and the US Constitution,* Santa Fe: Clear Light Publishers: pp. 73–124.

Venne, S. (1997) 'Understanding Treaty 6: An Indigenous Perspective' in M. Asch (ed.), *Aboriginal and Treaty Rights in Canada.* Vancouver: University of British Columbia Press.

—— (1998) *Our Elders Understand Our Rights: Evolving International Law Regarding Indigenous Rights.* Penticton, B.C.: Theytus Books.

Vincent, A. (ed.) (1997) *Political Theory: Tradition and Diversity.* Cambridge: Cambridge University Press.

Voget, F. W. (1951) 'Acculturation at Caughnawaga: A Note on the Native-modified Group', *American Anthropologist,* 53, 2: 220–31.

Wafer, J. (1996) 'After the field' in M. Jackson (ed.), *Things as They Are: New Directions in Phenomenological Anthropology.* Bloomington: Indiana University Press.

Waitangi Tribunal (1987) Report of the Waitangi Tribunal on the Orakei Claim (Wai 9). Wellington: Department of Justice.
—— (1995) *Kiwifruit Marketing Report*. Wellington: Brookers Ltd.
—— (1998) *Te Whanau o Waipareira Report (Wai 414)*. Wellington: GP Publications.
Waldron, J. (1992) 'Superseding Historic Injustice', *Ethics*. 103: 4–28.
—— (1999) *Law and Disagreement*. Oxford: Oxford University Press.
Walker, R. (1987) *Nga Tau Tohetohe: Years of Anger*. Auckland: Penguin Books.
—— (1989) 'Maori Identity' in D. Novitz and B. Wilmott (eds), *Culture and Identity in New Zealand*. Wellington: GP Books: pp. 35–52.
—— (1995a) 'Maori People since 1950' in G. W. Rice (ed.), *The Oxford History of New Zealand*, second edn, Auckland: Oxford University Press: pp. 498–519.
—— (1995b) *Nga Pepa a Ranginui: The Walker Papers*. Auckland: Penguin.
—— (1999) 'Maori Sovereignty, Colonial and Post-colonial Discourses' in P. Havemann (ed.), *Indigenous Peoples' Rights in Australia, Canada, and New Zealand*. Auckland: Oxford University Press: pp. 108–22.
Ward, A. and Hayward, J. (1999) 'Tino Rangatiratanga' in P. Havemann (ed.), *Indigenous Peoples' Rights in Australia, Canada, and New Zealand*. Auckland: Oxford University Press: pp. 378–99.
Warry, W. (1998) *Unfinished Dreams: Community Healing and the Reality of Aboriginal Self-government*. Toronto: University of Toronto Press.
Waters, M. (1990) *Ethnic Options: Choosing Identities in America*. Berkeley: University of California Press.
Weatherford, J. (1988) *Indian Givers: How the Indians of the Americas Transformed the World*. New York: Crown Publishers.
Weaver, S. M. (1991) 'A New Paradigm in Canadian Indian Policy for the 1990s', *Canadian Ethnic Studies*, 22, 3: 8–18.
Webber, J. (1993) 'Individuality, Equality and Difference: Justifications for a Parallel System of Aboriginal Justice' in Royal Commission on Aboriginal Peoples, *Aboriginal Peoples and the Justice System: Report on the National Round Table on Aboriginal Justice Issues*. Ottawa: Minister of Supply and Services, pp. 133–160.
—— (1994) *Reimagining Canada: Language, Culture, Community, and the Canadian Constitution*, Montreal: McGill-Queen's University Press.
—— (1995a) 'The Jurisprudence of Regret: The Search for Standards of Justice in *Mabo*', *Sydney Law Review*, 17: 5–28.
—— (1995b) 'Relations of Force and Relations of Justice: The Emergence of Normative Community between Colonists and Aboriginal Peoples', *Osgoode Hall Law Journal*, 33: 623–60.
—— (1996) 'Multiculturalism and the Limits to Toleration' in A. Lapierre, P. Smart and P. Savard (eds), *Language, Culture and Values in Canada at the Dawn of the Twenty-first Century*. Ottawa: International Council for Canadian Studies and Carleton University Press, pp. 269–79.
—— (1997) 'Beyond Regret: Mabo's Implications for Australian Constitutionalism', paper presented to Conference on Indigenous Rights, Political Theory, and the Reshaping of Institutions, Canberra, 8–10 August.
Webster, S. (1975) 'Cognatic Descent Groups and the Contemporary Maori: A Preliminary Reassessment', *Oceania*, 84, 2: 121–52.
—— (1989) 'Maori Studies and the Expert Definition of Maori Culture: A Critical History', *Sites*, 18: 35–56.

White, R. (1991) *The Middle Ground: Indians, Empires, and Republics in the Great Lakes Region, 1650–1815.* Cambridge: Cambridge University Press.

Whittaker, E. (1994) 'Public Discourses of Sacredness: The Transfer of Ayers Rock to Aboriginal Ownership', *American Ethnologist,* 21, 3: 310–34.

Wickliffe, C. (1995) 'Issues for Indigenous Claims Settlement Policies Arising in Other Jurisdictions', *Victoria University of Wellington Law Review,* 25: 204–22.

Williams, B. F. (1989) 'A Class Act: Anthropology and the Race to Nation Across Ethnic Terrain', *Annual Review of Anthropology,* 18: 401–44.

Williams, R. A. (1990) *The American Indian in Western Legal Thought: The Discourses of Conquest.* New York: Oxford University Press.

—— (1997) *Linking Arms Together: American Indian Treaty Visions of Law and Peace, 1600–1800.* New York. Oxford University Press .

Wilmer, F. (1993) *The Indigenous Voice in World Politics.* Newbury Park: Sage.

Wilmsen, E. N. and McAllister, P. (eds) (1996) *The Politics of Difference: Ethnic Premises in a World of Power.* Chicago: University of Chicago Press.

Windschuttle, K. (1994) *The Killing of History: How a Discipline is Being Murdered by Literary Critics and Social Theorists.* Paddington, NSW: Macleay.

Winichakul, T. (1996) 'Siam Mapped: The Making of Thai Nationhood', *Ecologist,* September–October.

Wiredu, K. (1997) 'Democracy and Consensus in African Traditional Politics: A Plea for a Non-party Polity' in E. Chukwudi Eze (ed.), *Postcolonial African Philosophy: A Critical Reader.* Oxford: Blackwell: pp. 303–12.

Wittgenstein, L. (1974) *On Certainty,* trans. G. E. M. Anscombe and G. H. von Wright, Oxford: Basil Blackwell.

Woenne-Green, S., Johnston, R. Sultan, and Wallis A. (1994) *Competing Interests: Aboriginal Participation in National Parks and Conservation Reserves in Australia: A Review.* Fitzroy: Australian Conservation Foundation.

Yeatman, A. (1994) *Postmodern Revisionings of The Political.* New York: Routledge.

—— (1998) 'Feminism and Citizenship' in N. Stevenson (ed.), *Cultural Citizenship.* London: Sage.

York, G. and Pindera, L. (1991) *Peoples of the Pines: The Warriors and the Legacy of Oka,* Toronto: Little, Brown and Co.

Young, I. M. (1990) *Justice and the Politics of Difference.* Princeton: Princeton University Press.

—— (1999) 'Two Concepts of Self-determination' in A. Sarat (ed.), *Human Rights and Post-colonial Legacies.* Ann Arbor: University of Michigan Press.

—— (forthcoming) *Inclusion and democracy,* Oxford: Oxford University Press.

Yu, P. (1997) 'Multilateral Agreements – A New Accountability in Aboriginal Affairs' in Yunupingu (1997): 168–80.

Yunupingu, G. (ed.) (1997) *Our Land is Our Life: Land Rights – Past, Present and Future.* St Lucia, University of Queensland Press.

Zerilli, L. (1998) 'Doing without Knowing: Feminism's Politics of the Ordinary', *Political Theory,* 26, 4 (August): 435–58.

Zines, L. (1997) *The High Court and the Constitution,* fourth edn, Sydney: Butterworths.

Cases and Statutes

A-G Commonwealth; Ex rel McKinlay v. *Commonwealth* (1975) 135 CLR 1.

Calder v. *AG BC* [1973] SCR 313.

Cherokee Nation v. *State of Georgia* (1831) 5 Peters 1.

Coe v. *Commonwealth of Australia* (1979) 24 ALR 118 [HC].
Coe v. *Commonwealth of Australia* (1993) 118 ALR 193 [HC].
Cooper v. *Stuart* (1889) 14 App Cas 286
Delgamuukw v. *British Columbia* (1997) 153 DLR (4th) 193 (SCC)
Gerhardy v. *Brown* (1985) 159 CLR 70
International Court of Justice (1975) *Western Sahara: Advisory Opinion of 16 October 1975*. The Hague: ICJ Reports: p. 12
—— (1995) *Case Concerning East Timor (Portugal v. Australia)*. The Hague: ICJ Reports
Mabo and Others v. *Queensland* (No. 2) (1992) 66 ALJR 408; 107 ALR 1.
MacMillan Bloedel Ltd v. *Mullin* [1985] 3 WWR 577 (BCCA)
Mahé v. *Alberta* (1990) 68 DLR (4th) 69 (SCC)
McGinty v. *Western Australia* (1996) 186 CLR 140
New South Wales v. *Commonwealth* (1975) 135 CLR 337
Pareroultja v. *Tickner* (1993) 117 ALR 206
Paterson, B. J. (1998) *Maori Fisheries Case: Decision on Preliminary Question Remitted by Privy Council*. Auckland: Auckland High Court
Re Southern Rhodesia [1919] AC 211
Report No. 31: The Recognition of Aboriginal Customary Laws vol. 1 (Canberra: Australian Government Publishing Service, 1986)
Simon v. *The Queen* (1985) 24 DLR (4th) 390 (CSCC)
Sparrow v. *R* [1990] 1 SCR 1075
Van der Peet v. *R* (1996) 137 DLR (4th) 289 (SCC)
Ward v. *Western Australia* (1998) 159 ALR 483 (FC)
Ward v. *Western Australia* (2000) FCA 191
Western Australia v. *Commonwealth* (1995) 183 CLR 373
Wik Peoples v. *Queensland* (1996) 141 ALR 129
Wi Parata v. *Bishop of Wellington* (1877) 3N2JR (NS) 72
Worcester v. *State of Georgia* (1832) 6 Peters 515 (US Supreme Court)
Yanner v. *Eaton* (1999) HCA 53
Yorta Yorta v. *Victoria* [1998] 1606 FCA (18 December 1998)

Aboriginal Land Rights (Northern Territory) Act (1976)
Children, Young Person, and Their Families Act (1989)
Maori Fisheries Act (1989)
Runanga Iwi Act 1990
The Indian Act (1985) Ottawa: Minister of Supply and Services Canada
The Treaty of Waitangi Amendment Act (1985)
Treaty of Waitangi (Fisheries Claims) Settlement Act (1992)

Index

difference (*contd.*)
  identity and, 5, 11, 14–17, 97, 138–40,
    147–50, 274n6, 275n16
  of interests, 165, 179
  internal, 79, 171–2, 179
  multiple, 191, 194
  politics of, 35, 47, 138–9, 147–9
  recognition of, 7, 41, 98, 122, 137–9,
    141, 143, 145–7, 149, 168, 170
  theorising, 139–40, 147
  working through, 89, 92–3, 97, 108
differentiation
  of people/groups, 19, 168, 199,
    275n8
  of rights, 6, 56, 170
discrimination, 3, 10, 93, 95, 150, 164–5,
  210, 224, 239, 266n16
dispossession, 1, 10, 33, 41, 48, 56, 86, 91,
  154, 159, 165, 171, 262n15, 266n16
diversity *see* cultural diversity
Dixon, Owen, 269
Dodds, Susan, 15–16
Dodson, Mick, 157
Dodson, Patrick, 269, 270
domination
  colonial, 91, 118, 157
  of indigenous people, 116, 156, 281n16
  political, 95, 119
  structures of, 37–8, 50, 57
Durie, Mason, 101–2

Edgeworth, Brendan, 69
education, 2, 39, 41–2, 56, 133–4, 173, 187,
  201, 205, 214, 219–20, 225, 244, 273,
  276
Elazar, Daniel, 225
equality
  of citizens, 18, 143
  of contestatory standing, 210, 213–15
  of electoral standing, 201, 203–4, 210,
    215
  of governmental treatment, 18, 202,
    209–10, 212–14
  of individuals, 76, 202, 212–14, 246
  institutional, 108, 206
  of nations, 44, 52–3, 222, 226, 263n24
  of peoples, 10, 18, 46, 51–4, 56–7, 95–7,
    186, 222, 246, 252, 263n24
  principle of, 2, 4–5, 18, 46–7, 53, 107,
    169–70, 202, 222, 241–2
  of sovereign status, 10, 18, 52–4, 95
  of rights, 170, 191, 201–4

ethnic
  conflict, 234–6
  groups, 19, 122, 216–17, 220, 229
  minorities, 7, 236
  nationalism, 221, 229, 231, 236, 280n22
  relations, 125, 216, 220, 222, 234–6
  see also postethnic
ethnicity, 97, 107, 128, 190–1, 216,
  immigrant, 219, 278n5
ethos
  of engagement, 18, 183, 190–5, 198
  pluralised, 195, 197
  Protestant work, 119–20
Europe
  colonisation, 38, 43, 46, 52, 157, 247
  culture, 156–7, 245
  derived societies, 43, 48
  descent, 197, 239, 245–6
  Eastern, 234–6, 280n22
  ethnography, 142, 153
  form of nationhood, 116, 119–20
  immigrants, 218, 220
  institutions, 4, 244–5
  jurisprudence, 27, 30
  nations, 12, 52, 238, 241, 246
  perception of indigenous people, 151,
    154, 241–2, 244
  settlers, 240, 244, 246, 257
  societies, 151, 242, 251
  tradition of political thought, 13, 27, 36
  Union, 255–6
extinguishment
  of rights, 40–1, 44–5, 50, 53, 64, 91
  strategies of, 40–1, 43, 50
  of title, 61, 63, 66–7, 73, 83
  treaties, 44, 53–4

federalism
  in Australia, 167
  of Britain, 225
  in Canada, 8, 219
  decentred, 253, 256–8
  democratic, 227, 238, 253, 256–8
  diverse, 253, 257–8
  and federacy, 225
  global, 256–8
  and indigenous people, 225
  Iroquois, 237, 241, 243
  multinational, 227, 280n25
  treaty-, 53
federation, 168, 184, 221, 227, 242, 258
  Australian, 59